Written *into* History

Written *into* History

PULITZER PRIZE REPORTING OF
THE TWENTIETH CENTURY FROM
The New York Times

EDITED AND WITH
AN INTRODUCTION BY
Anthony Lewis

TIMES BOOKS
HENRY HOLT AND COMPANY
NEW YORK

Times Books
Henry Holt and Company, LLC
Publishers since 1866
115 West 18th Street
New York, New York 10011

Henry Holt® is a registered trademark of
Henry Holt and Company, LLC.

Library of Congress Cataloging-in-Publication Data
Written into history : Pulitzer Prize reporting of the twentieth century from the
New York times / edited and with an introduction by Anthony Lewis.
     p.   cm.
  Includes index.
  ISBN 0-8050-7178-4 (pbk.)
  1. Journalism—United States.   2. Pulitzer Prizes.   I. Lewis, Anthony,
1927–   II. New York times.

PN4726 .W75 2001
071'.3—dc21   2001035555

First published in hardcover in 2001 by Times Books

First Paperback Edition 2002

Printed in the United States of America

1   3   5   7   9   10   8   6   4   2

CONTENTS

INTRODUCTION

In 1963 a young *New York Times* correspondent in Vietnam, David Halberstam, angered United States military and civilian officials up to and including President Kennedy. They wanted the American public to believe that the policy of preserving a non-Communist South Vietnam by arming and advising its forces was working, but Halberstam reported that the South Vietnamese were reluctant to fight and the Communist guerrillas were enlarging their hold on the countryside. President Kennedy asked the publisher of the *Times*, Arthur O. Sulzberger, to bring Halberstam home. Sulzberger rejected the suggestion—and canceled a scheduled vacation for Halberstam lest the *Times* seem to be yielding.

The next year, 1964, Halberstam won a Pulitzer Prize. He shared the prize for international reporting with a second young Vietnam correspondent who refused to parrot the official line, Malcolm W. Browne of the Associated Press. A third, Neil Sheehan of United Press International, later played a large part as a *Times* reporter in the Pentagon Papers reports on the origins of the Vietnam War, which infuriated President Nixon and won the *Times* a Pulitzer for meritorious public service in 1972. (Sheehan won his own Pulitzer in 1989 for his book on the war, *A Bright Shining Lie*.)

Pulitzer Prizes are the preeminent mark of achievement in American journalism. As the prizes for reporting on Vietnam in defiance of official wishes show, they also point to the press's view of its role in society. That view has changed substantially over the more than eighty years of the Pulitzer Prizes' existence. Exposing official corruption on a local level has always been part of what journalists see as their function. But today, more than ever before, they are ready to write critically about the policies of the federal government, even in the once sacrosanct areas of foreign and national security affairs. The result is that the press does not merely record but shape events—and journalists are eager to do so. Vietnam and Watergate are the classic cases of the press clashing with, and helping to force change in, high policy. But the phenomenon has not stopped there. When the Serbs of Bosnia turned on their Muslim and Croat neighbors, committing mass murder and other crimes, President Bush and then President Clinton wanted to keep the United States out of the conflict. But coverage of the horrors by reporters and television cameras eventually made that impossible. Reporters won prizes for their work in Bosnia, as for Vietnam and Watergate. The Pulitzers reflect the changing ethos of journalism, and the changing concerns of American society.

This book presents some great, and lasting, examples of American journalism. Lasting is a necessary qualifier, because journalism tends to be ephemeral. *Sketches in the Sand*, James Reston of the *New York Times* called a collection of his columns. These pieces have lasted. Some are firsthand history, others evocations of memorable people and situations. They appear here just as they were originally published and won Pulitzer Prizes, except for some cuts for reasons of space.

There can be no claim that this book canvasses the American press or the Pulitzer Prize record as a whole. It does not include the triumphs of other newspapers, such as the Watergate disclosures by Bob Woodward and Carl Bernstein that brought the prize for meritorious public service to the *Washington Post* in 1973. The *New York Times* alone is represented. But the *Times* and its staff have won more Pulitzers than any other paper or news service, and the pieces collected here are a fair sample of what the American press can do at its best.

It is inevitably an eclectic collection, spanning the work of decades as it does and ranging from reports of murders to commentary by critics of the arts. I alone, as editor, made the choices of what to include from the eighty-one Pulitzers won by the *Times* and staff members from 1918 to 2001. The selection was based on what would make good reading and what would throw light on the development of journalism and society over those decades.

In the beginning there was Joseph Pulitzer. (The accent is on the first syllable, pronounced like pull, not pewl.) He was an exemplar of the self-made man, an immigrant who came to the United States with little money and less English and within fifteen years owned the *St. Louis Post-Dispatch*. Born in Hungary in 1847 of a German Catholic

mother and a Hungarian Jewish father, he made his way to America
as a Union army substitute in the Civil War. (The draft law allowed
well-off draftees to pay for a substitute to serve instead.) He became
the owner of the *Post-Dispatch* in 1878, when he was thirty-one.
He married into society, mastered English and worked feverishly at
the paper.

Seymour Topping, who became administrator of the Pulitzer Prizes
in 1993, summarized Pulitzer's remarkable life in an introduction to
the 1999 book *Who's Who of Pulitzer Winners*, by Elizabeth A. Brennan
and Elizabeth C. Clarage. "Appealing to the public that his paper was
their champion," Topping said, "Pulitzer splashed investigative articles
and editorials assailing government corruption, wealthy tax-dodgers
and gamblers. . . . Pulitzer would have been pleased to know that in
the conduct of the Pulitzer Prize system, which he later established,
more awards in journalism would go to exposure of corruption than
to any other subject."

In 1883 Pulitzer bought the *New York World*, turning it into an
even more telling crusader. For a time it had the largest newspaper
circulation in the country, more than six hundred thousand daily. But
a circulation battle with the *Sun*, which attacked Pulitzer as "the Jew
who had denied his race and his religion," sapped his health. In 1890,
only forty-three years old, he gave up the editorship of the *World*.
Over the next twenty years he spent most of his time in isolation,
aboard his yacht or in one of his homes. But he kept his hand on both
the *World* and the *Post-Dispatch*.

The *World*'s exposure of illicit payments by the U.S. government to
the French Panama Canal Company brought menacing retaliation.
Pulitzer was indicted for criminally libeling, among others, President
Theodore Roosevelt. Criminal libel was a serious threat then, sixty
years before the Supreme Court held that the use of libel law to punish
criticism of government could violate the First Amendment. But Pulitzer refused to give way, and the courts dismissed the indictment: a
great victory for freedom of the press.

In a will drawn up in 1904, Pulitzer left $2 million to Columbia
University to establish a school of journalism. A quarter of that
amount was to be used to endow prizes. (The endowment has since
been enlarged from other sources.) In the will he explained what he
had done.

"I am deeply interested in the progress and elevation of journalism,"

Pulitzer wrote, "having spent my life in that profession, regarding it as a noble profession and one of unequaled importance for its influence upon the minds and morals of the people. I desire to assist in attracting to this profession young men of character and ability, also to help those already engaged in the profession to acquire the highest moral and intellectual training."

He made one other significant comment on his vision of a more enlightened journalism. The year he signed his will, 1904, he wrote in the *North American Review*: "Our Republic and its press will rise or fall together. An able, disinterested, public-spirited press, with trained intelligence to know the right and the courage to do it, can preserve the public virtue without which popular government is a sham and a mockery. A cynical, mercenary, demagogic press will produce in time a people as base as itself."

That warning is, if anything, more meaningful at the beginning of the twenty-first century than it was in 1904. In a far more dangerous world, with weapons of mass destruction that can be delivered thousands of miles away, and with the United States in a singularly powerful role, American democracy requires even more an able, disinterested, public-spirited press.

Of course there are elements in the American press today that are no more noble than the yellow press of Pulitzer's time. And technological change has brought a form of journalism that is inherently less reflective and more susceptible to the cynical, mercenary and demagogic: broadcasting. Pulitzer would surely regard extremist talk-show hosts and journalists who shout at each other on television, uttering before they have time to think, as perversions of the press's great function in a democracy. More recently, technology has given us a form of communication that is by nature both democratic and irresponsible: the Internet. Anyone can set up a Web site; that means an individual masquerading as a informed reporter can post the vilest rumors, unchecked and unaccountable. And the press must try to track them down.

Joseph Pulitzer died in 1911. In 1917 the advisory board designated by his will to administer the prizes chose the first winners. The board is a self-perpetuating body, appointing new members as terms expire. At the turn of the twenty-first century it included ten journalists and five academics.

There are Pulitzer Prizes—outside the scope of this book—in the arts as well as journalism: for drama, music and, in books, fiction, nonfiction, history, poetry and biography or autobiography. The journalism prize categories have been changed as newspapers have changed. Today there are fourteen, ranging from local reporting to international, criticism, cartoons and photography. The journalism prizes are only for work published in newspapers—or, as of 1999, on newspapers' Internet Web sites. Magazines have to look elsewhere for their kudos, as do broadcasters. But prizes in those fields do not approach the prestige of a Pulitzer. An article in *Brill's Content* in 2000 said: "The Pulitzer Prize: Win one, legend has it, and the first line of your obituary can be sent to the printer. It's the Oscar of the news business, the Nobel of journalism."

Joseph Pulitzer's comment in the *North American Review* that only a public-spirited press can preserve the public virtue "without which popular government is a sham and a mockery" was reminiscent of something said by James Madison, the author of the First Amendment, in 1822. "A popular government," Madison wrote, "without popular information, or the means of acquiring it, is but a prelude to a farce or a tragedy." In other words, democracy requires an informed public.

If Pulitzer was consciously paralleling Madison, it would be poetically appropriate. For it is fair to say that without Madison there could be no Pulitzer Prizes. Madison's vision of a society in which the governors are subject to uninhibited criticism by the governed—the vision made into law by the First Amendment and the judges who have interpreted it—has given us the freest press in the world. "A cantankerous press, an obstinate press, a ubiquitous press," Judge Murray Gurfein wrote when he ruled that the Nixon administration could not stop publication of the Pentagon Papers in the *New York Times*, "must be suffered by those in authority in order to preserve the even greater values of freedom of expression and the right of the people to know." No other country has a journalism profession as important (and occasionally, alas, self-important) as ours. And none has a journalism prize with the significance of the Pulitzer.

In Madison's day newspapers were nothing like today's serious papers. They were small, highly politicized and often scurrilous. Editors were sometimes in the pay of political parties. Madison had no illusions about the press's quality, but he still wanted to protect its right to print what it would. "To the press alone," he wrote in 1799, "chequered as it is with abuses, the world is indebted for all the triumphs which have been gained by reason and humanity over error and oppression...."

That extravagant praise for the press was voiced by Madison in the context of the first great struggle over press freedom in the United States. In 1798 the Federalist Party, which controlled Congress, pushed through a Sedition Act over objections from the Jeffersonian opposition. It was a criminal libel law, making it a crime to publish false, malicious comments about the president or Congress. (It did not punish nasty comments on the vice president, Thomas Jefferson.) The purpose was political: to silence the Jeffersonian press in the run-up to the election of 1800, when Jefferson would run against the Federalist president, John Adams. The act was used in just that way. Editors and owners of the leading pro-Jefferson papers were prosecuted—usually because they published mere political slanging against Adams rather than specific charges. James Callender was convicted and sentenced to nine months in prison, for example, for an 1800 campaign book that said voters had a choice between "Adams, war and beggary, and Jefferson, peace and competency." (After Jefferson was elected, Callender turned against him—for reasons of which we cannot now be sure. He first published the charge that Jefferson had fathered a child by his slave Sally Hemings.)

At the urging of Madison, the Virginia legislature in 1799 passed a resolution condemning the Sedition Act. The act, it said, "ought to produce universal alarm, because it is leveled against the right of freely examining public characters and measures, and of free communication among the people thereon, which has ever been justly deemed the only effectual guardian of every other right." The resolution said the Sedition Act violated the First Amendment, which had been added to the Constitution just seven years before, in 1791. But the Supreme Court never passed on the act's constitutionality before it expired, under its own terms, on Inauguration Day 1801.

In 1964 that history was brought to life by the Supreme Court, in the case of *New York Times v. Sullivan*. An Alabama jury, all white, had awarded five hundred thousand dollars to a Montgomery, Alabama, city commissioner who claimed he had been libeled by an advertisement in the *Times* criticizing Southern officials for brutality toward civil rights demonstrators—even though the ad did not mention Commissioner Sullivan's name. The Supreme Court reversed that judgment in an opinion by Justice William J. Brennan Jr. that analogized the penalty imposed on the *Times* to prosecutions under the Sedition Act of 1798.

"Although the Sedition Act was never tested in this Court," Justice Brennan wrote, "the attack upon its validity has carried the day in the court of history." With that, he effectively held unconstitutional a statute that had expired 163 years earlier. Under the First Amendment, he said, public officials must bear "robust [and] uninhibited" criticism. Even if a comment is false, its author is protected from libel suits by officials unless he made it knowing it was false or in reckless disregard of its truth or falsity.

New York Times v. Sullivan laid the legal foundation for the increasingly aggressive stance of contemporary journalism toward public officials and public policy, the "public characters and measures" that Madison said had to be discussed freely in a democracy. If the press prides itself today on speaking truth to power, it can thank James Madison and the Supreme Court for its power to do so without any meaningful constraint except its own sense of responsibility.

Near the beginning of this essay I remarked that Pulitzer Prizes can be a barometer of press attitudes from time to time. Nowhere is that more true than it is of the press's relationship with high public officials.

Until past midway in the twentieth century, reporters were instinctively respectful toward the president of the United States, even deferential. How different it was from today's skeptical White House press corps. Photographers made it a practice never to show Franklin Roosevelt in his wheelchair. When a new man took a picture of the president in the chair, the other photographers removed the film from his camera.

One Pulitzer Prize illustrates the change in attitude. It was awarded in 1938 to Arthur Krock, longtime chief of the *New York Times* Washington bureau and columnist, for what the citation called "his interview with the President of the United States, February 27, 1937." But readers must have been hard put to realize that it was an interview. The article began as follows:

WASHINGTON, Feb. 27—"When I retire to private life on Jan. 20, 1941," the President this week has been saying to his friends, "I do not want to leave the country in the condition Buchanan left it to Lincoln.

If I cannot, in the brief time given to me to attack its deep and disturbing problems, solve these problems, I hope at least to have moved them well on the way to solution by my successor. It is absolutely essential that the solving process begin at once."

This is his answer to those who have contended that the President has a third term in mind. . . .

Much of the Krock article dealt with Roosevelt's proposal, recently made, of what came to be called the Court-packing plan. Angered at the striking down of New Deal legislation by a five-to-four majority on the Supreme Court, he asked Congress for a law adding a justice for each member of the Court over the age of seventy. That would have taken the Court to fifteen justices in 1937 if none retired. (Congress defeated the proposal.) Krock described Roosevelt's defense of the plan in the third person, mostly without direct quotation. "The President believes it is necessary. . . ." Down in the piece he did disclose that he had talked with Roosevelt: "In the President's view—and discussion with him makes it clearer—the Supreme Court issue is but part of a larger problem. . . ."

That style, which today seems strangely arch, reflected the custom of the time—which was for reporters who saw the president not to quote him directly. Roosevelt met frequently with the press; reporters crowded around his desk in the oval office. But there were no stories beginning, "President Roosevelt said today that . . ." There were no radio broadcasts of press conferences, and television had not yet been invented. John F. Kennedy was the first president who allowed live telecasts of his press conferences.

As it happens, Arthur Krock was a conservative who was no softy when it came to Franklin Roosevelt. But such was his respect for the presidency that his story reads much like an apologia.

It was another world, scarcely imaginable now. And it did not altogether end in the 1930s. Until the 1960s the leading Washington journalists, the bureau chiefs and columnists, deferred greatly to presidents and their assistants on matters of foreign policy. So did the rest of us. Our assumption was that the president, the secretary of state and the other policy-makers were better informed than we were. We respected their superior knowledge and their good faith. And we shared the basic premises of policy: the need to stand up to the Soviet Union, for example, in the postwar period. All that ended in Vietnam.

It became clear that the president was less well informed than the young reporters on the ground. The secretary of defense at the time the American role was transformed into carrying the main fighting burden of the war, Robert S. McNamara, may have known the reality better than the president who gave the transforming orders, Lyndon Johnson. But McNamara deceived the public, and perhaps himself, into thinking there was light at the end of the tunnel. And the press could no longer be an unquestioning partner in a failed policy.

The change in the press's attitude toward the president and foreign policy did not come easily. When the *Times* learned in 1961 of plans for Cuban exiles to invade Cuba, it checked with the White House and at President Kennedy's request somewhat played down its scoop. (Two weeks later, after the invasion had disastrously failed, Kennedy told the paper's top editor, Turner Catledge, "I wish you had run everything on Cuba.") Then in 1963 Sulzberger said no to Kennedy's suggestion that Halberstam be pulled out of Vietnam.

The Pentagon Papers story in 1971 was the decisive test, for the *Times* and for the Pulitzer system. *Times* executives debated over many days whether to publish the articles and text excerpts. It was a tough decision for Sulzberger, an intensely patriotic former U.S. Marine. In the end he said yes. The next year the Pulitzer advisory board, after a tense debate, voted to give the *Times* the meritorious public service award for the series. But under terms of Pulitzer's will the board was only advisory; the prizes were actually awarded by the trustees of Columbia University. The trustees, dominated by conservative supporters of the Nixon administration, voted against giving a prize to the *Times*—or one to Jack Anderson, the syndicated columnist, for his disclosure of Henry Kissinger's efforts to tilt U.S. policy toward Pakistan in the Indo-Pakistan war. Only when the president of Columbia, William J. McGill, threatened to resign did the trustees back down. Three years later the trustees' role in the awarding of Pulitzer Prizes was dropped.

Vietnam provoked another Pulitzer conflict. In December 1966 Harrison E. Salisbury of the *Times* managed to get to Hanoi. In a series that began on Christmas Day he described, among other things, the civilian damage caused by American bombing of North Vietnam. It was a journalistic coup, but supporters of the war bitterly attacked Salisbury. When the *Times* submitted his series, the Pulitzer board split six to five against giving him a prize. It was not the Pulitzers' finest hour. (The Salisbury and Pentagon Papers episodes are described by John Hohenberg, Pulitzer administrator at the time, in his book *The Pulitzer Diaries*.)

"Given the subjective nature of the award process," Seymour Topping said, controversy over prize decisions was inevitable. Entries for the journalism prizes are so numerous—more than fifteen hundred a year now—that members of the Pulitzer board could not possibly read and judge them all. The board therefore appoints juries of five to seven members in each of the journalism categories to make preliminary judgments. The practice used to be for juries to indicate a first choice when reporting to the board. But sometimes the board overruled that choice, the story of what had happened naturally leaked and support-ers of the discarded jury choice were resentful. The board tried to deal with the problem by having each jury send up three choices, with no order of preference. But the board can still go beyond those.

Over the decades the Pulitzer process, like most things in American life, has become more complicated. College applications have become much more competitive in recent years; nowadays parents even strug-gle to get their children into nursery school. The same ratcheting-up seems to have happened with the Pulitzers.

Journalists are famously competitive anyway. The classic newspaper drama, *The Front Page*, by Ben Hecht and Charles MacArthur, shows the ruthless tricks used by warring Chicago papers in the 1930s— including hiding an escaped death-row prisoner in a rolltop desk in the city hall press room. Some of that competitive zeal has come to attend the quest for Pulitzers. Newspapers, at least the big ones, care-fully consider what entries to submit and in which categories their chances are best. And all the time the possibility of a prize glimmers for ambitious writers and editors. I do not mean that the editors of a paper like the *Times* plan articles with an eye on winning a Pulitzer; they do what they do out of concern for a better paper and a better society. But the thought of a prize undoubtedly crosses people's minds. And even on the *Times*, with its acknowledged position as the coun-try's leading daily and a long record of Pulitzer winners, the top editors and the news staff gather in the newsroom on the afternoon the prizes are announced to cheer *Times* winners—or condole if there are none.

The Pulitzer board's deliberations are secret. But there are leaks from time to time, and much speculative theorizing on the whys of who won and lost. Some editors of smaller papers suspect that the competition is tilted toward the *Times*, the *Washington Post*, the *Wall Street Journal* and other major institutions. When one of the majors is blanked out, its people may feel that the Pulitzer board thinks it has had too many prizes. Small papers are certainly not without hope of victory. The 1995 prize for meritorious public service, for example, went to the *Virgin Islands Daily News*, circulation 16,400, for stories on corruption in the islands' criminal justice system.

In a process run by human beings, there are always going to be decisions that in hindsight look like mistakes. The worst in Pulitzer history was the award of a prize in 1981 to Janet Cooke of the *Washington Post* for stories on how a small boy in the inner city of Washington, D.C., was caught up in the drug trade. Not long after the prize announcement the story unraveled; Ms. Cooke admitted that she had invented the small boy. She disappeared from the *Post* and journalism, and the prize was returned. The *Times*, too, has a blot on its Pulitzer record. In 1932 its Moscow correspondent, Walter Duranty, won for international reporting. But his work increasingly came to be seen as slanted toward the Soviet regime.

A nagging question is whether the Pulitzer board should itself check the truth of submissions before awarding them prizes. The 2000 *Brill's Content* article, by Seth Mnookin, criticized the board for not doing so. On the other hand, taking on that responsibility would probably require the board to set up a burdensome checking process. Would the board have to hire someone to telephone everyone quoted in a series of newspaper articles? If the board was considering an award for articles charging improper behavior, should it first invite comment by the person or institution accused? (Without any provision for such comment, some people who have been targeted by a newspaper have taken to writing the board, criticizing the paper's work, just in case it is considered for a prize.)

Both newspapers and Pulitzer Prizes have become more demanding over the years. No one is likely to win today for an interview with the president, as Arthur Krock did in 1938. (He also won a special Pulitzer commendation in 1951 for an exclusive interview with President Truman.) Nor is an editor likely to be excited if one of her reporters gets such an interview, at least not with a generally accessible president like Bill Clinton or George W. Bush. If the reclusive Richard Nixon had poured his innermost thoughts out to a reporter, that would have been reason for excitement.

The yearning today is not for an exclusive interview with the president or some other great figure but for an exclusive disclosure of his or her wrongdoing. Investigative reporting became the dream of many aspiring journalists after the success of Woodward and Bernstein in Watergate. They unseated a president, it was said—an accomplishment that fulfilled at the highest the desire of most contemporary journalists to help shape events, not merely record them. In truth, it was not Woodward and Bernstein who forced Richard Nixon's resignation in the end but our more formal institutions: a special prosecutor, a Senate committee, the Supreme Court. But without the *Washington Post* stories on Watergate, the process that exposed the wrongdoings of the president and his aides would probably never have got under way.

In a way, the word "investigative" is redundant. Much reporting has always involved investigation, going back to Émile Zola and his campaign to free Captain Dreyfus. Like Zola, American reporters have frequently aimed to right injustices. Jimmy Stewart was the dogged reporter in the 1948 movie *Call Northside 777*, working to free the wrongly imprisoned son of a cleaning woman, decades before the adjective "investigative" was used for reporters. In the age of Senator Joe McCarthy and other anti-Communist zealots, reporters won Pulitzer Prizes for proving that individuals had been wrongly tarred—and their lives ruined—by false charges of Communist affiliation.

Anthony H. Leviero of the *Times* won a Pulitzer in 1952 for exclusive stories on the undertakings General Douglas MacArthur gave President Harry Truman—and then broke—before Truman removed him from his command in the Korean War. But I think Tony Leviero's finest hour came at a press conference of President Dwight Eisenhower on November 11, 1953. The attorney general, Herbert Brownell Jr., had just suggested that the late Harry Dexter White, whom President Truman had named as the first U.S. executive director of the International Monetary Fund, was a Soviet spy. White had appeared before a grand jury, had answered all questions and had not been charged. Leviero asked Eisenhower:

Mr. President, I think this case is at best a pretty squalid one. But if a grand jury, under our system, has found a man—has in effect cleared the man or at least decided it has insufficient evidence to convict him or prosecute him, then is it proper for the attorney general to characterize the man, who is now dead, as a spy and, in effect, accuse a former president of harboring that man?

Eisenhower fended off the question, saying that he was not a lawyer and "the attorney general is here to answer it himself. Let him answer it." Leviero said: "He has refused to answer the questions, you see." I was at that press conference, and I remember the electricity in the room when Leviero used the word "squalid." Thirty-seven years later an official of the IMF, James M. Boughton, published a paper concluding, after intensive study of the White story, that the evidence "casts doubt on the case against him and provides the basis for a more benign interpretation."

After Watergate, editors and reporters focused more intensely on finding wrongdoing in government and large private organizations. It would be hard to prove that those institutions were more corrupt than they used to be. But their power over individuals was great, and the press may have been moved by a new sense of responsibility to hold that power accountable—as well as by the competitive urge to match the achievement of Watergate. The Pulitzer board recognized the trend, in any event, by establishing an investigative reporting category in 1985. Early awards were for stories on wrongdoing by police, sheriffs, courts and basketball teams.

In recent years the press has been increasingly concerned not only with individual wrongdoing but with systemic problems in government and the society. The two Pulitzer Prizes won by the staff of the New York Times in 2001 were for reporting of that kind. One, for beat reporting, went to David Cay Johnston for stories about the Internal Revenue Service and the federal tax code. They showed that, with a smaller enforcement budget and changing priorities at the IRS, the poor were for the first time more likely than the rich to have their returns audited. The other prize, for national reporting, went to the Times staff for an extraordinary series of articles on how race is lived in America. The series showed that, with all the progress in outlawing overt discrimination, Americans remain profoundly divided by race.

Another significant trend in journalism in the latter half of the twentieth century was fully recognized by the Pulitzer Prizes. That is the rise of analytical and contextual writing in newspapers. The old image of the print journalist as recording machine has faded. In its place is the journalist who tries to make sense, for the reader, of whatever world he or she is describing. It is a profound change, and it has been driven by a number of factors.

First, reporters and editors began to realize that merely repeating what someone said or did, without context, could be distorting. Senator McCarthy would announce, say, that he was about to expose shocking Communist infiltration of some agency. Simply to print that, without noting McCarthy's failure to back up similar previous claims, was to act in effect as his propaganda arm.

Second, there was a cultural change in the profession that contributed greatly to the transformation of American journalism. In the old days many reporters, probably most, had no college degrees but were wise in the ways of the city; they could talk knowingly to cops and scoundrels. They are the characters portrayed in *The Front Page*. (Why, incidentally, didn't the Pulitzer board of its day give the drama prize to *The Front Page*? Not elevated enough?) They drank whiskey and gambled. Today virtually every reporter has been to college, and some have graduate degrees. Their drink of choice is wine. Journalism, like the West Side of Manhattan, has been gentrified. Better-educated reporters have opinions and want to express them. Many would like to be columnists, so they can say whatever they think. Failing that, they write analytical pieces or explanatory comment. The line between analysis and opinion is a shadowy one, and critics of today's press complain that reporters too often cross it.

Third, there is a powerful economic reason for the change in print journalism. Technology has cost newspapers their old role as the prime source of breaking news. Broadcasting performs that function for most Americans now. Perforce, newspapers had to move to give the news a depth of meaning that broadcasters hardly ever supply. A television reporter can read out the last paragraph of the Supreme Court decision on the 2000 election—which is misleading. In the *Times* the next day, Linda Greenhouse explains (and dissects) the reasoning that made George W. Bush president.

Finally, there is an inescapable reality. The increasing complexity of the world around us demanded deeper journalism. Nuclear missiles, the human genome and the AIDS plague could not be treated effectively in the old ABC style of reporting. And so even the wire services that supply much of the national and international news for most American papers, though they are instinctively conservative in their approach to reporting, have become much more interpretive. (The wire services are eligible for Pulitzers, too.) Early Pulitzer winners tend to be unsophisticated pieces compared to today's.

The Pulitzer board recognized the movement toward contextual writing by adding new categories of prizes. In 1970 it began giving a prize for commentary. It went to columnists. (Before this category was created, the premier columnist of the century, Walter Lippmann, was awarded a special citation in 1958. James Reston, the great reporter and columnist of the *Times*, was praised for his columns in a 1957 prize for national reporting.) In 1985 the board added explanatory journalism as a category. Its prizes have been for such things as a 1985 *Times* series on President Reagan's Star Wars proposal for missile defense in space. The board also added a criticism category in 1970; the prizes under that heading have included wonderful writing on the arts and architecture, some of it reproduced in this book.

One more change should be mentioned, an unqualifiedly happy one. The writing in newspapers has greatly improved. Of course there was always some journalism with literary qualities: H. L. Mencken in the *Baltimore Evening Sun*, for a notable example. (Why didn't he win a Pulitzer?) But today I can be reading just about anywhere in the *New York Times*—to take what I know is a parochial example—and be struck by a beautifully written piece: witty, evocative, whatever.

That change made the job of editing this collection a pleasure. Time has robbed some *New York Times* Pulitzer winners of their raison d'etre, but many pieces are delightful, instructive, moving.

The editing job has had one less happy consequence. It made me remember, and regret, *Times* work that I think should have won Pulitzer Prizes but did not. One was the report by Peter Kihss, a great *Times* reporter, on the power failure that blacked out New York City and much of the Northeast on the night of November 9, 1965. All electricity was off in the city starting at 5:30 P.M.; eight hundred thousand people were trapped in the subways. Kihss sat at his desk, typing with the help of emergency lanterns, and told the story fluently and with remarkable completeness. (With the *Times'* typesetting and printing operations down, the paper of November 10 was produced at the plant of the *Newark Evening News*.)

Another veteran *Times* reporter who should have won a Pulitzer was A. H. Raskin, whose specialty was labor. At the end of a 114-day strike that closed the New York newspapers in 1963 he wrote a step-by-step account, more than a full page in the first post-strike *Times*, of why the strike happened and why it was not settled sooner. It was an extraordinarily courageous article, pointing out the failures of *Times* executives among others.

To overlook R. W. Apple Jr. the Pulitzer board must have been willfully blind. He was a *Times* correspondent in, among other places, London, Russia and Africa. He was for years the premier national political writer in America, the model for the trade. Then he undertook portraits of dozens of cities—their buildings, their people, their culture, their food. The first was about Cleveland. Reading it, I thought only Apple could make Cleveland interesting.

John Kifner's courage and tenacity in the search for truth produced stories worthy of a Pulitzer in this country and abroad. I shall limit myself to one example. On April 6, 1988, during the first Palestinian *intifada*, a fifteen-year-old Israeli girl was killed while walking in the occupied West Bank with other Jewish settlers. The Israeli army said that she had been stoned to death by Palestinian villagers. But the next day Kifner reported, exclusively, that an autopsy showed she had been killed by a bullet from the gun of an Israeli guard accompanying the group. A day later Israeli authorities confirmed that finding but, as Kifner reported, went ahead and punished the innocent Palestinian villagers by deporting six of them and destroying fourteen of their houses.

Celia Dugger should surely have won a prize, in my judgment, for her 1996 articles on Fauziya Kassindja, a young woman who fled from her native Togo and sought asylum in the United States to avoid the rite she was scheduled to undergo: female genital mutilation. The Immigration and Naturalization Service held her in jail, under harsh conditions, and an immigration judge found her story not credible. After Dugger's first report on the case, Kassindja was released from detention. The Board of Immigration Appeals found in her favor, granting asylum. Celia Dugger then went to Togo, found Kassindja's family and confirmed her story in detail.

Jason DeParle did the most complete and compelling reportage on welfare, the people and the system, to appear anywhere. He spent months with welfare clients who found work, succeeded and failed. He broke out of a common journalistic condition: short attention span. The human stories he related shed light on the underside of the most prosperous society in history. The *Times* submitted his work in 1995, 1998 and 2000, but there was no prize.

Steven Erlanger's reporting for the *Times* from Kosovo during the 1999 Serbian onslaught there was one of the great contemporary pieces of foreign correspondence, in my judgment—but the Pulitzer selectors did not see it that way. One report especially transfixed me. Erlanger drew on the biblical story of the exodus from Egypt, when the enslaved Jews marked their doorposts so the angel of death would pass over them as he smote the Egyptian firstborn, without making the parallel specific. "The evidence of ethnic purging here in Kosovo," Erlanger wrote, "is written upon the doorposts of their houses and upon their gates. . . . Many doors and storefronts bear a spray-painted Christian cross with a Cyrillic 'C' in each quadrant—the 'S' of Roman script—a widely understood sign that the owners and occupants are Serbs."

But those reporters have not sulked about missing out, and I can do no more than say that my enthusiastic judgments were confounded in those cases. In many more, as this book shows, *Times* reporters and editors were rewarded for work that honors our profession.

Newspapers are full of faults, as Madison said. But the prizewinning stories that follow prove that newspaper people can have noble ambitions, and work hard to fulfill them.

Written *into* History

ONE

What a Government Doesn't Want You to Know

A CHANGE OF ROLE

Immediately after the *New York Times* began publishing the Pentagon Papers series, on June 13, 1971, the publisher of the *Times*, Arthur Ochs (Punch) Sulzberger, and his wife, Carol, flew to London for a long-planned visit. I was the *Times* London bureau chief, and my wife and I joined the Sulzbergers for dinner at the Savoy Grill. Several times during dinner the headwaiter came to the table and said there was an international telephone call for Mr. Sulzberger. He left the table to take the calls, which were messages of encouragement from such friends as Katharine Graham, publisher of the *Washington Post*. Once, while he was gone, Mrs. Sulzberger said, nervously: "They're going to put Arthur in jail. I know it."

That was the level of tension surrounding the Pentagon Papers story. Sulzberger did not go to jail. But federal prosecutors presented evidence to a grand jury with a view to possible indictments. And when the lawyer retained to defend the paper, Alexander M. Bickel, met senior staff members, James Reston told him, "The fate of this institution is at stake." Bickel thought that was a correct statement.

For the *Times* to publish stories so strikingly against the wishes of the United States government was a profound departure from its practice. When Reston and his colleagues in the Washington bureau learned that the Soviets had put missiles in Cuba, in October 1962, the paper withheld the story at President Kennedy's request so that he would not lose the impact of his planned speech to the nation the next evening. Reston knew for years that the United States was sending U-2 spy planes over the U.S.S.R. but wrote nothing about it until the one piloted by Francis Gary Powers was downed in 1960.

Of course the government had been scooped by the *Times* before.

When the Dumbarton Oaks conference was held in Washington in 1944 to plan international organizations after World War II—the structure of the United Nations was agreed there—the meetings were secret. But Reston wrote a full report every day on what had been said, noting impishly in one story that the site was "surrounded by military police and barred to reporters." He won a Pulitzer Prize for that bravura performance. But his reports did not challenge the fundamental premises of an American policy.

The Pentagon Papers were quite different in character and size from the material disclosed in traditional newspaper scoops. Secretary of Defense Robert S. McNamara had ordered the preparation of a history of American involvement in Vietnam. It came to forty-seven volumes, made up of three thousand pages of analysis and four thousand of official documents. Every page bore a classified stamp of one level or another. Only fifteen sets of the study were made. The *Times* had all but four volumes.

The study went back to the Truman presidency. It showed that over all that time U.S. governments had acted in a consistent way against Vietnamese nationalists and then Communist-nationalist movements. While professing support for an independent, unified Vietnam, the U.S. secretly supported renewed French domination after World War II, helped the French in the subsequent war, sabotaged the Geneva settlement made by France as it withdrew from Vietnam, helped to create a separate regime in South Vietnam, took an increasing military role in support of that regime and, finally, escalated to an enormous war while denying that any change was taking place. The mass of detail threw light on such things as executive manipulation of Congress, the role of deception in forming public opinion and the inaccuracy of military reports on Vietnam.

The documents were obtained by Neil Sheehan near the beginning of April 1971. He and several other *Times* reporters were installed in the New York Hilton, in a suite of rooms with a guard outside the door. Over several weeks they read the papers and prepared a series of articles. But it was far from clear that they would be published.

A *Times* executive who thought publication might endanger the paper's existence asked for an opinion by the law firm that had been outside counsel to the paper for forty years, Lord, Day & Lord. Its senior partner was Herbert Brownell Jr., who had been President Eisenhower's attorney general. The firm told the *Times* that it would be a criminal offense to publish any of the texts or stories based on them. Indeed, the lawyers said mere possession of the documents was a crime; for that reason they had refused to look at the papers themselves.

But James Goodale, vice president and general counsel of the *Times*, did not agree. He advised the paper that what it should fear was not criminal prosecution but a civil suit to enjoin—prohibit—publication. He suggested printing everything in one issue of the *Times* or its Sunday magazine, but the editors thought that would look like running from the sheriff. Finally, Punch Sulzberger gave the go-ahead for a daily series of texts and articles.

The Pentagon Papers stories and accompanying texts are too long to be reproduced in this book, and too complex in their substance at this distance in time. What remains of signal importance is the legal battle over the right to publish them. Goodale was right in his prediction. After two days of publication, President Nixon's attorney general, John Mitchell, asked the *Times* to stop, claiming that further disclosures would "cause irreparable injury to the defense interests of the United States." Sulzberger, reached in London, rejected the request. A five-column headline the next morning said, "Mitchell Seeks to Halt Series on Vietnam but *Times* Refuses." A. M. Rosenthal, the managing editor, said later: "If the headline had been 'Justice Department Asks End to Vietnam Series and *Times* Concedes,' I think it would have changed the history of the newspaper business."

So the government asked the U.S. District Court in New York to stop publication. By chance—a spin of the wheel in the clerk's office—the case went to a new judge on his first day on the bench, Murray I. Gurfein. He had been a colonel in army intelligence. That, and his freshman status, made things look grim to the *Times*. Moreover, Lord, Day & Lord refused to represent the *Times* in court. Bickel, an eminent professor of constitutional law at the Yale Law School, was found by Goodale, the *Times* general counsel, at midnight the night before the case first came before Judge Gurfein.

Bickel had two lines of argument. First, he said, Congress had never passed a statute authorizing the government to seek an injunction against the publication of claimed defense material; that was in contrast to the Atomic Energy Act, which specifically allowed injunctions against disclosure of restricted nuclear data. Second, the First Amendment's language prohibiting abridgment of "the freedom of speech, or of the press" had been read by the Supreme Court especially to disfavor "prior restraints" like the injunction sought here.

Government lawyers had the forty-seven volumes of the Pentagon Papers wheeled into the courtroom, under military guard. At first Judge Gurfein seemed impressed by the potential danger of disclosure. But he kept asking the government lawyers and the officials to point to specific documents and potential damage—and they would not do so. Instead one said, "We are not talking about a stack of documents where you put one in one pile and one in another pile; we are talking about a total impact of documents and their interweaving and interpretation and evaluation in the light of past tactics as they bear on the future. . . ."

Empty generalities did not persuade Judge Gurfein in the end. On June 19 he rejected the request for an injunction, with an opinion that remains one of the best of the many issued in the Pentagon Papers case.

"The security of the nation is not at the ramparts alone," Judge Gurfein wrote. "Security also lies in the value of our free institutions. A cantankerous press, an obstinate press, a ubiquitous press must be suffered by those in authority in order to preserve the even greater values of freedom of expression and the right of the people to know. In this case there has been no attempt to stifle criticism. Yet in the last analysis it is not merely the opinion of the editorial writer, or of the columnist, which is protected by the First Amendment. It is the free flow of information so that the public will be informed about the Government and its actions."

James Madison would have agreed. But the *Times* had not yet won. Judge Gurfein's decision was stayed while the U.S. Court of Appeals for the Second Circuit considered the government's appeal. It ordered Judge Gurfein to hear more from the government about potential damage—in effect giving it a second chance to offer the specifics it had declined to give the judge. Meanwhile, the *Washington Post* had obtained copies of the Pentagon Papers, had started publishing and had been enjoined. The two cases now went to the Supreme Court, which decided them on June 30, just fifteen days after the government first sued in Judge Gurfein's court.

The Supreme Court decided in favor of the *Times* and the *Post*. There was a three-paragraph unsigned opinion for the Court, and all nine justices wrote separately on their own. Six agreed that the government's claim for an injunction should be dismissed; three dissented.

The majority relied on both of Alexander Bickel's arguments: that no statute authorized an injunction and that the First Amendment disfavored prior restraints. The most powerful opinion was by Hugo L. Black, the senior justice, in his thirty-fourth year on the Court. It was his last opinion, as it turned out; that summer he became ill, retired and died.

"In the first amendment," Justice Black wrote, "the Founding Fathers gave the free press the protection it must have to fulfill its essential role in our democracy. . . . The press was protected so that it could bare the secrets of government and inform the people. Only a free and unrestrained press can effectively expose deception in government. And paramount among the responsibilities of a free press is the duty to prevent any part of the government from deceiving the people and sending them off to distant lands to die of foreign fevers and foreign shot and shell. In my view, far from deserving condemnation for their courageous reporting, the *New York Times*, the *Washington Post* and other newspapers should be commended for serving the purpose that the Founding Fathers saw so clearly. In revealing the workings of government that led to the Vietnam War, the newspapers nobly did that which the Founders hoped and trusted they would do."

After the decision, two Columbia Law School professors, Harold Edgar and Benno Schmidt Jr., wrote that it marked the end of the "symbiotic relationship between politicians and the press." By publishing the Pentagon Papers, they said, the *Times* "demonstrated that much of the press was no longer willing to be merely an occasional critical associate devoted to common aims, but intended to become an adversary threatening to discredit not only political dogma but also the motives of the nation's leaders."

Officials did not claim that David Halberstam violated any legal principle by printing classified documents. Their complaint was that he wrote what he saw with his own eyes, which did not agree with the official view of how the war was going. The Halberstam article included in this chapter was a think piece, an analysis of the war at the end of his tour. It was published in December 1963—fifteen months before President Johnson in effect admitted that the war was being lost by sending in hundreds of thousands of American combat troops to take over the brunt of the fighting from the South Vietnamese.

A long reportorial tradition, on the *Times* and other papers, is for correspondents working in countries under totalitarian rule to fight censorship and repression by all means available. The classic example of the difficulty was in Stalin's Soviet Union, where censors reduced stories to pabulum that made it look as though correspondents were overlooking the dark side of Soviet life.

After suffering under that system, Harrison Salisbury left the U.S.S.R. and wrote a series of articles giving an unvarnished picture. The one reprinted here was on a most sensitive subject, the slave-labor camps so long hidden from the world.

Stories by three correspondents in Poland are included. Sydney Gruson's was one of the pieces cited by the Pulitzer board in giving the *Times* as a whole the prize for foreign news coverage in 1958. Gruson did what a correspondent occasionally could in Communist countries: obtain the text of a secret and revealing speech by a leader, in this case Mao Tse-tung. A. M. Rosenthal was expelled from Poland because his probing articles embarrassed its leaders. He, too, was able to write more freely then from outside. When, years later, a Communist leader imposed martial law and total silence on Poland, John Darnton was able to get a letter to the *Times*, which it published.

Finally, there are two examples of investigative reporting—really just good, intensive reporting on difficult subjects. John M. Crewdson discovered, and described, the terrible conditions in which desperate aliens who sneak into this country for work were being held by labor contractors. Philip M. Boffey's revealing story was one of ten by various reporters on the disaster of the space shuttle *Challenger* that won the *Times* the prize for explanatory journalism in 1987.

Russia Re-Viewed

HARRISON E. SALISBURY

September 27, 1954

This is the ninth of a series of articles by a correspondent of the New York Times *who has just returned to this country after five years in the Soviet Union. For the first time he is able to write without the restrictions of censorship or the fear of it.*

Half a mile from the outskirts of Yakutsk, on a muddy road leading to the main channel of the River Lena, there is a rather long building of log construction, about two and a half stories high.

Its walls have blank faces with no windows and it looks as if it might be a frontier fort or warehouse or, possibly, a place for storing ice.

The building is none of these things. It is, in fact, one of the most notorious prisons in the Soviet Union, a place of confinement for political prisoners who are regarded as being particularly dangerous.

This is the prison to which, it is said, Karl Radek, the writer and revolutionary who was known to many Westerners, was sent after he was convicted in one of the purge trials of the 1930s. And here he is said to have died in the later years of World War II, the victim, so the story goes, of a fellow prisoner who killed him in a rage or quarrel. Gregori Sokolnikov, the veteran Soviet diplomat who got ten years along with Radek in 1937, was another victim of this prison.

A glimpse of this prison was one of many terrible and chilling sights that this correspondent encountered in a trip to the Soviet north and eastern Siberia. It was probably the most extensive survey of this grim region by an American since the journey in the late 1880s of George Kennan, granduncle of George F. Kennan, former United States ambassador to Moscow.

It is sometimes said that everything in Siberia is run by the MVD. This is not quite correct. Novosibirsk and western Siberia are generally free of directly operated MVD enterprises. On the other hand, the MVD runs most of the north and the Arctic and large areas of Central Asia, as well.

If you were to draw a map of MVD-land, the capital would be

at Khabarovsk, a grim, gray city on the Amur, six hours ahead of Moscow in time zone and nearly forty-eight hours distant by plane.

Khabarovsk is the administrative center of Russia's great empire-within-an-empire, the slave state of prison labor and forced residence workers that extends twenty-seven hundred miles west to Novosibirsk, nearly two thousand miles from the Arctic Ocean south to the Manchurian frontier, and six hundred miles east to Sakhalin.

Great Central Asian areas also fall within MVD-land—the coal basin and booming steel works of Karaganda, the copper mines of Balkhash, potash works in Uzbekistan, uranium mines in Tadzhikistan.

It is a fluid state and a superstate, imposed upon the ordinary civil apparatus with tentacles like those of an octopus, doubling back on itself and entwining half of Russia in its grasp.

The direction of this sinister superstate is housed in a great gray building of modernistic design that occupies a block or more of frontage on Volochayevskaya Street just off the main thoroughfare in Khabarovsk. This is the headquarters of the eastern administration of the MVD, the biggest and most powerful single administration in the Soviet Union and one of the biggest and most powerful in the world.

This correspondent, partly by chance and partly by management, happens to have traveled through more of this vast area of MVD-land than any other foreigner.

There are vast areas still unvisited by any outsider—the Magadan goldfield regions on the Sea of Okhotsk, Sakhalin with its oil fields and fisheries, Kamchatka, the Arctic fringe, the desert mining areas of Central Asia and scores of other areas, most of which are firmly closed to foreign visits.

It is most difficult to generalize about conditions in an area so vast as this. It must also be remembered that impressions of a traveler are a highly subjective thing. For example, the last two Americans to see Yakutsk before this correspondent were the late Wendell L. Willkie and Henry A. Wallace. Both were favorably impressed. Ten years later, in which time it may be deduced that such changes as occurred in Yakutsk were for the better, this correspondent got a decisively unfavorable impression.

Mr. Wallace's trip to Siberia in 1944 was one of the most unusual that ever occurred.

He saw things that no foreigner had seen before and few will ever see again—the Magadan goldfields for example; Yakutsk, as mentioned above; Karaganda, the Balkhash copper fields and a good many others. He was escorted from point to point by old Gen. Sergei A. Goglidze, whom Mr. Wallace praised for his gentleness and humanity.

But what Mr. Wallace did not realize until several years later was that good old Sergei Goglidze was the chief of the MVD for all this enormous area. He was the biggest police boss in the world. He was the man who sat in those gray offices on Volochayevskaya Street and ran the whole thing. Mr. Wallace rode in General Goglidze's private railroad car and ate at his table every day. And never knew who his host was.

General Goglidze is gone now. He went to his death with his boss, Lavrenti P. Beria, in December 1953, presumably in one of the execution chambers under the old insurance building on Lubyanka Hill in Moscow, the main headquarters of the MVD, or possibly in some army stronghold.

In any event, a new MVD general runs the Volochayevskaya Street headquarters in General Goglidze's place. Someone else sits in his seat in the Supreme Soviet, representing the Jewish Autonomous Oblast, one of the minor dependencies in the MVD empire. Another man holds General Goglidze's place on the Central Committee of the Uzbekistan Communist Party.

There has been a big reshuffling of chairs since Beria's arrest at the end of June 1953.

But nothing materially has changed on Volochayevskaya Street.

There is a special atmosphere in this gray prison land where the MVD is master. This is not a subjective thing, nor do you have to be foreign to feel it. For instance, an airplane on which this correspondent was traveling had motor trouble and had to make an unscheduled landing at Karaganda, the big prison coal center in Kazakhstan. As the passengers walked from the runway to the airport buildings one Russian said to the stewardess, who had announced that we would have to stop overnight: "Please tell the local *vlast* [powers] that we are not staying here because we want to. I haven't any visa for Karaganda on my passport and I don't want to be *rasstrelyan* [executed by shooting]."

This was the passenger's idea of a joke. But a pretty serious joke, at that. Foreigners make plenty of remarks about persons being sent to Karaganda. But you don't often hear Russians making the same kind of remarks.

We spent about eight hours in Karaganda and the Russian passenger's fears were needless. No one, Russian or foreign, was allowed off the airport grounds. It was the first time an American had had a glimpse of Karaganda since Mr. Wallace was there. Without the advantages of a personal escort of top MVD authorities, it was difficult to get more than a general impression of the place. But, even from the air, it was possible to ascertain that it had expanded enormously in recent years and a few more details could be garnered from the people at the airport.

At Yakutsk, the prison occupies a fairly extensive plot of land. It is surrounded by an eight-foot wooden fence, topped with four rows of barbed wire on stringers. At each corner and at intervals of about two hundred feet on all sides are typical Russian wooden sentry towers, manned by MVD soldiers with bayoneted rifles. A large searchlight on a swinging base is mounted at each tower.

The prison buildings themselves, like almost everything in Yakutsk, were of plain log construction with canted, tarpaper-covered roofs. The sides of the buildings were blank and windowless. Just below the eaves were long narrow slits, possibly a foot wide and three feet long, marked by a vertical row of bars. There was no other access for light or air. No door or entrance to the buildings was visible from the street.

Adjacent to the prison and also within the protective wooden fence and guard posts were wooden barracks for MVD troops and smaller individual residences for MVD officers and what apparently were office buildings.

This prison is the biggest single institution in Yakutsk. Its presence was not mentioned by local authorities, but, on the other hand, no special effort was made to keep it secret. Or at least there were no compunctions about driving past it with a visiting foreign correspondent. Possibly the authorities thought he wouldn't know what it was. But more likely they had just seen it so often it didn't register any more.

Prisons are an old, old institution in northern and eastern Siberia. In the Yakutsk local museum there are pictures of the *ostrogi*, or prisons, where the Czarist police used to keep their political captives. The buildings look very much like the long house in Yakutsk, but the modern prison has one refinement the Czar's jailers overlooked.

The old Czarist jails had ordinary windows that let in light and air. The new Soviet jails keep light and air to a minimum.

In the days just after the 1917 Revolution, the Bolsheviks had a poster they put to very effective use in Siberia and Central Asia and other backward areas. It showed an underground pit, in cross section. At the bottom were prisoners, shackled, working with bent backs in a cavern too low for upright posture. Just above them was another layer of workers with a little more shoulder room. Above them, petty officials with space for comfortable breathing. Above them, the clergy and nobles and at the top of the pyramid the Czar.

The poster is still to be seen in dim corners of dusty provincial museums—like that at Yakutsk. It has been many years since it had been posted on street walls or fences and probably just as well, so far as the regime is concerned. The public might see too plain a parallel with present conditions.

The fact is that when you get out into northern and eastern Siberia there is nothing very secret and nothing very much concealed about prisons, prisoners, labor camps, prison labor, forced residence, forced settlement and all the rest of the grim and horrible apparatus of the MVD.

Prisoners and the police apparatus are so routine, common and ordinary a part of life in these regions that local residents seem not to have the slightest embarrassment about such phenomena.

Actually, there is so little difference between the life of prison labor and the life of "free" labor in the north and the east that the whole question of the labor camp and forced labor suddenly seems to be legalistic and scholastic.

Americans, in particular, and Western-oriented people in general would be quick to note that there is a spiritual difference between working under the ever-present muzzle of a tommy gun in the hands of an MVD guard and free labor; between going home at night to a barbwire-encircled camp and to your own room.

Having seen the free workers and the slave workers, having seen them doing identical tasks, except for the presence of the guards; having seen the barracks in which the free labor for the most part lives, this correspondent has considerable doubts as to the existence of any great spiritual differences. In fact, the conditions of life are such as to leave very little room for things of the spirit, regardless of the technical status of the individual.

The editor of the Yakutsk paper felt no reluctance in showing the visiting correspondent from New York a new printing plant being built to house the two Yakutsk newspapers and the local publishing institution. The fact that the plant was being constructed by prison labor, working under guards carrying tommy guns, did not strike him as embarrassing or a circumstance that should be concealed.

Elsewhere in eastern Siberia the same attitude was apparent.

At Chita there is a prison camp not far from the airport. You can't drive from town to the flying field without going right past it. While not quite so grim a sight as Yakutsk's prison—it was composed of a series of one-story wooden barracks with typical barred, slit windows just under the eaves—the Chita camp did not look like a health resort.

But I doubt that the Chita officials who drove me past the place four times even noticed it any more than they paid the slightest heed to gangs of women working in a nearby potato patch with the inevitable tommy-gunned MVD escorts or the gangs of men in another field a little farther up the road where the MVD tommy gunners were mounted on Mongolian ponies, or the mixed gangs of men and women digging drainage ditches along the side of the highway while their guards lolled in the shade of a cottonwood clump, resting their chins on the stocks of their guns.

And, certainly, slave labor does not bring any blushes to the cheeks of the citizens of Khabarovsk, the great Far Eastern capital. The main street of Khabarovsk is Karl Marx Avenue and the principal square of the city is named for Lenin. In six blocks along this street five large construction projects are in progress—office buildings, dwellings and a hospital.

Each project is being built by prison labor. Each is surrounded by board fences with tommy gunners of the MVD mounted in guard towers at each corner. At one building the construction crew was almost entirely women, but the guard was just as large as at those buildings where the construction force was a mixed group of men and women or entirely masculine.

This correspondent drove a good many miles through the streets of Khabarovsk and was much impressed by the volume of new building going on, particularly of new apartment-house construction.

He was even more impressed by the fact that every construction job he saw was being carried on by prison labor—except for a dozen or so buildings that were being put up by regular Soviet Army troops.

In the whole city of Khabarovsk, out of forty or fifty building projects *not one* was being carried out by ordinary free, civilian labor.

This correspondent stood for a while in Lenin Square, across the street from a fine-looking hospital to which a large addition was being constructed. The annex was being built, of course, by prison laborers, most of whom appeared to be women. There were MVD tommy gunners right beside the sidewalk at an entrance to the construction site for trucks, and hundreds of people, men and women, were strolling past.

The citizens of Khabarovsk streamed steadily past the building site. No one averted his eyes. No one looked away. In ten minutes of watching I saw no sign of interest, no sign of curiosity in the faces of the passersby.

1955 PULITZER PRIZE FOR INTERNATIONAL REPORTING

Mao Text Shows Reds "Liquidated" 800,000 Since '49

SYDNEY GRUSON

Warsaw, Poland
June 13, 1957

Chinese Communist security forces "liquidated" eight hundred thousand persons between October 1949 and the beginning of 1954.

Mao Tse-tung, Chinese chief of state, disclosed this figure in a speech he made to Chinese party leaders in Peiping last February. He added that terror had since given way to persuasion.

However, he added that methods of terror were halted in 1954 and that persuasion and education were substituted.

His remarks were made in the first of two speeches, delivered by Mr. Mao last February 27 and March 12, in which he laid down his new Marxist theory that contradictions or conflicts could and did arise between the rulers and the ruled in a Communist state.

The texts of Mr. Mao's two addresses have not been published.

However, a summary of Mr. Mao's remarks, including textual excerpts, has now become available.

Mr. Mao's new theory has aroused widespread attention. Soviet doctrine has long contended that conflicts between the rulers and the ruled existed only under capitalism and vanished in Communist society.

In his recent television interview, Nikita S. Khrushchev denied the existence in the Soviet Union of such contradictions. The denial of the Soviet party secretary was suppressed by censorship and did not appear in the version of his remarks circulated in the Soviet Union and China.

Among the principal points made by Mr. Mao in the version of his remarks obtained here were the following:

- Contradictions, including those between the leaders and the people, exist under Communism. Stalin's mistaken understanding of this point led to a rule of terror in the Soviet Union and the liquidation of thousands of Communists.
- Persistent use of terror within a nation sets up internal antagonisms that produce the kind of results demonstrated last autumn in the revolt in Hungary.
- In the Hungarian crisis, the Communist Party simply disappeared "in a matter of a few days" and the whole state threatened to disintegrate.
- The Hungarian uprising had a positive side, as do all events, in that it demonstrated the mistakes that arise from great-power feelings and chauvinism.
- Small-scale strikes and demonstrations are "beneficial" danger signals, revealing trouble that needs correction. Persuasive methods, not coercion, must be used in such instances. General large-scale strikes directed against the regime are another matter.
- There is no danger of a new world war for at least fifteen years.
- Because of food and other problems, China's population must be stabilized at about six hundred million, its present level. China does not have sufficient funds for adequate wages.
- Communist populations must be exposed to a certain amount of negative propaganda if they are to understand the nature of the struggle between Communism and capitalism. Generalissimo Chiang

Kai-shek's works and some Voice of America presentations will be published in China.

The summary of Mr. Mao's speech deals with five major topics and some questions and answers.

The first section was devoted to the problem of conflict within a Communist society. It includes the following excerpts:

"These problems are new in Marxism-Leninism. Marx and Engels did not know about these problems for obvious reasons. Lenin mentioned them but did not enlarge upon them because during his lifetime, as a result of foreign intervention, it was difficult to speak about internal problems only.

"As for Stalin, his opinions can be considered only negatively. The experience of the Soviet Union in this respect shows that Stalin made the mistake of substituting internal differences for external antagonism, which resulted in a rule of terror and the liquidation of thousands of Communists.

"In dealing with enemies it is necessary to use force. We in China also have used force to deal with enemies of the people. The total number of those who were liquidated by our security forces numbers eight hundred thousand. This is the figure up to 1954.

[The eight hundred thousand are believed to include mainly opponents of the regime killed in civil warfare after 1949, as well as persons executed on charges of spying and counterrevolution.]

"Since then we are no longer using methods of terror. Instead we have substituted persuasion and education. If one persists in using the methods of terror in solving internal antagonisms, it may lead to transformation of these antagonisms into antagonisms of the nation-enemy type, as happened in Hungary.

"But the method of persuasion must go together with an analysis of the bad side of the problem, with the making of suggestions, that take root in the mistakes committed. This is the old method of meetings and discussions. Many people laugh at us because we have too many meetings. But this old and tried custom of allowing everyone to have his say has frequently given good results and is the most democratic procedure.

"The internal differences are not and must not be antagonistic even

if they are the antagonisms between the proletariat and the bourgeoisie. If we stand on the platform of national unity, the solution of
these differences must be based on criticism designed to strengthen
that unity.

[In other words, differences should be kept within the family and
not be embittered to the point of physical struggle.]

"A good example is the attitude of the Chinese Communist Party
toward the bourgeoisie, which resulted in the bourgeoisie's joining the
constructive work of building a Socialist state. Of course, we do not
say this applies to every other country, which may be born under
different conditions, but in the Chinese experience this way of solving
problems has proved most useful."

Following are excerpts of the second part of the speech, dealing
with strikes:

"The internal antagonisms should be dealt with as soon as they
appear. But what to do if this is hampered by bureaucracy, which in
turn leads to demonstrations and strikes? Such incidents should be
considered as warning signals to sectors of the administration where
bureaucracy has made its nest.

"In this respect it can even be said that small strikes are beneficial
because they point to mistakes committed. Of course big general
strikes cannot be considered in the same way because they are not
fought to rectify mistakes or satisfy rightful grievances but are directed
against the regime itself.

"Small strikes, if correctly dealt with, can be a good way to avoid
big strikes. But it also must be pointed out that we should use persuasion to dissuade workers from using these methods. Strikes are
never beneficial to the working class because they result in less goods
for the market, that is for the workers themselves. But we should use
only persuasion and never administrative methods of force.

"Another aspect of this situation is the question of pay. We do not
have at present enough funds to increase the pay even for those who
rightly claim more for their work. It is known that the wages given to
three workers must suffice for five persons at least. So what can be
done? The best solution seems to divide the work so that everyone gets
something, both in the way of work and pay. We must try also to get
everyone who wants it the possibility of engaging in outside work."

The third part of the speech considers the population problem.

According to official Chinese statements made earlier this year the annual population increase is between thirteen million and fifteen million.

Mr. Mao said that the number of births, now thirty million a year, was a "sign of great progress made in medical service and the general rise in living standards, especially in the countryside and of the faith people have in the future."

"But this figure must also be of great concern to us all," he said, continuing:

"I will quote two other figures. The increase in grain harvest for the last two years has been ten million tons a year. This is barely sufficient to cover the needs of our growing population.

"The second figure concerns the problem of education. It is estimated that at present 40 percent of our youth have not been placed in primary schools. Steps must therefore be taken to keep our population for a long time at a stable level, say, of six hundred million. A wide campaign of explanation and proper help must be undertaken to achieve this aim."

The fourth section of the speech dealt with what Mr. Mao called "the double aspect of all occurrences." Some excerpts follow:

"Each problem must be considered in its entire complexity. Everything has two sides, a good side and a bad side. For instance, the Japanese attack [on China in the 1930s] was a bad thing because it meant war. But, on the other hand, it resulted in good because the struggle against Japanese aggression made it possible to mobilize the whole nation around the Communist Party, which led the struggle, and ultimately made for the Communist victory.

"The tragedy of Hungary was also bad. But the Hungarian tragedy had its positive result because it made us conscious of the mistakes that spring from great-power feelings and chauvinism and taught us to beware of them. World War II also had its positive as well as its negative aspects. The war brought upon the world much destruction but at the same time it crushed the old imperialists [an allusion to the end of colonial rule in many countries] and made clear that a new war would mean the overthrow of capitalism. But we do not want a war though the possibility of it must not be excluded."

Following are excerpts from the fifth section of the speech, dealing with Communist theory:

"Marxism-Leninism is not afraid of criticism and does not fear discussion. It is the compass of the party that built a Socialist China. Marxism-Leninism must come out to meet criticism head-on because only in this way can it be strengthened and become a really great power and not a new religion or a taboo. The party believes that Marxism-Leninism will win more sympathizers if it conducts an ideological struggle based on the principle of unity-criticism-unity.

[Under this principle, criticism of decisions is encouraged, but unity must again be restored once the criticism has been taken into account.]

"The opinions against the policy of a hundred flowers are the result of a fear of criticism, fear of losing the monopolistic position. They are an example of dogmatism. Marx never said that he should not be criticized. To those who do not follow that teaching of Marx I would address an old saying: 'He who does not allow himself to be criticized during his life will be criticized after his death.' "

[Mr. Mao calls his new doctrine, "Let a hundred flowers bloom, let a hundred schools of thought contend."]

"There need be no fear that the policy of a hundred flowers will yield poisoned fruit. Sometimes it is necessary even to have this poisoned fruit to know what it is that we are fighting against. For this reason too, it has been decided to publish the full works of Chiang Kai-shek and even a volume of some of the Voice of America broadcasts. It is not enough to attack reactionaries. We must know exactly what the reactionaries want and what they represent."

Mr. Mao was asked a question about the possibility of a new war and replied:

"A new war is a possibility we must always bear in mind. There are different reasons why the capitalists may want to start it. But personally I do not believe we need fear such a possibility for at least the next fifteen years."

To a question on the problem of solving the difference between the immediate needs of the people and the needs to safeguard industrial progress, he replied:

"The one-sided drive to build in a hurry the heavy industry needed by the country aggravated this problem. But an analysis made it possible to reduce the proportion of funds devoted to heavy industry from 9.1 percent to 6.1 percent and there is a possibility of still further reductions."

He was asked whether it was really necessary to publish General Chiang's works and Voice of America broadcasts. He replied:

"The new generation, which did not fight face to face with imperialism and reactionaries, must know why we are calling on them to continue that fight. And another reason. We cannot breed flowers in a hothouse. Such flowers will be neither beautiful nor healthy. We must strengthen and harden them if their fruits are to be lasting."

Replying to a question of how far China could use Soviet experience, Mr. Mao said:

"The Soviet Union has many experiences that can be used for the benefit of our country, especially in regard to industrial progress. But other experiences of the Soviet Union cannot be neglected and we have to consider them if only not to repeat the mistakes."

Asked about Hungary, he replied:

"The Hungarian party was weak because it stressed the methods of repression instead of persuasion. The weakness of the party came out during the tragedy of October when the party simply disappeared in a matter of a few days. The use of Soviet forces was necessary because there was fear that the disintegration would not be confined to the party alone but to the whole state, though it is regrettable that the situation made such an intervention necessary."

Mr. Mao's views on the contradictions between leaders and masses in a Communist society were explained in an article in the Chinese Communist newspaper *People's Daily*. The following is taken from the Russian translation of the article, which appeared in *Pravda* last April 15.

"Why can there arise contradictions between the masses and their rulers? This is determined by the different situation which they occupy in the life of the state. The masses take direct part in productive activities and are occupied primarily with physical labor, and usually it is difficult for them to realize directly their right to administer. The position they occupy leads them comparatively easily to examine problems from the point of view of partial facts of a given moment and a given place, to put more attention on current interests and interests which are of a partial character. It is with difficulty that they understand the entire picture and all the difficulties of Socialist construction.

"On the other hand, rulers directly realize the right to administer and usually are rarely engaged in physical labor. They in general can understand the overall future and general interests, but at the same time they comparatively easily leave out of account the concrete situation and vital requirements of the popular masses.

"However, the contradictions between the masses and the rulers, like other contradictions among the people, are nonantagonistic contradictions that arise on the basis of the unity of primary interests. They are completely unlike the contradictions between us and our enemies, contradictions arising on the basis of conflict of primary interests."

1958 PULITZER PRIZE FOR INTERNATIONAL REPORTING

Polish Reds Turn Bitter over Rule

A. M. ROSENTHAL

Vienna, Austria
December 1, 1959

This is the second of five articles on Poland by a correspondent of the New York Times *who was recently expelled from that country for having "probed too deeply" into Polish affairs.*

Poland's Communist Party, placed in power and kept in power only by Soviet might, has been thrown into confusion and bitterness by a leader it once followed out of hope and now follows out of desperation.

In a Warsaw newspaper office, three Communist journalists were teasing a fourth Pole because he was the only member of the editorial board who did not belong to the party.

"Aren't you afraid for your job?" they kept asking him.

"Not at all," the nonparty man answered lightly. "I am the only one of us who feels secure. They have to keep me. I am the only one who represents the people."

Everybody smiled, but not very broadly. In his mocking way, the nonparty man had touched a painful nerve that prevents Polish Communists from feeling politically at home in the land they control. It is the awareness that the Communist Party of Poland is a party of a small minority, kept in control by the existence of a foreign power, which has never been able to bridge the gap of distrust that separates it from the people of Poland.

But this is an old story in all the Eastern European Communist countries, and in Poland the Communists have learned to live with it.

Some of them live with it proudly—"We are part of the forces of history." Some cover it with a layer of cynicism—"If they don't like us in Poland, all they have to do is move the country to the moon." Some accept with a mixture of hope and stoicism—"We are working for a better Poland and some day we will be understood."

But in the last few months the Polish Communist Party—officially, the United Workers Party—has been stumbling badly under additional troubles, troubles that few Polish Communists really understand.

Polish Communists find themselves denounced with bitter scorn by the man they brought back to power with their surge of hope in 1956, Wladyslaw Gomulka. Then they find themselves ignored by M. Gomulka until the time comes for another denunciation.

They find men coming back to power whose very names chill them with memories of the past—and of the people's reaction to the past. They find that more and more of the men who recalled the hope of 1956 are being dismissed and sometimes they refuse to believe, because it is too painful to believe or because nobody bothers to inform them.

"I tell you Hochfeld cannot have been dismissed!" said the editor of a leading Polish Communist weekly to a Western correspondent. "I'll bet you a hundred zlotys he has not been dismissed."

Julian Hochfeld, a Socialist spark of the 1956 intellectual upheaval, had been dismissed as head of the Institute for International Affairs a full week earlier. No one had bothered to tell the editor of the weekly that is M. Gomulka's forum.

Poland's Communists are not liberals or social democrats; they are Communists. But many of them are men who believe deeply in socialism and had believed deeply that socialism could be achieved under a considerable degree of freedom—and in 1956 risked their necks to prove it. They did not think there would be a swift rush toward complete freedom, but they thought there would be a steady move toward it.

In 1956 they saw themselves as part of a movement that might not be liked by the people but was right for Poland and would be accepted by the people. Now they see that there will be restrictions in the range of liberty. It may not be as bad as it was in the days of Stalinism, but having tasted a measure of freedom, even Communists are not happy with smaller dollops.

They are not happy, but as Communists they would accept much more easily if they understood fully or believed fully in what their leader was doing. They neither understand fully nor believe fully.

For one thing, most of the members of the party have lost all contact with M. Gomulka. For the first time since 1956 they refer to him not just by his underground nickname of Wieclaw but as "Wieclaw the dictator."

"Even in the Stalinist days we were consulted more," said a party member in Warsaw. "Now it's Gomulka this and Gomulka that and keep your damned mouth shut."

The party follows M. Gomulka. It has no other choice. The Communists know in essence what he is driving at—instilling discipline into the party, trying desperately to give it roots in the country, prodding the people and the party into coming into contact with each other.

But many party members are filled with a heavy fear that he is going about it the wrong way. Perhaps peasants in the countryside or workers in a provincial town do not care much which Communists are appointed to high places. They lump most Communists together and would be happy to pack them all off.

For a party member there are not many more important things than the men who rule the apparatus. The personalities and philosophies of the leaders determine the tone of life for the rank and file.

Now men who most Polish Communists took it for granted were destroyed by 1956 are coming back to places of influence, men like Julian Tokarski, the Stalinist target of the workers' wrath in 1956, now recalled from obscurity to the post of deputy premier.

For a long time the party has been trying to dilute the memory of 1956. At the last party congress in March 1959, official history was rewritten to make the Soviet Union the inspiration of 1956 instead of the main opponent of it.

But the trends set in motion by 1956 still exist in Poland and the government has not yet turned its back on some of the principal achievements of 1956—the truce with the Roman Catholic Church, the removal of Polish terrorism, private ownership of land.

The fear is heavy in the party ranks that M. Gomulka is so intent about establishing the power of the party and so heavy-handed that, whether he wills it or not, he is re-creating the influence of the Stalinists.

Poland is a small country, and to the outside world only absolutes seem to count. If it is not Stalinism it does not matter much. To Poles, especially Polish Communists, variations, trends, nuances, are of supreme importance because they determine how a man lives.

M. Gomulka was enormously successful in the days after 1956, successful in Communist terms. He found himself a leader of a shattered party and re-created it.

But in the last two years, most particularly in the last few months, he has made one enormous error. He has failed to give the party the line.

The line for a Communist party is a combination of ideology, directive, officially accepted causes and remedies and, most of all, a clearly understood political atmosphere.

These days none of the component parts of the line is available for the Polish Communist to cling to. The result is that Communists have a feeling of being cast adrift from their political moorings.

There are days of jumpiness in Warsaw when newspapermen compare the number of tranquilizers being swallowed in their offices: "On Jerozolimskie Street it's just like Madison Avenue."

Then days come when nothing happens, and in the steamy cafes people tell each another it is all a passing fuss.

"You know," a Polish teacher said comfortingly, "in Poland the Communists always have to act tougher than they intend to get because otherwise who would pay any attention to them?"

But nobody really knows because nobody knows the line.

Tough men who favor strict centralization are brought into the government. But Polish Communists hear of a speech by another leader saying decentralization is really not bad. What is the line?

M. Gomulka screams at the propaganda chiefs for failing to get out there and pitch. Party editors go to the next briefing prepared to hear the whip crack. But Edward Ochab, the new propaganda boss, merely talks mildly about the need for "studies." What is the line?

And the Russians, what to think about them?

Every time something unpleasant happens in Poland, or is about to happen, Polish Communists whisper to their Western friends that it is all the Russians' fault.

This time virtually all the politically minded say that it is M. Gomulka himself who quickened the tempo of the movement to the Right that he believed in all along. Still, it is possible the Russians did not have a hand in persuading M. Gomulka to bring back a man as detested as Lieut. Gen. Kazimierz Witaszewski, known as "General Gaspipe." What is the line?

Then there is agriculture. Everybody says that is the key. Everybody, knows that the peasant cannot be cajoled into collectivization and cannot be forced into it. Agricultural production is stumbling and something obviously has to be done. What is the line?

The party has troubles that go deeper than the current crisis. It is virtually without prestige in the country, and outside the big cities a Communist is often a social outcast. ("Just remember one thing," a Polish bride-to-be said to her Western bridegroom. "No Communists at the wedding.")

The party has failed to attract youth, except those interested in picnics, hikes and free movies. University students are contemptuous of it and so are most intellectuals. Periodically the official publications of the United Workers Party complain that the workers are staying away in droves.

And there are deep troubles inside the party, inherent in its nature and history. Its leadership generally is a leadership of second-raters and newcomers. The first-rank men and the veterans' cadre of the party before World War II were murdered in Moscow in Stalinist purges or killed by the Germans.

The party before the war had only a few thousand members. Now it has more than a million—but it is a membership that makes its leaders shudder.

"The first thing a Communist party should do after attaining power is to close its doors for a while to keep out opportunists," said a leading Communist. "We opened them wide because we were still fighting the Socialists and the peasant parties. You ask and write about the party. You call this a Communist party? We have almost no real Communists, just a collection of churchgoers and job-seekers."

Apathy and sloth are party problems—nobody wants to work for the party, the newspapers complain from time to time—and so is anti-Semitism.

Some of the party's leaders are Jews and many of its organizers, killed in the purges, were Jews. The Polish Communist government has fought anti-Semitism in the country and has a better record on that score than any other Communist government.

But deep-seated anti-Semitism is a part of Polish life and the party apparatus reflects it. A Polish Jewish Communist official once told this reporter that Polish Jewish Communists had learned that the party wanted them to fade into the background so as not to "run counter to opinion."

"I think more than twice myself about hiring a Jewish stenographer," he said.

The party still follows M. Gomulka. The reservoir of admiration has not completely dried up—"and who else is there?" But three years after it renewed its hold on power in a flush of enthusiasm and hope, the Polish Communist Party is confused, lethargic, worried and heavy with the realization of its own isolation and ineffectiveness.

1960 PULITZER PRIZE FOR INTERNATIONAL REPORTING

Crucial Point in Vietnam

DAVID HALBERSTAM

Saigon, Vietnam
December 23, 1963

The long and bitter struggle to keep South Vietnam from being taken over by Communism has reached a critical point.

For a year the war there has been going poorly for the anti-Communists, and the tough, well-armed Communist guerrillas are stepping up the conflict. Facing them is a new and uncertain military government. The Communist guerrillas, known as the Vietcong, hold the initiative, militarily and psychologically, in most rural areas. In regions they effectively control, they levy taxes, obtain food, redistribute land and recruit reinforcements. They are strong in the Mekong River delta, the country's rice bowl, stronger than they ever were during the French Indochinese war, some experienced Vietnamese observers believe.

Secretary of Defense Robert S. McNamara paid his most recent visit to Vietnam last week and the seriousness of the situation there is said to be acknowledged now at the highest American military and civilian levels in Washington and Saigon.

A thousand United States servicemen, their specific jobs completed, came home this month, but plans to end the rest of the 16,500-man American military advisory and support mission by 1965 are reported to have been abandoned.

Despite this, experienced Western observers in South Vietnam warn that unless the new military junta in Saigon takes drastic action in the coming dry season, it may lose a last chance to turn back the Communists. The dry season, which begins in January and lasts about four months, makes operations against the guerrillas, particularly pursuit, easier.

Some observers believe that the Ngo Dinh Diem regime, which was toppled by the junta at the beginning of November, never adequately employed its military strength and the mobility represented by such United States equipment as transport helicopters and armored personnel carriers.

The resources to turn back the Vietcong are available, these observers say, but what is in doubt is the nation's willingness to pay the price for victory. If the junta is to win, they say, it must wage a bitter and costly war in the next six months; it must actively seek out, engage and pursue the guerrillas; and it must accept casualties far heavier than the Diem regime would accept, testing to the utmost the strength of the nation in fratricidal conflict.

Yet the junta has not shown the sense of urgency that some Westerners believe is required.

True, the heavy political atmosphere of recent years has lifted. Gone are the rigid pride and vanity of the Diem regime, which induced subordinates to tell the late president what he wanted to hear.

For example, while the situation in the two provinces south of Saigon was deteriorating alarmingly, the commander there was reporting that government forces controlled 95 percent of the area.

The new junta, moreover, seems willing to discuss serious problems seriously, and the inability of the United States to get a real hearing for its view may have ended. But the problems, particularly the immediate military problems, are immense.

With considerable skill the Communist guerrillas have expanded their control in rural areas, particularly in the delta, pressing their military and political initiative, slowly driving the government forces back into district capitals. In recent weeks there has been a sharp increase in mine-laying and sabotage incidents along main routes right outside district headquarters.

As to the increase in mine-laying, one knowledgeable Vietnamese province chief said, "They have us back in the caves and want to keep us there."

A prolonged trip through the lush delta these days is a sad journey for someone who also traveled there more than a year ago. Those earlier trips took place in an area where the government had a good chance of victory. Now the signs of government neglect and the Vietcong's presence are everywhere.

There are district capitals where government troops do not move from their posts and where they face the night uneasily. There are villages, formerly government-controlled, where children look away when government troops arrive. There are government airstrips where light planes land through Vietcong sniper fire. In one village an American officer and a newsman found a Vietcong flag flying from the roof of a small Roman Catholic church.

The officer asked the young priest to explain.

"It is very simple, captain," the priest said. "You and the government come here once every three or four months and you have tea with me and then you leave. But the Vietcong are here every night and this is the price they exact for the survival of my church. They are very clever, I think."

When the government troops left, the flag was still on the church.

One aspect of the situation in the delta is this: The government must fight to wrest initiative and control from the Vietcong before it can persuade the villagers that it offers them a better deal than the Diem regime did.

In the delta and elsewhere, with the dry season approaching, the Vietcong cannot afford psychologically to have the government smash their main units and force them into a less effective type of guerrilla war.

Rather there is evidence that the Vietcong guerrillas see themselves at a point of no return. There are reliable reports of an increase in cadres for main-force units infiltrating the country. Also there are reports of heavier weapons, such as 75-mm recoilless rifles, and large amounts of ammunition being brought into the country through Cambodia and down the Mekong River into the delta.

The key question remains how deeply the South Vietnamese people want to win the war and how heavy a sacrifice they and their new leaders are prepared to make. The Western, particularly non-American, observers in Saigon who doubt the will of the people and their leadership believe that the Vietnamese are unaware of how tough the fighting ahead will have to be to turn the tide of the conflict.

The outlook is that the situation will deteriorate unless the government can wrest the initiative from the guerrillas. Unless it can, there appear to be only two likely alternatives.

One is a neutralist settlement. The other is use of United States combat troops to prop up the government.

Despite President de Gaulle's idea of a neutral Vietnam free of American influence and with closer ties to France, most observers believe that a neutralist settlement would leave a vacuum in South Vietnam that could be exploited by Communist North Vietnam. These observers say that a Communist takeover in the south would probably follow a neutralist settlement in about two years.

The use of United States troops for combat, rather than for advisory, support and training missions, would pose major problems. Some think that nothing would please the Communist world more than the sight of American troops fighting the Vietcong.

Furthermore, many guerrilla-war experts believe that the Vietnamese rice paddies would swallow up the United States troops, that the population would turn on them and help the Vietcong and that the Americans would face a situation like the one that defeated the French in the 1945–54 Indochinese war. With France's defeat, French Indochina was divided into North and South Vietnam, Laos and Cambodia.

There is a general impression that the current war in South Vietnam was envisioned by North Vietnam at the time of the Geneva settlement of the Indochinese conflict, a settlement that partitioned Vietnam. The struggle in South Vietnam began in earnest in the late 1950s.

The prevalent view is that while the Vietcong are almost all South Vietnamese, the guerrilla war is directed from North Vietnam and cadres are sent there for training.

The Vietcong strategy, especially in the last year, has been aimed not so much at all-out military victory—the guerrillas do not have the strength for that—as at forcing a new Geneva settlement, one that would neutralize South Vietnam and enable the Communists to take over.

This strategy has included a major military offensive in the provinces right around Saigon—Long An, Dinh Tuong and Binh Duong—to choke off the capital and hold all the countryside around it.

This would make the local and foreign residents in Saigon edgy, create a psychological impression of vast Vietcong control, and presumably result in a greater willingness to seek a neutralist settlement. The Vietcong offensive in these provinces, American and Vietnamese military observers believe, was singularly successful.

In a sense, one chapter has ended in Vietnam and another is about to start. The last chapter began in late 1961, when the country, faced by a grave challenge, appeared unable to resist Communist subversion. That was the time, according to one American, "when you went to bed at night and didn't know whether there would still be a country there when you woke up."

In October of that year President Kennedy sent General Maxwell D. Taylor, then his special military adviser and now chairman of the Joint Chiefs of Staff, on a special mission. General Taylor found Vietnam prepared for a war it was not fighting and unprepared for one it was fighting. He recommended drastic measures designed to give the Vietnamese army the means and mobility with which to resist a guerrilla war.

What has become clear is that the Americans and the Ngo Dinh Diem regime differed widely on their priorities. To the Americans, the number one priority was winning the war. For the Ngo family it was different: Its survival in a postwar Vietnam held the top priority.

What also became clear was that although the United States mission in Vietnam was primarily advisory, the government was far more interested in American gear and money than in American advice.

This seemed particularly true at the highest level. Last September Ngo Dinh Nhu, the president's brother and chief adviser, said to an Australian visitor that the war would be won faster if the Americans went home and left their equipment in Vietnam.

President Diem and Mr. Nhu are known to have disliked American advice, which placed considerable emphasis on direct confrontation and meant that the attacking government forces must be prepared to accept relatively heavy casualties.

President Diem, though extremely sensitive about losses suffered by his main-force units when attacking, did not seem to feel so strongly about losses when an outpost was overrun by the Vietcong.

Though there are no official statistics on this, some well-informed United States military officials believe that between 70 and 80 percent of government casualties were suffered in static positions. This indicates the kind of war that was fought in the last year.

The United States military command was in a difficult position. It was caught between an ally that was not taking its advice and an administration at home that was exerting pressure for results.

Perhaps because the ally at times paid lip service to accepting United States tactical doctrines, perhaps because the weapons statistics appeared good, the United States military mission in Vietnam expressed optimism and apparently, right up until the coup that overthrew the regime, believed that the war was going well.

Western authorities on guerrilla warfare believe that what happened in Vietnam in the last year and a half was something like the following:

The Vietcong, caught off guard by the American-aided buildup, and having underestimated American willingness to make a commitment in Vietnam, took a beating through mid-1962. Then, as the year ebbed, the guerrillas adjusted to the situation; they learned how to stand and fight instead of running from the helicopters and fighter planes. They regained their confidence.

The government troops failed to follow up aggressively. Rather, commanders became too dependent on the new machinery, relied too much on air and artillery. They lost the momentum they had, and by the end of 1962 the favorable statistics were beginning to taper off. The Vietcong forces were beginning to exploit the situation.

This continued through the beginning of 1963. It was most noticeable in the Mekong delta region, where confrontation with the enemy can be a regular thing if a commander really seeks it. By February some United States field advisers were warning that the signs were ominous.

What it amounted to was this: Despite all the talk about fighting guerrillas there was little antiguerrilla fighting in Vietnam.

The Special Forces, with their montagnard trainees in the highlands, encouraged some small-unit fighting. But in the heartland of the war, the delta, there was little fighting at night, little attempt to try guerrilla tricks on the Vietcong themselves, little emphasis on patrols, mobile defenses or ambushes.

Because mistakes were regularly repeated—for instance, the guerrillas were allowed to help themselves constantly to good weapons at the small outposts—victory is further away, not closer, than it was a year ago. And the price in blood will be considerably higher.

The Vietcong men did not repeat their mistakes—they exploited the government's lack of aggressiveness, and consequently improved their abilities more than the government troops did.

Fifteen months ago the Americans would say about the elusive Vietcong, "If we could only make them stand and fight." Now the Vietcong are often standing and fighting. The problem has changed drastically. It has become one of how to face a well-armed, dug-in enemy in a rice paddy and tear it up without taking a disproportionate number of casualties.

Eight times this year, government soldiers have come upon Vietcong battalions in rice paddies. Though they inflicted sizable casualties on the guerrillas, they never really sealed off an area, destroyed a battalion or performed as the American advisers feel Vietnamese are capable of performing.

Just how much the ruling junta is going to improve on this situation is the key question in Vietnam today.

The generals, one American asserted, "are good men, but good isn't enough." He added: "They damn well better be great men. We don't have time for anything else."

So far the American advisers appear to like the three top generals in the junta but, as an embassy official noted, it is "more a matter of liking their promises than anything specific—they haven't done that much."

In particular, the Americans seem to like Major General Duong Van Minh, chairman of the junta. There is a marked feeling that whether the junta succeeds depends to a great degree on whether he becomes a bold figure and tries to become a popular leader.

So far neither General Minh nor any other member of the junta has emerged sharply. Some Vietnamese see the difficulty as stemming, in part, from the junta's uncertainties and divisions.

A basic division is reported among the regime's top four generals. On one side are General Minh, Major General Le Van Kim and Major General Tran Van Don, the defense minister. On the other is Major General Ton That Dinh, along with a few other lesser-known officers.

General Dinh was for long a loyal supporter of President Diem. He was a particular favorite of the late president and is not really trusted by the others. He reciprocates this suspicion. In style, manner and age, the audacious General Dinh is different from the others.

Many observers feel that a break within the junta is inevitable. But for the present the split has taken the form of uneasy maneuvering, primarily over command appointments.

As the generals maneuver, each seems hesitant to move too quickly to seize power lest this alarm the others. The result has been to neutralize some of the leadership potential of the junta, and leave it with less of a sense of direction than is needed in Saigon.

Yet there is a realization in Vietnam of the urgency of the war situation, and some Americans believe that part of the most recent McNamara visit was an attempt to impart that urgency to the generals.

For there is little time and little optimism left in South Vietnam. As one member of the American mission said, "It is no longer a question of not knowing the problems. We are down to looking for the answers."

1964 PULITZER PRIZE FOR INTERNATIONAL REPORTING

Thousands of Aliens Held in Virtual Slavery in United States

JOHN M. CREWDSON

Immokalee, Florida
October 19, 1980

Uncounted thousands of Spanish-speaking aliens who flee to this country each year to escape the crushing poverty of their homelands are being virtually enslaved, bought and sold on sophisticated underground labor exchanges. They are trucked around the country in consignments by self-described labor contractors who deliver them to farmers and growers for hundreds of dollars a head.

Exactly how many find themselves bound to employers who take advantage of their illegal status, their naivete and their cultural alienation is not known.

But dozens of Immigration and Naturalization Service officials, migrant aid lawyers, prosecutors, social workers, farm union organizers and others who work closely with migrant laborers said in interviews that they believed the practice, while not common, was probably a growing one involving thousands of migrants from the tomato fields of Arkansas to the apple orchards of Virginia, from the cotton fields of north Texas to the orange groves of Florida.

"You're not talking about something isolated," said William Burk, an assistant Border Patrol chief in Del Rio, Texas. Humberto Moreno, a senior official of the immigration service, agreed. "There's a significant amount of that going on," he said.

Five years ago the immigration service caught seventy-six thousand aliens who had been smuggled into the United States by "coyotes," as the smugglers call themselves; last year it apprehended 211,000. And as the organized smuggling of illegal aliens increases, officials say, so does the possibility that an alien will find himself forced to work for little or nothing.

As a result, the immigration service and the Justice Department, which until recently were mainly concerned with keeping illegal aliens out of this country, are now broadening their focus to include the smugglers, the labor contractors and the growers who prey on the aliens once they are here. Earlier this month the Justice Department brought its first peonage case in nearly a year, against the owner of a seafood processing plant near Houston.

The Justice Department's civil rights division has assigned a lawyer to coordinate cases of involuntary servitude with the immigration service and the Department of Labor, which enforces federal law governing the hiring and transporting of migrant farmworkers. Moreover, the immigration service recently began instructing its antismuggling agents in the intricacies of the Reconstruction-era slavery laws, which prohibit involuntary servitude and peonage, or the forcing of a laborer to work off his debt to the employer.

"We're telling them to 'think peonage,'" said Moreno, who heads the antismuggling section of the immigration service. That the authorities have no certain figures on such cases does not surprise some who know the problem well. "This country does a better job of counting its migratory birds than its migratory workers," said Gary Bryant, a lawyer with Migrant Legal Action in Washington.

Formal complaints about involuntary servitude are relatively few. Last year the Justice Department conducted twenty-one investigations into possible violations of the antislavery laws, and there have only been nine such inquiries so far this year. In both years, most involved blacks in eastern states, not migrant Hispanic workers.

Daniel F. Rinzel, chief of the criminal section of the Justice Department's civil rights division, said his office received relatively few complaints of "illegal aliens held against their will."

The government's principal difficulty in finding and trying such offenses, said Bruce Berger, who left two weeks ago as the Justice Department's "involuntary servitude" coordinator to go into private practice, "is in finding people who are willing to come forward."

"Most times the victims are very afraid," he said. "We're aware of the problem, and I don't think we've found any satisfactory way of dealing with it."

Vincent Beckman, a lawyer with Michigan Migrant Legal Services, agreed. "Usually, the people are just so intimidated they don't do anything about it," he said.

Even when potential witnesses overcome their reluctance, federal investigators said, there may be a host of other obstacles to a successful peonage prosecution. Frequently illiterate and often intimidated by the American legal process, illegal aliens do not make the best courtroom witnesses, investigators say. Jailed by the government as "material witnesses," they may grow hostile by the time a trial begins.

The clandestine nature of involuntary servitude may make it difficult to gather independent evidence, as can the determined anonymity of the coyotes and labor contractors who often enforce it. An alien may not even be aware that the sort of indentured service that might be tolerated in rural Mexico qualifies in this country as a violation of the peonage or involuntary servitude laws. Most frustrating of all, some of the larger growers may have the political connections to get an investigation squelched, some investigators say.

In this context, several Border Patrol agents mentioned a south Texas grower whom one described as "a big operator" and "a pretty rough customer." He added, "He was shooting at aliens, holding their money, anything he could to keep them from running off. We tried every way we could think of to get at him under the peonage statutes, but he was very well connected politically."

Existence is hard enough for the illegal aliens who toil in the fields from sunup to sundown, picking lemons in Arizona, lettuce in California or melons in south Texas for a few dollars a day, cooking over open fires, sleeping in the fields at night and watching, always, for the green-uniformed agents of *la migra*, the United States Border Patrol.

But for those who unwittingly stumble into the underworld of the slave traders, life can be infinitely worse. Shackled with inflated debts they can never repay, they may find themselves locked up by night and guarded by day, beaten or threatened with harm or even death if they try to escape, their children held hostage to insure their continued servitude. Sometimes the workers held in bondage are little more than children themselves.

Under federal law, involuntary servitude occurs whenever a worker is compelled, by whatever means, to work at a job he does not want. If he is forced to work off a debt to his employer, the offense becomes peonage. The size of the debt does not matter, and it also makes no difference whether the peon initially agreed to take the job, or whether he was paid.

And, according to recent court decisions, the law takes no account of the means of compulsion. Physically restraining a worker, harming him or threatening to harm him may be sufficient grounds for a charge of involuntary servitude, as might the withholding of his pay or the holding of his relatives as hostages. Even if a worker failed to take advantage of opportunities to run away because he feared the consequences, servitude might be considered to exist.

Court records, immigration service files and other sources are filled with descriptions of such abuse. In Bartow, Florida, two Mexican girls, aged twelve and fifteen, are allegedly held prisoner by a labor contractor who hires them out as field-workers to neighboring farmers. Federal agents burst into the contractor's house and take the girls away. The girls file a civil lawsuit against the contractor.

In Colorado, a frantic Mexican mother seeks help from the authorities, saying a rancher holds her thirteen-month-old child hostage to insure her return to a forty-dollar-a-week job tending the rancher's cows and pigs. The authorities storm the ranch and recover the child unharmed.

Another typical case is that of Jose Corona, a young Mexican who worked in 1978 and 1979 for Ted Cisnero, an orange grower in La Belle, Florida, twenty miles north of here. In an affidavit, Corona said he received no wages for the first month he worked for Cisnero, his salary going only for food and to repay the two-hundred-dollar "transportation fee" Cisnero had given the coyote.

"Mr. Cisnero and his sons constantly warned and threatened me and other members of the crew not to try to leave his employ or his camp," Corona said in an affidavit. "They threatened us with death or the possibility of being sent back to Mexico. On several occasions Mr. Cisnero or his sons pointed guns at members of the crew, warning them not to try to escape."

When the workers were taken into town to buy food once a week, he said, they were closely watched by one of the Cisneros, who "would often force many of the younger members of the crew to buy them 'gifts' while they were shopping." Cisnero promised to send his workers' salaries directly to their families in Mexico, Corona said, but when one worker discovered that his family was not receiving any money and asked what had happened to it, the only reply he received was a beating.

Along with two other workers, Corona, who said he was finally "able to escape from Cisnero's camp" in December 1978, is suing Cisnero, alleging that his conduct violated the federal peonage statutes. The Justice Department is also investigating the allegations.

Cisnero could not be reached for comment. His telephone has been disconnected, and lawyers for Florida Rural Legal Assistance, who are handling Corona's lawsuit, said Cisnero had not yet retained an attorney.

The Justice Department's first successful peonage prosecution involving illegal Mexican aliens was recorded only last November. Connie Ray Alford, a forty-one-year-old Truxno, Louisiana, chicken farmer, pleaded guilty to chaining two of his workers, Isaul Mata and his brother Fidel, in a chicken coop at his Welcome Home Ranch to keep them from running away. According to court records, the Mata brothers, like their nine coworkers, had incurred debts of of $250 each for their transportation from Mexico to Louisiana that had not been worked off. Alford was convicted and given five years' probation and incarcerated for three months.

The Mata brothers and their coworkers are suing Alford for $3 million, charging that they were held captive for four months, menaced with guns and forced to work twelve hours a day, seven days a week, for substandard wages.

Peonage, though it exists on farms and ranches of the Southwest, is relatively uncommon there because of the proximity to the Mexican border. California, Arizona and Texas are flooded with illegal alien workers, and "there just isn't that much excess demand for labor here," said Lupe Sanchez of the Arizona Farmworkers Union.

Rather, it is in the citrus and winter-vegetable belts of Florida and the potato fields of Idaho and on the tobacco farms of Virginia and North Carolina that farmworkers are at a premium, so much so that the coyotes who smuggle them north or east can easily command fees of five hundred dollars a worker.

A principal route of the underground alien-smuggling railway, investigators say, is between Arizona and Florida. They say the system operates this way:

Workers earning perhaps fifteen dollars a day in the lemon groves around Phoenix are easily lured eastward by a coyote with the promise of wages of five hundred dollars or more a week picking oranges or tomatoes. The smuggler, through a series of late-night calls between public telephones, has already received a Florida farmer's order for a specified number of workers. When the workers are delivered, the farmer pays the coyote between three hundred and five hundred dollars a head.

But when the worker arrives he is told by the farmer that he is not free to leave until he has repaid that sum from his wages, and as he works the debt grows larger with charges for room, board, clothing, cigarettes and alcohol, all sold by the grower at what Rob Williams, who heads the Florida Rural Legal Services office here, calls "really inflated prices."

The worker is given perhaps five dollars a week for pocket money, with the rest of his "earnings" credited against what he owes. The arrangement is legal.

It is only when the worker tries to leave that he may run into trouble and find himself threatened with physical harm or exposure to immigration agents by the farmer because of the unpaid debt. "They make sure that anybody who's planning to run away doesn't," Williams said. "That's the way the system works. It really is peonage." And that is when the federal laws can be brought into play, though they seldom are.

Of the twenty-five thousand or so agricultural workers who come to Florida at the peak of the winter harvest season, Williams estimates, perhaps two thousand are "trapped in camps where they can't leave."

"A lot of people try," he said, "especially when they find the working conditions not to their liking, and that brings in the nastier elements of violence."

When the harvest ends, the worker, if he is lucky, is set free, often with only a few dollars to show for weeks of labor. If he is not so lucky he is sold by the farmer to another farmer for several hundred dollars, and the process begins again.

Federal officials say one of the largest smuggling operations is run by two Florida men who operate a tomato farm. They are under investigation by the immigration service and the Justice Department, and a federal grand jury is hearing evidence in the case.

Until recently, the vast majority of farmworkers in the South and Southeast were black. But the makeup of the farm labor force is changing rapidly all along the eastern seaboard.

In North Carolina, according to William Geimer, the former director of a Farmworkers Legal Services office there, the percentage of Hispanic workers has increased in the last two years to the point where they now number one worker in five.

In south-central Florida the change is evident everywhere, as on a recent morning here in Immokalee, where clusters of young Mexican men sat talking and drinking beer along the sidewalks of the town's tiny main street. Surrounded by Mexican restaurants and bakeries, by public notices in Spanish and by local markets stocked with tortillas, chorizo and canned beans, they might as easily have been passing the time in a dusty little village along the Mexican border fifteen hundred miles away.

As more Mexicans and other Hispanic workers find their way east, cases of suspected peonage are coming to light. After the Alford prosecution, federal agents in Louisiana were flooded with unsolicited tips about other alien workers held in similar situations. A. Martin Stroud III, the assistant United States attorney who prosecuted the case, said then that investigators were "tracking down other leads" involving farmers "all over northern Louisiana." But in a recent interview in his Shreveport office, Stroud said the investigation had been curtailed, primarily because of a shortage of immigration service funds.

The Alford case "revolted" him, Stroud said, but he also understood the economics that created such situations. "Where else do you get farm labor?" he asked, adding, "You take thirty workers at $250 a head, that's an expensive proposition. The farmer's got to hold them to get his money back. What's he going to do if they start to run off—sue them?"

And the workers, he said, were generally "easy prey" because "they don't understand our society, they don't understand our customs."

Few farmers resort to chains and shackles to prevent their workers from running away, as Alford pleaded guilty to doing. But violations of the peonage and involuntary servitude statutes require only the threat of force. Immigration officers told of instances in which farmers had armed guards patrolling their fields to keep workers from leaving.

In the cattle and cotton country of the Texas Panhandle, according to Trini Gamez of the Texas Rural Legal Assistance agency, workers are sometimes simply locked up at night. "They're not allowed to come to town, and the boss will bring them food and so on," she said, telling of a sugar beet farmer who held his workers in a large barn.

"The men had their cots in there," she said. "At night the door was locked. They couldn't leave the place at all." But she said that Legal Aid lawyers had been unable to investigate because of regulations prohibiting them from soliciting cases, and because the workers involved were not free to come forward and complain to the authorities.

The threat to turn an alien worker in to the immigration service if he attempts to leave is most common, officials said. Federal courts have long held that such a threat does not constitute a sufficient ground for a charge of forced labor, although recent decisions may have opened the way for a test case.

Some employers resort to withholding a worker's pay until the harvest is complete or threatening to have him charged with some real or imagined crime in the event he runs away. Federal investigators are looking into a recent incident in Tucson in which Arthur M. Burris Jr., a twenty-eight-year-old truck driver and part-time rancher, was arrested and charged by the state with false imprisonment.

Burris was charged with chaining a twenty-year-old alien worker to a tree overnight without food or water. Pima County sheriff's deputies said Burris told them he had suspected the worker, Manuel Hernandez, of stealing some tools, a theft that a friend of Burris later confessed. But Hernandez told the authorities that, although Burris had promised to pay him seven dollars a day when he was hired August 21, he had not received any money.

Not all of the Hispanic newcomers who find themselves in forced-labor situations are necessarily illegal aliens. Two farm labor contractors are being sued by more than two dozen Puerto Rican workers, some as young as sixteen, who are alleging that they were forced to work up to ninety hours a week on farms in Delaware, New Jersey and Pennsylvania, in some cases for as little as one cent a week in net pay. They were threatened with harm, they say, and even death, if they tried to leave.

Often, officials say, the aliens are enslaved long before they reach the farms and ranches. Because they are a precious commodity to the smugglers, they are forcibly held in decrepit "drophouses" until someone is found who will pay their ransom. "Generally, it's relatives or a farmer who come up with the money," said Leon D. Ring, the chief Border Patrol agent in Livermore, California, near San Francisco.

Last March, twenty-eight Mexicans were found by immigration service officers in a ramshackle Houston house, its windows boarded up, where they had been held under armed guard by smugglers for two weeks. Officers say they have found as many as fifty aliens held captive in tiny one- or two-room shacks for long periods with no mattresses or sanitary facilities and very little food. The immigration service recently acquired a videotape, made in an undercover surveillance, showing aliens being roughly unloaded from a truck and, with kicks and punches from their coyotes, herded into a drophouse in east Los Angeles.

Immigration service files are filled with such descriptions of cruelty as these: In Los Angeles, a tearful Honduran woman tells the police that her daughters, fifteen and sixteen, are being held by a smuggler demanding seven hundred dollars for having guided the family across the border. The smuggler is threatening to strip the girls of their clothing and abandon them in the desert if he is not paid, she says. The police and federal officers rescue the girls and arrest a suspect.

In a Mexican border town, a Peruvian woman arranges with a smuggler to bring her and her three-year-old grandson to the United States for five hundred dollars. At the border the child disappears. When he is recovered seven weeks later by the immigration service, the boy says he has been "beaten by a man very often" and "forced to beg money in the streets."

Another reason the relatively small number of prosecutions for peonage and involuntary servitude does not provide an adequate picture of the scope of such offenses, officials say, is that it is often easier to prosecute on the more easily proved offense, such as smuggling or harboring illegal aliens.

Durward (Woody) Woosley pleaded guilty to alien smuggling in San Antonio in 1978. According to federal investigators and investigative files that are part of the court record, from January to August that year Woosley bought and sold more than five thousand alien workers, paying recruiters thirty dollars a head to bring them north from the Mexican border, then shipping them out to growers in the East for up to five hundred dollars apiece.

"Farmers in Arkansas were buying an alien from Woosley for four hundred dollars and withholding wages until the four hundred dollars was paid off," said Hugh Williams, who recently retired as the Border Patrol chief in Del Rio, Texas. "Then they would sell the alien to somebody else for four hundred dollars. The alien never saw any cash. In effect, each farmer was getting free labor. There were cases where we found Mexicans who were at their third or fourth farm and hadn't made a penny the whole time they were in the U.S.—peonage, that's really what it was."

Letter from Warsaw

JOHN DARNTON

December 18, 1981

Following is a letter received yesterday from John Darnton, Warsaw bureau chief of the New York Times, *addressed to Robert B. Semple Jr., the paper's foreign editor. Normal communications from Warsaw have been shut by the authorities since Sunday.*

Dear Bob,

At least twice in the past twenty-four hours the official Polish press agency has used the word "normalization" to apply to events here. For Poles and other East Europeans this is a dreaded code word.

"Normalization" is what happened to Czechoslovakia after a Warsaw Pact invasion crushed the "Prague Spring" of 1968. In the peculiar jargon of Communist officials, in which words can mean their opposite, it is the restoration of orthodox authority. To people it is the almost unbearably painful process of watching the dismantlement, piece by piece, of freedom and liberties painstakingly won.

A major part in that process is fear, and fear, it is clear, has become of the new military Poland. [As written.] It is strange; perhaps the one defining trait of the Polish "renewal" of the past sixteen months was the absence of fear.

With a massive show of manpower and equipment and a calculated campaign of intimidation, the military authorities here are trying to break the spirit of resistance of the workers' movement.

Yesterday evening, a caravan of 273 police cars, trucks, water cannons and other hardware moved slowly through the city at rush hour. Thousands of onlookers were forced back on the sidewalks, dark figures waiting on dirty snow banks and trees in the cold. It seemed a parade of brute force.

This morning at an early hour three secret policemen barged into the small apartment of a Polish journalist. They insisted that he sign a document asserting that he would no longer "act in a manner to oppose socialism in Poland." He resisted and was bundled away. His wife pleaded with the policemen as they dragged him down the stairs.

One of them responded, "Don't worry, we'll be back tomorrow for you to sign it."

The fear campaign is working in some respects. Already people open their doors just a crack, to inspect who is there. They play the radio loudly while talking, or set the water running—old devices from the Stalinist 1950s to foil the eavesdropper.

For someone who has lived here for almost three years, it is as if a door that was gradually opened has been suddenly shut.

"I can't see you now," whispers a Polish friend, as he answers his door and steps into the hallway, closing it behind him. "Didn't you hear? I was detained. I just got out. I'm sure you're being observed."

"We can't talk here," says another Polish friend standing in a stairwell, with a glance at a man nearby, who said he was a taxi driver waiting for a customer. He may, or may not, have been listening.

It takes a long time for fear to go away, weeks, or months even, in which people slowly learn that they can speak out or, emboldened by others, write more forcefully and honestly in the newspapers. But fear can come back as quickly as a door slamming.

The full extent of the strike protest to the imposition of martial law cannot be determined with all communications down all over the country. But in areas where foreign journalists have been able to reach, factories in the Warsaw region, what broke the backbone of the protest was fear. The authorities mounted an overwhelming show of force— surrounding factories with tanks and armored cars and simply waiting for darkness and curfew to unsettle the demonstrators inside.

Workers who gave up said afterward that they felt isolated, with no idea of what was going on in other parts of the country. They were worn down, sometimes hungry, and began thinking of their children. Women among them began weeping. When the troops and policemen burst in, they were offered a chance to leave, unharmed, if they would separate themselves from their leaders.

"We really had no other choice," said one worker at the Huta Warszawa steel mill. "They had live ammunition and their guns were raised. They seemed as scared as we were."

In other regions, resistance is still going on and some workers are apparently determined to repel an armed attack. But what the outcome will be cannot even be guessed.

"Poles always called the Czechs cowards for not resisting in '68," said one foreign visitor here who travels frequently throughout Eastern Europe. "Now they will have to eat their words. The Czechs were invaded by five armies, the Poles did it all by themselves."

A major factor in the ease with which military rule has been established so far is the Polish love and respect for the army. The army, like the flag and church, is a symbol of nationalism.

"All this time we were all looking at the army and saying that because it is mostly made up of conscripts it might not be loyal to the government," said one European diplomat. "What we didn't see was the other side of the coin. Because the army contains so many sons and brothers, people were reluctant to move against it."

The most telling scene in the capital over the past three days, perhaps, occurred yesterday morning when busloads of soldiers moved into the Polish Academy of Sciences to break up a strike by some of the country's most eminent thinkers. The crowd was sullen and angry as the troops led away men in rumpled suits and spectacles and loaded them into a bus. But no one even threw a snowball. Minutes afterward, a truckload of soldiers goes past and, surprisingly, some of them waved to the crowd, for all the world like liberating soldiers, not agents of repression.

The military decree that was promulgated the morning after the army moved in was Draconian, and it was prominently displayed on posters and the two newspapers allowed to publish. Penalties range from two years to death, for seemingly minor infractions. It simply overwhelmed people.

Soldiers posted at intersections throughout the city turned cars away and let others through, rerouting traffic without any logical rhyme or reason. It was effective psychological harassment.

One Polish journalist, sitting at a cafe and talking to a foreign colleague with a nervous glance over his shoulder from time to time, displayed the demoralization and depression that most Poles seem to be feeling. It was, he said, the intellectuals who would feel the backlash. All his journalist friends, he said, were now out of work. One by one, he predicted, new newspapers would open up and one by one his friends would be offered jobs, if they were judged reliable. "Now comes the time for true courage," he said. "I wonder how many will measure up. It's either that or going to the work center for a job as a street cleaner."

"We are back to 1951 and '52," he continued, referring to the Stalinist years. "It would take us twenty years to rebuild what we had here."

Solidarity, he suggested, has talked a great line, but at no time over the past sixteen months did the union really prepare a plan to counter a massive display of force. It was not envisaged that things could turn around so quickly, he said. Nor was it even thought that fear could come back so quickly.

Yours sincerely,
John Darnton

1982 PULITZER PRIZE FOR INTERNATIONAL REPORTING

NASA Had Warning of a Disaster Risk Posed by Booster

PHILIP M. BOFFEY

Washington, D.C.
February 9, 1986

The space agency was warned last year that seals on the space shuttle's solid-fuel booster rockets might break and cause a catastrophic accident, according to documents from the agency's files.

The documents show that engineers at the headquarters of the National Aeronautics and Space Administration and its Marshall Space Flight Center in Huntsville, Alabama, were concerned that leaks might occur where segments of the booster rockets are mated.

Such leaks would allow hot gases and flames to escape through the side of the rocket instead of through the nozzle that channels the gases out the rear, possibly causing severe damage to the shuttle or an explosion, according to space experts.

One NASA analyst warned in an internal memorandum last July that flight safety was "being compromised by potential failure of the seals." He added: "Failure during launch would certainly be catastrophic."

A 1982 "critical items list" for the booster also warned that if the seals should fail the result could be "loss of vehicle, mission, and crew due to metal erosion, burnthrough, and probable case burst resulting in fire and deflagration," or rapid, intense burning.

It is not clear what action, if any, NASA might have taken in response to the warnings in the documents, but the issue was listed as a matter of concern in agency documents as recently as December.

The internal documents describing problems with the seals were made available to the *New York Times* by a solid-fuel rocket analyst who has worked closely with propulsion engineers from the Kennedy Space Center in Florida, which assembles the booster rockets; the Marshall center in Alabama, which is responsible for their design; and NASA headquarters in Washington.

Although no one knows exactly what caused the explosion that destroyed the *Challenger* on January 28, space agency officials have said that the leading theory, based on films of the flight, is that a plume of flame emerged from one side of a booster and set off an explosion of the shuttle's giant external fuel tank.

Space officials have said they cannot identify precisely where the plume emerged and thus do not know whether it burned through a seam or through the metal side of the rocket. "It did appear to happen at least near a seam," Dr. William R. Graham, acting administrator of the space agency, said last Sunday. He said the plume appeared to start "near one of the field joints" but that measurements had not yet established whether the plume occurred "at the seam or just near the seam."

The safety of the seals also became an important issue Thursday at the first meeting of a presidential commission that is investigating the causes of the accident. The space agency acknowledged that it had consulted with the rocket's manufacturer, Morton Thiokol Inc., about concerns that cold weather at the launching site might have weakened the seals. But an agency official told the commission the manufacturer had concurred that the launching should proceed.

The official, Judson A. Lovingood, deputy manager of shuttle projects at Marshall, also acknowledged that there had been concern after previous shuttle flights about erosion damage to some of the seals, but he indicated that this problem had been thoroughly investigated.

The seals are needed because the booster is not a single long structure but rather four large cylindrical segments that are bolted together, along with other components, at the Kennedy Space Center when the rocket is being prepared for launching. Although the side of the rocket may look leakproof to the naked eye, there is room for gases to escape at the seams. Thus rocket engineers have devised a series of seals and other barriers to keep the gases in.

The two most important seals are O rings, essentially large doughnut-shaped pieces of synthetic rubber that fill the tiny gap between two cylindrical segments that are bolted together. The O rings are themselves protected from heat and flame damage by an initial barrier of putty.

If flames and hot gases are to escape through the joint between segments of the rocket, they generally must first pass through the putty, then through the primary O ring, and finally through the backup ring. The rubbery O rings are designed to seal especially tight when they are hit by the high-pressure gases, much as a rubber washer on a faucet seals tight to prevent water from leaking.

At the presidential commission's meeting Thursday, Lovingood, from the Marshall space center, was asked if experts had looked at the joints in the reusable boosters after previous shuttle flights to see if there was any evidence of leakage. "We have seen some evidence of erosion of those seals, the primary seal," he said. "We've never seen any erosion of a secondary seal. But we have seen evidence of soot in between the two seals."

When asked if this was a cause for concern, he replied: "Oh, yes. I mean that's an anomaly and that was thoroughly worked, and that's completely documented on all the investigative work we did on that."

The possibility that cold weather might weaken the seals, by causing shrinking or stiffening or through some other effect, is not explicitly addressed in the internal documents. Instead, those memorandums focus on erosion and heat effects observed on the seals after previous flights. One memorandum does suggest, however, that "environmental effects such as moisture" could be an indirect factor in causing erosion.

A memorandum prepared within the comptroller's office at NASA headquarters last summer used dire terms to describe the potential problems of charring and erosion that might damage the effectiveness of the seals. The memorandum, dated July 23, 1985, was addressed to

Michael B. Mann, head of the resources analysis branch for the shuttle program, from Richard C. Cook, a subordinate.

Cook warned that "the charring of seals," which had been observed on recent shuttle flights, posed "a potentially major problem affecting both flight safety and program costs." In the joint between the nozzle section of the rocket and the adjoining segment, the memorandum said, "not only has the first O ring been destroyed, but the second has been partially eaten away." The memorandum did not say how often this had occurred.

The joint referred to in the memorandum is the one nearest the spot where the plume of flame was seen to emerge from the side of the rocket just before the explosion that destroyed the *Challenger*.

The memorandum said the cause of the erosion problem had not been determined. "There is little question, however, that flight safety has been and is still being compromised by potential failure of the seals," it said, "and it is acknowledged that failure during launch would certainly be catastrophic."

The memorandum said the leadership of the space flight program "is viewing the situation with the utmost seriousness."

Another memorandum prepared at roughly the same time by Irving Davids, an engineer in the shuttle rocket booster program at NASA headquarters, described a visit he made to the Marshall Space Flight Center on July 11, 1985, to discuss "seal erosion problems" that had affected the O rings on several shuttle flights.

This memorandum said there had been "twelve instances during flight" where there had been some erosion of the primary O ring at the seam where the nozzle segment of the rocket is bolted to the adjacent segment.

The memorandum said that in two cases soot actually blew by the primary seal, and in one case the backup seal showed erosion as well. Both this observation and Cook's memorandum appear to contradict Lovingood's assertion that no erosion of a secondary seal had been observed.

The document added that the prime suspect in causing the erosion was the type of putty used. It said Morton Thiokol, the manufacturer of the booster rocket, believed that the putty, made by another, unidentified manufacturer, could develop holes under certain conditions and that these holes would have a "jetting effect," an indication, apparently, that the holes could focus hot gases on the seal. "There doesn't appear to be a validated resolution as to the effect of the putty," Davids wrote.

The memorandum also described erosion of the O rings at the joints between other major segments of the rocket. It said there had been five occurrences during flight where the primary ring showed erosion and one case where the backup ring was affected by heat although not actually eroded.

One critical problem, it added, was that rotational forces generated as pressure builds up within the rocket caused a "lifting off" or "unseating" of the secondary ring, a problem that "has been known for quite some time." One proposal for eliminating this problem, the memorandum said, was a "capture feature," not otherwise described, which would prevent the seal from lifting off.

The memorandum from Davids was addressed to Moore, the associate administrator for space flight.

Through the rest of the year, the O rings continued to be a concern to some engineers and budget analysts.

On August 21, 1985, a budget briefing prepared for top-level NASA officials listed charring of the rings as one of the top "budget threats" to the solid-fuel booster program, apparently a reference to the fact that fixing the problem could become costly.

On September 10, 1985, a status report and briefing prepared by NASA's propulsion division said that the most recently completed shuttle mission showed "one minor erosion" on the primary ring at the joint between the nozzle and the adjacent segment but no such damage at the other joints. It also listed charring of the rings at the top of a list of "solid-rocket booster issues."

In December 1985, a monthly status report again listed ring charring as one of seven issues regarding the booster.

Concerns about the seals had been expressed in agency documents at least as far back as 1982. A "critical items list" for the solid-fuel booster rocket, dated December 17, 1982, described the joints as in the most important category.

The document also said that "joint rotation" as the pressure rose in the rocket might knock out the backup ring. This was the same problem that, according to Davids's memorandum, had still not been solved in July 1985, although it had been "known for quite some time."

TWO

In Danger

SERVING HISTORY

Journalism can be a dangerous business. In the savagery of the twentieth century—"this terrible century," Hannah Arendt called it—reporters and photographers often risked their lives. Totalitarian rulers regarded a free press as a potential enemy, to be suppressed without mercy when necessary. Reporters trying to be detached were caught, too, in the bitter ethnic and religious conflicts, the guerrilla wars and the drug killings that increasingly characterized armed struggles.

Every year the Committee to Protect Journalists, an organization founded by U.S. reporters and editors concerned about their colleagues in other countries, lists a significant number of journalists who have been killed or imprisoned for doing their job. In this country, reporters have the First Amendment and the tradition of press freedom to protect them. But when they go abroad to report on armed conflict or the doings of repressive regimes, they are at risk.

This chapter gives some examples of work done by *New York Times* reporters under dangerous conditions. The stories won prizes not just because of the danger but because they told readers important truths about troubling situations.

Sydney Schanberg covered Cambodia for the *Times* in the last months of the cruel war between its rightist government, supported by the United States, and the Khmer Rouge rebels. The world knew little about the Khmer Rouge then except that it was a Communist movement. We learned. When the rebels won the war, in April 1975, they executed members of the former government and drove the entire population of the capital, Phnom Penh—including hospital patients—out of the city. In the ensuing years hundreds of thousands of Cambodians were executed as suspect intellectuals or dissidents.

Schanberg ignored his editors' instructions to leave while it was safe and stayed to the end. The Khmer Rouge kept him and other foreigners in the French embassy until, after two weeks, he and others were taken by truck to Thailand. Before the fall, Schanberg reported on the appalling human costs of the war. Some of the damage was done by bombs dropped in error by American B-52s on civilian targets. Some, as in the story from Neak Luong reprinted here, resulted from indiscriminate Khmer Rouge shelling.

Thomas L. Friedman was a *Times* correspondent in the Middle East for seven years—on both sides of the conflict. That extraordinary achievement required both courage and a sympathetic ability to understand the passions that animate Arabs and Jews.

Friedman won his first Pulitzer as the Beirut correspondent. He was there during the vicious Lebanese civil war that saw Beirut divided between Christian and Muslim sectors, and then during Israel's 1982 invasion of Lebanon. The danger of that time is illustrated by a terrible event. As the Israeli invaders approached Beirut, Friedman moved for safety reasons from his apartment in west Beirut to the Commodore Hotel, where most foreign reporters were staying. It was unwise to leave the apartment empty, because Palestinians fleeing refugee camps on the southern fringe of Beirut were taking over empty apartments. His driver and news assistant, Mohammed Kasrawi, volunteered to have his daughters, Azizza, twenty, and Hanan, seven, stay in the flat. On Friday evening, June 11, 1982, while Mohammed's wife Nazira was visiting the two girls, someone planted a bomb in the hallway outside the apartment. The building was blown in half, and Mohammed's wife and daughters killed.

The article used as an example of Friedman's work in Beirut is an account of how Yasir Arafat, under pressure from Lebanese Muslims caught in the Israeli siege, finally agreed to leave for Tunis with his PLO forces. No other reporter had the drama of that turning point.

In 1984 Friedman drove south from Beirut, across military lines and the Israeli border, to become the *Times* correspondent in Jerusalem. Three years later he was covering the *intifada*, young Palestinians' stone-throwing revolt against Israel's long occupation of the West Bank and Gaza. There were dangers in that conflict, met as it was by strong acts of Israeli repression. But Friedman found an entirely different kind of tension in Israel: between Jewish religious extremists and other Jews. His report from Bnei Brak told readers about a profound internal division that few had understood.

Physical danger was an inescapable fact of life for John Burns as the correspondent in Sarajevo, the Bosnian capital, when it was under siege by the Serbs. From the hills around the city, they shelled hospitals, the great national library, mosques—and the Holiday Inn, where Burns was staying. Snipers picked out targets, including children, to kill. All normal communications and transportation routes were cut. Burns filed stories on an early version of a satellite telephone, awkward and heavy. His story on what the citizens of a once-beautiful European city did as it was destroyed by men who had been their neighbors was what the headline said: an elegy for Sarajevo. But it and others Burns wrote were more than that. They made Americans aware of the Bosnian tragedy.

Successive U.S. presidents, George H. W. Bush and Bill Clinton, wanted to stay out of the conflict in Bosnia. Reporting by Burns, Roy Gutman of *Newsday* (who also won a Pulitzer) and a handful of other correspondents made that impossible in the end. When Americans knew what was happening—men murdered in thousands because of their religion, women held in rape camps—they were sickened. The pressure of outrage led President Clinton finally to order the bombing of Serbian forces until their leaders agreed to a cease-fire and the Dayton Conference ended the war. It was one of American journalism's finest hours.

Four years later Burns was covering Afghanistan after the Taliban, the fanatical Muslim movement, had taken over. It is an understatement to say that offending the Taliban was dangerous. Burns took that risk when he wrote the story reprinted here, on the stoning to death of an adulterous couple. That terrifying primitivism is part of reality in our world, and we rely on courageous reporters to tell us what we must know.

The 1998 Pulitzer Prize for international reporting went to the *Times* as a whole, for a series of eight articles on the effects of the drug trade in Mexico—corruption, kidnapping, murder. The reporters were Julia Preston, Sam Dillon, Tim Golden and Craig Pyes. Their reporting, about such things as the involvement of Mexican officials in the drug world and killings, put them in great danger.

In a Besieged Cambodian City, Hunger, Death and the Whimpering of Children

SYDNEY H. SCHANBERG

Neak Luong, Cambodia
January 16, 1975

Every fifteen minutes or so a shell screams down and explodes in this besieged town and another half-dozen people are killed or wounded. It goes on day and night.

The tile floors of the military infirmary and civilian hospital are slippery with blood. They have long since run out of painkilling drugs. Bodies are everywhere—some people half conscious crying out in pain, some with gaping wounds who will not live. Some are already dead and, in the chaos, just lie there with no one to cover them or take them away.

Fifty yards away, behind a wall, another shell bursts. Those who are conscious jump involuntarily. The seriously wounded are too weak to react.

Inside the infirmary a seven-year-old girl, a filthy bandage over the wound in her stomach, lies on a wooden table. The only doctor in the town feels her pulse. It is failing.

Suddenly her father appears, a soldier. He has come from the spot where another of his children, a five-year-old girl, has just been killed by a mortar shell. His wife was killed three years ago by shelling in another town.

He picks up his daughter in his shaking arms; his face, bathed in a cold sweat, contorts as he tries to hold back the tears that come anyway.

"I love all my children," is all he says as he walks away with the dying child—heading for the helicopters that are too few to carry all the wounded to Phnom Penh.

There is deep hunger in Neak Luong, too. The soldiers here are getting by, for American and Cambodian transport planes are dropping some food by parachute for them—but there is none for the civilians.

By today, the thirty thousand or more refugees who have fled to Neak Luong from outlying areas as the Communist-led insurgents have advanced toward the town have been reduced to subsistence on the thinnest of rice gruel. Every day it becomes thinner. Many are living in the open and it rains almost every night.

Yesterday the Catholic Relief Services, whose dogged Cambodian staff has stayed in Neak Luong to run gruel kitchens, tried to send a barge with twenty-five tons of rice down the Mekong River the thirty-eight miles from Phnom Penh to the isolated town. But at the last minute, the barge was ordered to stay in Phnom Penh. The Cambodian military said the situation was too dangerous and the barge would probably be sunk if it tried to run the insurgents' gantlet.

"They're going to have to airdrop more food," said one disheartened relief worker. "That's all there is to it. Otherwise people will starve."

Already, as one walks around the shell-marked town, one hears everywhere the sound of children whimpering.

The military situation here, though grave, does not seem to be deteriorating. Government reinforcements continue to pour in by helicopter and, while the Cambodian insurgents are right across the Mekong from Neak Luong, on the western bank of the river and also very close on most sides of the town itself, it does not appear likely at this point that they can overrun the town.

Yet until the government troops do more than just hold on—that is, until they push the insurgents back far enough to take the town out of shelling range—the human misery here, with shells raining in indiscriminately, will continue.

The government's determination to save Neak Luong stems from the town's importance as virtually the last government position on the lower Mekong. If it fell, the government would lose all hope of getting supplies into Phnom Penh by way of the Mekong.

With all other surface routes cut long ago in this five-year war, the American-backed government is now dependent on the Mekong for 80 percent or more of its supplies from the outside world.

Even now, the Mekong is temporarily blockaded. The rebels, in the annual dry-season offensive that began New Year's Day, have seized control of so much of the river and its parallel road, Route 1, that the Americans have been forced to postpone indefinitely all the supply convoys—which come up from Thailand and South Vietnam.

Amid all this, there was at times a preposterous normality.

In the market, where a few Chinese-run shops were open for those who still had money, a colonel who had just flown in with his fresh troops was examining a bottle of French cologne with a discriminating air. His boots were highly polished, his uniform starched, his neck scarf just so. He squeezed the atomizer, sniffed the spray, then put it back and walked away disdainfully.

Last night the insurgents began increasing their shelling—with mortars, recoilless cannon and rockets. Through the night, the casualties rose.

At dawn, with the explosions heaviest in the southern sector of town, where most of the refugees had been huddled in the streets, a pagoda and a primary school, the refugees began fleeing with their sackfuls of belongings to the northern fringe of Neak Luong, which was not safe but at least safer.

There was squalor, fear and bedlam. But there was also the traditional Buddhist fatalism of the Cambodian people. Some of this trapped population, which totals at least 250,000 counting the refugees, seemed almost to accept that being caught here is simply their lot.

The colonel was an incongruity in Neak Luong today. The norm was blood-soaked stretchers, the smashed bodies of infants attached to plasma bottles, wounded soldiers being dragged or dragging themselves from every lane, and a meadow on the northern edge of town where the wounded who still had a chance were carried to await the evacuation helicopters.

1976 PULITZER PRIZE FOR INTERNATIONAL REPORTING

Weeks of Siege

———————————•———————————

THOMAS L. FRIEDMAN

Beirut, Lebanon
August 20, 1982

In a sense, after July 3 it was all over but the shooting. It was on that humid Saturday evening during the Moslem holy month of Ramadan that Yasir Arafat, the chairman of the Palestine Liberation Organization, first agreed in writing to leave Beirut.

Between then and today much blood was spilled, many speeches made and much negotiating done, but it is now clear that on July 3 the fate of the PLO in Lebanon was sealed.

The setting for such a historic moment was a fitting one—the white, three-story palace of former Prime Minister Saeb Salam, built by his father in 1912 when he was a deputy in the Ottoman Parliament. On that Saturday afternoon the eight leading Sunni Moslem figures of west Beirut, including another former prime minister, Takeddin al-Solh, gathered in Salam's marble-floored dining room to discuss how to persuade the PLO to leave besieged west Beirut. Arafat and his top political adviser, Hani al-Hassan, were invited to join the group at 12:30 P.M.

When Arafat arrived, wearing his tightly creased pea-green army uniform and cap, he and his aide were ushered into the dining room and seated around the long Chippendale English table lighted by an antique chandelier.

Salam, a still crafty seventy-seven-year-old politician, opened the discussion in a praising tone, reaffirming to the guerrilla leader that his men had fought the good fight against impossible odds and had performed better than anyone could have predicted. The PLO had covered itself in honor, Salam said firmly, and now was the time to leave with honor.

Arafat was sitting to Salam's right with his cap removed, revealing his bald head. He listened intently to the remarks of the various Moslem figures who controlled west Beirut, and responded with counterarguments of his own. The dignity and honor of the PLO was at stake, he declared. This was a question of "saving face" and he and his men would never lose face before the Israelis. They would prefer, he said, to die fighting street-to-street than quit west Beirut in disgrace.

Seeing that his soft-spoken approach was not having its intended effect, Salam began to raise his voice. The military battle was obviously over, he shouted, and now was the time for the PLO to transform itself into a purely political entity outside Lebanon, for its own sake and for the sake of west Beirut.

Clearly hurt and on the defensive, according to people who were there, Arafat began shouting back: "Do you want to push us out? Is that it?"

"With all of the sacrifices we have made for you and your cause," stammered Salam in a still louder voice, "you cannot say that about us. It is better for you and for us that you go, with your honor."

The discussions continued in this tone for four and a half hours, with others occasionally interjecting remarks to cool things down. At one point a crew from Lebanese television arrived to take some posed footage of the meeting, but even as the camera was running, the talks exploded into another shouting match between Arafat and the others. One of the notables at the meeting had to use his influence to get the film cassette back from the government-run television before it could be shown on the nightly news.

At 5 P.M. Arafat agreed to study what had been discussed with his colleagues in the PLO leadership and return with some kind of answer. As it was Ramadan, Salam invited Arafat to join him that evening for the *iftar* meal, the traditional breaking of the daylong Ramadan fast.

At 7:15 P.M. Arafat and Hassan returned, joining the Salam family and the other notables around the dining-room table. Everyone agreed that there should be no talk of politics during the meal of ground meat, cold yogurt and eggplant. Arafat listened as the others exchanged anecdotes, eating little except for the black olives set in the middle of the long wooden table.

After dinner Arafat asked if he could be excused to perform the evening prayers alone. He went into Salam's den, faced south toward Mecca and performed the ritual prayers on the white carpet in solitude.

When he returned to the dining-room table, Arafat said he had something to deliver. He removed the ever-present green notepad from his pocket and slipped out a folded piece of white PLO stationery. Putting on his black glasses, Arafat began to read from the document, written in his own hand under the letterhead of the PLO commander in chief.

His voice full and resonant, Arafat read, "To our brother Prime Minister Shafik al-Wazzan"—to whom the note was officially addressed—"With reference to the discussions we have had, the Palestinian command has taken the following decision: the PLO does not wish to remain in Lebanon."

Arafat then proceeded to outline in a very general fashion the security guarantees the PLO was demanding for the 650,000 Palestinian refugees who would remain in Lebanon.

When he finished reading the crucial lines Arafat handed the note to Salam, who immediately had it photocopied. Arafat then took it back and delivered it later that evening in an even more emotionally charged meeting with Wazzan. The prime minister eventually conveyed its contents to the American special envoy, Philip C. Habib, the man for whom the note was truly intended all along.

The rest, as they say, is history.

No one ever quite got the name of this war right. The Israelis called it the Peace for Galilee operation, but it was clearly more than that. The Lebanese tended to call it the Israeli invasion of Lebanon, but that never really captured what was at stake either. In retrospect, the events of the past summer clearly have much deeper historical roots.

In talking to the Palestinian guerrillas one always got the sense that they were fighting the war against the Jews that their fathers and grandfathers failed to fight in Palestine in 1948. The battleground may have been Lebanon, but to them this was the real Palestinian-Israeli war finally being fought thirty-four years later, with no Arab states getting in the way.

That feeling of a battle long-delayed came through most powerfully in an interview with Dr. George Habash, the leader of the Marxist Popular Front for the Liberation of Palestine and the founder of the Arab nationalist movement. The pediatrician-turned-guerrilla has futilely been fighting the Israelis since 1948, when he was twenty-one. Easily the most charismatic of the Palestinian, and probably Arab, leaders, Habash met this reporter in an underground bunker at his west Beirut headquarters a few days after the Israeli army had overrun all the guerrilla bases in southern Lebanon.

The air was stale and musty and "Dr. George" sat erect behind a small table, surrounded by a knot of young guerrilla devotees. To him the fact that the battle in south Lebanon had been lost was totally insignificant. The most important point was that there was a battle at all.

His silver hair standing out in the dim light, Habash punctuated all of his comments by slamming his left arm down on the table, sending little puffs of dust into the air.

"I thank God," he shouted, oblivious to the irony of the great Arab

Marxist appealing to the Almighty. "I thank God," he continued, bringing his fist down on the table. "I thank God that I lived to see the day that a Palestinian army fought an Israeli army. Now I can die. I don't need to see anymore."

Waving his arm around at his young followers, he added, "I feel sorry if anything happens to these young men, but now I can die, for we really fought them."

Whatever their pride in having battled the Israelis alone, there was nonetheless a deep and seething bitterness among Palestinians over the fact that not a single Arab country lifted a finger to help them militarily. The Palestinians finally gave a war and nobody came. Nobody but the Israelis.

A few weeks into the conflict, after the negotiations had begun, a reporter asked a Palestinian professor at the American University of Beirut, if he were going to give a party for all of the PLO's friends when this was over, whom would he invite?

"The French," said the professor straightaway, "definitely the French. Then maybe a few Americans, some other West Europeans and maybe even some Egyptians for the help they have been in Washington. I might let the Saudis be the waiters. No Soviets allowed."

In the last days of the Beirut siege, some difficult weeks later, a reporter asked the professor the same question. This time he thought longer. Again, he said, the French could come, maybe a few Americans in Washington, but no Arabs whatsoever. "Not a single one," he said. "I would not even let the Saudis clean up after the meal."

It was inevitable that this bitterness would eventually express itself in the form of graffiti, particularly as the siege wore on. Someone calling himself "Ayub" began putting up crudely written Arabic posters in shop windows on the side streets off west Beirut's main Hamra thoroughfare. Most of them were addressed to the Arabs.

"There are two kinds of Arabs today," read one sign. "The Arabs of fear and the Arabs of sheep. But we alone in west Beirut are making history. Ayub."

"Today we are in shelters," read another poster, "but tomorrow the Arab leaders will be on shish kebab skewers. Ayub." Finally, the one that captured the truly existential sense of abandonment felt by many Palestinians and even Lebanese read: "Tell your children what Israel has done. Tell your children what the Arabs have done. Tell your children what the world has done. Ayub."

In an interview in the first month of the war, Arafat told a reporter that the Arab inaction was only temporary. "How long," he asked, "will the Arabs remain silent?" Clearly, it was much longer than either he or the anonymous Ayub ever expected. Ayub, incidentally, is the Arabic name for Job, the biblical figure of endlessly patient suffering.

War, like politics, makes for some strange bedfellows. In the early weeks of the Israeli invasion correspondents who had lived and worked in PLO-controlled west Beirut for their entire careers suddenly found themselves nose-to-nose with Israeli soldiers and officers besieging the capital. There was a certain attractive novelty to these meetings at first. Reporters used to go for a day to Christian east Beirut or the surrounding hills just to "talk to an Israeli," and sniff them over as if they were some kind of strange beings. The favorite watering hole for these close encounters was Emille's Restaurant in Baabda.

One afternoon a group of west Beirut-based reporters trundled off to Emille's to meet some of their colleagues from Jerusalem and an Israeli officer. Included in the west Beirut contingent was a Jewish reporter from a Communist European paper, one of the very few Jewish correspondents working out of the western half of the capital.

When they arrived at Emille's, the Israeli officer went around the table introducing himself and shaking hands with each correspondent, until he got to the Communist reporter. The Communist refused to shake the Israeli officer's hand, saying, "I will not shake the hand of an occupier."

The Israeli officer shrugged off the slight and the group proceeded with its lunch. Over coffee, the west Beirut reporters began pressing the Israeli officer for his assessment of whether or not the Israeli army would storm west Beirut and, if it did, what would happen to all of the correspondents living there in the Commodore Hotel. The officer told them not to worry, that no harm would come to any journalists— but they kept pressing him. Finally, the exasperated officer said, "If I have to, I will personally drive my own car into west Beirut and take you all out safely.

"All except this one," he added, pointing his finger at the Communist correspondent who had snubbed him. "But," chimed in the other reporters, "he is the only Jew among us." Said the Israeli officer, "I should have known."

The first thing one develops after living in Beirut for any length of time is a sense that all violence is localized. Because so many shooting incidents between rival gangs used to break out at any moment around town, people began taking them in stride. If it was not happening on your street, outside your door, then it might as well not be happening at all. Life would go on as usual, only a bit noisier.

This somewhat blasé attitude toward violence carried over into the first weeks of the Israeli invasion, when one could find Israeli fighter jets attacking Palestinian positions on the southern outskirts of the city, while across town people were sitting in seaside coffeehouses taking in the entire drama with the aplomb of spectators at the Paris air show. There was also an unspoken understanding—which later evaporated—that somehow the Israelis knew what they were doing and whom they were hitting. People actually moved about freely during the first air raids, counting on the reknowned accuracy of Israeli pilots.

"I was going out one afternoon in the middle of an air attack," remembered Nawaf Salam, a university researcher, "and my parents told me, 'Stop, don't go out, the planes are everywhere.' I told them, 'Look, this is not Bashir Gemayel and the Phalangists. This is Sharon.' Right away they knew what I meant and let me go. Only later, when the Israelis started hitting everywhere, did this break down. Then, everyone felt he could be a victim."

One of the most fascinating things one could observe during the siege, and nearly daily bombardments of some magnitude or another, was how, despite it all, people remained for the most part so very human. Just when you expected people to be paralyzed by fear, they reacted in just the opposite way—especially the Lebanese, who have a certain anarchic resistance to disorder.

The editor of a widely known Beirut newsletter tells the story of being in his apartment with his college-age daughter the night of a particularly heavy bombardment of west Beirut by Israeli artillery and gunboats. Their apartment is directly across from that of a senior PLO official. Shells were whistling back and forth and Israeli planes were crisscrossing the night sky, dropping orange flares that hung over the Palestinian refugee camps like spotlights over a boxing ring. There was no electricity, and the editor and his daughter were lodged in the middle of the apartment trying to avoid the rattling windows.

Suddenly they saw a mouse. It had crawled out from behind a sideboard and its two little eyes were flashing right up at them. "Well, let me tell you something," remembered the editor. "We forgot about everything going on around us. I can stand the bombing, but I cannot stand a mouse in the house. My daughter grabbed a flashlight and I found a big fly swatter, which was the only weapon we had in the apartment, and we chased that little mouse all over, even out onto the balcony. We didn't give a damn about the planes. Fear for us came from that little mouse."

Ever since the last week in June the Israelis have been trying to get the estimated five hundred thousand civilians in west Beirut to leave so that they would not come under fire when the Israeli army attacked the six thousand to nine thousand guerrillas trapped in the western half of the capital. They made repeated radio broadcasts and twice dropped multicolored leaflets warning people to flee for their lives. This, however, was easier said than done.

Many husbands sent their wives and children out, but stayed behind to protect their apartments and property from the thousands of squatters looking for shelter. Many people would leave and come back as soon as the fighting died down, because they could not afford to live in a hotel or rented apartment in east Beirut or the mountains. Almost all of the wealthy left, many of them leaving their apartments behind in the hands of Indian, Ceylonese or Eritrean maids whose passports they would take away with them to insure that the servants did not abandon west Beirut.

But there was one group of people who could not leave even if they wanted to—the two hundred thousand civilian Palestinian refugees. The people whose houses, property and lives were the most battered by the Israeli attack could not leave, with some exceptions, because the Christian Phalangist militiamen of east Beirut would not let them through the crossing points.

After the Israeli bombardment of Sunday, August 1—dubbed by the west Beirut press as "Black Sunday" because of the intensity of the shelling—the leftist Beirut daily *As Safir* carried the story of a fifty-year-old Palestinian refugee with official papers from the Lebanese government. The man could no longer stand life in besieged west Beirut and decided to take his chances and try to cross to the Christian eastern half of the capital, having heard that some people were being let through.

When he came to the museum crossing point, he first encountered an Israeli checkpoint. The Israeli soldiers examined his papers and waved him through. A few hundred feet down the road he came to a Phalangist checkpoint, the paper said. The Phalangist militiamen took one look at his documents and turned him back.

Lugging a single suitcase with all of his belongings stuffed inside, the man trudged back to the Israeli checkpoint. Just as he got there sniping broke out along the crossing point, between Palestinian and Israeli troops. The man ran for cover, leaving his suitcase sitting in the middle of the road outside the Israeli position.

When the shooting stopped, the Israeli soldiers emerged from their outpost and found the suitcase sitting there. Fearing that it was some kind of booby-trapped object, they riddled it with machine-gun fire, the paper reported. By this time the old man had returned to claim his belongings. The Israelis were apologetic. The old man bundled together his tattered luggage and shredded identity papers and shuffled back to west Beirut.

In the final days of the Beirut siege the top officials and military officers of the PLO, including Yasir Arafat, all but disappeared from public view. Almost no interviews were being granted, and the normally gregarious Arafat was not being pictured in any papers for days at a time. Palestinian officials said the guerrilla chieftains were taking extraordinary security precautions to avoid possible Israeli "hit squads" or attempted assassination by fighter planes.

The anti-Palestinian Christian Phalangist radio took to broadcasting the names of buildings where they said Arafat was sleeping at night, as part of their own psychological war against the guerrillas.

A leading Lebanese politician, who was acting as a central intermediary between Arafat and Habib, said that even he had not seen the guerrilla leader since August 1. He said Arafat would no longer communicate by telephone and sent all his messages through written notes by way of two trusted aides. Answers to his messages have to be communicated through the same aides, who can be reached at a special phone number.

Arafat is understood to sleep at a different location every night and to travel around in at least a dozen different armor-plated automobiles of various sizes and shapes.

His fears are not without some foundation. On August 6 two Israeli fighter planes prowled around the central west Beirut skyline in the early afternoon and out of nowhere swooped down and blew apart a single six-story apartment bloc in the heart of the city. Scores of civilians were crushed to death in the building, and it is strongly rumored that some PLO officials might have been using the apartment bloc as a type of auxiliary office. It was the only building bombed by the Israeli jets the entire day and was nowhere near the front.

Just how cautious Arafat has become was reflected in an incident that took place in late July, in the middle of the negotiations. Arafat was at the home of a distinguished Lebanese politician, holding talks in his living room while his guards and the Lebanese politician's guards stood watch in an adjacent sitting room.

Suddenly the phone rang. It was a friend of the Lebanese politician calling from Israeli-occupied east Beirut. The man was told by one of the Lebanese politician's guards that his boss was not available now because he was meeting with Arafat. As soon as those words were out of his mouth one of Arafat's guards scribbled out a note saying that his location had just been revealed to someone calling from east Beirut. The note was slipped to Arafat in the meeting, he read it, passed it on to his host and immediately asked to be excused. Within a minute he was gone.

The most fascinating aspects about reporting events in Lebanon are the insights it affords into human nature. It is only at the frontier, under extreme conditions, that you see how people are capable of behaving both positively and negatively. Lebanon today is the frontier. In besieged west Beirut you find out which one of your neighbors will share his last bottle of cooking gas with you and which gas-station owner will take advantage of the shortage and charge you ten times the price. They are all here, mixed together in the same city.

Of all the images from the summer, none stands out more vividly than the one from June 5—the day before the actual invasion began. A reporter and his assistant were driving to south Lebanon along the coastal highway running out of Beirut. A few miles south of the capital they stopped to pick up a bottle of water. While they were halted, two Israeli jets dive-bombed the highway only a few miles ahead, near Naameh, turning a five-hundred-yard stretch of road into a field of crushed asphalt and twisted cars.

The reporter and his colleague rushed to the scene of the attack and by the time they arrived a group of volunteer civil defense workers were already busy trying to pry people out of the mangled cars and a school bus.

One group was gathered around a half-buried Mercedes, out of which two feet were protruding. The workers pushed away the boulders covering part of the twisted wreckage and slowly began to extract the body.

It was a teenage girl. She was wearing blue-jean overalls, with a blue and white striped T-shirt. Her head had been blown off, leaving a bloodied stump of neck.

Moaning "Allah Akbar, God is great," the civil defense workers gently placed the girl's body on a stretcher and took it away, her arms dangling limply from both sides.

The reporter could never get the picture of that girl out of his mind. She came to represent the thousands of nameless, faceless, literally headless Lebanese and Palestinian civilians who died in this war—whatever it will finally be called and whatever it will truly prove to be about. He often wondered what her name was. Where was she going? And, most importantly, what was the meaning of her death?

In reflecting on that question the reporter was always reminded of a conversation about the brutality of life in Lebanon that he had had before the war with Charles Rizk, the president of Lebanese television.

"In Lebanon," observed Rizk, "death is at its most absurd and scandalous, because when you die here you really die for nothing."

1983 PULITZER PRIZE FOR INTERNATIONAL REPORTING

Fight Builds Over the Shape of Religious Future in Israel

THOMAS L. FRIEDMAN

*Bnei Brak, Israel
June 29, 1987*

Until six months ago, Shimon Tsimhe had the hottest newsstand business in Bnei Brak—before the bombing. Now he ekes out a living selling falafel sandwiches.

"I used to sell lots of newspapers—lots," Tsimhe said nervously, looking over his shoulder. "But there were threats."

"They told me it would be better if I didn't sell newspapers," he added. "They said it would be better if I sold falafels."

Down the street in this Tel Aviv suburb, a center for the deeply religious Jews generally referred to here as the "ultra-Orthodox," Leah and David Green's newspaper kiosk also did a brisk business selling daily Israeli newspapers—before the bombing.

They still sell secular papers, but quietly, through the backdoor, with the stealth that a small-town American drugstore might use to sell *Playboy* or *Penthouse*.

Tsimhe and the Greens, who are all Zionist religious Jews, had their shops damaged by a group of deeply Orthodox Jews who reject the modern state of Israel, from its army to its newspapers. They have either bombed or intimidated virtually every news seller in Bnei Brak into removing all daily Israeli papers from their shelves.

The Bnei Brak newspaper war is symptomatic of a national religious power struggle under way in Israel. At stake is who will determine the Jewish religious character of Israel.

Will it be the non-Zionist ultra-Orthodox, who do not see in the reborn state an event of major religious significance and who believe instead that a Jewish state will be worth celebrating only after the Messiah comes and the rule of Jewish law is total? They make up about 5 percent of the population.

Or will it be those Zionist Orthodox Jews who see in Israel's creation an important religious event and believe that Judaism, when reinterpreted for the twentieth century, can flourish in a modern state? These Jews make up about 15 percent of the population.

If recent trends are any indication, religious and political power among Israel's strictly observant Jews is gravitating to the non-Zionist minority, while the Zionists are increasingly on the defensive. If this trend continues, it will have a major effect on Israeli society and on Israel's relations with Jews overseas.

"American Jews, who have often been concerned about rising Christian or Moslem fundamentalism, must recognize that a serious Jewish fundamentalist revival is gaining strength in Israel as well," said Daniel J. Elazar, an expert on religious politics.

The nonreligious Israeli majority, represented largely by the Labor Party and the Likud bloc, is watching and waiting to make political deals with whatever religious parties emerge strongest and most able to deliver votes in exchange for concessions on religious issues.

Although there has been a strong ultra-Orthodox community in this land since before the Zionists immigrated, these people, who are known in Hebrew as *Haredim* or "those who are God-fearing," always lived secluded from the rest of the society. Until recently, they made little attempt to integrate or dominate. But in the last few years, according to Menachem Friedman, a Hebrew University expert on *Haredi* society, "the *Haredim* have begun to feel confident enough to present themselves as a real alternative model to the 'evil' modern society of Israel."

The majority of *Haredim* in Israel, who include Hasidic sects related to those in the United States, do not engage in the violence that has taken place in Bnei Brak. Rather, their newfound active role is channeled through peaceful means.

One symbolic effort has been a recent attempt by *Haredi* yeshivas to "convert" Israeli fighter pilots, who are widely considered to be the elite of the Israeli military and society, into giving up their wings and taking up a life of Torah study. Nearly a dozen pilots are reported to have quit the air force under these conditions, and their pictures have quickly been put up on posters in religious neighborhoods as signs of success.

"Slowly, slowly I see every day more and more people in the land of Israel having the knowledge of God," said Rabbi Menachem Porush, a seventy-two-year-old leader of the *Haredi* party Agudat Israel.

"When I look at my great-grandchild, I say to myself: In twenty years he will live in a real holy land, with a real holy people. It will be a different parliament from the one we have today. Remember, the past is ours; the future is ours. We just have to bridge the present."

What distinguishes the *Haredim* from other Israeli Jews is not only their dark black coats, long sideburns and black fur hats, which they wear just as their ancestors did in seventeenth-century Eastern Europe, but also their conviction that the Zionist revolution has not constituted any important change in Jewish life. That life, they feel, is ideally practiced today in its Orthodox form just as it was one hundred or one thousand years ago.

They do not celebrate Israel's Independence Day. For them, independence day is, as it always was, Passover, which marks the Jewish liberation from Egypt three thousand years ago.

The *Haredim* believe that it was loyalty to the Torah and its religious code for living, not nationalism, that kept the Jews alive through the ages and gave meaning to Jewish communal life. They see Zionism, with its avowed aim of making the Jews "a nation like all other nations," as destroying the singular religious identity of the Jewish people.

The *Haredim* seek to justify not serving in the Israeli army, while enjoying the security that it provides from hostile Arab neighbors, by arguing that they too are protecting the country by keeping the "authentic" Jewish heritage and spirituality alive.

While nonreligious Israelis may feel their ways of life threatened by *Haredi* demands to close movie houses, remove pictures of bikini-clad women from bus-stop advertisements or ban soccer games on Saturdays, the *Haredim* see things differently.

Many have family roots in Israel that date long before the first Zionists arrived, when the only Jews who lived here were religious. In their view it is their way of life that has been besieged by modern Israeli society, said Rabbi Porush. His family has lived in Israel for eight generations.

When Israel was founded thirty-nine years ago, the secular Zionist majority was ready to accept the *Haredi* groups because they reminded them of their grandfathers and because the Zionists felt certain that these people, speaking Yiddish and dressed in Eastern European attire, would wither away in a generation.

According to the Jerusalem Institute for Public Affairs, the average number of children in *Haredi* families is eight, compared with 3.5 for religious Zionists and 2.2 for secular Zionists. The majority of new immigrants today are deeply Orthodox Jews from North America and Western Europe, while Western liberal Jewish immigrants are a mere trickle.

"I just read that 250,000 Israelis are living in the United States," Rabbi Porush said. "I can tell you that none of those leaving are religious Jews. The Zionists say Israel should be a nation like all others. So if things don't work out here, they just go elsewhere. Our people are coming here and staying here because this is a holy land, and only here can you fulfill certain commandments of the Torah."

In the 1977 elections, the Zionist National Religious Party won twelve seats in Parliament; today it has four and in the next election could hold even fewer. The ultra-Orthodox party Shas, which did not exist in 1977, has four seats today, and Agudat Israel has two.

The *Haredi* communities have been gaining strength not only through numbers, but also through religious leadership.

What they have done is to establish their own rabbinical courts and religious authorities, believing them more observant and knowledgeable about religious affairs than the state-appointed chief rabbis or Zionist religious parties.

In their view, the notion of a chief rabbinate appointed and paid by a secular state is repugnant to the traditional Jewish notion of the rabbi whose authority grows from his own piety and knowledge.

For example, the chief rabbi's office is responsible for deciding what food is kosher, but the *Haredim* will eat food only if their own rabbis have stamped it "strictly kosher." The Israeli press recently reported about a salt factory that has five rabbis at the end of its production line, some from the chief rabbi's office and some from the *Haredi* community.

The *Haredi* rabbis have told the management of some luxury hotels that they will hold bar mitzvah and wedding celebrations there only if the hotels hire *Haredi* rabbis to supervise their kosher kitchens. The hotels have generally agreed, because by hiring such a rabbi they can open up a new, growing market and not lose the other more moderate religious markets, whose members also recognize *Haredi* kosher supervision.

Once a hotel is signed up, the *Haredi* rabbis go to their suppliers and explain to the butchers and bakers that if they want to continue selling to the hotels, they will have to adopt *Haredi ḳashrut* supervision. This process goes on down the line of suppliers.

The *Haredim* have also used their influence to affect how Israelis study their traditions and educate their children.

As a result of the *Haredim*'s devotion to Jewish learning and the building of new yeshivas, they and their rabbis, not the religious Zionists, now set the standards for what it means to be a *talmid hacham*, or learned Jewish scholar.

The religious Zionists have "lost their way," Rabbi Porush said. "They carried two flags, one of nationalism and another of Torah. They were always torn between the two. We have one flag: the Torah. That is why the power is in our hands now."

The Israeli government runs a network of Zionist religious schools, which educate about 30 percent of the country's youth, conduct prayers in the classroom and teach religious and secular subjects.

But in recent years these high schools have found themselves short of religious Zionist faculty and have sought help from the growing number of learned *Haredim* to teach their children religious subjects. As a result, the state religious schools today have many faculty members who do not believe in the state of Israel or the possibility of integrating Jewish tradition with modernity.

"In the old days, the principals of the state religious schools looked to the Zionist National Religious Party for spiritual guidance," said Eliezer Shmueli, former director general of the Ministry of Education. "Now many of them look to the *Haredi* rabbis."

"For a long time we watched this happening very passively," said Yehuda Ben-Meir, a leader of the religious Zionist camp. "We tolerated it because we may have had a hidden inferiority complex that the *Haredim* really were more religious than us. When they were proselytizing secular Jews, we thought it was fine, but when they started taking our own children and questioning the religious legitimacy of our own yeshivas, it was too much. We have started to fight back."

Because the *Haredim* now dominate the religious bloc and because the religious bloc in Parliament holds the balance between Labor and Likud, it is the *Haredim* whom the secular politicians are increasingly seeking to placate.

"The *Haredi* politicians know how to play the political game very well," Elazar said. "They know how to work the halls, build alliances and to use the system to their advantage. While they take an interest in secular issues, they mainly focus on their own religious bread and butter."

Unlike the Zionist National Religious Party, which was ready to compromise with the secular majority on some issues of synagogue and state, the *Haredim* used their power in Parliament for one purpose only—to get the Israeli democratic state to accept their religious agenda.

"The *Haredim* live in ghettos," Ben-Meir of the National Religious Party said. "They don't come in contact with the secular population and they don't care about them. All they care about is keeping their own people happy, and the more extreme they are, the happier they are.

"The religious Zionists like us come in contact with the rest of the public—at the university, at work and in the army. So while we never compromise on basic religious values, we are ready to make political compromises in order to live together."

This was illustrated during the recent debate over the issue of *shmitta*, or the sabbatical year.

The Torah enjoins that every seventh year Jewish farmers in Israel let their land lie fallow as a sabbath. When the Zionists returned to Israel in the twentieth century, however, observance of the sabbatical was not economically feasible. So the religious Zionists, led by Rabbi Abraham Kook, ruled that a Jewish farmer could "sell" his land for the year to an Arab, with a fictional contract, and his land would then not be Jewish-owned. That would allow him to eat of its harvest.

But this year when the chief rabbis, following Rabbi Kook, advised Israelis to "sell" their land to the Arabs, the *Haredim* denounced this as a religious fraud. They insisted that the state instead sell the entire crop of Israeli-grown wheat abroad and import American-grown wheat in its place.

The Minister of Industry, Ariel Sharon of Likud, bowed to the increasing electoral power of the *Haredim* and agreed to try to work out a solution along the lines they stipulated, thereby enraging religious Zionists.

During the cabinet debate on the subject, the minister of religion, Zevulun Hammer of the National Religious Party, was quoted as saying, "The *Haredim* deserve support, but there is no justification for all the arrangements regarding *shmitta* to be carried out in opposition to the chief rabbis."

Sharon reportedly said, "I respect religion and the rabbis."

This prompted minister of absorption Yaacov Tzur, a member of the Labor Party, to retort about the *Haredim*: "I also respect them, but there are other questions. This is a group of people for whom our national anthem, the flag, Independence Day and serving in the Israeli army mean nothing. It is not a problem of *shmitta*, or wheat, but of blackmail."

In a few weeks Parliament is again scheduled to debate the issue of who is considered a Jew. The *Haredi* parties want Parliament to reactivate a pre-1948 law governing changes in religious status that would empower the rabbinate to determine the religious status of any convert to Judaism who immigrates to Israel.

Since the *Haredi* parties do not recognize American-style Reform or Conservative Judaism, anyone converted by a Reform or Conservative rabbi would not be considered Jewish or eligible for automatic Israeli citizenship.

In a deal struck in May between Shas and the Likud bloc, Likud, which is led by Prime Minister Yitzhak Shamir, agreed in principle to back such an amendment.

"If this bill passes, it will mean that a person who was converted by a Reform or Conservative rabbi, who may have been living as a good Jew all his life, will be considered a non-Jew the minute he fulfills the Zionist dream and comes to Israel," said Rabbi Richard Hirsch, representative of the Reform movement in Israel.

The Likud accepted such a bill as part of a deal in which Shas agreed not to throw its support behind efforts by Foreign Minister Shimon Peres, leader of the Labor Party, to call an international peace conference on the Middle East. Had Peres offered Shas the same deal on the Jewish identity issue that Likud did, Shas would have supported an international conference.

"The only interest Labor and Likud have in religion is which rabbi can deliver to them the most votes to stay in power," said David Hartman, the modern Orthodox Israeli philosopher.

"But once these ultra-Orthodox have finished off the religious Zionists, they are going to take on the nonreligious Zionists—that is, Labor and Likud—and make this state an uninhabitable place," he added.

"Unless the modern Zionists wake up and assume responsibility for articulating a view of Judaism that can live with the modern world, they will be digging their own grave," Hartman said. "They will be left with a Judaism that repudiates modernity and will, in the end, undermine the whole Zionist structure that has been built here."

1988 PULITZER PRIZE FOR INTERNATIONAL REPORTING

Elegy for Sarajevo

———————————◆———————————

JOHN F. BURNS

Sarajevo, Bosnia and Herzegovina
June 8, 1992

As the 155-mm howitzer shells whistled down on this crumbling city today, exploding thunderously into buildings all around, a disheveled, stubble-bearded man in formal evening attire unfolded a plastic chair in the middle of Vase Miskina Street. He lifted his cello from its case and began playing Albinoni's Adagio.

There were only two people to hear him, and both fled, dodging from doorway to doorway, before the performance ended.

Each day at 4 P.M., the cellist, Vedran Smailovic, walks to the same spot on the pedestrian mall for a concert in honor of Sarajevo's dead.

The spot he has chosen is outside the bakery where several high-explosive rounds struck a breadline twelve days ago, killing twenty-two people and wounding more than one hundred. If he holds to his plan, there will be twenty-two performances before his gesture has run its course.

Two months into a civil war that turns more murderous by the day, Sarajevo, the capital of Bosnia and Herzegovina, is a skeleton of the thriving, accomplished city it was. It is a wasteland of blasted mosques, churches and museums; of fire-gutted office towers, hotels and sports stadiums; and of hospitals, music schools and libraries punctured by rockets, mortars and artillery shells.

Parks have been pressed into service as emergency cemeteries, and the pathetic lines of graves march ever farther up the hillsides toward the gun emplacements.

What is happening here, in a European city that escaped two world wars with only minor damage, is hard to grasp for many of those enduring it.

It is a disaster of such magnitude, and of such seeming disconnectedness from any achievable military or political goals, that those who take shelter for days in basement bunkers, emerging briefly into daylight for fresh supplies of bread and water, exhaust themselves trying to make sense of it.

Many, like Smailovic, who played the cello for the Sarajevo Opera, reach for an anchor amid the chaos by doing something, however small, that carries them back to the stable, reasoned life they led before.

Smailovic, thirty-six years old, spoke over the blasts of the shells that have poured down on the city unremittingly for the last forty-eight hours. The barrages by the Serbian forces seem to be a paroxysm of fury at their failure to capture the city after weeks of dumping thousands of tons of high explosives from the hillsides.

He could have been speaking for all the survivors trapped here, in defiance of the Serbian nationalists' insistence that only the ethnic partitioning of the city, and of the republic, can bring them security.

"My mother is a Muslim and my father is a Muslim," Smailovic said, "but I don't care. I am a Sarajevan, I am a cosmopolitan, I am a pacifist." Then he added: "I am nothing special, I am a musician, I am part of the town. Like everyone else, I do what I can."

In Sarajevo, as in many cities, towns and villages across this former Yugoslav republic, Serbs, Muslims and Croats, the third major ethnic group in the population of 4.4 million, have lived for centuries side by side, so much so that their cultures, families and lifestyles have grown into each other—creating a society of striking depth and variety.

They have done so in a landscape that is one of the most beautiful in Europe, a place of Alpine mountains and blue-green rivers, of terra-cotta-roofed houses that cling to precipitous hillsides, of white stone mosques with green copper domes and pencil-slim minarets.

Sarajevo, in a narrow valley bordered on all sides by mountains, has long been the symbol of this richly textured life, enchanting generations of travelers since the present city was established by a Turkish sultan in 1462.

Now it is a symbol of another kind—of a place where Muslims, Serbs, Croats, and other religious and ethnic minorities, including Albanians and a tiny population of Jews, suffer together. They endure the gunfire of Serbian nationalists who believe that the independent nation of Bosnia and Herzegovina proclaimed on March 2, and led by Muslims and Croats, will dominate and eventually persecute Serbs.

From this conviction—met with increasing ferocity in many parts of the republic by Muslims and Croats, some of whom have adopted tactics as brutal as those of the Serbs—has grown the war that is draining the life from Sarajevo.

The conflict here had small beginnings early in April, when decisions by the European Community and the United States to recognize the new nation led to barricades being thrown up around the city by rival ethnic militias.

Early in May, it got out of control after Alija Izetbegovic, the Muslim who is president of the new republic, was kidnapped by the Serbian forces, and Muslim and Croatian troops retaliated by ambushing a convoy of the Serbian-led Yugoslav army as it evacuated an army headquarters in the city.

The president, who was released in exchange for guarantees of safe passage for the convoy, was out on Marshal Tito Street in the center of Sarajevo this afternoon. He walked gingerly around piles of broken glass and rubble from the shattered facades of apartment buildings built during the time before World War I when Sarajevo was an outpost of the Austro-Hungarian Empire.

The sixty-seven-year-old leader, a lawyer and economist who spent nearly ten years in prison under Yugoslavia's Communist rulers for his writings on Muslim beliefs, sought to reassure scattered groups of people he met along the way. But he made no effort to hide his own anxiety after weeks of heavy shelling.

"Are you scared?" he asked a group of militiamen standing guard with Kalashnikov automatic rifles under an archway leading into the Solomon Palace, a six-story apartment building that was once home to some of the city's leading Jews, many of whom died in the Nazi terror.

"A little," one militiaman replied, shifting nervously in a denim jacket embroidered with the fleur-de-lis badge that is the emblem of the new republic.

"I am afraid too," replied Izetbegovic, who has spent long periods in a basement bunker in a nearby government building. "But we must hold out."

For many here, that has become a prospect of appalling bleakness. Although the United Nations on Friday reached the outline of an agreement to take control of Butmir Airport, on the city's outskirts, from the Serbian forces and to open a corridor into town, there is little confidence here that the Serbs will carry it out.

By lifting the siege, the Serbs would effectively acknowledge that they have lost the city, many in Saravejo believe. Already, all but a few of Sarajevo's suburbs are controlled by Bosnian territorial forces made up of Muslims, Serbs and Croats.

But if relief supplies do not arrive soon, desperation may turn to catastrophe. Only a handful of government services still operate, and those in skeletal state. No one seems to know how many people remain, but it appears to be at least half the city's prewar population of 560,000—possibly many more.

The Serbian nationalist forces allow no food to pass through their roadblocks on the periphery of town, and supplies that have been sneaked past their gun positions on the hills have been minimal. Most families have only loaves of bread baked by the single bakery that continues to function, using reserve supplies of flour from silos that are in a part of town under Izetbegovic's control.

To this, some families have added a thin gruel made of water and nettles taken from the lower slopes of the surrounding hills. With inventive cooking, and private supplies of flour, Sarajevans produce the likes of French bread and a sugared Turkish cake called *kevlici*.

But no one outside the government knows how long the flour supplies might hold out, and fear of starvation is widespread. When two Western reporters entered the city on Friday, one of the first people they encountered was a professor of biophysics from the medical faculty of Sarajevo University, Dr. Hamid Pasic.

"I am hungry!" he said. "I am seventy-six years old, I am a professor, and I am hungry!"

Those who venture out for food do so at great risk. Although some of the gunnery appears to be aimed at military targets, most of the rounds land in densely populated parts of the city. The sections of town taking the worst punishment include the central district and Bascarsija, an old quarter of mosques, narrow alleyways and wooden-front workshops and boutiques.

The toll has risen rapidly, particularly this weekend, when the Serbian gunners began their most merciless barrage. Every minute or two, with only a few pauses, shells slammed into apartment buildings and the remnants of commercial districts, each volley hitting with a blast that could be heard miles away.

At night, the skyline was a facsimile of Baghdad during the Gulf War—with gunners' flares lighting the high-rises of the city center in silhouette, and tracer fire skipping across the sky.

From a vantage point in the old town, fires blazed at every point of the compass, some of them huge conflagrations that burned for hours.

The number of dead and wounded was another unknown, but gravediggers were hard-pressed to keep up with the new bodies arriving by the hour.

At Kovlaci Park above Bascarsija, 185 new graves, each with a coffin-shaped wooden marker bearing the Muslim emblems of a star and a crescent moon, lay row upon row on the hillside. The graves were piles of freshly turned earth beneath clusters of wild roses, carnations and violets.

Shells hitting the hillside drove a steam-shovel operator who was digging the graves into the cover of a ridge abutment. While he took shelter there, two middle-aged women carrying plastic bags of bread were hit by a new blast. Both were killed.

For Kemal Aljevic, the forty-five-year-old owner of a bar in Bascarsija called Alf, after the American television puppet character, the sight of the Kovlaci graves was too much. With tears streaming down his cheeks, Aljevic said that the Serbian gunners appeared to be repeating the destruction of Vukovar, the Croatian town of forty-five thousand that was reduced to rubble by artillery fire last year.

"This will be three times worse than Vukovar," he said.

As in Vukovar, the Serbs seem to use the heaviest weapons of the Yugoslav army, which formally withdrew from Bosnia and Herzegovina three weeks ago and turned at least fifty-five thousand men over to a new force of Bosnia's ethnic Serbs.

One of two Sarajevo newspapers still being produced, *Oslobodenje*, quoted Yugoslav army officers who had defected to the Bosnians as saying that weapons being used in the barrage included 155-mm howitzers, 120-mm mortars, 104-mm tank cannon and 132-mm multiple-rocket launchers. The paper said a total of four thousand tons of high explosives had been fired into the city.

Some of the artillery shells are coming from a former Yugoslav army barracks at Hampjesic, twenty miles east of Sarajevo, the officers reportedly added.

The destruction has reached every quarter of Sarajevo, and almost every landmark. Fifty of the city's eighty mosques have been damaged or destroyed, including the oldest in the Balkans, Tabacki Mesdid, which dates to 1450. The Morica Han, a fifteenth-century Turkish inn stop for caravans, and the Islamic Theological Faculty, also from the fifteenth century, were damaged.

The main synagogue and the Roman Catholic cathedral have been hit, though only lightly damaged. The main broadcasting center and its transmitter have been repeatedly shelled; repairs at feverish speed have kept the radio and television stations on the air.

The Serbian nationalists seem to have taken little care to avoid buildings of historic importance to the ethnic Serbs who live here, 38 percent of the city's population before the fighting.

One building was extensively damaged by a shell that pierced its glass dome. It was the National Library, formerly the city hall, where in 1914 Archduke Franz Ferdinand of Austria-Hungary attended a reception minutes before he and his wife, Sophie, were assassinated by a nineteen-year-old Serbian nationalist, Gavrilo Princip. Half a mile away, at the site of the assassination, the museum dedicated to Princip has now been destroyed.

The main Serbian Orthodox church in the city center has also been extensively damaged.

Sites linked to the 1984 Olympics have come under fire, too. Both cupolas have been destroyed atop the former United States Consulate building, a neoclassical structure on a rise above the city center, which served as the Olympic museum. Its roof was penetrated by a shell, and all its windows were shattered.

The hospitals are packed with the wounded, many with amputated limbs from shrapnel blasts. Doctors report an unusually high incidence of heart attacks and of psychological distress.

With gasoline unavailable, many of the doctors walk miles to work through streets where every intersection offers clear sightlines to snipers in the hills. Along the way, hundred of cars, buses and trams lie destroyed, many of them burned-out hulks.

A lung specialist who walks back from the Vrazova Health Center every day spends her nights in a shopping-center storage room in the city's old quarter with her husband, a cardiologist.

With them, on mattresses on the floor, are a taxi driver, dentist, fireman, electrical engineer, waiter and computer scientist, together with their families—a cross section of Sarajevo life, pressed together as they rarely were before the fighting. Amid occasional tears, there are moments of joy over chess games, crossword puzzles and surprise meetings with old friends from other parts of town.

"You're alive!" a professor exclaimed to another who appeared in a shopping arcade on Saturday night, hugging him tightly for a full minute as both wept.

On a radio broadcast that was frequently drowned out by exploding shells, an announcer urged people to turn up the volume on the station's Bosnian patriotic songs and Beatles music. "We cannot kill these maniacs with guns," he said, "so let's kill them with love and music."

In an apartment nearby, with only a candle burning to deny the gunners a target, the sixteen-year-old daughter of a Muslim electrical engineer and his architect wife, Meliha Dzirlo, lingered at a piano into the small hours playing Beethoven's "Pathetique" sonata and a polonaise by Chopin.

Everywhere, when they were not arranging forays for food or water or exchanging names of those killed or wounded, people appealed for help from the outside world. After listening to a shortwave-radio account of the United Nations plans for relief convoys, Asim Hadzic, a thirty-year-old Muslim who is a food-company salesman, shook his head.

"It would be a good start but it isn't enough," he said. "We want military intervention."

The doctor who walks every day to the Vrazova Clinic, a Muslim who, fearing for her house, asked not to be identified, took a wider view.

"I can't believe this is all real," she said, gesturing toward a pile of rubble from an apartment building. "Here we are on the eve of the twenty-first century—in Europe, in a beautiful city and a country that offered people every possibility of a good life. How can such a thing happen? And how can a so-called civilized world allow it to continue?"

1993 PULITZER PRIZE FOR INTERNATIONAL REPORTING

Stoning of Afghan Adulterers

JOHN F. BURNS

Kandahar, Afghanistan
November 3, 1996

When the Taliban religious movement decided to stone to death a couple caught in adultery, it chose a blazing afternoon in late August.

The suffocating desert heat had pushed temperatures past 100 degrees, but those who were there remember how the townspeople came by the thousands to witness a spectacle not seen in the city of Kandahar for decades.

Long before the condemned couple arrived on the flatbed of a truck, their hands and feet tightly bound, every vantage point around the forecourt of Id Gah Mosque was taken. Still, according to the Muslim traditions of Afghanistan, space was made so that relatives of the condemned pair, including small children, could have a clear view of the type of justice imposed by the Taliban, who now control three-quarters of the country.

The condemned woman, Nurbibi, forty, was lowered into a pit dug into the earth beside the outer wall around the mosque until only her chest and head were above ground. Witnesses said she was dressed in a sky-blue *burqa*, the head-to-toe shroud with a gauze panel for the eyes that the Taliban require all women to wear outside their homes.

Nurbibi's stepson and lover, Turyalai, thirty-eight, was taken to a spot about twenty paces away, blindfolded and turned to face the Muslim cleric who was their judge.

Those close enough to have heard said the cleric spoke briefly about the provisions for stoning adulterers in the *Sharia*, the ancient Muslim legal code imposed by the Taliban since they began their rise to power in Kandahar two years ago.

Then, those witnesses said, the judge, following tradition, stooped to pick up the first stone from one of two piles that had been prepared, one for each of the condemned pair.

The first stone, the witnesses said, was thrown at Nurbibi. Quickly, Taliban fighters who had been summoned for the occasion stepped forward and launched a cascade of stones, each big enough to fill the

palm of a hand. One of the men who responded to Taliban appeals
to step forward and join the stoning, Rahmatullah, twenty-five,
recalled that neither Nurbibi nor Turyalai had cried out.

Turyalai, he said, appeared to be dead after ten minutes, but the
killing of Nurbibi took longer, past the point where one of her sons,
stepping forward to check, turned to the judge to say his mother was
still alive.

"The son was crying," Rahmatullah said. "I could see it."

At that point, several witnesses said, one of the Taliban fighters
picked up a large rock, advanced toward Nurbibi and dropped it on
her head, killing her.

Toward dusk, when most of the crowd had dispersed, family members recovered the bodies and took them away for burial in two of
the stony plots that serve as cemeteries.

Nurbibi, family members said, was laid next to her father, while
Turyalai was buried beside his father, Nurbibi's husband, in a plot
bounded by the rubble that is all that is left of much of Kandahar.

Among the score of people who gathered before the mosque to offer
their recollections of the stoning, none expressed dismay. To the con-
trary, all—men and boys, since women in Kandahar are forbidden by
Taliban rules to linger in public or to speak to strangers—spoke with
enthusiasm of the killings.

"It was a good thing, the only way to end this kind of sinning,"
said Mohammed Younus, sixty, a teacher.

Mohammed Karim, a twenty-four-year-old Taliban fighter, picked
up several stones and threw them in a reenactment of the executions.
"No, I didn't feel sorry for them at all," he said. "I was just happy to
see *Sharia* being implemented."

Court-ordered executions of adulterers by stoning have been
reported occasionally in revolutionary Iran, and in the Sudan, but since
World War II this punishment has been imposed only rarely in
Afghanistan—until the Taliban took power in Kandahar and imposed
a harsh version of the *Sharia*, under which they have also ordered the
amputation of hands and feet of thieves.

The Muslim cleric who led the investigation that resulted in the
stoning of Nurbibi and Turyalai, Mohammed Wali, says the incident
was at least the third stoning for adultery in the Kandahar Province,
one of thirty-three in Afghanistan, since the Taliban took power. Others have been reported in several of the twenty other provinces under

Taliban control, although none so far in Kabul, the capital, which the Taliban captured five weeks ago.

Wali heads the Taliban's religious police, the Office for the Propagation of Virtue and the Prohibition of Vice. Visitors encountered him relaxing with a dozen of his investigators under a mulberry tree in the Kandahar courtyard where the religious police maintain a dumping ground for smashed television sets, stereo systems and cameras, all banned by the Taliban. Wali, who is thirty-five, is typical of many Taliban, having been educated in a religious school that offers little but years of studying the Koran. He stroked his beard for a few seconds when he was asked about the stonings, then said that they had given him great satisfaction.

"When I see this kind of thing, I am very happy, because it means that the rule of Islam is being implemented," he said.

The Taliban take care to see that foreigners, especially non-Muslims, are kept away from stonings and amputations, which Taliban leaders like Wali describe as religious occasions not to be witnessed by nonbelievers. But the executions of Nurbibi and Turyalai were openly discussed with the visitors outside the mosque and in the Id Gah bazaar, just down the road, where Turyalai, after years as a guerrilla fighting the Soviet forces that occupied Afghanistan in the 1980s, earned a living selling and repairing secondhand motorcycles.

But a first attempt by Western reporters to talk to the family of the victims was angrily aborted by the Taliban. Making their way to the Naido district of the city, an area where thousands live among rubble left when Soviet aircraft carpet-bombed the southern districts of Kandahar in 1986, the reporters found a small boy who led them up an alleyway to a heavy wooden door in a ten-foot-high mud wall.

Moments later, an elderly woman, Sidiqa, who identified herself as Turyalai's aunt, appeared at the door and, with neighbors, began to relate the story of the stoning.

But two young Taliban fighters who had been posted to keep watch on the district, one armed with a Kalashnikov rifle, quickly arrived, ordering the foreigners to leave. When they delayed, one of the fighters turned to the gathering crowd. "Pick up stones," he said.

The visitors retreated, followed by angry youths throwing stones and rotting corncobs. But at dawn the next day, a visit to the family went unnoticed by the Taliban. Family members and neighbors appeared eager to talk, gathering around to speak of Nurbibi and Turyalai and how their relationship led to death.

By the family's accounts, the events that led to the stoning began thirteen years ago, when Turyalai's father died of a stomach ailment. Nurbibi, the father's second wife, was more than twenty years younger than her husband, and was left with two young sons. She remained in her husband's home, with Turyalai, who was the son of her husband by his first wife.

Under Muslim tradition, any intimate relationship between Nurbibi and her stepson was forbidden, and in any event, Turyalai was married and had a growing family of his own.

Nazaneen, Turyalai's wife, who spoke from inside the family home through a half-opened door, said she had long known of the close relationship between her husband and Nurbibi but had not been concerned about it until recently.

"I knew that they were intimate with each other, but I felt it was the relationship of a mother and a son," she said. "But then I became suspicious of them, and finally my suspicions were confirmed."

"Of course," she added, "I know that Turyalai was not in love with her, but some evil force must have drawn them together."

Some neighbors hinted that the tip-off to the Taliban came from Nazaneen. But she appeared distressed at her husband's death, hurrying back into her house to fetch an old identity card with a faded passport-sized picture of him during his days as a guerrilla fighter. "It is the only photograph we have," she said. But a man who said he was a cousin of Turyalai said the Taliban had been alerted by Nurbibi's two teenage sons, Habibullah and Asmatullah, who were angered by their mother's infidelity.

"The two boys went to the Taliban and told them that their mother was having a sexual relationship with her stepson," he said.

A few nights later, several family members said, a group of men from the Taliban's religious police hid themselves on the roof of an adjoining house. In summer, many Afghans relax and sleep at night on the flat roofs of their homes, and Nurbibi and Turyalai were alone together on the roof when the Taliban sprang from their hiding place.

"They caught them red-handed," one man said. "There wasn't any doubt about it."

Under the *Sharia*, conviction for adultery requires four witnesses;

in this case they were the men from the Taliban. Family members say the couple were imprisoned immediately and held for a month before the Thursday in August when they were taken out and stoned. Between them, Nurbibi and Turyalai left ten children, and all of Turyalai's eight children were aged twelve or under.

The oldest daughter, Gulalai, twelve, stood listening to accounts of the stoning with her youngest brother, Nadirjan, three months, swaddled in her arms, then burst out with her own account.

"I saw it," she said. "I was on a truck and I saw it." Then she turned, tears in her eyes, and fled into the house.

1997 PULITZER PRIZE FOR INTERNATIONAL REPORTING

A Toll of "Disappearances" in Mexico's War on Drugs

SAM DILLON

Ciudad Juárez, Mexico
October 7, 1997

The disappearance here earlier this year of Manuel Hernandez, a Texas drywall contractor and former marijuana dealer, with two relatives began like many others. Uniformed federal policemen smashed into a working-class home and dragged the men away, in full view of municipal police officers and frightened neighbors.

Then came the official denials. Hernandez's wife, Maria Elba, trudged for days from police stations to hospitals and morgues, everywhere getting the same brusque treatment: nobody knew anything about Hernandez. Although he is an American citizen, the United States Consulate was not much help either.

Nine months later, Hernandez is still missing. His case is part of a pattern unfolding just across America's southwest border: the disappearance of scores, perhaps hundreds, of people at the hands of Mexican security forces. Human rights groups say many of the disappearances appear to be part of a dirty war against people suspected of being drug traffickers.

In Juárez alone, a gritty border city that is a crossroads in a multibillion-dollar drug trade, nearly ninety people have vanished, including eight United States citizens. Like Hernandez, many have had at least peripheral ties with the narcotics underworld.

The evidence in some cases suggests that the victims were arrested and killed by Mexican police officers or soldiers who were hired by traffickers to eliminate rivals or punish debtors. In other cases, the victims appear to have been detained for interrogation by antidrug agents before they vanished.

The Mexican authorities say they are looking into the disappearances and have appointed a special investigator, but not one case has been resolved. Nowhere in the world have so many people disappeared in the context of drug-related violence, human rights groups say.

"There's just no parallel to what's happening in Mexico's northern states," said Morris Tidball Binz, who heads Amnesty International's programs in Latin America. "We're seeing disappearances of the type seen in the 1970s, and the number of reported cases has shot up over the last year and a half.

"The person vanishes, and even though the police or the military are responsible, there is absolute denial from the authorities."

To combat official stonewalling, relatives of scores of the missing have joined a newly formed Association of Relatives of Disappeared Persons. Its members include people from Juárez and El Paso, which together form one metropolitan area straddling the border. Their aim is to press the authorities for a full accounting, but they complain that officials have remained unresponsive.

Two Americans, Jaime F. Hervella, an El Paso accountant, and Saul Sanchez, a retired Labor Department employee from Laredo, Texas, founded the association after a fruitless three-year search for Sanchez's son, Saul Sanchez Jr. A thirty-five-year-old United States Navy veteran, Sanchez disappeared in Juárez with his wife, Abigail, in May 1994 while selling microwave communications equipment to Mexico's federal police.

"The authorities treated us as if to say, 'Look, your relatives are gone, and that's just too bad,' " said Hervella, the missing man's godfather.

This summer the two Americans placed newspaper advertisements inviting others with loved ones lost in Juárez to get in touch with the association's office, which is next to Hervella's accounting business in an El Paso shopping center.

The response has been stunning. In recent weeks, dozens of relatives, including Mrs. Hernandez, have called in to tell of the disappearance of more than fifty people in the last three years, most of them after detention by Chihuahua State or federal police.

A list of people who have disappeared in Juárez since 1993, compiled by a local newspaper, *Norte,* bears fifty-six names.

Reports of disappearances have emerged recently in other important drug marketplaces across northern Mexico as well. In the states of Baja California, Sonora and Sinaloa, families have reported that since mid-1996 about twenty relatives have vanished after detention.

But nowhere have so many cases been reported as in Ciudad Juárez, possibly because Mexico's largest drug cartel is based here. The Chihuahua authorities have compiled a list of one hundred people who have disappeared in the state this year alone.

These disappearances are in addition to the scores of bodies dumped in ditches and fields around Juárez every year, most of them victims of drug or sexual violence.

The disappeared people include a wealthy onetime government prosecutor whose wife now drives to association meetings in a Mercedes-Benz, an adviser to a congressman from Mexico's governing party, a recently retired Chihuahua state policeman, a former Mexican army lieutenant and an assembly-line worker whose grieving mother lives in a dirt-floor shack.

Opening the association's office in El Paso seems to have been crucial for its success. Many relatives say that they are terrified, and that locating the association in Juárez would have been unthinkable, for fear that its offices would be attacked. But the association has registered with the Mexican government and holds meetings in Juárez.

For its part, the Clinton administration largely appears to have turned a blind eye toward the disappearances, consistently praising the Mexican government's antidrug efforts. Officials at the United States Consulate say their involvement has been limited because the families of only two of the eight missing Americans have sought help. In those two cases, family members said consular officials had acted sluggishly on their behalf.

But consular officials denied that. "Protecting American citizens is the most important thing we do here," said David C. Stewart, the consulate's number two official.

Who is responsible for the disappearances? "I wish I knew," the mayor of Ciudad Juárez, Juan Ramon Galindo, said in an interview. "But I wouldn't be surprised to find that federal police are involved.

"One of our problems is that our officers can be bought. These are Mexican, not American police, and they reflect Mexico's problems: the lack of education, poverty. We can't hope that they will act like police from other places."

Juárez was the main gateway used by the drug cartel controlled by Amado Carrillo Fuentes until his death in July. Many of the abductions appear to have been carried out by corrupt police officers on the cartel's behalf, to settle scores, punish informants or protect its turf against rivals. Other abductions appear to have been committed by Mexican security officials in overzealous antidrug operations.

"What worries us enormously is the involvement of men with federal or state judicial police credentials or uniforms," said Alberto Medrano Villarreal, president of the Juárez Bar Association. "Just because people are suspected of involvement in the drug trade does not mean you can allow them to be seized and killed without trial. Our entire system of law is being violated."

The Bar Association published open letters in Juárez newspapers this year, including one during a recent visit by President Ernesto Zedillo, urging him to intervene.

Earlier this year, Jorge Madrazo, Mexico's attorney general, quietly appointed a seventy-two-year-old lawyer, Francisco Hernandez Vazquez, as a special prosecutor to investigate the disappearances.

"In the majority of cases, there are signs of the involvement of armed elements, who people believe belong to one of the police forces because they use uniforms or insignia or vehicles associated with the police," Hernandez Vazquez said in an interview.

But he added: "There is nothing to prove that the disappearances reflect a policy of the Mexican state. They just appear to reflect the actions of certain police groups."

The armed men appear to wield tremendous influence, however. No one interferes with them.

In February 1995, for example, after a Colombian man was acquitted of drug charges in a federal trial in El Paso, American agents escorted him to the international bridge to Juárez and released him to his Mexican lawyer.

As the two men began walking toward Juárez, six men drove up, waved Mexican federal police credentials and dragged them into their car. Hours later, the federal police acknowledged to relatives of the men that they were in custody, but they were never seen again.

Agents of the National Institute to Combat Drugs, Mexico's now-defunct antinarcotics agency, were implicated in the disappearance in November 1995 of two brothers who owned a Juárez steak house, along with an employee.

A man who washed cars in a police garage testified that two days after the three were reported missing, he saw federal agents shove the restaurant worker into a vehicle at the garage.

The governor of Chihuahua, Francisco Barrio Terrazas, acknowledged the government's involvement in that case. "We've found that there were officers from the institute that carried them off, apparently without having an arrest warrant," Barrio said weeks after their disappearance.

In June 1996, Chihuahua police searching for a missing Juárez man found his Suburban parked outside a restaurant. Inside were several agents of the antidrug institute—as well as the missing man, who was lying on the floor in the rear.

It appeared that the federal agents were using him to identify the restaurant's customers. His family never received further information about his whereabouts.

In fact, no relatives have learned anything reliable about the whereabouts of their disappeared loved ones, although their fears have fueled speculation.

Several families said they believed that their relatives had been arrested and turned over to the Drug Enforcement Administration and were being held incommunicado in the United States.

James J. McGivney, a spokesman for the agency, said: "That is an absurd claim, just nonsense."

Hernandez Vazquez, the government investigator, said police officers in Juárez had told him, "The desert around Ciudad Juárez is a vast cemetery."

And Manuel Hernandez's wife said a government detective had told her that traffickers had murdered her husband on a distant ranch. "He told me they use a big oven to cremate the disappeared," she said.

THREE

Around the Globe

DISPATCHES FROM ABROAD

Reporting on the world outside the United States has been a particular commitment of the *New York Times*. Its first Pulitzer Prize, in 1918, was a public service award for reporting on World War I. Between 1918 and 1999 the paper and its reporters won twenty-five Pulitzers for foreign correspondence.

The first individual *Times* foreign correspondent to win was Walter Duranty, who got the prize in 1932 for his reporting from the Soviet Union. That prize has come under a cloud, as indicated in the introduction to this book. In the *Times* building in New York there is a corridor lined with photographs of Pulitzer winners. With each picture is a brief note of the year and nature of the prize. Duranty's says the prize was for "his series of dispatches on Russia*." The asterisk adds: "Other writers in the *Times*, and elsewhere, have discredited this coverage."

Duranty wrote, in 1931: "Stalin is giving the Russian people—the Russian masses, not Westernized landlords, industrialists, bankers and intellectuals, but Russia's 150 million peasants and workers—what they really want, namely, joint effort, communal effort. And communal life is as acceptable to them as it is repugnant to a Westerner." Such reporting ignored the reality of Stalin's mass murder. Duranty did note some of the cruel realities. He wrote that the Stalinist slogan "liquidation of the kulak as a class" (kulaks were prosperous farmers) meant that "five million human beings, one million of the best and most energetic farmers are to be dispossessed, dispersed, demolished, to be literally melted or 'liquidated' into the rising flood of classless proletarians." But then he added, ludicrously in light of what we later learned: "Rank may replace class in the Bolshevik cosmogony to satisfy human needs, but rank based on merit, not on wealth or birth."

When Duranty reported from Moscow, the United States had no diplomatic relations with the U.S.S.R.—and no diplomats there. A young U.S. Foreign Service officer, George F. Kennan, watched from Riga in neighboring Latvia. In 1932 he wrote a memorandum that was brought to light in 2001. He said the Soviet Union was a country "where fifteen to twenty million people have been killed in military operations, exiled to prison camps, forced [to] emigrate or deprived of all civic rights for political reasons—where the ideals, principles, beliefs and social position of all but a tiny minority have been forcibly turned upside down. . . ."

The totalitarian brutalities that marked the century were brilliantly captured by Frederick T. Birchall's reporting from Germany, which won a Pulitzer in 1934. Day after day he described Hitler's relentless oppression of the Jews, the Nazi use of violence, the suspension of democracy and legal rights.

Otto D. Tolischus was the *Times* correspondent in Germany later in the 1930s. He focused less on Hitler's repression than on his maneuvering toward war. One of the reports that won him a Pulitzer Prize was a remarkable prediction. On May 7, 1939, Tolischus raised the possibility of a pact between Nazi Germany and Communist Russia. The Nazi-Soviet Pact became reality on August 23, opening the way to World War II.

The early prizewinning foreign correspondence, in its particularity, does not lend itself to excerpting. This chapter gives in full, or with modest cuts, more recent examples.

Max Frankel won the prize in 1973 for his reports on President Nixon's path-breaking visit to China. Each day during the trip he wrote the lead story, then a sidebar entitled "Reporter's Notebook" that described some of the surprises of life in Communist China—a China that had been closed to American reporters for a generation. One of those Notebooks is reprinted here.

The Soviet Union gradually became more open to foreign reporters after Stalin's death in 1953. Censorship ended. But penetrating that society still presented formidable difficulties to correspondents. One way to understanding was through the dissidents who began to appear in Soviet life. The greatest of them—one of the great figures of the century—was Andrei Sakharov, the subject of Hedrick Smith's 1973 *Times Magazine* article. Seven years later Sakharov was sent into internal exile in Gorky; in 1986 Mikhail Gorbachev set him free.

Gorbachev, the first Soviet leader to recognize the decrepit state of the country's economy, sought to improve it by policies of glasnost (openness) and perestroika (restructuring). In the end he failed, and the Soviet Union collapsed. That denouement came as a startling surprise to the world. But not long before it happened Bill Keller, Moscow correspondent of the *Times*, wrote a series of articles that showed the enormous obstacles in the way of Gorbachev's reform formula. They were obstacles not only of economic structure but of culture and human expectations. All that is made graphic in the article, reprinted here, from Ilyichevsk on the Black Sea.

One of the tragic aftermaths of the Vietnam War was the fate of Vietnamese who had supported the South in the war or who were otherwise regarded by the victorious Communist government as suspect. Thousands were sent to reeducation camps, where they lived in grim conditions for years. Others tried in whatever way they could to escape the new Vietnam. The only way, for most, was extremely risky: by boat across pirate-infested seas to other Asian countries that did not want them. The phenomenon of the boat people was brought to the world's attention by Henry Kamm of the *Times*. One of his prize-winning stories focused on the inhospitable response of Japan to the refugees.

In the old days the *Times* had a rule against a husband and wife both working for the paper. The odd result, at least once, was to have the husband a *Times* correspondent and the wife a correspondent—in the same country—for the *Washington Post*. Did they compete? Nowadays the rule has been abolished. Indeed, one can almost say it has been reversed, because there are so many husband-wife correspondent teams. One of them, Nicholas D. Kristof and Sheryl WuDunn, covered China at the time of the great protest and then the massacre in Tiananmen Square, Beijing. Their reports won the Pulitzer Prize in 1990.

The most dramatic signal of the change brought to the Soviet world by Mikhail Gorbachev was his decision to let the Berlin Wall be breached and then to let the two Germanies reunite. Reunification was a triumph for West Germany, political and psychological. But it presented formidable economic problems because the two states had such different systems and East Germany was so much poorer. Serge Schmemann explored the differences in reports from two nearby towns, on opposite sides of the east-west border, just before reunification. A decade later the problems he described have still not been wholly overcome.

Rugged Barriers

MAX FRANKEL

Peking, China
February 24, 1972

There is talk of exchanges in the air—of people, performers, ideas and goods—that makes it timely to consider the difficulties as well as the opportunities such contacts offer to both Americans and Chinese. Starting the relationship, though it took more than twenty years, may turn out to have been the easy part of the exercise.

One fair example is Mrs. Richard M. Nixon's encounter yesterday with the manager and workers at Peking's Glassware Factory, an amalgam of fifty formerly independent handcraft shops that employs more than five hundred workers and produces glass toy animals, flowers, fruits and potted plants.

Watching the assembly of glass flowers, the First Lady asked, naturally enough, "Do they use their own judgment on what they mix together? Can they just take a little bit of this and a little bit of this?"

Mrs. Chao Mei-yun, the roly-poly chairman of the factory's revolutionary committee, took care of that bit of bourgeois fantasy with a simple, firm reply: "They have a certain design."

They certainly do, not only in flowers, but also in responses to questions in the quasi-public surroundings in which all conversations so far have had to occur.

At one point Mrs. Nixon asked Mrs. Chao whether the young women worked at the factory for a lifetime or whether they tended to go on to other jobs. The question was routine, perhaps even delivered by rote. But the answer, or rather the nonanswer, had that certain design. Before liberation, said Mrs. Chao, meaning the coming of Communism in 1949, the shops were faced with bankruptcy and there was no steady work. But now there is, she added.

The first problem of contacts here is that the list of approved places for visits is relatively short and that requests to stray from the pattern—say, from reporters wishing to visit a newspaper office—though never denied, seem to be dying of neglect.

Life as the member of a delegation whose program and logistics and escorts can be arranged in advance can be rewarding. But efforts to stray from the flock, to break the routine and above all to communicate person to person instead of people to people, though not forbidden, are often prevented by the hosts' inflexibility and the travelers' ignorance.

No one in this land of eight hundred million people, give or take fifty million, is ever really alone and there is an especially strong urge toward collective security when dealing with foreigners. There is a strong tendency toward speeches, therefore, and also a universal urge to respond to questions with little more than quotations from the trusty chairman, Mao Tse-tung, with or without attribution.

There are certainly signs that many Chinese weary of this routine as quickly as their guests, and do not really deem it a substitute for communication. But coping with the Americans can be a trying experience. At the moment there are three hundred of them here who two weeks ago would have paid a healthy ransom for the mere privilege of entering the People's Republic. And now, after seventy-two hours on the ground, they are already bending every effort to beat down the next line of barriers.

Needs Keep Growing

They want taxis when there are not enough, because they want to dash from one end of town to the other. They want interpreters, and not only interpreters but the kind that will translate without really watching, and preferably guides whose instant loyalty can be transferred from employer to traveler.

The language itself is an enormous barrier, as even the president and Mrs. Nixon are discovering in their well-planned touring. "Ni hao" (Hello), the president said to Premier Chou En-lai at the start of yesterday's conference, almost as if to underscore the sense of strangeness Americans feel here.

"Ni hao," a reporter mumbled a hundred times in walking the labyrinthine old quarters of Peking, nodding and smiling toward the puzzled faces and the grinning but fleeing children along the dusty lanes and behind the low but formidable gray walls around each home. Only two men, old men of pre-liberation habit, tried to communicate surprise or bewilderment and welcome through the welcome barrier.

"I started to learn Chinese, but I was so busy," Mrs. Nixon told her interpreter today. "I wanted to. Next time I come back I'll be a real expert."

It will help.

The real barriers seem to be neither linguistic nor official, but genuinely semantic and philosophical.

If the experience of three reporters at Peking University is any clue, these barriers can be breached, but it will take time and effort.

The Chinese are hospitable to a fault—only the swift mastery of "bao le, bao le, bao le" can call a halt to the piling of irresistible delicacies upon your plate. The Chinese are also respectful of any genuine dedication to study—really willing to talk for hours about their views and ideological persuasions even though they are unaccustomed to the brash expressions of curiosity.

These two traits alone would seem to suffice for a beginning, once Americans can come to live here and pursue friendships and insights at a more leisurely pace than the Nixon travelers have had.

OFF THE BEATEN PATH

But the stranger will have to know his Mao—not only to avoid mistaking a slogan for an answer but also to break down the explanations by finding contradictions and citing Chinese history to keep the discussion moving. As Premier Chou himself cautioned a visitor last summer, don't pay so much attention to the slogans.

Combining some of their knowledge and their persistence, the three reporters at the university were able to break off from a tour of laboratories and language classes and engage the members of two former rival Red Guard factions and assorted party cadres and teachers in an extensive conversation about the turmoil that overturned the education system here during the Cultural Revolution. They talked also about the lost frames of reference by which Americans and Chinese might judge each other's society and about the difficulties posed by such terms as "correct line," "capitalist roaders," "bourgeois," "capitalism" and "middle class."

The formal briefings at the university, about the "revolution" in education to bring workers and peasants into higher schools, were not nearly so instructive as the private conversation on cultural lag that now poses the same problem for teachers here as the open-admission concept does in America.

The official accounts of the new line in teacher-student relations was not nearly so illuminating as the private account of the "chaos" that resulted from officially inspired student uprisings in 1966, the seizures of buildings and combat with fists and iron pipes.

Why was the bloodshed allowed to continue for ten months without mediation or suppression? Because the conflict made it easier to fully expose enemies who had sneaked into the proletariat.

Then why does Chairman Mao now say that violence is not the way? Because violence is not the way.

How can it be both good and not good? Something can be undesirable but useful.

Are not some factional fights mere struggles for power? Only bourgeois elements fight for individual power; other factions fight for the correct mass line.

But how can a citizen or student know which line is correct when factions are contending all around him? By the study of Mao.

And if the rivals all speak from Mao? "Things are complicated here," said one of the hosts as he sent away the waiting bus, offered a magnificent lunch and then led an elaborate postlunch discussion of social justice in China and the United States.

Not until four hours into this conversation did the talk lapse into sterile speeches.

1973 PULITZER PRIZE FOR INTERNATIONAL REPORTING

The Intolerable Andrei Sakharov

HEDRICK SMITH

Moscow, U.S.S.R.
November 4, 1973

In person, Andrei Sakharov hardly seems the man to stir an international furor. Almost automatically now, he is paired with Aleksandr Solzhenitsyn—vilified in the Soviet Union as a "renegade and turncoat" who has slandered and betrayed with "black ingratitude" the motherland that nurtured him; sanctified in the West as a champion of individual rights, a beacon of free-thinking liberalism, a symbol for humanizing détente.

Yet Sakharov and Solzhenitsyn are immensely different men. Sakharov does not have the imposing presence, commanding personality or combative temperament of Solzhenitsyn. Where Solzhenitsyn self-confidently thrusts to the center of the conversational stage, Sakharov hovers in the wings, a shy, almost homely, unpretentious man, content to listen and reflect, head rolled thoughtfully to one side until he feels sufficiently at home with newcomers to converse freely.

The Solzhenitsyn of barrel chest, lined and ruddy face, work-worn hands, mahogany beard and penetrating eyes is physically as well as mentally powerful. Having overcome the trauma of Stalin's labor camps and endured the agony and awful uncertainties of cancer, he fought for eminence late in life as he fought in earlier years for life itself and when it has suited him, he has relished prestige and the limelight. So well is he recognized that his rare public appearances cause a stir; he is a palpable presence.

The contrasts with Sakharov abound at every turn. He is a tall but slightly stooped figure, with high intellectual forehead and two patches of thinning gray hair bordering his baldness, large hands unscarred by physical labor, and sad compassionate eyes. He is an inward man, a Russian *intelligent*, an intellectual through and through.

In his reticence and his conversational lapses, one senses the solitary thinker. His own natural penchant for privacy has been deepened by two decades of enforced privacy in the Soviet nuclear-research program, where outside contacts were forbidden. His unprecedented Soviet awards and decorations won him no public fame, since they were bestowed in secrecy. Even today, he can walk into a grocery, unshaven and in a rumpled raincoat looking for something to celebrate the birth of his first grandchild, and pass all but unnoticed and unrecognized.

A theoretical physicist of the stature of Oppenheimer and Teller, Sakharov gained eminence naturally, easily and early in life as one of the fathers of the Soviet hydrogen bomb. His meteoric career (Doctor of Science at twenty-eight, full member of the Academy of Sciences at the unheard-of age of thirty-two) earned him position, a fortune, private bodyguards and direct access to the pinnacle of the Soviet system. One of his first acts of dissent was a note scribbled to Khrushchev during a Kremlin meeting. For a decade he voiced his misgivings only within the rarefied atmosphere of the Soviet elite.

Abroad, his name was unknown until his manifesto, "Progress, Peaceful Coexistence and Intellectual Freedom," advocating an end to the arms race and convergence of the socialist and capitalist systems, leaked out to the West in 1968. Only thereafter did Sakharov begin to use his intellectual eminence in a public way, and then sparingly at first. Unlike Solzhenitsyn, he avoids the limelight. For months he refused to grant press interviews or permit journalistic portraits. Only with reluctance, feeling cornered and falsely accused, did he take his own problems to the world press this fall.

A kind of Grant Wood–American Gothic simplicity and modesty permeates Sakharov's life. He is modest in gesture, in manner, in dress, in surroundings. He seems as plain as an off-duty night watchman as he pads about his apartment, not bothering to change when guests arrive. As a concession to social convention, Sakharov dons a charcoal-gray suit with a nondescript, clip-on four-in-hand tie over a white, or even gray, work shirt, to go to the theater or on other public occasions.

His apartment is as unpretentious as Sakharov himself. He shares two rooms and a kitchen with his second wife, Elena, her son and her mother. For morning callers, bedclothes are tucked away to convert a modest master bedroom into an equally modest living room: a foam-rubber double-bed-couch on a faded oriental rug; a typewriter and an old-fashioned phonograph piled near a glass-front bookcase; a pan tied to a window radiator to catch drips. Because of the inevitable Russian space squeeze, skis are stored standing next to the flush bowl in a tiny toilet. Ice skates dangle overhead.

The first time someone took me to his apartment, we arrived to find it in total turmoil for repairs. With instinctive Russian hospitality and a brief apology for the mess, he led us directly to the kitchen where an enamel-topped table was littered with dishes, teacups and stray saucers. Andrei Dmitriyevich, as Russians call him, using his first name and patronymic, was drinking tea sweetened—or rather flavored—with chunks of little, hard, green apples.

"It's my favorite way of drinking tea," he remarked in answer to a curious glance.

"They used to say that the nobility had tea with lemon and the cooks had tea with apples," volunteered his wife. "So this is cook's tea."

Gently, Sakharov urged me to try his cook's tea, and I did. One cup was enough. I had the next cup with sugar. A box of plain biscuits was produced and then a box of motley candies, a few odd chocolates mixed with large gumdrops from some other package. Everything was very plain. Seven people squeezed around the little table. In a thoroughly Russian way, visitors were absorbed into life as it was and made to feel at home. No one made any effort to dress things up unnaturally.

Private, reticent, soft-spoken and kindly as he is, Sakharov wears his heart on his sleeve. When moved, he has a vibrant sense of outrage at injustice, a quick and deep compassion for the suffering of others, a naive directness in action and speech, almost heedless of the consequences for himself.

In years past, when he was less outspoken and his work on the hydrogen bomb was better remembered, the authorities used to play up his streak of naive idealism when trying to discredit his unorthodox views among other intellectuals. He was ridiculed as a naive eccentric, a well-meaning but hopelessly unrealistic, unworldly professor. The recent, sharper campaign against him even stirred some sentiments for putting him in a mental hospital, reminiscent of the treatment of the nineteenth-century Russian biologist and philosopher Pyotr Chadayev, whom the Czar had declared insane after Chadayev had condemned Russia as a backward society.

Sakharov, who has a good enough sense of humor to smile at the irony of being a prophet without honor in his own country, has joked with friends about being treated as a half-sainted, half-demented maverick. He once called himself "Andrei Blazhenny," a play on the ambiguities of the Russian word "blazhenny," which can mean saintly but in a crazy, capricious and quixotic way. And he has enough perspective about the limits of his influence and the ineffectuality of the Human Rights Committee, which he formed with two other physicists in 1970, to have kiddingly dismissed it as "The Pickwick Committee," a jibe at its practice of gathering and issuing papers that make not one dent in the Soviet system.

This modest side of Sakharov's personality is disarming and misleading. Some Westerners who meet him have come away wondering why so powerful a regime as the Soviet treats a man like Sakharov as dangerous. Others have asked aloud how so meek-mannered a soul suddenly brought down on his own head the orchestrated wrath of the Soviet establishment, as he did this fall.

The questions underestimate the force of Sakharov's thoroughly unconventional views. For he has gone well beyond other Soviet dissidents in his strong indictment of Soviet society and his blunt critique of the leadership's cherished policy of détente. From the regime's point of view, his independence of mind is an extremely dangerous example for other Soviet intellectuals when détente and broadening contacts with the West are likely to expose the Soviet body politic, especially other scientists, to the virus of Western ideas and habits of freethinking.

Perhaps more significantly, Sakharov has challenged the jealously guarded monopoly of the Communist Party in the realm of politics and ideas, which is a threat to the bedrock foundation of the Soviet system. For if in the modern age, managers and engineers are capable of running the economy, and administrators and bureaucrats can manage the government and diplomacy, the party is left without legitimacy and a raison d'etre. This is why the party hierarchy brooks no ideological opposition, no matter how small. And precisely because Sakharov's dissent is philosophical as well as topical and pragmatic, it becomes intolerable—more intolerable, some insiders say, than anything Solzhenitsyn has said or written.

Sakharov's judgments on Soviet society in the past year have been harsh and sweeping. He has attacked the vaunted Soviet system of free education and medical care as an "economic illusion" based on underpaid doctors and teachers, which actually offers services of "very low" quality. He has condemned the "pernicious" effects of the "hierarchical class structure" of Soviet society, in which a party-government-intellectual elite enjoys "open and secret privileges" such as better schools, clinics, rest homes, special stores and even "a system of supplemental salaries in special envelopes." He has voiced his dismay that among lower social strata drunkenness is "taking on proportions of a genuine national disaster, a symptom of the moral degradation of our society."

He has accused the leadership of perpetuating regional inequities by making Moscow and other large cities "privileged zones" for consumer goods, comforts and cultural activities. He has charged the regime with "cruel and persistent" religious persecution and "deliberate sharpening of the national problem," or frictions between Russian and non-Russian nationalities. He has declared that "militarization of the economy" poses a threat to peace, asserting flatly that "in no other country is the proportion of national income that goes to military needs as high as it is in the U.S.S.R.—40 percent."

"I am skeptical of socialism in general," he declared in a Swedish radio interview this summer. "I don't find that socialism has brought anything new in the theoretical plane, or a better social order . . . we have the same kinds of problems as the capitalist world: criminality and alienation. The difference is that our society is an extreme case, with maximum lack of freedom, maximum ideological rigidity, and— this is most typical—with maximum pretensions about being the best society, although it certainly is not that."

Sakharov's philosophical differences with the Soviet system are those of a modern Western liberal concerned with problems posed by the awful weapons of the twentieth century and unchecked political and economic power. "Philosophically, I am a liberal and a humanist," he explains. "Although not everything in official doctrine seems right to me, my objection is not to doctrine but to negative influences in life, such as intolerance, great-power chauvinism, nationalism, hypocrisy, brutality, illegality, egoism, conformism."

"We used to have Marxism but now that is only for form, for facade," he says. "Now we have pure pragmatism. If that pragmatism were good, I would not object to it."

His ideal is to see Soviet society reformed and evolving toward something between Sweden and West Germany today, a mixed economy, an open society, a free press, several parties. Here that stands out as heresy. "You Americans should remember what it was like in your McCarthy period," said one Russian bitterly. "Weren't people upset then if someone stood up and said your system was wrong? Wouldn't they have been outraged if someone had told the Soviet Union then not to negotiate with the United States? Remember those things and you see how people here can feel about Sakharov."

On foreign policy, Sakharov's challenge to the leadership was equally sharp. Lately, he has urged the American Congress to impose conditions on granting trade concessions to Moscow (no equal-tariff treatment unless the doors are thrown wide open to free emigration). And he has warned the West not to accept the Kremlin's type of détente. To a group of Western reporters, he declared:

"Détente without democratization [in the Soviet Union], détente in which the West in effect accepts the Soviet rules of the game, would be dangerous. It would not really solve any of the world's problems and would simply mean capitulating in the face of real or exaggerated Soviet power. It would mean trading with the Soviet Union, buying its gas and oil, while ignoring all other aspects.

"I think such a development would be dangerous because it would contaminate the whole world with the antidemocratic peculiarities of Soviet society, it would enable the Soviet Union to bypass problems it cannot resolve on its own and to concentrate on accumulating still further strength.

"As a result, the world would become helpless before this uncontrollable bureaucratic machine. I think that if détente were to proceed totally without qualifications, on Soviet terms, it would pose a serious threat to the world as a whole. It would mean cultivating a closed country where anything that happens may be shielded from outside eyes, a country wearing a mask that hides its true face."

"I would not wish it on anyone to live next to such a neighbor, especially if he is at the same time armed to the teeth," Sakharov said at a press conference poignantly timed for the fifth anniversary of the invasion of Czechoslovakia.

It was this that touched off the avalanche against Sakharov. In retrospect what is surprising is not that his dissent finally triggered a Niagara of inspired and menacing denunciations in the controlled media but that the onslaught did not come sooner. The real question is how Sakharov has managed to get away with his dissent when others were banished to harsh prisons in Siberia for lesser challenges to the system.

First of all, Sakharov has gained protection from the immense prestige he enjoys at home and abroad, especially as a member of the Academy of Sciences elected for discoveries that made enormous contributions to Soviet defense. Second, Sakharov has been spared the fate of those persecuted under Stalin because of very real changes in Soviet society since the dictator's death. For all its conservatism, the present leadership has not re-created Stalinist terror; it feels some restraints.

Finally, Sakharov's immunity from arrest thus far rests significantly on the regime's sensitivity to Western criticism at this particular time. The main anti-Sakharov campaign was suspended on September 9 after pointed protests from such European neutrals as Austrian Chancellor Bruno Kreisky and Swedish Foreign Minister Krister Wickman and such sympathetic Western statesmen as West German Chancellor Willy Brandt, because the leadership dared not jeopardize its détente push in Europe. The Kremlin was presumably equally sensitive to the kind of clear warning sent by Philip Handler, the head of the American Academy of Science, to Mstislav Keldysh, his Soviet counterpart, that "harassment or detention of Sakharov will have severe effects upon relationships between the scientific communities of the U.S.A. and U.S.S.R. and could vitiate our recent efforts toward increasing scientific interchange and cooperation."

In a very real sense, Sakharov, like Solzhenitsyn, gains some measure of safety from the fact that the regime has made use of him. Each of today's two great Soviet dissenters won his initial platform for criticizing important aspects of Soviet life by loyally serving the leadership—Solzhenitsyn as author of the first powerful anti-Stalinist novel, and Sakharov as one of the fathers of the Soviet hydrogen bomb. This loyal service gave them stature at home and made them listened to by foreigners. Only later did they break with the system and become ostracized dissenters, albeit of very different kinds—Solzhenitsyn, the Russian nationalist, and Sakharov, more akin to the modern Western progressive.

With hindsight, the evolution of Sakharov's dissent seems as natural and logical as his rapid rise as a theoretical physicist. Born in 1921, the son of a physicist who wrote textbooks and taught at Lenin Pedagogical Institute, young Sakharov quickly made his mark. By the age of twenty-six, he was embarked on cosmic-ray research that foreshadowed his later contributions to the Soviet hydrogen bomb. Three years later, in 1950, he and Dr. Igor Y. Tamm, who later won a Nobel Prize, had established the theoretical laws of controlled nuclear fusion, the basis for the H-bomb.

The rewards, by Soviet standards, were immense. Sakharov won a Stalin prize and eventually became one of a handful of mortals to win three awards as Hero of Socialist Labor, the nation's highest civilian decoration. He had a special, cabinet-set salary of two thousand rubles a month ($26,500 a year) and by 1969 had accumulated a fortune of 139,000 rubles ($153,000), which he donated to cancer research, evidently feeling that it was blood money.

As someone within the highest reaches of trust in the Soviet system, he lived a celibate life, cut off from normal social contacts except with fellow scientists. From 1950 to 1968 he lived in a city far from Moscow. He had a bodyguard at all times who slept with him, or nearby, and who went everywhere with him, even on vacations or in swimming. Once, Sakharov later recollected, he gave the guard the slip early one morning by getting up while the guard was still asleep. "I went off to ski," Sakharov said with puckish satisfaction.

In the early years, when the Soviet Union under Stalin was trying to catch up with America and overtake its atomic lead by becoming the first to detonate a hydrogen bomb, Sakharov took satisfaction in his work. "Twenty-five years ago, when I began working on this terrible weapon, I felt subjectively that I was working for peace, that my work would help foster a balance of power and that it would be useful to the Soviet people and, even to some extent, to mankind as a whole," he said recently. "That was the way I felt at the time. It was a natural point of view, shared by many, especially since we actually had no choice in the matter."

But later he felt pangs of conscience, much as had Oppenheimer, the American physicist. "I gradually began to understand the criminal nature not only of nuclear tests, but of the enterprise as a whole. I began to look on it and on other world problems from a broader, human perspective."

He became particularly concerned over the long-term dangers of radioactive fallout from nuclear tests and of the need to halt such tests. He made this the topic of his first real protest, a confidential letter to Igor Kurchatov, the chief scientific administrator of the weapons program at the time. In October 1958, after a six-month hiatus in Soviet atmospheric tests, Sakharov wrote Kurchatov urging cancellation of some scheduled Soviet tests. Kurchatov agreed and flew to see Premier Nikita Khrushchev, then vacationing at Yalta. But Khrushchev was unyielding; the tests went ahead.

Sakharov's next protest was more personal, and it provoked Khrushchev's irritation. In September 1961, the Soviet leadership had planned a series of huge nuclear tests leading up to a whopping 100-megaton explosion to coincide with the end of the twenty-second Communist Party congress. On the eve of the congress, Khrushchev invited top scientists to meet with the party leadership to discuss the tests and international policy.

During the meeting Sakharov was unable to contain himself and jotted a note to Khrushchev. He urged that the tests be called off, arguing that they were technically unnecessary and that it was vital for Moscow not to violate unilaterally the three-year-old atmospheric-test moratorium. The world then knew nothing of Khrushchev's plan to order the building of the Berlin Wall later that year, but people at the meeting were informed of it. And Sakharov, in his note, observed that "breaking the moratorium on atomic testing is a far more serious matter than building a wall in Berlin." He passed the note up to Khrushchev, who barely looked at it and stuck it in his pocket.

Later, when the participants had gathered for a small Kremlin reception, Khrushchev had obviously read the note and mentioned Sakharov's views to others. Again, he was unmoved. "Sakharov is a good scientist," the burly Soviet leader is reported to have commented. "But he is trying to teach us politics and we know politics better than he does. You have to be clever and tough and use blackmail with the imperialists."

Sakharov's third protest on this issue was the most crucial for him personally because it marked an important sense of breaking with the system. A big Soviet test was scheduled for September 25, 1962, but Sakharov had opposed it for much the same reasons.

"Our minister, Slavsky [Yefim Slavsky, the official who has since 1957 run the Soviet nuclear-weapons program under the cover title of minister of medium machine-building] had promised me they would not have it," Sakharov later explained. "But I found out that he had deceived me and they were going ahead. So I called Khrushchev personally. We had special telephones. We could do that. He was in Ashkhabad. I got him there. When I told him that I opposed the test, he said, 'Excuse me, I will have to clarify this with Kozlov.' Frol

Kozlov was his deputy at the time. Kozlov called me back but by that time they had moved forward the time of the test and it was too late. The test had already occurred by the time I talked with Kozlov on the phone."

It was a shattering experience for Sakharov to feel tricked by his superiors on his own project. "It was terrible," he recalled. "I had an awful sense of powerlessness. I could not stop something I knew was wrong and unnecessary. After that, I felt myself another man. I broke with my surroundings. It was a basic break. After that, I understood there was no point in arguing."

The 1963 Soviet-American agreement banning atmospheric tests relieved some of his sense of frustration, in part because Sakharov felt he contributed to it. Immediately after the test that he had opposed, Sakharov recalls having gone to Slavsky and recommending that the Soviet Union pick up an old American fallback position put forward in February 1959 by President Eisenhower. It called for a ban on nuclear testing in the atmosphere, in space and under water, the three environments in which tests could be readily detected. The idea evidently went up the hierarchy, but Sakharov now feels the initiative was his.

The test-ban treaty did not, however, halt the evolution of Sakharov's dissent. His superiors thought his protests were perhaps motivated by career dissatisfactions or unhappiness over conditions at work, but he felt a growing moral concern. "The atomic question was always half science, half politics," he mused one day, talking in a low voice, stretched across the bare, gray-green foam-rubber mattress of his bed, unshaven, in an old blue sweater, recalling his challenge to the top leadership as if it were an ordinary occurrence. "The atomic issue was a natural path into political issues. What matters is that I left conformism. It is not important on what question. After that first break, everything later was natural."

Actually, Sakharov slid into political dissent by stages, once again incurring Khrushchev's disfavor. In 1964, Sakharov opposed the election to the Academy of Nikolai Nuzhdin, a close aide of Trofim Lysenko, the biologist who had purged and suppressed genetics studies under Stalin and Khrushchev. Other prestigious academicians sided with Sakharov and Nuzhdin was rejected. Soon thereafter, Sakharov was crudely attacked in the press as "a complete ignoramus" on biology and, insulted, he protested to Khrushchev in a letter that renewed his criticism of Nuzhdin and Lysenko, who was a favorite of Khrushchev.

The letter evidently angered the leader for he reportedly showed it to some high-level party colleagues, including Mikhail Suslov, the chief ideologist, to whom he is said to have blustered: "First, Sakharov did not want to test the bomb. Now he mixes in the Lysenko affair." Khrushchev is said to have told the secret-police chief to find some compromising material on Sakharov "to teach him a lesson," but Sakharov was spared by Khrushchev's fall from power.

Nonetheless, Sakharov was demoted a notch for his outspokenness. This in turn enabled him to broaden his social contacts. In the mid-1960s, he met Solzhenitsyn for the first time. In 1966, he joined twenty-four other outstanding intellectuals in appealing to the party leadership not to rehabilitate Stalin at the twenty-third party congress. And on December 5, 1966, he took part in a one-minute vigil in Pushkin Square commemorating international Human Rights Day, his first public act of dissent.

By early 1967, he had begun to intervene in a few cases of such dissidents as Alexander Ginzburg, Yuri Galanskov and Yuli Daniel, privately protesting to party leaders over their arrests or the harsh conditions in their labor camps. None marked an irreversible break with the establishment, but each pushed him further into the arena of social protest.

Higher-ups disapproved of his activities and removed him as chief of a section in the nuclear program, thereby cutting his salary in half. But by the first half of 1967, he had already begun collecting thoughts for his famous "Progress, Coexistence and Intellectual Freedom" essay that first brought him world attention and marked his firm break with the system.

By comparison with Sakharov's later statements, this was moderate, couched in language intended to appeal to establishment liberals. He offered a broad social vision with two basic themes—the division of mankind threatens it with destruction, and intellectual freedom is essential to society. Sakharov balanced off criticism of American policy in Vietnam with reproof of Soviet Middle East policy, urged an end to the arms race and a cooperative campaign against world hunger, suggested reforms for both West and East, predicting and proposing the ultimate convergence of the two systems. Perhaps most significantly, he began with a tribute to the "lofty ideals of socialism" and affirmed his own "profoundly socialist viewpoint."

But he also set out some sharp critiques of Soviet society. He opposed efforts to export revolution and condemned such mass myths as "the myth about the sharpening of the class struggle and proletarian infallibility." Even then, he decried "the formation of a distinct class— a bureaucratic elite from which all key positions are filled and that is rewarded for its work through open and concealed privileges." And he declared battle with "the ossified dogmatism of a bureaucratic oligarchy and its favorite weapon, ideological censorship."

Within the Soviet Union, the essay found a wide audience. According to other intellectuals, it circulated widely in scientific institutes of major cities. Some estimate that thousands upon thousands of intellectuals read it and passed it on, regarding it as less risky than other unofficial, underground material because it carried the prestigious name of an academician and a highly decorated scientist.

But unofficial retribution was swift when the essay was first printed in the West in June 1968. Sakharov was fired from the nuclear program. One morning he was merely forbidden to enter the classified working area. His security clearance was lifted. When he inquired, he was told he was no longer needed. For a few months, his salary continued to be sent to his savings bank. But for nearly a year, he had no job.

Only in May 1969, forced into what was considered the indignity of an open academic competition for a job well below his status, he was taken back as a senior researcher at the Lebedev Institute of Physics, where he had begun his civilian career more than twenty years earlier. He has worked there ever since, going on Tuesdays in a chauffeur-driven car (one of the perquisites of being an academy member) to take part in a seminar on quantum theory and elementary particles.

Totally cut off from the nuclear program, Sakharov was now drawn into a career as a campaigner for civil rights. In 1970, 1971 and 1972, he issued lengthy new essays on broad social problems, each one sharper in tone than the previous. Beginning in 1970, he signed scores upon scores of personal protests and appeals for less well known dissenters—Grigorenko, Amalrik, Bukovsky, Ginzburg, Galanskov, Daniel, Lyubarsky, Shikhanovich, Pluyush, Feinberg, Borisov. He

stood vigil outside trials to assert the principle of open trials and rule
of law.

At one vigil, in October 1970, he met Elena Georgevna Bonner, a
gregarious, energetic, half-Armenian, half-Jewish pediatrician whose
mother was sent to sixteen years in camp and exile at the peak of the
Stalinist purges in 1937 and who had spent a lifetime sending food
packages to relatives in prison. She is the aunt of Eduard Kuznetsov,
a young Jew given a death sentence—later reduced to fifteen years—
in the December 1970 Leningrad hijacking trial. Sakharov's first wife
had died in 1969, and in a few months he married Elena, who started
his activism.

Together with her children, Tatyana and Alyosha, among others,
he went to the Lebanese embassy in September 1972 to protest the
killing of Israeli athletes at the Munich Olympics by Palestinian com-
mandos—and was detained for the first time. Squads of police awaited
the demonstrators. There was no clash, no scuffle. Demonstrators were
simply motioned into parked buses as they arrived at the scene. Sakharov was interrogated—politely, he later said—and quickly released.
What depressed him most, he said, were some sharply anti-Semitic
remarks by the onlookers.

It is impossible to judge how much sympathy there is among intellectuals for Sakharov's views today (until recently the common man
did not know of him and now presumably accepts the regime's charges
that he is a turncoat). It seems clear, however, that as Sakharov has
become increasingly active, his influence among establishment liberals
has declined. In part, they have withdrawn because of tightening controls and a sense of futility over the lack of impact of earlier protests.
Sakharov's official ostracism and dismissal made it riskier for people
to read and pass on his later essays, and their audience is widely
reported to be a mere fraction of the audience that read the 1968 essay.

His insistence on the need for greater intellectual freedom, less censorship, easier access to Western publications, freer scientific inquiry
is reported to have found a sympathetic audience in a fairly wide
scientific community. A smaller group presumably shares his concern
over heavy military expenditures at the cost of better housing, school-
ing, clothing or medical care. Still fewer are likely to share his resentment against the privileged elite, since a fair number of scientists are
part of it themselves.

Some now privately voice the suspicion that Sakharov has sharp-
ened his criticism to provoke the authorities into letting him emigrate,
a path closed to them. "When his first essay came out, many people
felt he was speaking for all of us," said one natural scientist. "Now,
if he really wants to emigrate, some people feel he is speaking more
for himself and not the rest of us."

Sakharov's own explanation for his sharpening dissent is his sense
of frustration at what he sees as a broadening pattern of official repression, which is being ignored by the West because of its own preoc-
cupations and its interests in political détente and trade with the Soviet
Union. More than once he has remarked that he felt the situation had
become worse for freethinking Soviet intellectuals since President
Nixon's first summit visit to Moscow in May 1972. Indeed, over the
past twelve to eighteen months, a determined secret-police campaign
has produced scores of arrests and left dissidents demoralized and in
disarray. Their underground publications have been shut down. And
other intellectuals are cautious.

Sakharov denies that there ever was such a thing as a dissident
movement in the sense of a group, or groups, pursuing a political goal
and giving the authorities any serious reasons for concern. "I have
always considered it mainly as an effort to protest against unfair trials,
unjustified commitments to mental institutions, to help the families of
the persons concerned," he said. And he acknowledged that even
"these ranks have been thinned."

Although Sakharov himself has thus far avoided trial and incarcer-
ation, he has paid a price that serves as a deterrent for others. He still
receives a good salary of 750 rubles, more than half of it his guaranteed
stipend as an academy member. But at fifty-two, he feels unproductive
as a theoretical physicist, having spent so many years in applied rather
than theoretical fields and now being troubled by what he calls his
"inner unrest" over social issues.

At work, other scientists tend to shy away from Sakharov. Socially,
his circle has narrowed. He maintains a dacha, awarded him under
Stalin, in the scientists' suburb of Zhukhovka. But he visits much less
with other senior academicians than in years past. Colleagues and
friends who share his views have been harassed. The two young physicists who joined him in forming the Committee on Human Rights
in 1970 lost their jobs. One, Valery Chalidze, came under such sharp

police pressure that he chose to accept an invitation to visit the United States, where Soviet authorities lifted his citizenship.

Sakharov's family relations are strained. His three children by his first marriage, two daughters and a son, rarely ever see him. The daughters, both married, disapprove of his politics and shun contact with him. His sixteen-year-old son lives with the oldest daughter and, to Sakharov's great personal disappointment, also stays away from him.

His stepchildren have come under official pressures. Nearly a year ago, Tatyana was abruptly expelled from the sixth and final year of the evening department of the journalistic faculty of Moscow State University on a rarely invoked technicality. Her husband was later advised to quit his job as an engineer or face dismissal.

This spring, Sakharov was jolted when his sixteen-year-old stepson, Alyosha, a boy with an excellent school record, was flunked on one entrance exam for the university. Friends inquired and found evidence that his Russian literature paper had been unfairly downgraded despite his high marks in other subjects. After a delay of several months, he was allowed to take exams for the Lenin Pedagogical Institute, got almost straight A's, and is now enrolled.

Sympathizers believe this fall's campaign against Sakharov was intended to oust him from the Academy of Sciences, thereby preparing ground for a trial. The timing and nature of the warning given him in August by the deputy procurator general (the Soviet assistant attorney general) tends to support this notion. More than once, the Party Aktiv (the party members among the academy) was reported to have been summoned to meet with higher party officials to see how an expulsion could be arranged. One such meeting was said to have lasted until 2 A.M. Allegedly, the higher party officials were told that any number of signatures could be produced for denunciations of Sakharov but there was no way to guarantee his expulsion in the required secret ballot. Moreover, by academy rules, Sakharov would be entitled to speak in his own defense.

The episode points up the peculiar and important standing of the Soviet Academy as a unique organization able in some limited way to resist the party's writ. By tradition, no one is expelled and the members fear a dangerous precedent if action is taken against Sakharov. Unable to expel him, the authorities drummed up a press campaign to discredit and isolate him, obtaining the signatures of many of the nation's best-known scientists, writers, composers, artists and other intellectuals. Ironically, Sakharov was spared its first shock effect because he was not in Moscow when the first thunderous letters appeared—including one signed by forty other members of the academy. He was vacationing in the Crimea. His wife, Elena, overheard others on the beach reacting to the press campaign, denouncing him and asserting that such a man should be "put in a mental hospital." She rushed off to warn her husband to leave the beach. But he returned and, unrecognized by the people, fell into conversation with them, asking whether they personally knew Sakharov. When they said no, he suggested, "perhaps Sakharov is a good man after all" and then left.

In general, the campaign was so heavy-handed that it not only provoked protests abroad but galvanized a few of the previously demoralized and recently inactive dissenters. They quickly felt, as the writer Lydia Chukovskaya put it, that Sakharov was "the captain of our ship," and rallied around him. In part, their efforts were aided by the fact that the Soviet Union had just stopped jamming the Voice of America and other Western radios, meaning that more people could hear of Western reactions to the campaign as well as Western broadcasts on the few Soviet statements defending Sakharov.

But the present situation represents no more than an uneasy truce. Sakharov has become a central symbol in the tug-of-war over the nature of détente. He symbolizes the liberalization the West would like to see and that the Soviet leadership is determined to prevent.

On the surface, it appears as though the West has won an important battle by rallying to the defense of Sakharov and Solzhenitsyn, but this may be a delusion. Sakharov and Solzhenitsyn are two unique personalities in Soviet society. They are so well known in the West that Western politicians and liberals react when actions are taken against them.

But Soviet authorities, who renewed sporadic attacks against Sakharov in October, evidently count on Western opinion to be too disorganized and forgetful to follow consistently the issue of civil rights in the Soviet Union. Sakharov and Solzhenitsyn have themselves observed that repressions have continued against other, less well known, freethinkers. Sakharov's own protests on their behalf find almost no echo abroad. He and others fear that it is not the civil rights advocates who have prevailed but Soviet conservatives, who cleverly muted their anti-Sakharov campaign before it turned human rights into a burning and permanent issue in the evolution of détente.

The present situation represents no more than an uneasy stalemate. Westerners, who see Sakharov as a symbol of the liberalization they hope will occur along with détente, have risen to Sakharov's personal defense but have achieved little more. The Communist establishment, determined to prevent the kind of liberalization that Sakharov symbolizes, has now better insulated its intelligentsia against outside infection, though it has been unable to silence Sakharov personally. Ironically, some of the very latest attacks have for the first time exposed Soviet readers to some of Sakharov's ideas, acquainted them with his contributions to the Soviet hydrogen bomb and even reported his efforts to limit Soviet nuclear tests.

His personal future, however, remains uneasy and uncertain, isolated as he is from establishment liberals, unable to do productive work, and worried about his family. He seems genuinely not to fear for himself. By his doorbell, there is posted a little cartoon of a hedgehog, crouching in the bushes, on guard against snakes, and the caption says: "This is a hedgehog. Do not try to take him by hand"—a warning that Sakharov will raise a furor if he is threatened again. But what really troubles him is the quiet, unseen but unrelenting pressures on his family.

"I have not been afraid personally for myself," he said not long ago. "I am mostly afraid of a kind of pressure being directed against my family, my wife's family and relatives."

But he was clearly shaken when two Arabs claiming to be from the Black September terrorist group came to his house on October 22 and threatened to kill him if he made another statement sympathetic to Israel and harmful to the Arabs. The threat grew out of an earlier interview, during the Arab-Israeli fighting, in which Sakharov saw Israel as fighting for its life and the Arabs motivated by less compelling needs and in which he urged Western aid to Israel to match Soviet aid to the Arabs. "We never give two warnings," the Arabs told him.

Nonetheless, moved by personal convictions, he is not one to desist from speaking out, even though his civil rights activities have had no noticeable impact. With a spirit that links him to other dissenters in Russia's past, he asserts the need to be true to one's self.

"You always need to make ideals clear to yourself," he told someone who asked why he kept going this way. "You always have to be aware of them, even if there is no direct path to their realization. Were there no ideals, there would be no hope whatsoever. Then everything would be hopelessness, darkness—a blind alley."

1974 PULITZER PRIZE FOR INTERNATIONAL REPORTING

Vietnam Escapees Wait in Limbo as the World Turns a Deaf Ear

HENRY KAMM

Tokyo, Japan
June 7, 1977

A month after setting out on the open sea in a small fishing boat under cover of night from the port of Vung Tau, near Saigon, thirty-seven Vietnamese refugees are docked in the small Japanese port of Handa aboard the freighter that picked them up at sea.

The Liberian-flag, Swiss-operated freighter, *Los Andes*, arrived in Japan eight days ago, but authorities have not allowed the refugees to come ashore, even temporarily. Unless the Liberian or Swiss government guarantees that it will accept responsibility for getting the thirty-seven people out of Japan if no country offers them permanent refuge, Japan will not let them land.

And as long as there is a possibility that responsibility can be passed on to someone else, Vietnamese refugees have been waiting in limbo throughout Asia, tasting the bitterness of having staked their lives on the remote chance of survival at sea for the sake of finding a freer life outside their country and finding instead a world that shows them by its inaction that it wishes they had stayed where they came from.

"As a government policy, we don't accept refugees," a high Foreign Ministry official said, explaining the Japanese attitude. Because of the disproportion between Japan's wealth and the small number of refugees that reach Japan's waters, their icy reception here is a token of the full measure of the distress of the approximately one hundred thousand Indochinese refugees in Asia.

Since the Vietnam War ended more than two years ago, Japan has received 689 refugees who escaped by the only available means: small boats that set out on the open sea with as much water, food and fuel as they could cram aboard in addition to the passengers and the hope that, if their own countrymen do not catch them and the boat can stay afloat on the high seas, their supplies will not give out before a passing ship acknowledges their SOS and picks them up.

How many of them are caught as they set out or are picked up by vessels from Communist countries and returned, or perish at sea, will never be known.

Of the 689 who have found temporary refuge in Japan, 258 have gone on to permanent immigration elsewhere, mainly the United States. But countries ready to take Indochinese refugees are getting increasingly rare. The United States now issues visas to only one hundred persons and their immediate families a month for what it calls "boat survivors" throughout Asia, and stays in "temporary" havens are taking on the air of indeterminate waits for word from an embassy.

By allowing the refugees to wait in Japan, the Japanese government makes it clear that it considers it has carried out its humanitarian obligations. It does not feed, clothe or shelter them, extends no medical, educational or social services and allows no refugee to work to provide for his or her own needs.

The refugees are cared for by religious charitable organizations, principally the Roman Catholic Caritas group. They are supported by the United Nations High Commissioner for Refugees, who represents the refugees in dealing with the Japanese government and tries to find permanent homes for them, as well as paying a daily stipend of 900 yen ($3.21) per refugee and some medical expenses.

"The refugees are granted a temporary stay to give them breathing space before going on to a final accommodation," said Shunji Kobayashi, chief of the general affairs section of the immigration control bureau, the principal official concerned with the problem. "We are limited by the lack of basic facilities and people to look after them."

Mr. Kobayashi and the Foreign Ministry official emphasized in interviews that Japan had no tradition of receiving foreigners, which seems to disregard the hundreds of thousands of Koreans and Taiwanese brought here when their countries were conquered by Imperial Japan.

"We don't have government facilities for refugees," the Foreign Ministry official said coolly. "This is a very new thing for us, and we have enough problems looking after ourselves for housing." There are now 431 Vietnamese in Japan, a nation of 113 million.

Asked why the Japanese government did not contribute to the refugees' support, the official said that since there was no provision for refugees in Japanese legislation, no budget appropriation could be made. Mr. Kobayashi went on to cast doubt on the refugees' authenticity as political refugees and suggested that they were leaving Vietnam for their material advancement, like the great number of Korean illegal immigrants here.

The Foreign Ministry official said that while Japan made no direct contribution to the refugees' living, it was a leading contributor to the United Nations High Commissioner. A Foreign Ministry specialist said that Japan made an annual contribution, which was $70,000 last year and will be $80,000 this year. In addition, he said, Japan had made a special contribution of 600 million yen ($2 million) for Indochinese refugees in 1975 and 175 million yen ($583,000) last March.

The Immigration and Foreign Ministry officials both expressed concern over the mounting number of Vietnamese nearing the coasts of Japan. In addition to the refugees of *Los Andes*, eighty are reported inbound on three vessels.

If they are to be allowed to land, these conditions must be met, said Hitoshi Mise, Japan's representative here of the United Nations High Commissioner: The United Nations must guarantee the costs of their stay and their eventual transport to another country as well as their adherence to Japanese law. This includes abstention from political activities, which is interpreted to mean that they must not speak out about conditions in the country from which they fled.

Asked whether Japan feared complications in the relationship it hoped to develop with Hanoi, a Foreign Ministry source thought a long time before saying that he didn't know. But he pointed out that the Tokyo-Hanoi relationship was quite new and in a sensitive stage. A European banker here, blunter, said that the market of fifty million Vietnamese was the strongest magnet to business and banking in Asia today, that few countries would risk offending Hanoi for the sake of humanitarian considerations.

The problem that they have provoked by surviving until they

entered Japanese waters has caused only a thin echo among the thirty-seven refugees on *Los Andes*. They are still recovering, with the customary absence of self-pity that distinguished the millions of Vietnamese displaced by both sides, from their ordeal at sea.

This group is typical of the broad range of people fleeing Vietnam, Laos and Cambodia, and it resembles in variety those, for example, who fled Hungary in 1956 or other Communist countries since World War II. Except for one former sergeant in the Saigon air force who has strong anti-Communist views, they displayed no ideological commitment but rather deep unhappiness over an increasingly restrictive life, arbitrary arrests for "reeducation" at forced labor with no provision for release and a sense of being cut off from the world and their relatives and friends abroad.

The bulk of the group is made up of the fifty-seven-year-old owner of the fishing boat, his wife, their four sons, one daughter, one daughter-in-law and two nephews, fishermen and farmers from Vung Tau. There is the wife of a former South Vietnamese army physician who has been undergoing "reeducation" for two years and her six-year-old son. Their closest friend, a Saigon secretary, came with her. And there is a Saigon high school student hoping to finish his education in France.

When asked about their escape, they spoke softly of the night they spent hiding in the forest near the place where the boat was tied up, admonishing their children to be quiet. They recall how seasick they all were, especially the two pregnant women and the thirteen children. They tell how ten days out their motor broke down and they drifted for two days, losing hope.

With their boat drawing a lot of water and their strength to bail it out waning, they were joyous when a freighter stopped for the SOS, but crushed when after long deliberation it did not take them aboard, instead lowering a vessel for them to continue the voyage on their own.

Soon after, the motor of that craft broke down and the men rowed with the oars that had been provided. Again they drifted as their strength flagged. Days passed. Then a Philippine freighter stopped. But instead of taking the exhausted people aboard, its crew gave them a map that marked their position near Okinawa and told them, falsely, that they were only nine miles from land and to keep rowing. "We

were crying," the former sergeant said, because they had no strength
to row.

Then came *Los Andes*.

Capt. Carlo Guidi, an Italian, has accommodated his passengers as
best he can, although they outnumber his crew and far outstrip his
facilities. He does not know what he will do if Japan refuses to accept
the refugees. His next stop is Argentina, a voyage of perhaps thirty-
five days around Cape Horn. In their eagerness to get rid of the
refugees, he said, port authorities at his first Japanese stop persuaded
them to continue on his itinerary, although with sixty-six persons
aboard and lifeboats for only forty, *Los Andes* is in clear violation of
safety rules.

Captain Guidi said there was no way he could set out for Argentina
with his passengers.

"We don't understand Japan," said the Saigon high school student.
"They call themselves a country of freedom."

Mr. Kobayashi, the immigration official, said he hoped the problem of Vietnamese knocking on Japan's door would diminish rather
than grow.

1978 PULITZER PRIZE FOR INTERNATIONAL REPORTING

Soviet Change vs. Worker's Scrutiny

———————————————•———————————————

BILL KELLER

Ilyichevsk, U.S.S.R.
May 10, 1988

Mikhail S. Gorbachev's new economic reality visited this Black Sea
port city last year, passing like an unexpected tremor through the rock-
stable lives of longshoremen, crane operators, mechanics and clerks.

Early in the year port executives informed the workers that, in
keeping with the new drive for profit and efficiency, 634 of them

would be laid off or retrained for different jobs, or pushed into retirement.

Anxious rumbles swept through this city not far from Odessa. So this was the bright future Mr. Gorbachev calls perestroika, or restructuring. No vodka, no meat, and now, no jobs.

"It was so unexpected," said Mikhail Matiyets, a truck driver, who took a pay cut. "It was a shock, really."

Serafima Gorozhankina, a technical librarian who found her library organized out of existence, said: "Everybody was afraid. Nobody knew who would be on the list."

The port personnel director, Pyotr G. Sibalo, recounting the anxieties of a workforce raised to think of the employer as a lenient parent, said, "In some cases I was close to tears myself."

But in the end, what many feared would be a painful upheaval was almost an anticlimax. For this was a Soviet-style layoff, in which cold-blooded economic sense gave way to the realities of a long-standing social contract.

Everyone displaced was offered another job, with no loss of benefits. The few workers who complained about their new places were given jobs more to their liking. Yulian Serebrisky, offended at losing his job as a mechanic, sued in the local court to get his place back, and won. The workers who stayed in their old jobs were given new promises of job security.

Profit took a back seat to labor peace: for every ruble the port saved by the cutbacks, it spent four rubles on generous pay raises designed to keep the workforce contented.

Gorbachev's economists tell him that if he is to lift this backward country to a modern standard of living and make it competitive in the world, the Soviet Union will have to begin loosening the safety net of cheap prices, job guarantees and cradle-to-grave entitlements that stifle initiative.

In principle, Gorbachev agrees. He argues that people should be rewarded for their work and for their initiative, not for simply showing up—and that society should not coddle those who refuse to pull their weight.

But the ruthlessness of the marketplace violates the sense of justice and equality reinforced by seventy years of Soviet rule.

Perhaps more than any of the obstacles looming before Gorbachev— the intractable bureaucracy, the degraded state of technology, the legions of managers who have never been taught to manage, the legacy of corruption, the entrenched interests of those who have privileges and cling to them—it is this social contract that presents the most serious challenge.

The Soviet people expect, as a matter of basic right, something most economists believe is impossible: that perestroika should bring them a better life without risk, without discomfort.

The Soviet economy is run along the lines of an Appalachian coal company town. The company—in this case the state—is the source from which all material blessings flow. That is critical to understanding why ordinary citizens find Gorbachev's program so disturbing.

In Ilyichevsk, a city thrown up haphazardly around a new cargo port in the 1950s, the company is the Ministry of the Merchant Marine Fleet, known as Morflot. Those who do not work for the port itself work for something related—the maritime technical school, the ship repair yard, the electronics plant built to provide jobs for port wives.

Because of the imported goods the sailors bring in, and because of the gentle Black Sea climate, life is somewhat better than in other places. It is immeasurably better than the grinding poverty of most of the nation's villages, where it is still common to find housing—and even hospitals—without hot water. But the average American would find little to envy in the living standards of Ilyichevsk's seventy thousand residents.

As in much of the country, newcomers must wait ten to fifteen years for a separate apartment. In the meantime they live in shabby hostels where single workers double up and share communal kitchens and showers, and a family of five occupies a ten-by-fifteen-foot room.

Meat and fruit are scarce, except in the unregulated farmers' markets, where a chicken or a slab of stewing beef costs several times the official price, and where a precious lemon sells for up to five dollars in late spring.

Perestroika has done little so far to brighten the life of consumers. The latest national economic report, for the first quarter for 1988, is a litany of shortages: meat, dairy products, shoes, clothing—even that bulwark of the Soviet diet, potatoes.

Ilyichevsk has one of the new cooperative cafes that have sprung up under recent laws permitting private enterprise, and there are several more in nearby Odessa, but "you know what the prices are in those places," said Lyudmila Matiyets, a warehouse clerk, who has enough trouble keeping two growing daughters in clothes.

But if life in Ilyichevsk is not luxurious, it is at least heavily subsidized and relatively secure, assuring most residents a basic level of comfort with little regard for an individual's talent or effort. The necessities of life are provided as perks accumulated on the job.

Serafima Gorozhankina, who has worked at the port for twenty-five of her fifty-three years, recited the benefits that have accrued to her and her husband, a seaman, as a result of this system.

Their apartment, two cozy rooms in the port complex, takes only twenty-seven rubles of their monthly 350 rubles in combined income, including rent, all utilities, and a telephone. The apartment is small, but it is theirs for life unless they move away.

The couple's basic medical care in the port clinic is free, as are the nursery schools and kindergartens their son and daughter attended. They can ride to work on port buses—transportation throughout the country is heavily subsidized—and vacation in port-owned homes or on travel vouchers provided at discount prices by their trade union.

When Gorozhankina needed a new refrigerator, she borrowed three hundred rubles from the port, interest-free. When the state stores are empty of meat and fish, she can often buy a chicken or piece of fish through the port cafeteria, "not the fish I would like, but fish all the same." Soon she will have a garden plot to grow her own vegetables—another perk from the port.

"There are little things you are so accustomed to you don't even notice them," she said. For example, she subscribes to all her newspapers and magazines through the port, because that way she can pay on the installment plan.

The port plays an almost parental role in the life of its workers.

If Gorozhankina, who has traveled to Bulgaria and Romania, wants to go abroad again, it is the Communist Party committee at her workplace that certifies she is trustworthy to be let out of the country.

"If they agree that I have no reprimands, that I don't drink and that I am a good mother, then I can go," she said.

"You see why we were so concerned" when word of the layoffs spread last year, Gorozhankina added, as she poured cups of strong tea for visitors. "We receive practically everything from the port."

In such a system, more money is not necessarily the key to a dramatically higher standard of living. It cannot usually buy a better apartment—only patience or privilege can bring better housing.

It cannot buy a car, because there are not enough cars to go around. The government newspaper *Izvestia* reported last year that if the shortage of cars were suddenly eliminated, a million people in the Russian republic alone would turn up at sales outlets ready to pay cash. The right to buy a car, like housing, is bestowed on workers as a reward for patience or a senior position.

Money is, to be sure, an essential lubricant in the Soviet system of bribery and *blat*, or pull. A hospital patient expects to pay the nurse a few rubles for an extra blanket, and someone languishing on an apartment waiting list may advance his position with a well-placed gift.

But for most workers, what counts is not so much a higher paycheck as staying put and hanging on.

This is the boat Gorbachev has started to rock.

Gorbachev's strategy is to reduce the subsidies and perks, while giving people more money and more good things to spend it on. In time, he hopes, people will begin to understand the connection between harder work and a better quality of life.

One approach is to reorganize the pay system in each workplace so the eager worker is not limited by arbitrary wage norms set by a ministry in Moscow and the lazy worker pays a price.

Some workers clearly relish the new opportunity, but many are wary.

As Stanislav S. Mikhailyuk, the Ilyichevsk port director, says, they are still accustomed to the old system, by which "we paid people, to a certain extent, for their blue eyes."

"The hardest thing of all is to make changes in the head," he said, "to teach people that there is a difference between receiving money and earning it."

When Soviet officials talk of tampering with this system of entitlements, they risk the charge that they are straying from basic socialist doctrine. In Soviet parlance, the phrase "human rights" does not mean freedom of speech or emigration; it means guarantees of housing, job security, medical care and so forth.

During a meeting with port officials, Boris Kondratsky, a young official of the local county executive committee, raised an obvious question: how can a worker really learn the value of a ruble when most of his necessities are seen as gifts bestowed by the state?

"True, to a certain extent it spoils people," the port director replied. "But it's also one of our advantages," allowing the port to hold on to good workers.

But suppose, Kondratsky suggested, that the worker got more cash in his pocket, and had to pay the real value of his housing, his medical care, his children's kindergarten?

"Then it would be not socialism, but capitalism," the director replied without hesitation.

The reluctance to take on greater risk and responsibility is compounded by a widespread suspicion, reinforced by decades of unfulfilled promises, that things will not really get better after they get worse.

Perhaps when Gorbachev talks of the illogic of price controls— where bread is so cheap, he says, you sometimes see children using a loaf as a football—people get his point. But when he vows that ending subsidies will be painless, because everyone will get compensatory pay increases, they are skeptical. They already see prices creeping up as a result of a partial deregulation of farming.

Gorbachev's initial calls last year for "radical price reform" caused a panicky public reaction, hoarding and anxious letters to the press, so the Soviet leader agreed that state controls on consumer prices would not be lifted before 1990, despite the advice of his economists that price controls hamper other aspects of his economic program.

Nothing frightens Soviet workers quite so much as the specter of unemployment, and not just because it means being cut off from a reliable source of material benefits. This is, after all, a country where the best-selling newspaper is called "work," where a job is not only guaranteed by law but required, where someone without work is officially a "parasite."

Soviet officials insist that unemployment on any significant scale is not an immediate danger in the Soviet Union.

The country has a chronic manpower shortage exaggerated by the vicious cycle of the welfare state: workers have had little reason to exert themselves because they could not be dismissed, so that factories needed more workers to do the same job, so that even lazy workers became indispensable, encouraging them to perform badly.

Even if the average Soviet worker began to produce at Western levels, the country has many underutilized factories that could be run on two or three shifts, many working women who would be happier to stay home and tend their children, and a desperate need for people to provide basic services.

But repairing the Soviet economy will require massive dislocations. Soviet economists predict that sixteen million people will have to be relocated or retrained by the year 2000, as the country tries to trim the fat from its factory workforces and create a service industry.

At Ilyichevsk, the layoffs last year entailed a six-month process of meetings, job placement, hand-holding and negotiations.

Port officials prepared the lists of which sections must be cut, and sent them to meetings of the "worker collectives" at each division of the port, where the workers themselves were told to choose who would go and who would stay.

For the most part, the layoffs were carried out according to the rules of the social contract, keeping the people who needed the jobs, not the people the company needed most.

"In our collective, first they took into account who has enough money, who is better off," recalled Fyodor Lobadrov, sixty-three, who worked as a tallyman keeping track of cargo on the docks. "Second, those of pension age were asked to go. If a person had only a year or two until pension, of course he stayed. If someone had two or three children, he stayed. Or if a person could not learn another trade he stayed."

A third of the tallymen had to be eliminated, so Lobadrov took a less demanding job supervising a boiler room.

Some workers say the cutbacks gave the remaining workers a new attitude toward their jobs, at least for now. The pay increases, workers say, had much less to do with this than the whiff of expendability.

"You can feel it," Gorozhankina said. "People are more diligent in their jobs and they don't try to evade work. Maybe people are more afraid, afraid they will be fired if another cutback happens."

This disturbs Nikolai M. Grishin, the director's assistant, who feels people should be working better not out of fear but out of a sense that it will bring them a better life. At Ilyichevsk, he said, the jury is still out on this fundamental question.

"People are still thinking about whether it is advantageous to work harder," he conceded, adding, "When they develop a taste for money, perhaps that will be a decisive factor."

Since the layoffs at Ilyichevsk, employers have been given somewhat greater freedom, under new economic laws, to lay off unneeded workers. Job training and placement centers are being upgraded, and laid-off workers are being encouraged to look for work in cooperatives or other private business ventures.

So far the new thinking has produced widespread anxiety, but little real change in the economic landscape.

In Moscow, for example, thousands of workers have been laid off as government ministries were abolished or merged in a shuffle intended to break the bureaucratic habits of an economy dictated from Moscow.

At the recently dismembered Ministry of Machine-Building for light and food industries and household appliances, which supervised the production of machines for food processing and other consumer industries, the corridors are dim and ghostly as the last workers clean out their desks.

Where have the 495 workers gone? How are they coping with the adjustment to less prestigious jobs, or to life away from the cultural and material attractions of Moscow?

"No one was forced to leave Moscow," said Anatoly M. Yershov, a deputy minister and chairman of the liquidation committee, in an interview at the office he will occupy for a few more weeks. "We cannot just tell a person he has to move. Nothing like that has happened."

In fact, most of the workers were simply, as one Moscow newspaper put it, "shifted from one armchair to another," shuffled to other government offices, or to the administrations of Moscow industrial enterprises and research institutes previously overseen by the abolished ministry.

This attitude has slowed the growth of private business, which is a critical component of Gorbachev's economic strategy. Private business is supposed to quickly satisfy the public craving for better goods and services, while providing employment for many of the surplus workers in industry.

Private enterprise now employs some four hundred thousand people, according to the State Committee on Statistics, including those who moonlight doing repairs and driving taxis, and those who work in cooperative cafes, construction companies, beauty parlors and other businesses.

The new law has already spawned a small, energetic entrepreneurial class, mostly young people who have the appetite for Western-quality consumer goods and some exposure to Western ideas of commerce.

Here, too, economic change runs up against a prodigious sense of fair play.

In the Soviet Union, Horatio Alger would be called a "money-grubber," Donald J. Trump a "speculator." Americans believe the early bird gets the worm. Russians say the sunflower that grows tallest is the first to have its head lopped off.

Those who venture into private business recall from their history books the last great Soviet experiment of this kind, the so-called New Economic Policy that began in 1921, legalizing private trade. By the end of the decade, the private traders had been crushed, many of the "nepmen" arrested and put on trains for Siberia, often with the enthusiastic support of a public who despised the nepmen even as they patronized their shops.

Today the Soviet leadership is beginning to portray NEP in a more favorable light, but the basic bias against the "money-grubber" remains, evident in letters to the press and the complaints and personal slights often directed at new entrepreneurs.

"Some people don't understand," said Konstantin Kadtsi, who converted a warehouse in Odessa into a cafe offering cherry dumplings and Western videos. "Some people are very cautious. Some people are unhappy about the higher prices. Some expect real magic. It's not part of our everyday life yet."

"The most serious obstacle to the cooperative movement is not bureaucratic, it is psychological," said Vladimir Y. Yakovlev, a twenty-eight-year-old former journalist who runs Moscow's only consulting service for new entrepreneurs.

"A person starts working in a cooperative, and at first he works like a dog," Yakovlev said. "Because he's begun to make a lot of money, he works very hard—for the first two months. Then he gets used to the money, and automatically starts trying to work as little as he would in a state enterprise.

"The person is used to the idea that there's this enormous state, in which he is just a tiny cog, and the state pays for his every step, his trips, his health care and so on. And bankruptcy, or millions in profits—that's not his concern, that's the concern of the state."

A few blocks away from Kadtsi's cafe, Arkady and Tatyana Sakh-
nevich have found another niche in the new economic thinking. Under
a contract with the state, the family operates a simple grocery store.

The store is unassuming, offering only a half dozen kinds of vegetables and a small fruit-juice bar. But on closer inspection it is a step
up from ordinary state stores.

The produce is picked clean of rotten leaves and scrubbed. Customers can pick out their own and weigh it on electronic scales to avoid
cheating. The sales clerks smile and say good day, which is enough to
draw doubletakes in any Soviet enterprise. Prices are set daily according to quality and demand, and while they are a bit higher than state
stores they fall well below the farmers' markets.

The Sakhneviches, a cheerful and industrious couple who employ
much of their family in the shop, say customers are enthusiastic. And
yet many react as if this family venture had fallen to earth from
another planet. They scratch their heads at the sight of the store director unloading trucks or clerks scrubbing the floor.

"Yes, there are some people who envy, who do not understand, who
try to interfere," said seventy-seven-year-old Arkady Shvarts, a family
friend who serves as a consultant to the store. "There are some suppliers who try to make trouble."

The family is convinced, however, that a proliferation of private
ventures will bring down prices and win converts. A recent poll by
Leningrad sociologists found that in Tallinn, the Estonian capital,
which has one of the largest concentrations of cooperatives, popular
approval is much higher than in Leningrad, where cooperatives are
few. Younger people support them more than the older generation by
a wide margin.

The people who have ventured into this alien world so far are
hopeful. Shvarts, who lived through the New Economic Policy, says
this time it will be different because customers are fed up with the
old way of doing business.

He has heard all the talk about the intractability of the Soviet system, the pampered Russian worker, but when he runs up against a
farm director who refuses to sell his vegetables to a small businessman,
or hires a twenty-year-old worker who quits after a few days of washing potatoes because it smacks of real work, he thinks of the famed
Russian circus trainer, Vladimir Durov.

"If Durov can teach bears to dance," he said with an impish laugh, "why can't we learn perestroika?"

1989 PULITZER PRIZE FOR INTERNATIONAL REPORTING

Crackdown in Beijing: Troops Attack and Crush Beijing Protest

NICHOLAS D. KRISTOF

Beijing, China
June 4, 1989

Tens of thousands of Chinese troops retook the center of the capital early this morning from pro-democracy protesters, killing scores of students and workers and wounding hundreds more as they fired submachine guns at crowds of people who tried to resist.

Troops marched along the main roads surrounding central Tiananmen Square, sometimes firing in the air and sometimes firing directly at crowds of men and women who refused to move out of the way.

Early this morning, the troops finally cleared the square after first sweeping the area around it. Several thousand students who had remained on the square throughout the shooting left peacefully, still waving the banners of their universities. Several armed personnel carriers ran over their tents and destroyed the encampment.

Reports on the number of dead were sketchy. Three Beijing hospitals reported receiving at least sixty-eight corpses of civilians and said many others had not been picked up from the scene. Four other hospitals said they had received bodies of civilians but declined to disclose how many. Students said, however, that at least five hundred people may have been killed in the crackdown.

Most of the dead had been shot, but some had been run over by armored personnel carriers that forced their way through barricades erected by local residents.

The official news programs this morning reported that the People's Liberation Army had crushed a "counterrevolutionary rebellion" in the capital. They said that more than one thousand police and troops had been injured and some killed, and that civilians had been killed, but did not give details.

Changan Avenue, or the Avenue of Eternal Peace, Beijing's main east-west thoroughfare, echoed with screams this morning as young people carried the bodies of their friends away from the front lines. The dead or seriously wounded were heaped on the backs of bicycles or tricycle rickshaws and supported by friends who rushed through the crowds, sometimes sobbing as they ran.

The avenue was lit by the glow of several trucks and two armored personnel carriers that students and workers set afire, and bullets swooshed overhead or glanced off buildings. The air crackled almost constantly with gunfire and tear-gas grenades.

"General strike!" people roared, in bitterness and outrage, as they ran from Tiananmen Square, which pro-democracy demonstrators had occupied for three weeks. "General strike!"

While hundreds of thousands of people had turned out to the streets Saturday and early today to show support for the democracy movement, it was not clear if the call for a general strike would be successful. The government had been fearful that a crackdown on the movement would lead to strikes, but its willingness to shoot students suggested that it was also capable of putting considerable pressure on workers to stay on the job.

The morning radio news program reported that it would be "very difficult" to hold a meeting of the National People's Congress standing committee as scheduled. The committee, which had been scheduled to meet June 20, has the power to revoke martial law and oversee the government, and many members of the panel are known to be deeply upset by the crackdown.

The announcement by the Beijing news program suggested that Prime Minister Li Peng, who is backed by hard-liners in the Communist Party, was still on top in his power struggle for control of the Chinese leadership. The violent suppression of the student movement also suggested that for now, the hard-liners are firmly in control, and that those who favor conciliation, like party leader Zhao Ziyang, at least temporarily have little influence on policy.

It was too early to tell if the crackdown would be followed by arrests of student leaders, intellectuals who have been critical of the party, or members of Zhao's faction. Blacklists have been widely rumored, and many people have been worried about the possibility of arrest.

Students and workers tried to resist the crackdown, and destroyed at least sixteen trucks and two armored personnel carriers. Scores of students and workers ran alongside the personnel carriers, hurling concrete blocks and wooden staves into the treads until they ground to a halt. They then threw firebombs at one until it caught fire, and set the other alight after first covering it with blankets soaked in gasoline.

The drivers escaped, but were beaten by students. A young American man, who could not be immediately identified, was also beaten by the crowd after he tried to intervene and protect one of the drivers.

Clutching iron pipes and stones, groups of students periodically advanced toward the soldiers. Some threw bricks and firebombs at the lines of soldiers, apparently wounding many of them.

Many of those killed were throwing bricks at the soldiers, but others were simply watching passively or standing at barricades when soldiers fired directly at them.

Two groups of young people commandeered city buses to attack the troops. About ten people were in each bus, and they held firebombs or sticks in their hands as they drove toward lines of armored personnel carriers and troops. Teenage boys, with scarves wrapped around their mouths to protect themselves from tear gas, were behind the steering wheels and gunned the engines as they weaved around the debris to approach the troops.

The first bus was soon stopped by machine-gun fire, and only one person—a young man who jumped out of a back window and ran away—was seen getting out. Gunfire also stopped the second bus, and it quickly caught fire, perhaps ignited by the firebomb of someone inside. No one appeared to escape.

It was also impossible to determine how many civilians had been killed or injured. Beijing Fuxing Hospital, 3.3 miles to the west of Tiananmen Square, reported more than thirty-eight deaths and more than one hundred wounded, and said that many more bodies had yet to be taken to its morgue. A doctor at the Beijing Union Medical College Hospital, two miles northeast of the square, reported seventeen deaths. Beijing Tongren Hospital, one mile southeast of the square, reported thirteen deaths and more than one hundred critically wounded.

"As doctors, we often see deaths," said a doctor at the Tongren Hospital. "But we've never seen such a tragedy like this. Every room in the hospital is covered with blood. We are terribly short of blood, but citizens are lining up outside to give blood."

Four other hospitals also reported receiving bodies, but refused to say how many.

In addition, this reporter saw five people killed by gunfire and many more wounded on the east side of the square. Witnesses described at least six more people who had been run over by armored personnel carriers, and about twenty-five more who had been shot to death in the area. It was not known how many bodies remained on the square or how many people had been killed in other parts of the capital.

It was unclear whether the violence would mark the extinction of the seven-week-old democracy movement, or would prompt a new phase in the uprising, like a general strike. The violence in the capital ended a period of remarkable restraint by both sides, and seemed certain to arouse new bitterness and antagonism among both ordinary people and Communist Party officials for the government of Prime Minister Li Peng.

"Our government is already done with," said a young worker who held a rock in his hand, as he gazed at the army forces across Tiananmen Square. "Nothing can show more clearly that it does not represent the people."

Another young man, an art student, was nearly incoherent with grief and anger as he watched the body of a student being carted away, his head blown away by bullets.

"Maybe we'll fail today," he said. "Maybe we'll fail tomorrow. But someday we'll succeed. It's a historical inevitability."

On Saturday the police had used tear gas and beat dozens of demonstrators near the Communist Party headquarters in Zhongnanhai, while soldiers and workers hurled bricks at each other behind the Great Hall of the People. Dozens of people were wounded, but exact numbers could not be confirmed.

It appeared to be the first use of tear gas ever in the Chinese capital, and the violence seemed to radicalize the crowds that filled Tiananmen Square and Changan Avenue in the center of the city. The clashes also appeared to contribute to the public bitterness against the government of Prime Minister Li.

The violence on both sides seemed to mark a milestone in the democracy movement, and the streets in the center of the city were a kaleidoscope of scenes rarely if ever seen in the Chinese capital: furious crowds smashed and overturned army vehicles in front of Zhongnanhai, and then stoned the Great Hall of the People; grim-faced young soldiers clutching submachine guns tried to push their way through thick crowds of demonstrators near the Beijing train station; and the police charged a crowd near Zhongnanhai and used truncheons to beat men and women disabled by tear gas.

"In 1949, we welcomed the army into Beijing," said an old man on the Jianguomenwai bridge, referring to the crowds who hailed the arrival of Communist troops at the end of the Communist revolution. Then he waved toward a line of fifty army trucks that were blocked in a sea of more than ten thousand angry men and women, and added, "Now we're fighting to keep them out."

Most Chinese seemed convinced that the tanks and troops had been ordered into the city to crush the pro-democracy demonstrations once and for all. The immediate result of the first clashes was to revitalize the pro-democracy movement, which had been losing momentum over the last ten days, and to erase the sense that life in the capital was returning to normal. But the use of tanks and guns came later, and it was not clear if they would succeed in ending the movement or would lead to such measures as a general strike.

The tension was exacerbated by an extraordinary announcement on television Saturday night, ordering citizens to "stay at home to protect your lives." In particular, the announcement ordered people to stay off the streets and away from Tiananmen Square.

"The situation in Beijing at present is very serious," the government warned in another urgent notice read on television. "A handful of ruffians are wantonly making rumors to instigate the masses to openly insult, denounce, beat and kidnap soldiers in the People's Liberation Army, to seize arms, surround and block Zhongnanhai, attack the Great Hall of the People, and attempt to gather together various forces. More serious riots can occur at any time."

There were some reports that the Communist Party's ruling Politburo had met Friday and given the Beijing municipality the authority to clear the square and end the protests. The *People's Daily* and the television news on Saturday took a hard line against the unrest, and the evening news warned that "armed police and troops have the right to use all means to dispose of troublemakers who act willfully to defy the law."

The clashes and enormous outpouring of support for the students were an unexpected turnaround for the democracy movement. Just a few days ago, the number of students occupying Tiananmen Square had dropped to a few thousand, and students seemed to be having difficulty mobilizing large numbers of citizens to take to the streets. The government's strategy, of waiting for the students to become bored and go home, seemed to be leading to the possibility of a resolution to the difficulty.

Then a police van crashed into four bicyclists late Friday night, generating new outrage against the government. One cyclist was killed instantly, and two died in the hospital Saturday, while the fourth seemed less seriously hurt.

Rumors were less meticulous about detail, and word spread early Saturday morning through the capital that four people had been killed by the police. Tens of thousands of people took to the streets to protest, and immediately found themselves confronting more than two thousand unarmed troops who were marching toward Tiananmen Square.

The troops retreated, but that confrontation seemed to set the tone for the massive demonstrations later Saturday and early today.

1990 PULITZER PRIZE FOR INTERNATIONAL REPORTING

Crackdown in Beijing: In the Streets, Anguish, Fury and Tears

SHERYL WUDUNN

Beijing, China
June 4, 1989

As the crackle of automatic weapons filled the air today on the Avenue of Eternal Peace, tens of thousands of Beijing residents, even elderly men and women, rushed out to see what they could do to turn back the troops.

"The citizens have gone crazy," said a driver watching as a tank plowed its way down the main thoroughfare. "They throw themselves in front of the tank, and only when they see it won't stop, they scatter."

The driver himself was shaken by what he had seen: A tank had rammed into an army truck used as a barricade. As the truck turned over, it crushed a man to death. Elsewhere, he had seen three bloodied bodies lying in the street. Several soldiers still standing in their trucks were crying.

Students and workers threw beer bottles, gasoline bombs, lead pipes, whatever they could find, at the tanks and armored personnel trucks, which nevertheless continued rumbling down the avenue. One truck drove back and forth along the east side of the Changan Avenue, as the Avenue of Eternal Peace is known in Chinese, and did not stop when people stood in its path.

Amazement had already turned to fear and defiance earlier in the evening as citizens saw the military convoys entering the city. Some troops from other provinces practically paraded their AK-47 rifles as they stood in their trucks, stranded by the human blockades that had formed around the trucks.

By dark, tensions had soared throughout the city. Hundreds of thousands of people were impelled outdoors by their disbelief and anger, yet brought back to their homes by fear of the violence. The sound of tanks whizzing by and reports of open firing fanned their fears.

"You beasts! You beasts!" shouted the people at the troops.

Around a convoy of about forty-five military trucks in the eastern part of the city, people pushed and shoved their way to the troops, shouting and urging them to consider their role as fellow citizens. But the sympathy that had characterized the troops last week was gone; the soldiers seemed to have a certain resolve.

"Will you shoot at us if they order you to?" was a question asked by many of the people surrounding the truck. The soldiers gave weak assurances to the people that they would not fire, but they also admitted that they had to follow orders.

"We have to obey orders because we are soldiers," said one uniformed trooper who was driving a truck. "Otherwise, we will be punished. In any case, there's no way they will order us to shoot the people."

His platoon commander was firm. "We don't fear being beaten by you people," he said as he climbed out of the truck. "We just fear that our guns will be taken and then we will have chaos." Everywhere in the vicinity of the convoy was the sound of hissing, as people let out the air from the tires of as many trucks as they could.

"Why do you have guns?" shouted one man.

"A man is not a soldier without his gun, is he?" came the reply of a soldier carrying an AK-47 automatic rifle.

An old man took up the cause. "I tell you, there will be no good end for you if you follow your order loyally," he screamed as though his life depended upon it. "You have parents, you have brothers and sisters. You should not beat your fellow citizens under any circumstances."

The nearly crazed citizens were climbing onto the trucks, trying to intimidate the soldiers. But everywhere in the vicinity, anger was mixed with horror as the people saw how the soldiers handled their rifles and watched as several tanks pulled up.

"Is this the way Li Peng shows how martial law protects the people?" said an old man sitting on a rail.

Another young man said, "When they shoot with real bullets, it will be doomsday." Only hours later did the troops open fire.

In the afternoon, the scene near the walled-in Communist Party compound, where about thirty tear-gas bombs were released, had been the first site of violence. But now that seemed tame. A twenty-minute conflict between three hundred to four hundred riot policemen and hundreds of citizens seemed to have galvanized the citizens. They began to believe that the government was willing to use force—rubber bullets, broken bricks, truncheons—against the people.

"I couldn't keep my eyes open because of the dense tear gas," said

Lu Baochun, a twenty-six-year-old assistant engineer. "It was the troops that first used bricks and tiles to attack, and the citizens fought back."

Lu had rushed back out to the scene, a chaotic swirl of thousands of people darting back and forth inspecting broken bricks and glass and examining the white powderlike splotches on the street apparently from the tear gas.

"When I went into the house of a nearby citizen to wash my eyes with fresh water, I saw several children lying on their stomachs on a bed," said Lu, whose own face and neck were reddened from the gas. "They had wet towels covering their mouths, and an old woman was beside them weeping."

He was standing at the Communist Party headquarters shouting with rage now at the two dozen military troops with long truncheons and green helmets, sweating in their heavy green uniforms under the pelting sun.

Some citizens gathered in small huddles around people they thought had been witnesses to the attack. Others crowded together discussing the event, many apprehensive about how far the government would go.

"They are simply ruffians and bandits," said a young well-dressed woman who had gotten caught in the cross fire of bricks and stones as she was on her way to the office. "They bit people just like mad dogs."

A Chinese journalist was trying to comfort her. "We are shocked," he said. "We thought that this kind of thing only happened during the reign of the corrupt government of the Kuomintang. Yet this happened in our People's Republic. The troops and the police, they are supposed to be our brothers."

1990 PULITZER PRIZE FOR INTERNATIONAL REPORTING

A German Divide Fades, but Two Towns Still Feel It

SERGE SCHMEMANN

Bad Harzburg, West Germany
September 23, 1990

It is once again a pleasant thirty-minute drive from Bad Harzburg to Wernigerode through a classic German landscape of wooded mountains and half-timbered villages. The two towns share a common heritage; people used to speak the same dialect and were reared on the same legends of the Brocken, the nearby mountain where witches dance on Walpurgis Night.

On October 3, the two towns will again be part of the same country. But for forty years they stood on opposite sides of an all-but-impregnable divide, each at the fringe of a different world. New generations grew up in Bad Harzburg facing west, and if they turned to the east at all it was to show tourists the fences, tank traps, watchtowers and unsmiling guards of the East German border. In Wernigerode, people came under a paternalistic police state, secure and protected as long as they never ventured into the three-mile-wide security zone to reach the land beyond.

Now, on the verge of reunification, the people of the two towns, and of the two Germanys, look on one another and their impending union with mixed and troubled feelings.

WESTERNERS PROTECT WHAT IS THEIRS

Everybody in Bad Harzburg has stories of the euphoria last November, when the border at Eckertal, a few miles to the east, suddenly fell open.

"At first it was a small hole, and they kept chipping away, and then the first Trabi drove through," Heinz Sinkemat, the deputy city manager, recalled. Tears and sparkling wine flowed freely, and people from both sides were seized with feelings of kinship and pride.

Now, with unity just weeks away, the residents of Bad Harzburg look to their eastern neighbors with something of the condescension and irritation that a comfortable burgher might feel toward a poor relative come to stay.

Sinkemat said that at first, when visitors from East Germany took their first stunned walks along Herzog Wilhelm Street, the elegant pedestrian mall of this resort town, so-called Westies pitched in to buy groceries or trinkets for Ossies—or easterners, sometimes also referred to as Zonies, the more derogatory name derived from the Soviet occupation zone in which they lived.

But before long, people began to gripe about the traffic and the sputtering Trabant sedans, about the East Germans clogging supermarket lines, about the cost of unity. Recently, Sinkemat said, an East German with a full shopping cart angrily turned to complaining West Germans behind him and shouted, "We waited in line for forty years. Now you can wait."

Stereotypes have hardened. To hear people on the street, the Easterner dresses shabbily, acts timid, overruns discount stores, works badly and has a rude Saxon accent. He wants to have all the television sets, cars and washing machines for which the West Germans worked for forty years, and he wants them now.

"They think that because they haven't had anything for forty years they can demand it all now," said Karin Lutz, a forty-eight-year-old jewelry salesclerk. "They want to have everything in one day if possible. You just want to say to them, you can't be lazy and stand around here, you have to build up your country and not rely on the West so much."

Lutz would probably acknowledge, as most people do at some point in a conversation, that the people "over there" are relatively poor not because they were less industrious, but because of Communism.

Yet the sight of easterners in their trademark stonewashed jeans hauling washing machines and refrigerators while West Germany pays out billions to keep their economy afloat seems to foster indignation among people who have achieved so exemplary a level of security and prosperity through thrift and hard work.

Some say that at the core of West Germans' attitude is a basic satisfaction with their life and resistance to changing it. For West Germans, reunification seems more duty than joy, and that duty is to assimilate East Germany quickly into the Federal Republic with as little change as possible.

Hans-Magnus Enzensberger, a West German author, critic and editor who lives in Munich, said a reluctance to change explains why much of the public enthusiasm for unity has been in East Germany, not West Germany.

"I haven't seen a single rally in this half where flags were waved, no public meeting that can be described as patriotic, jingoistic, as happened in East Germany," he said. "People accept unity, maybe welcome it, but there is no trace of euphoria. It's a marriage of convenience."

A recent poll in the news magazine *Spiegel* found that 29 percent of West Germans were either "rather opposed" or "very opposed" to unification. The poll showed that 67 percent of West Germans accepted that unity would require sacrifices, but only 38 percent were willing to make them.

How long such attitudes survive probably depends on how rapidly East Germany becomes economically viable. But early predictions of a second "economic miracle" have given way to pessimism as the disintegration of the Communist economy becomes more apparent. As many as four million East Germans may be unemployed by year's end, and experts now say it will take ten to fifteen years for them to reach Western living standards.

Most West Germans have also accepted that their taxes will rise to pay for reunification, though Bonn denies there will be an increase. While the booming West German economy should prove up to the task of restoring the East, Germans are known as a people who place a great premium on stability and security.

"There's going to be a lot of class conflict," Enzensberger said. "Poor relations and rich relations are never on the best of terms, and there's a lot of resentment boiling up here."

EASTERNERS BRACE FOR FUTURE AS "SECOND CLASS" GERMANS

Henny Berner still remembers the humiliation of her first business trip to West Germany last spring.

As director of the new Deutsche Bank branch here, she was invited to a luxurious hotel in Neustadt for a seminar with new managers. At their first breakfast, Berner said, she overheard West Germans commenting on the East German cars parked outside.

"They were saying, 'How can anyone from East Germany dare to stay at a hotel like this,' that they would rather help Afghanistan or Africa than East Germany," she said. "Even now, every time we hear West Germans talking about unity, it's always, 'What will it cost?'

"We're second-class citizens, and it won't stop on October 3," she said. "It will really start on October 3. We're helpless here. We all studied Russian, and we suddenly need English. I spent ten years studying economics, and I've had to learn the free-market economy in a three-month crash course."

Berner's story was one of many illustrating the growing sense among East Germans that they are facing a long stretch as second-class citizens in a united Germany. Nobody wants the clock turned back, but for many, the long-awaited unity has proved a mixed blessing: the open borders and West German marks have brought cars, travel and freedom, but they have also brought home the poverty of the East, and with it a loss of confidence.

Only a few miles from the West German border and graced with a stunning castle and lovely half-timbered houses, Wernigerode has drawn tens of thousands of Western visitors since the border opened last November. They prowl the winding streets, visit the castle and hike in the surrounding forests. But most return to spend the night in Bad Harzburg or one of the other West German resorts on the other side of the border, leaving Wernigerode little of their spending money.

At the same time, Wernigerode's electric-motor factory, the biggest local employer, has laid off many workers and put others on "zero hours," a common East German arrangement in which employees are paid full salaries but do no work. The deal is considered a gimmick devised by Chancellor Helmut Kohl to conceal soaring unemployment rates until the all-German elections in December. Many workers suspect that after that, West German subsidies will dry up and many East German factories will die.

So far, the official unemployment rate here is only 3.3 percent, but more than a third of the workforce is on short hours, and some local officials expect the rate to reach 40 percent to 50 percent by next spring.

The experience of Wernigerode is shared, in varying degrees, across much of East Germany as it braces for formal union with the West.

After forty years of dreaming about the promised land beyond the strictly guarded three-mile security zone along the border, they had welcomed the fall of the Berlin wall with patriotism and hope.

Yet early on, the dream began to sour. The first waves of West Germans flowed over not to embrace their long-suffering kin, but to buy up cheap East German goods and food, emptying towns like Wernigerode.

Monetary union in July gave East Germans the West German mark. But the currency only underscored their poverty and new dependence, and their rush to buy Western goods only accelerated the disintegration of East German industry and agriculture.

The mountain is open to visitors again, but the shriek of powerful winds blowing through the Soviet equipment atop the magic mountain seems to confirm that the dark forces of the past have not yet been exorcized.

The Rev. Gottfried Werther, pastor of the town's main Protestant church, St. Sylvester, said that many more parishioners were turning to him with problems. Mr. Werther was active in the demonstrations last fall that led to the collapse of the Communist government, but like many other leaders of the original popular movement, he is unhappy at the direction things took.

"They gave us currency union, but not social unity as they had promised," he said of the West. "Of course, we are very happy to be rid of the Communists. We have no reason to complain there, but there were hopes that should not have been awakened. Now we will have to be the poorhouse of Germany for a while, and this is the start of a minority complex."

Werther said Chancellor Kohl had asked all churches to ring their bells on October 3. But he declined, arguing that it was not proper for the church to celebrate for the state.

Yet when asked directly, most citizens of Wernigerode said they probably would celebrate unity.

"Certainly there are fears and complexes," said Rita Ahrens, a town official. "But the feeling of being one unified nation is overwhelming."

At a crowded, smoke-filled pub near the electric-motor factory, Klaus-Dieter Fessel downed another beer. He has been on zero hours for several weeks now and expects to be laid off soon. He is forty-three years old and has no idea what will happen next.

Yes, he agreed, unity is an exciting prospect. "It's just that we didn't want it to be so harsh," he said.

1991 PULITZER PRIZE FOR INTERNATIONAL REPORTING

FOUR

The Public Advocate

TAKING A POSITION, GIVING CONTEXT

In European newspapers, both Continental and British, news stories often have a strong point of view. Even in reporting public events, the paper may advance the cause of a political party. A delicious example was the way the *Sun*, Rupert Murdoch's best-selling tabloid, dealt with the 1992 British election. Murdoch favored the Conservatives. On election day, the *Sun* had a large picture of the Labor Party leader, Neil Kinnock, on page one. Above and around it was this headline: "If Kinnock wins today will the last person to leave Britain please turn out the lights."

In the early days of the American press, newspapers exhibited equally unashamed bias. Editors were often in the pay of one party or another. That was what James Madison had in mind when he said he favored freedom for the press despite its abuses. But in the twentieth century most newspapers became more detached in their reporting. The dominant journalistic ethic was separation between news and opinion. The news columns told the reader what was happening, in as neutral a way as human beings could achieve. The editorial page told the reader what to think.

In time, editors came to feel that something was needed aside from the neutral news story and the anonymous institutional voice of the editorial: something more individual, more distinctive. The result was the columnist, an American invention. A writer was given the freedom to express his or her own viewpoint in his or her own style. Inevitably, there was a wild diversity of styles and opinions, and readers could be outraged. Charles Evans Hughes, chief justice of the United States, called them "calumnists."

A parallel development took place beginning in the 1930s. In its

"News of the Week in Review" section on Sunday, the *Times* published articles by its regular reporters that strove to put the news in context. The reporter could step back and give the larger meaning of events. Analysis was what the great Sunday editor of the *Times*, Lester Markel, called those pieces—not opinionated like a column, more explanatory than a news story. In time, the concept moved into the daily paper, where explanatory pieces were labeled "news analysis."

One of the early masters of the genre was Anne O'Hare McCormick, who won a Pulitzer in 1937 for her news and analytical pieces from Europe. She went on to become an editorial page columnist, a remarkable achievement in an age of total male newspaper dominance. Unfortunately, her articles deal with subjects too obscure now to be reproduced to effect.

James Reston was a phenomenon: a hardworking reporter who joined the *Times* in London during World War II, diplomatic correspondent in Washington, columnist, Washington bureau chief, executive editor of the paper. As a columnist he had a unique authority that I think stemmed from personal goodness. You could not imagine him thinking, much less expressing, a mean thought. Not that he was uncritical; he just respected everyone's flawed humanity. His columns were often owlishly funny, making a point by getting under the reader's guard.

My own *Times Magazine* article is included as an example of how beat reporters had opportunities to discuss the news in a deeper historical context. I covered the Supreme Court of Chief Justice Earl Warren—a court, I wrote, that had become the conscience of the country. How different it looked when Linda Greenhouse won a Pulitzer Prize decades later for her coverage of the Supreme Court. It was a court then that increasingly turned its back on concern for individual rights. Americans became newly aware of how much it mattered who took a seat on the Supreme Court, as the conflict over Robert Bork so dramatically showed.

Some of the best writing in American newspapers has always been about sports. Scotty Reston began as a sportswriter. And sports columns have wide readership. The columns included here, by Red Smith and Dave Anderson, show why. Of course both deal with much more than sports.

Since 1970, when the *Times* began publishing its op-ed page, editorial columnists have appeared on that page. The examples included in this chapter demonstrate the diverse nature of the column form. William Safire's piece is the column as scoop and political arrow. Safire's prizewinning series of columns on Bert Lance, a Georgia banker brought to Washington by President Carter as his budget director, produced much news and ended with Lance's departure.

Russell Baker was nonpareil as columnist and writer of books. At least for me, it is impossible to characterize them and do justice to Baker's poetry. His two columns here, from the collection that won the prize in 1979, speak for themselves.

Anna Quindlen brought her own life and her family's into her column. As the one included here shows, she was uniquely able to talk to all of us through the personal about very large issues. Maureen Dowd, with her corruscating wit, skewered Kenneth Starr as she has so many pompous figures.

Then, finally, in the commentary category, there are editorials. The ones reproduced in this chapter show how much less sententious— and more interesting—*Times* editorials have become in modern times. Jack Rosenthal won a prize in 1982 for, among other things, these editorials on President Reagan's war against the poor; Robert Semple won for a series of pieces on the environment—of which the one on Alaska is a telling example. Editorials do not always make a difference. These did.

Washington: The One Vessel That Leaks from the Top

JAMES RESTON

Washington, D.C.
June 24, 1956

Want to know how things work in this town?

One day last July Bob Donovan, a nice guy who covers the White House for the *New York Herald Tribune*, was approached by a White House official with an interesting suggestion.

How would Mr. Donovan like to write a book on the Eisenhower administration, the official asked. Specifically, how would he like to write one if he had access to the records of the Eisenhower cabinet meetings?

This was a little like asking Mickey Mantle how he would like to have all the pitchers in the American League throw 'em easy from now till September so he could break Babe Ruth's home-run record. Mr. Donovan, always an obliging and cordial gentleman, readily agreed.

The book was in the hands of reviewers this week—*Eisenhower: The Inside Story*—and immediately there were charges that this was strictly campaign propaganda, leaked out by the administration for political advantage on the basis of executive documents that the administration refused to show to anybody else, including an inquiring Congress.

Richard Rovere of the *New Yorker* staff asked how the executive branch of the government could sustain its argument in Congress about the sanctity of executive documents after passing them out to a reporter.

He also wanted to know how cabinet members could be expected to talk freely in future cabinet meetings if the records of the meetings were to be made public. And, of course, the Democrats on Capitol Hill immediately took up the cry.

All this is fascinating to a student of hypocrisy in the nation's capital. Of course the documents were made available in the hope of presenting the administration in a friendly light during a presidential election, but what's new about that?

Every president since Washington has given inside dope to friendly reporters, and some of them have even had the good judgment to give it to unfriendly reporters.

President Truman gave another White House correspondent, William Hillman, access to what Mr. Hillman called "all his diaries, his private papers and correspondence." This was in 1951, while Mr. Truman was still in the White House.

Mr. Truman even allowed John Hersey, the novelist, permission to sit in on some of the most private official meetings in the White House while Mr. Hersey was preparing a series of articles for the *New Yorker*. In fact, Mr. Hersey was actually in one of those meetings when the news reached the White House that the Chinese Communists had invaded North Korea in force.

Arthur Krock of this newspaper received access to the files of all United States ambassadors' reports to the State Department in the critical periods before the German invasion of Poland in 1939 and before the Japanese attack on Pearl Harbor in 1941. And by the Roosevelt administration yet!

Also there have been some low charges that the *New York Times* printed the Yalta papers!

There was, besides, an avalanche of books by officials after the war that purported to "tell all" (usually written by some penurious ghost). These were written not primarily in the interest of history or political advantage but for cash.

The Donovan book is different from all these, but only in degree. That is to say, the degree of calculated political advantage and of unblushing hypocrisy was greater in this case.

Mr. Donovan was not responsible for this. Actually, given the circumstances, he has written a book with a minimum of political propaganda. It is not what you would call an exhaustive account of this administration's three years, but Donovan is an honest man who has done the best he could without impairing his reputation as a good reporter.

The hypocrisy lies with the officials in the White House. They have done in this case what other administrations have done, only more so. The only basic difference is that this administration has a weakness for striking high moral poses and claiming that it is above all the old political tricks.

More than any other administration in memory, this one has emphasized the sanctity of executive papers. It has claimed that it was giving an honest count on everything, which no administration ever does, while it was managing the news to its own advantage.

When James C. Hagerty was asked about the Donovan book Friday, he refused to comment. When he was asked whether he would "find out" who authorized it, he smiled and said "no."

Moral of the story: A government is the only known vessel that leaks from the top. Moral number two: Nobody is immune to the diseases of politics, not even Crusaders.

1957 PULITZER PRIZE FOR NATIONAL REPORTING

Historic Change in Supreme Court

ANTHONY LEWIS

Washington, D.C.
June 17, 1962

A historic term of the Supreme Court is drawing to a close. It rates that adjective because of a single momentous decision—the decision in *Baker v. Carr*, opening the doors of the federal courts to legal attacks on the apportionment of seats in state legislatures.

The apportionment case was decided just three months ago, on March 26. But it has already started to remake the political map of the United States. In Georgia and Alabama, federal courts have ordered rural forces to relax their ancient hold on the legislatures. In Maryland the legislature, acting under a judicial ultimatum, has redistricted its lower house for the first time in forty years. In two dozen other states legal or political action is under way on reapportionment.

A lawyer who has been a student of the Supreme Court's work for many years remarked soon after March 26 that the decision in *Baker v. Carr* had been "inevitable." Then he added: "But twenty years ago, or even ten, it would have been inconceivable."

From "inconceivable" to "inevitable" in a decade or two—so swiftly does the course of decision run. But why the change? That is the great question posed by the apportionment case. What had happened to Court or country that made the justices see the issue differently in 1962 from the way they might have, indeed had, seen it a few years earlier?

In this respect the apportionment case is part of the larger question of change in the Supreme Court. For of course it is not the only example of a revolution in constitutional doctrine in recent years. Two others come quickly to mind: the standards of fairness imposed on state criminal proceedings and, best known to the public at large, the Court's attitude toward racial segregation.

Recall, first, the dominant mood of the Supreme Court a generation ago. The issues then were the right of the states to set maximum hours and minimum wages, the right of the federal government to use its tax and commerce power to deal with the Depression. In short, the

Court's concern seemed to be with property, not what we today would call human liberty.

It was in that setting, in 1936, that the Court for the first time in history set aside a state criminal conviction because the defendants had been mistreated. The case was called *Brown v. Mississippi*, and it is worth recalling the facts set out in Chief Justice Charles Evans Hughes's opinion.

Three Mississippi Negroes were charged with murder. One was hanged from a tree and told he would hang there until he confessed; at the trial he still bore the marks of the rope on his throat. The two others "were laid over chairs and their backs were cut to pieces with a leather strap with buckles on it. . . . In this manner the defendants confessed the crime, and as the whippings progressed or were repeated, they changed or adjusted their confession in all particulars of detail so as to conform to the demands of their torturers."

The Supreme Court decided that convictions based on confessions obtained by such methods denied the "due process of law" guaranteed by the Fourteenth Amendment.

Since 1936, in a steady progression of cases, the Court has struck at the use of coerced confessions. It has outlawed psychological as well as physical coercion. And in many other aspects of criminal law, despite protests from state officials and from dissenters within the Court, new restraints have been put on the states.

In 1956, over strong dissent, the Supreme Court said that a state that allows appeals in criminal cases cannot deny the right just because a prisoner is too poor to buy a trial transcript; it must supply the transcript or an adequate substitute. The Conference of State Chief Justices charged gloomily that the decision threatened "an almost complete breakdown in the work of state appellate courts," but nothing like that has occurred.

Just a year ago the Court, again by a narrow division, overturned the well-established rule that state courts were free to admit illegally seized evidence. It has put down for argument next year the question whether it should now require the states to supply free counsel to impoverished defendants in all criminal cases, abandoning the present rule assuring counsel only in cases involving the death penalty.

The course has been clear in the area of criminal law: despite resentment at new restrictions on the freedom of the states, and despite some misgivings within the Court from time to time the Supreme

Court has moved steadily in the past twenty-five years to impose uniform national standards of fairness on state criminal proceedings. State law enforcement faces federal judicial scrutiny today to a degree unthinkable a generation ago.

Why?

It seems evident, first, that in moving against the third degree and other forms of unfairness and inequality in the criminal law, the Court was reflecting a national moral sentiment. Perhaps this arose from the experience of totalitarian brutality in other countries. Whatever the reason, Americans were plainly less willing to tolerate police misbehavior in any state, regardless of the political niceties of federal-state relations, than they were in earlier years. Many Americans have a national conscience that is injured by any state's misbehavior. And more and more the national ideal is prevailing over state orientation.

A second point to be made is that, if higher national standards were to be imposed on law enforcement in this country, the Supreme Court was the only agency that could do the job.

The inmates of state prisons hardly had the kind of political power likely to spur legislative reforms. State courts tended to be dominated by local feelings and dislike for criminals. One of the happy effects of intervention by the Supreme Court has in fact been growing sensitivity on the part of local courts and political groups to the needs of fairness in criminal procedure. Intervention has spurred self-reform.

In 1938, two years after *Brown v. Mississippi*, there came a significant decision in the racial area. For the first time the Supreme Court emphasized the "equal" aspect of its 1896 rule that a state could provide "separate but equal" facilities for Negroes. Over bitter dissent, the Court held that Missouri did not meet the rule by sending Negroes to an out-of-state law school; it must provide legal training within its own borders.

There followed a series of unanimous decisions on higher education tightening the "separate-but-equal" standard. Finally, in 1950, the Court all but made segregation a legal impossibility. It held that Texas had not provided equality by establishing a separate law school for Negroes. In directing the (white) University of Texas Law School to admit a Negro applicant, Chief Justice Fred M. Vinson wrote:

"[The white law school] possesses to a far greater degree those qualities which are incapable of objective measurement but which make for greatness in a law school. Such qualities, to name but a few, include reputation of the faculty, experience of the administration, position and influence of the alumni, standing in the community, traditions and prestige."

It took no great thinker to realize that, when such intangibles were placed in the scale, no segregated school for Negroes was ever likely to be found "equal." Four years later the Court cut through the legal web and held that segregated schools were inherently unequal and denied the "equal protection of the laws" guaranteed by the Four-teenth Amendment.

The school decision followed other great victories for the Negro in the Supreme Court—cases establishing the right to vote and serve on juries and buy property without discrimination. But schools were by far the most inflammatory issue in the South, and the Court was well aware of that. Nevertheless, it decided against segregation, and unan-imously.

Why?

Once again no complicated motive need be sought. The Supreme Court was reflecting a national moral consensus on segregation—per-haps anticipating a feeling that had not yet fully taken shape.

In 1896, in establishing the "separate but equal" rule, the Supreme Court had relied on the sociology of its day. It said there was nothing invidious to the Negro in segregation unless "the colored race chooses to put that construction upon it."

But after Adolf Hitler and South Africa, no court could say with a straight face that separation of human beings on account of race or color was a stamp of inferiority only if the segregated so regarded it. Most of the world knew, and the United States was at least coming to know, that segregation was intended as a demonstration of one race's superiority over another.

Moreover, there was again the fact that unless the Supreme Court acted there would be no action. Discrimination made the Negro polit-ically powerless in his own state. Ever since Reconstruction, Congress had happily left to the Supreme Court the enforcement of constitu-tional guarantees against racial discrimination. The federal legislative path to reform was blocked by the South's power in the Senate. Clos-ing of the judicial path might produce intolerable social pressures.

The Senate Majority Leader, Mike Mansfield, made the point dur-ing the recent Senate civil rights debate. Our recent constitutional history, he said, "makes clear that progress toward the equalization in practice of the ideals of human freedom will not be halted indefinitely. When one road to this end fails, others will unfold. If the process is ignored in legislative channels, it will not necessarily be blocked in other channels—in the executive branch and in the courts."

Finally, the problem of legislative districts. It is an old problem; rural areas have refused for decades to relinquish the power given to them by unrepresentative districts in state legislatures.

In 1946 the Supreme Court seemed to close the doors of the federal courts to the aggrieved city dwellers. Justice Felix Frankfurter said the districting question would lead the courts into a "political thicket." The cure, he said, would have to be a political struggle by the disenfranchised.

A dozen times since 1946 the Court had held to the hands-off attitude on apportionment and related questions. Then, last March, it abruptly changed direction. The extraordinarily swift reaction to *Baker v. Carr* helps to suggest why the Court decided as it did.

Here, in contrast with the much less than deliberate speed with which school segregation has been abandoned, the Supreme Court's lead has been followed with exuberant enthusiasm by lower federal and even state judges and by political figures. No recent constitutional decision has had such widespread effects so fast.

It seems evident that on the issue of legislative apportionment a moral explosion was waiting to be set off. Almost everyone, including the beneficiaries of the evil, knew that an evil existed. But Justice Frankfurter's advice to work for political change was useless; the political system provided no way of escape. The Supreme Court supplied the key, opening the way for political as well as legal forces to work for orderly change.

Perhaps in 1946 it still seemed possible that the rural oligarchies in control of state legislatures would listen to reason. But by 1962 that hope had passed. It was plain that only the Supreme Court could cure the disease of malapportionment eating away at the vitals of American democracy.

There, then, are our three examples of dramatic change in Supreme Court doctrine during the past quarter century. Surely they do suggest some generalizations about why the Court has shifted as it has in its own view of its role.

One constant in the three examples was the ethical element. In intervening on behalf of the abused criminal suspect, the Negro, the citizen disenfranchised by malapportionment, the Supreme Court has been responding to what it deemed to be a moral demand—a demand of the national conscience. Moreover, the national conscience had found no way to express itself except through the Supreme Court. The Court moved in only when the rest of our governmental system was stymied, when there was no other practical way out of the moral dilemma.

The conclusion is that the Supreme Court has tended in recent years to act as the instrument of national moral values that have not been able to find other governmental expression. If the Court has changed, it is because we have changed.

The unhappy recent history of the world has rearranged Americans' hierarchy of values, and so it should be no great surprise that the Supreme Court emphasizes interests different from those of the past. We are more concerned, now, about abuse of official authority, mistreatment of racial minorities and sabotage of democracy than we are about the state powers in a federal system.

This is not to say that everyone agrees on moral goals, much less ones that are judicially attainable. The nine justices cannot be expected to march in happy unanimity toward a legal heaven whose definition all applaud.

Only in the field of race relations—where, ironically, public reaction has been the most divisive—have the justices been regularly in agreement. They have apparently found the moral imperative more obvious. But even here it seems doubtful that unanimity can long be preserved as the Court reaches the difficult questions of how to distinguish "private" from "public" discrimination.

Outside the racial area the Court has been deeply divided. Justice Frankfurter has been the principal spokesman for the view that the Court should be hesitant to impose its moral idea in a complex political structure. He dissented not only from *Baker v. Carr* but, for example, from last year's decision outlawing illegally seized evidence in state criminal trials.

Justice Frankfurter, of course, is not alone in his doubts about an expansive role for the Supreme Court as keeper of the national conscience. Most of today's critics of the Court are disaffected only because they dislike some particular result—say, the outlawing of school seg-regation. But there are some who, like Justice Frankfurter, have deeper and more general philosophical objections.

One is that judges are not necessarily competent to make broad moral judgments. Law school trains a man to work his way through conflicting principles in construing a contract or a statute. But does it equip Supreme Court justices, or the lower court judges who must carry out their decisions, to pass judgment on great social questions such as race relations and legislative districting, where there are few guidelines—few easily defined principles?

Even more strongly pressed is the thesis that reliance on the courts to cure society's ills saps the strength of democracy. The late Judge Learned Hand put it most colorfully when he said that he did not care to be ruled by "a bevy of Platonic guardians."

The more citizens rely on the courts, it is argued, the less will they fight issues out where they ought to be fought out in a democracy—in the political forum.

Those who believe in the moral role that the Supreme Court has increasingly come to play would not deny the difficulty of the job it gives to judges. But they make the point that it is a duty compelled by a written Constitution. The framers of the Constitution and its amendments deliberately chose to use phrases such as "due process" and "equal protection"—phrases that express no more than moral ideals, that must be given content by each generation. It is our judges who have been designated to supply that content, and their sources of inspiration must be national values.

The Court has not been a Platonic dictator and could never success-fully be that. When it has tried to stand against the tide of history, as in the 1930s, it has failed. Its great success has been as a moral goad to the political process—when it has urged politicians to do what they have avoided doing but knew in their hearts they should, as in race relations and apportionment.

There is every indication that the Supreme Court more and more sees its constitutional function in those terms. Slowly but perceptibly, with occasional retreats but with the overall direction clear, the Court is taking up the role of conscience to the country.

1963 PULITZER PRIZE FOR NATIONAL REPORTING

How to Get the City Out of Hock

WALTER WELLESLEY "RED" SMITH

New York, New York
June 4, 1975

New York City is tapped out like a broken horseplayer and nobody—
not Abe Beame nor the town's smartest bankers nor the best fiscal
brains in Albany and Washington—knows what to do about it. This
helplessness in high places is mystifying, for there is a simple solution
so obvious that it should have occurred to somebody in authority long
before this. The city should take over loan-sharking, prostitution and
narcotics traffic just as it has taken over gambling. We are assured by
all reliable authorities that there is more than enough profit in these
fields to make up the $641 million deficit in next year's budget, and
in the unlikely event that Mr. Beame still came up short, why, there
are other untapped sources of revenue such as labor racketeering and
bank robbery.

Prudery should not stand in the way of solvency for the greatest
city in the world. A few years ago when there were moral objections
to the city's making book on the races, they were hooted down by
Honest John Lindsay, the friendly bookie, and his chief sheet-writer,
Howard Samuels. Be realistic, they told us, gambling was a biological
urge that legislation could not suppress; therefore, was it not desirable
that the profits go to support schools, hospitals and deserving politicians rather than the criminal underworld?

Moreover, we were told, illegal gambling provided the treasury
from which the underworld financed such activities as loan-sharking,
prostitution and dope-pushing. History tells us that organized crime
was starved to death in New York starting at 10:52 A.M. on Holy
Thursday, April 8, 1971, when the Offtrack Betting Corporation
opened for business.

GO AND SIN NO MORE

Is it not incumbent upon enlightened city officials who eradicated the
cancer of illegal horseplaying to follow their own example and drive

out the unlicensed Shylocks, pimps and pushers? Especially if it will ease Abe Beame's headache and save the jobs of firemen, cops and teachers?

American politicians have a single solution for fiscal crises—tax sin. However, in order to convert human frailty into cash, it is necessary to encourage widespread sinning. It doesn't do merely to pass a lottery law, you've got to tempt the public with ads on buses and in newspapers and gussie up the lottery with gimmicks called New Chance, Summer Special and The Colossus.

Offtrack betting has required equally insistent and expensive promotion. Although we were told that the public's consuming passion for gambling was producing underworld profits running into hundreds of millions, the city made only $3,138,654 out of bookmaking in 1971, OTB's first year. "Bet more!" the ads have clamored ever since. "Bet till it hurts! Come on, suckers, don't you want to get rich?" Exhorting and expanding, OTB has built up business steadily, without ever approaching the volume its proponents promised.

One reason for the city's financial bind is that making book on the races has been nowhere near so profitable as expected. Citizens were told it would produce $200 million a year for the city. Last year it reached $54,070,647. Instead of $800 million for four years, OTB has returned $112.3 million. That's a gap of $687.7 million, which is bigger than the current budget gap.

Racing dates have been extended to generate additional business. The 1974 thoroughbred season closed on January 4, 1975, and Aqueduct was dark only until February 24. Exotic forms of betting have been introduced because the take-out on them is 25 percent instead of the normal 17 percent. Sunday racing starts at Belmont next week. What next?

Who Mentioned Yankee Stadium?

Well, Paul Screvane, successor to Howard Samuels at OTB, is echoing his predecessor's argument in favor of handling action on baseball, football, basketball and other sports in addition to racing. Paul would like to put in something like "Pick It," the state-operated numbers game in New Jersey. The New York State Racing and Wagering Board, which has already approved an arrangement whereby New

York races will be televised into Connecticut betting parlors, is urging that Saratoga races in August be piped into Aqueduct, where mutuel windows would service players who can't get up to the Spa.

This week Robert Abrams and Percy Sutton, borough presidents of the Bronx and Manhattan, plumped for legalization of dog racing with pari-mutuel betting. They ran a couple of mutts across Bryant Park in a demonstration.

"We wanted New Yorkers to see the beauty of these great animals," said Abrams, patting a greyhound over its pea-sized brain. In a forecast reminiscent of the promises made for OTB, Abrams said a hundred nights of dog racing would produce "at least" $17.5 million. Whatever business the dogs did would, of course, be reflected in reduced revenue from Yonkers and Roosevelt Raceways. As the racing and wagering board points out in its annual report:

"New York's harness tracks found themselves in a serious struggle for the entertainment dollar, the competition including overlapping sports seasons, functioning mostly at night, New York City's standard superb variety of entertainment, prime-time TV, Monday night football and the spread of offtrack betting facilities with the telephone making race betting possible in every home."

"It might help pay for Yankee Stadium," Abrams said of dog racing. Maybe right now he shouldn't have reminded New Yorkers about that $50 million and up they're spending on a playground for George Steinbrenner.

1976 PULITZER PRIZE FOR COMMENTARY

Boiling the Lance

WILLIAM SAFIRE

Chicago, Illinois
July 25, 1977

When Sherman Adams made a phone call to inquire of a federal official about the status of a Bernard Goldfine request, outraged Democrats pointed to a vicuña coat and demanded the scalp of President Eisenhower's chief of staff.

When Howard "Bo" Calloway was accused (falsely, as the current *Harper's* magazine reveals) of using his government job to help along a private project, editorial voices boomed and President Ford's campaign manager was forced to resign.

But they were Republicans. Since Democrat Bert Lance, President Carter's most influential adviser, was revealed to have used his public job to line his pockets, the trumpets of rectitude have been muted.

Lest loyal Carter men complain that a charge of using public office for private gain is excessive, let us count the ways the president's chief financial man cut his corners:

The sweetheart loan. Mr. Lance's bank put two hundred thousand dollars of its depositors' money in the First National Bank of Chicago, at no interest. Within three months, and after being appointed to the Carter cabinet, Mr. Lance turned to Democrat Robert Abboud, who runs the Chicago bank, and personally borrowed $3.5 million.

First Chicago's spokesman at first told reporters that officials of Lance's bank "came to us as a result of the correspondent banking relationship" to borrow Mr. Lance's money. Evidently every lawyer in the bank landed on that harried fellow's neck, because he tells me his words were "misinterpreted"—but an investigator from the Controller of the Currency spent all day Friday at First Chicago to determine whether an illegal "compensating balance" can be proved.

Despite denials, the full record will show that Bob Abboud's loan was one sweet deal for Mr. Lance. One hopes Senator Ribicoff's committee will insist on a detailed, comparative analysis of that loan's terms—and its underlying collateral, which a prudent bank is obligated to examine—by the Controller of the Currency, else why

did not the original lender—New York's Manufacturers Hanover—
"Manny Hanny"—compete for the business?

The Teamster connection. How can an itty-bitty bank, with a tiny
trust department, latch on to $18 million in Teamster Central States
Pension fund money in a presidential year? By flexing political muscle,
as detailed in this space last week, that's how.

The Butcher appointment. Thanks to the investigative reporting of
John Berry, Jack Egan and George Lardner Jr. of the *Washington Post*,
who also broke the no-interest deposit story, a vivid picture emerges
of the way Mr. Lance uses his political clout to shore up his financial
house of cards.

The Butcher brothers, Jake and C. H., own a few banks in Knoxville and Nashville. Their old friend Bert Lance is into one of their
banks for $443,466 on terms not likely to be available to the average
borrower.

Now that their debtor has the run of the White House, the Butcher
boys thought it would be a dandy idea to get on a first-name basis
with the secretary of the treasury, Michael Blumenthal.

So they called friend Bert. "We asked for the appointment," blurted
C. H. Butcher, not realizing how the truth would hurt, "because we
had never met him [Blumenthal] and he does regulate our business as
treasury secretary."

That candor caught Mr. Lance in the middle of a cover-up. He had
enlisted his press spokesman in concocting a story that gave a quasi-
public purpose to the Butchers' meeting with Secretary Blumenthal:
some folderol about promoting a Knoxville exposition, which is, of
course, of enormous concern to the secretary of the treasury.

But Mike Blumenthal knew nothing about the exposition, or why
he had been asked to glad-hand these particular two bankers. Mr.
Lance had never confided the real reason to his cabinet colleague: He
owed the Butchers $443,000 (skip the change), and wanted to show
them he could put them on a first-name basis with the man who, in
C. H.'s phrase, "does regulate our business."

Yet here is Bert Lance using his office to protect and improve his
personal fortunes with impunity. Worse than that: One week ago, the
president of the United States sent the Senate a letter about Mr.
Lance's finances that was patently misleading. Who drafted that letter?

The unhappy Government Affairs committee wants to "confront"

Mr. Lance with a few newspaper clippings, let him make ringing, self-serving denials, and then claim the Senate has discharged its responsibility.

But Mr. Lance's appearance should be the beginning, not the end, of a serious investigation. Illinois Senator Percy, who will come under great pressure from well-connected Chicagoan Abboud, bears a heavy burden; he should insist the GAO be assigned to audit the truthfulness of the asset statements Mr. Lance submitted at his confirmation.

On the other hand, senators and editorialists can agree that Mr. Lance is too amiable a guy, and Mr. Carter too new and clean a president, to charge with such tawdry abuse of power. In the event of such a whitewash, let the Senate at least vote a single-standard resolution of exoneration for Sherman Adams.

1978 PULITZER PRIZE FOR COMMENTARY

Why Being Serious Is Hard

RUSSELL BAKER

April 30, 1978

Here is a letter of friendly advice. "Be serious," it says. What it means, of course, is, "Be solemn." The distinction between being serious and being solemn seems to be vanishing among Americans, just as surely as the distinction between "now" and "presently" and the distinction between liberty and making a mess.

Being solemn is easy. Being serious is hard. You probably have to be born serious, or at least go through a very interesting childhood. Children almost always begin by being serious, which is what makes them so entertaining when compared to adults as a class.

Adults, on the whole, are solemn. The transition from seriousness to solemnity occurs in adolescence, a period in which Nature, for reasons of her own, plunges people into foolish frivolity. During this period the organism struggles to regain dignity by recovering child-hood's genius for seriousness. It is usually a hopeless cause.

As a result, you have to settle for solemnity. Being solemn has almost nothing to do with being serious, but on the other hand, you can't go on being adolescent forever, unless you are in the performing arts, and anyhow most people can't tell the difference. In fact, though Americans talk a great deal about the virtue of being serious, they generally prefer people who are solemn over people who are serious.

In politics, the rare candidate who is serious, like Adlai Stevenson, is easily overwhelmed by one who is solemn, like General Eisenhower. This is probably because it is hard for most people to recognize seri-ousness, which is rare, especially in politics, but comfortable to endorse solemnity, which is as commonplace as jogging.

Jogging is solemn. Poker is serious. Once you can grasp that dis-tinction, you are on your way to enlightenment. To promote the cause, I submit the following list from which the vital distinction should emerge more clearly.

1. Shakespeare is serious. David Susskind is solemn.
2. Chicago is serious. California is solemn.
3. Blow-dry hair stylings on anchormen for local television news shows are solemn. Henry James is serious.
4. Falling in love, getting married, having children, getting divorced and fighting over who gets the car and the Wedgwood are all serious. The new sexual freedom is solemn.
5. *Playboy* is solemn. *The New Yorker* is serious.
6. S. J. Perelman is serious. Norman Mailer is solemn.
7. The Roman Empire was solemn. Periclean Athens was serious.
8. Arguing about "structured programs" of anything is solemn. So are talking about "utilization," attending conferences on the future of anything, and group bathing when undertaken for the purpose of getting to know yourself better, or at the prescription of a swami. Taking a long walk by yourself during which you devise a foolproof scheme for robbing Cartiers is serious.
9. Washington is solemn. New York is serious. So is Las Vegas, but Miami Beach is solemn.
10. Humphrey Bogart movies about private eyes and Randolph Scott movies about gunslingers are serious. Modern movies that are

sophisticated jokes about Humphrey Bogart movies and Randolph Scott movies are solemn.

Making lists, of course, is solemn, but this is permissible in newspaper columns, because newspaper columns are solemn. They strive, after all, to reach the mass audience, and the mass audience is solemn, which accounts for the absence of seriousness in television, paperback books found on airport bookracks, the public school systems of America, wholesale furniture outlets, shopping centers and American-made automobiles.

I make no apology for being solemn rather than serious. Nor should anyone else. It is the national attitude. It is perfectly understandable. It is hard to be Periclean Athens. It is hard to be Shakespeare. It is hard to be S. J. Perelman. It is hard to be serious.

And yet, one cannot go on toward eternity without some flimsy attempt at dignity. Adolescence will not do. One must at least make the effort to resume childhood's lost seriousness, and so, with the best of intentions, one tries his best, only to end up being vastly, uninterestingly solemn.

Writing sentences that use "One" as a pronoun is solemn. Making pronouncements on American society is solemn. Turning yourself off when pronouncements threaten to gush is not exactly serious, although it shows a shred of wisdom.

Heck on Wheels

RUSSELL BAKER

November 14, 1978

Norman Rockwell and I never saw things eye to eye when we worked together on the *Saturday Evening Post*. Norman was illustrating covers and I was trying to sell the finished product. The selling was hard labor.

I would strap on my roller skates, sling a canvas bag containing two dozen *Saturday Evening Post*s over my shoulder and begin by ringing doorbells. The sales pitch was simple: "Want to buy a *Saturday Evening Post*?" As the week progressed, it became tinged with subtle pathos: "You don't want to buy a *Saturday Evening Post*, I suppose?"

During the final day or two of each week's sales campaign, when the imminent arrival of next week's batch of *Post*s loomed like the *Wehrmacht* massing on the borders of the soul, I would post myself at a strategic traffic light and dart among idling cars shouting, "*Saturday Evening Post!*"

In good weeks, the sales profit ran as high as twenty-three cents, which, even though a nickel could buy three apples in those days, did not strike me as the kind of revenue that was going to induce J. P. Morgan to put out the red carpet when I arrived to establish a line of credit.

It was clear to me that the fault was largely Norman's. Although I was only eight, or nine, or ten at the time, I had seen enough of the mass market to realize that Norman's vision of reality was hopelessly askew. The world whose doorbell I rang hungered for tales of illicit passion, gore and depravity, and was shameless about saying so.

Mounting three flights of stairs on wheeled feet, banging an apartment door, flashing Norman's vision of America, I would be met by a slattern in beer fumes declaring the only magazine she wanted was *True Confessions*.

Men sat around the house in their undershirts growing whiskers in that America. Permanent unemployment tends to make a man indifferent to the dictates of *Gentlemen's Quarterly* and sour of temper toward midgets on roller skates peddling Norman's wholesome folks.

"Why don't you sell something good like *True Detective*?"

". . . *Spicy Adventure*?"

". . . *Doc Savage*?"

I never told Norman what the world was really like out there. The *Saturday Evening Post* did not tolerate its business officers trying to interfere with its editorial content. Consequently, Norman never drew a boozy woman in bare feet at the front door announcing her preference for tales of adultery, nor the look in the eye of an unshaven man in his undershirt when he tells you that he'd really rather look at pictures of mutilated bodies (preferably female).

The disagreement between Norman and me was never expressed.

As a result, Norman went on painting dogs as winsomely lovable pooches instead of nasty, snarling carnivores ready to pounce at the first sound of a roller skate wheel on the front porch.

Long afterward it occurred to me that if I had gone to him and said, "Look, Norman, I'm dying out here trying to sell these wholesome characters and phony mutts you're painting," he would have smiled and painted me as an apple-cheeked nine-year-old with a patch on my corduroy knickers and innocence sticking out all over my cowlick. He was that insistent about refusing to see the world as it is instead of as it should be.

When he died the other day, people who have to comment on such things stated that despite his mass audience—perhaps the largest any painter has ever had—he was not an artist but an illustrator. I don't know. There are many definitions of art. Somebody has said that art is a lie that helps us to perceive the truth, and it seems to me that this pretty well expresses what his work was about.

His paintings are graphic fairy tales about Americans. They speak of a people unbelievably decent and innocent. That we were not during the age he painted is beside the point; the fact is that Americans in that time thought of themselves as such. And, indeed, acted on that assumption when the age culminated in World War II.

In *Not So Wild a Dream*, one of the definitive books for students of World War II, Eric Sevareid writes that he was frequently astonished and appalled by the innocence in which American soldiers went to death for a purpose of which they understood nothing except that it was fundamentally decent.

This old sense of innocence, which we have now lost, had bleak political consequences, beginning with our refusal to set realistic war aims in the 1940s and ending with the triumph of the notion that the alternative to innocence must be cynicism.

I didn't understand Norman's significance in the old days. All I could see was that he didn't know what it was like trying to sell the *Saturday Evening Post* on roller skates. He saw things truer than I did. It was an honor to work with him.

1979 PULITZER PRIZE FOR COMMENTARY

The Food on a Table at the Execution

DAVE ANDERSON

New York, New York
November 22, 1980

Near the door of George Steinbrenner's office in Yankee Stadium yesterday, there were two trays of bite-sized roast beef, turkey and ham sandwiches, each with a toothpick in it. As soon as fourteen invited newsmen entered his office for the execution of Dick Howser as manager and the transfer of Gene Michael from general manager to dugout manager, Steinbrenner, the Yankees' principal owner, looked around.

"Anybody want any sandwiches?" he asked. "We've got a lot of sandwiches here."

Gene Michael had piled four little roast beef sandwiches on a small plastic plate and he had a cup of coffee. But as he sat against the far wall, under a huge Yankee top-hat insignia and several enlarged photos of memorable Yankee Stadium moments, he was the only one eating when Dick Howser suddenly appeared and walked quickly to a chair in front of the table with the sandwiches.

"Nobody wants a sandwich?" George Steinbrenner asked. "Nobody wants a drink?"

One of the newsmen ordered a glass of white wine from the bartender, but that was all. Then there was a momentary silence as George Steinbrenner, husky in a soft-blue shirt with a navy blue and green striped tie, sat at a big tan vinyl chair behind his shiny round desk. On the desk was a gold numeral one, maybe several inches high, and a small sign announcing, "Lead, Follow or Get the Hell Out of the Way," and a miniature brass ship's telegraph.

"During the season it's always pointed to full speed ahead," he would explain later. "But in the off-season it's on standby."

To the owner's right, about ten feet away, Dick Howser sat stiffly. His legs crossed, he was wearing a beige shirt, a brown tie, brown pants and brown cowboy boots. He was staring out away from George Steinbrenner, staring blankly at the white draperies that had been drawn across the huge window that overlooks the grassy geometry of the ball field where Dick Howser no longer would work. Most of the time he had his left index finger up against his left cheek, as if to keep from having to look at the Yankee owner, who now was discussing the managerial situation that had been simmering for several weeks.

"Dick has decided," George Steinbrenner began, "that he will not be returning to the Yankees next year. I should say, not returning to the Yankees as manager."

Dick has decided. That would be the premise of George Steinbrenner's explanation. Dick has decided. Ostensibly he suddenly decided to go into real estate development in Tallahassee, Florida, and be the supervisor of Yankee scouts in the Southeast after having been the manager for the Yankee team that won 103 games last season, after having been in baseball virtually all his life as a major league infielder, major league coach, college coach and major league manager of baseball's most famous franchise.

But baseball's most famous franchise also has baseball's most demanding owner. When the Yankees were swept in three games by the Kansas City Royals in the American League championship series, George Steinbrenner steamed. And now Dick Howser is in real estate and is a Yankee scouting supervisor.

"At no time," George Steinbrenner said yesterday, "did I lay down rules or commandments that Dick would have to live by if he returned as manager. The door was open for him to return, but he chose to accept this business opportunity. It took so long because he wanted to make sure he was doing the right thing."

All the while Dick Howser stared at the drawn draperies.

"But could Dick," somebody asked George Steinbrenner, "still be the manager if he wanted to be?"

"Yes."

"Dick, why don't you want to be?"

"I have to be cautious here," Dick Howser said staring straight ahead. "But the other thing popped up."

"Were you satisfied that you could have returned without conditions?"

"I'd rather not comment on that," Dick Howser said.

"If you had won the World Series instead of being eliminated in the playoffs," he was asked, "would you have taken this real estate opportunity?"

"That's hard to say."

"Were you fired, Dick?"

"I'm not going to comment on that," the former manager said.

"I didn't fire the man," the owner said.

Maybe not, but it is reasonable to believe that George Steinbrenner suggested that Dick Howser look for employment elsewhere. That way George Steinbrenner could put Gene Michael, whom he considers a more combative manager, in the dugout. Perhaps to soothe his conscience, he disclosed yesterday that Dick Howser would be paid his reported one-hundred-thousand-dollar salary for each of the remaining two years on this three-year contract.

"I feel morally and contractually obligated to Dick and his wife, Nancy," the owner said. "I took him out of Florida State, where he was the baseball coach and where he could have stayed for life. If it hasn't worked out, maybe it's my fault."

If it hasn't worked out. Until then it had been, "Dick had decided." But perhaps on a slip of the tongue it was, "if it hasn't worked out." Anybody who knew George Steinbrenner knew that all along. And anybody who knew Dick Howser knew that, if given a choice, he would not decide to go into real estate development rather than be the Yankees' manager.

But still George Steinbrenner persisted.

"I think it's safe to say," he said at one point yesterday, "that Dick Howser wants to be a Florida resident year-round, right, Dick?"

Dick Howser didn't even answer that one.

Say this for Dick Howser—instead of going along with George Steinbrenner's party line yesterday, he declined to comment. By not answering questions, he answered them. Anybody could see that. And anybody could see through George Steinbrenner's scheme.

"What advice," Dick Howser was being asked now, "would you give Gene Michael?"

"To have a strong stomach," Dick Howser replied, smiling thinly, "and a nice contract."

Minutes later, the execution was over. Dick Howser got up quickly and walked out of the room without a smile. Behind his round desk, George Steinbrenner looked around.

"Nobody ate any sandwiches," the Yankee owner said.

1981 PULITZER PRIZE FOR COMMENTARY

Charity

———————————————•———————————————

JACK ROSENTHAL

Editorial
March 29, 1981

What has Ronald Reagan declared war on? If, as first appeared, the enemy is America's economic straits, then many of us, suspending neutrality or partisanship, are willing to enlist. But increasingly we're dogged by the suspicion that he also has another enemy in mind: the philosophy of social justice this country has evolved over the last fifty years.

"I don't think people are entitled to any services," says Budget Director Stockman. Martin Anderson, the president's chief domestic adviser, says, "People are quite benevolent. That's good. But it's quite a different thing for people to demand that they have a right to a certain amount of income or services." And elsewhere the administration says that services chopped out of the federal budget can be supplied by the states, or business or volunteers.

In other words, there is no such thing as social obligation. There is only charity—someone else's charity. If that is the administration's philosophy, it deserves to be denounced.

First, some semantic business. Standing alone, the budgeteers' word "entitlements" certainly does sound arrogant. The poor are not constitutionally entitled to any services they deem necessary. But there are some things people should not have to beg for.

Food, for instance, or safe housing, or a lawyer when there's trouble. Would Mr. Stockman or Mr. Anderson deny a sick person access to a hospital emergency room? Surely not. Is that an *entitlement* to medical services? Call it what you will.

Americans are a generous people, exceedingly generous. Carl Bakal has written that our collective private philanthropy comes to about $180 a day for each man, woman and child in the nation. In Canada, it's thirty-five dollars. There is a vast role for private philanthropy; there may even be a case for enlarging it. Maybe, when federal job programs are chopped back, industry could help pick up the slack. Maybe, when funding for legal services is eviscerated, private law firms could step in. Maybe. But two problems get in the way.

If this idea of charity, of supplanting federal social justice with private voluntary action, is sincere, then why does the administration not pursue it?

The genial host, corporate persuader and Great Communicator in the White House needs no lessons in stimulating the private sector. Has he invited the heads of the one hundred biggest companies to the White House to encourage them to create a private job program large enough to offset his budget cuts? Has he assembled partners from large law firms and urged them to provide surrogate legal services?

No. Which raises the suspicion that his administration is much less interested in proving theories than in abandoning social welfare altogether.

Even if the administration now injected action into this theory of voluntarism, it would not suffice.

Deep down, society knows that. Consider jobs. Franklin Roosevelt wrote to a friend in 1934 that "I cannot say so out loud yet, but I hope to be able to substitute work for relief." In 1965, Lyndon Johnson and Henry Ford II launched their then-celebrated, soon-forgotten JOBS program. Richard Nixon, Gerald Ford and Jimmy Carter all had similar ideas. One after another, under the pressure of this merger or that retrenchment, they disappeared.

But assume that a voluntary jobs program could work. How much more can voluntarism do, generally? Federal spending constitutes three-fourths of the total spent for social welfare. Even if Mr. Reagan could mobilize every one of the eight-hundred-thousand-odd charitable institutions, he could not begin to replace government's role in providing services that help people ranging from alcoholics to lactating mothers.

The federal government has undertaken so many services because society has learned that the states alone cannot combat hunger, that volunteers alone cannot provide minimal medical care. Society has turned to the federal government because it is the logical place to address such needs, through the organization of voluntary programs like VISTA, or the Foster Grandparent program that Mrs. Reagan has taken to heart.

That Washington is the logical place doesn't mean it is necessarily efficient, or effective, or even humane. But to say "no entitlements," or "let the states do it," or "let the private sector do it" is a barely varnished way of saying "Don't do it." And that is not a war against inflation. It is a war against the poor.

The War against the Poor

JACK ROSENTHAL

Editorial
December 27, 1981

Ronald Reagan's antipoverty program has three fronts. One is the social safety net, protecting "those with true need." A second is voluntarism, private charity to offset federal cuts. The third and most important is economic recovery, the rising tide that John Kennedy said would lift all the boats. As the administration ends its first year, the poor are losing on all three fronts—and so badly that a question begins to reverberate: what is Mr. Reagan warring against, poverty or the poor?

We will continue to fulfill the obligations that spring from our national conscience. . . . All those with true need ran rest assured that the social safety net of programs they depend on are exempt from any cuts.

That was how the president introduced the safety net last February. Its seven programs were only a partial net to begin with, protecting some middle-class benefits while omitting programs that, on their face, help the very poor.

Even so, there have been sharp cuts even in the exempt programs. School lunch and breakfast programs were in the safety net. Yet about three hundred thousand poor children no longer get lunch in school. Summer youth jobs were in the safety net. Those funds have been cut 27 percent.

Meanwhile, programs that should have been in the net have also been cut, even savaged. Since the Nixon administration, it has been national policy to eliminate hunger. Food stamps have been a well-targeted way to meet that goal. Yet a million people in need will lose their food stamps altogether and most of the 22 million recipients will suffer reductions.

With the same energy that Franklin Roosevelt sought government solutions to problems, we will seek private solutions.

Big government is not the only way, the president told a business audience in October. Exactly right: there is a deep strain of decent, charitable instincts in American society and Mr. Reagan has appointed a fourteen-member commission to find new ways to reach private resources. It is a commendable exercise. It is also a fig leaf.

How much can private supplant public services for the poor? Few of them send their children to private schools, use limousines and taxis or hire guards. They lose most from cuts in federal funds for elementary and secondary schools, or urban mass transit or law enforcement. Governors and mayors understand the cuts; poor people feel them.

In all, Mr. Reagan has so far cut about $25 billion in social spending. If business giving, $2.7 billion last year, were to *double*, it would barely fill 10 percent of the gap. Even the administration acknowledges the point. "I wish the words 'fill the gap' had never been used," says Mr. Reagan's assistant for voluntarism.

Our aim is to increase our national wealth so all will have more, not just redistribute what we already have, which is just a sharing of scarcity.

When the president said that last February, the inflation rate was nearly 12 percent. Now it is down below 10. Much to the good—but at what price? The unemployment rate was 7.5 percent a year ago; it is 8.4 percent now. That means about a million more people are out of work (and extended unemployment insurance benefits are no longer as readily available). An ebbing tide lifts no boats.

Mr. Reagan believes that, if the administration persists in its program, the tide will turn. A more apt maritime image is offered by Herbert Stein, economic adviser to President Nixon: "If the captain of the ship sets out from New York harbor with a plan of sailing north to Miami, 'Steady as you go!' will not be a sustainable policy, and that will be clear before the icebergs are sighted."

*   *   *

For poor people, the issue is not an abstract matter of ideology, or whether the administration is right to keep the faith and wait. For them, the questions are simple: what do *they* do in the meantime? Why, when the administration is so willing to increase windfall oil profits or reduce inheritance taxes, is so much of the burden heaped on *their* backs? In short, what safety net? What voluntarism? What rising tide?

There is only one way in which Mr. Reagan's poverty program has provided for the poor. It is the way prescribed by Reaganaut theoreticians, notably George Gilder in *Wealth and Poverty*, the book widely circulated in the administration earlier this year. "In order to succeed," he wrote, "the poor need most of all the spur of their poverty."

1982 PULITZER PRIZE FOR EDITORIAL WRITING

Believe in Magic

ANNA QUINDLEN

November 9, 1991

The last time we heard so much about a smile was when those ridiculous buttons surfaced a decade ago, the ones with the happy face and the legend "Have a nice day." Those were phony; Magic Johnson's smile is real, a grin that says feelgood as surely as the rest of him says basketball.

Some basketball players, because of their height and a certain hauteur, seem to demand genuflection. Magic Johnson always looks to me like a guy you should hug. That was especially true when he told the world he was infected with the AIDS virus, said he was going to become a national spokesman and flashed the grin nonetheless. What a man.

This is what AIDS looks like—good people, lovable people, people you want to hug. Are we finally ready to face that truth? Are we finally ready to behave properly instead of continuing to be infected by the horrible virus of bigotry and blindness that has accompanied this epidemic?

This is what AIDS looks like—good people who get sick. Artists, actors, soldiers, sailors, writers, editors, politicians, priests. The same issue of the *New York Times* that carried the astounding story of Magic Johnson's announcement carried the deaths of four men with AIDS: an educational-testing expert, an actor, a former dancer and choreographer, and a partner in a law firm. "Loving nature," said one death notice. "Generosity of spirit," said another. Beloved by family and friends.

In the ten years since five gay men with pneumonia became a million people who are HIV-positive, this illness has brought out the worst in America. We obsess about "lifestyle" in the midst of a pyramid scheme of mortality, an infectious disease spreading exponentially.

Over the last year, we have witnessed the canonization of one AIDS patient, a twenty-three-year-old woman named Kimberly Bergalis who says that she "didn't do anything wrong." This is code, and so is her elevation to national symbol. Kimberly Bergalis is a lovely white woman with no sexual history who contracted AIDS from her dentist. She is what some people like to call an "innocent victim."

With that single adjective we condemn those who get AIDS from sex and those who get it from dirty needles as guilty and ultimately unworthy of our help and sympathy. We imply that gay men deserve what they get and people who shoot up might as well be dead. It's a little like being sympathetic to the health-conscious jogger who dies of a heart attack during a stint on the Stairmaster but telling the widow of the couch potato, "Well, if he hadn't eaten all those hot dogs, this wouldn't have happened."

It's not how you get it; it's how you spread it. And we know how that happens and what to do about it. Education. Conversation. Prevention. I don't want to hear any more about how condoms shouldn't be advertised on television and in the newspapers. I don't want to hear any more about the impropriety of clean-needle exchanges or the immorality of AIDS education in the schools.

On Thursday night our eight-year-old asked about safe sex after he heard those words from Magic Johnson's mouth. And I was amazed at how simply and straightforwardly I was able to discuss it. Because I don't want to hear any more about good people who aren't going to live to their fortieth birthday, about wasted talent and missed chances and children who die long before their fathers and mothers do. I'm far less concerned about my kids' lifestyles than I am about their lives.

How are all those parents who denigrate "queers" and "junkies" going to explain this one? How are all those pious people who like to talk about "innocent victims" going to deal with the lovable basketball star, the all-time sports hero, who stressed safe sex when he told the world he was HIV-positive? Will this finally make them say to their kids, "It could happen to you," finally make them stop relying solely on chastity and start dealing with reality?

"Marc will be greatly missed," said one of the death notices. Who cares where it began; this is where it ended, in small black letters on the obituary page. One good person after another, infected, then sick, and finally dying. Magic Johnson, with that engaging personality, that athletic legerdemain, that grin—this is what AIDS looks like. Why can't we learn to deal with our national tragedy with as much dignity and determination as this good man brings to his personal one?

1992 PULITZER PRIZE FOR COMMENTARY

In Alaska, Nature under Siege

ROBERT B. SEMPLE JR.

Editorial
August 28, 1995

Every state in the union will suffer in one way or another from the Republicans' relentless effort to undermine twenty-five years of legislation designed to protect the environment. But Alaska faces a double insult. If bills now moving through Congress receive final approval, the pristine Arctic National Wildlife Refuge would be opened to oil drilling and the Tongass National Forest—the country's largest— would be exposed to ruinous logging.

All this is courtesy of Alaska's congressional delegation, which consists of three Republicans. They are Representative Don Young, Senator Ted Stevens and Senator Frank Murkowski, who would also extend his fervor for logging to the old-growth forests of the Pacific Northwest. [Senator] Murkowski and [Representative] Young are men with legendarily retrograde views on the environment. By a stroke of ill fortune known as the 1994 midterm elections, they now preside over the two key natural resources committees in the Senate and House.

They argue that opening up the refuge and the forest will create jobs and revenue for the state. If oil is found in the refuge, there will indeed be new jobs and an infusion of cash to every Alaskan citizen. For these reasons, Alaskans as a whole would like to see drilling proceed. They are far less enthusiastic about increasing the timber harvest in Tongass.

Conservationists oppose exploitation of both the refuge and the forest. We agree. The short-term benefits of drilling and logging are not worth the long-term degradation of the environment.

The Tongass National Forest is a vast expanse of islands and lush valleys covering most of the Alaska Panhandle. It is home to grizzly bears, bald eagles and countless salmon. It also includes magnificent stands of old-growth trees coveted by timber companies. After years of rapacious logging in the forest, Congress passed a bill in 1990 that set aside one million acres as protected wilderness, imposed strict land-management rules in other parts of the forest and sharply reduced federal subsidies to the timber companies.

Murkowski now seeks to overturn that act with legislation requiring the Forest Service to increase the yearly "harvest" to provide enough timber to guarantee a minimum of twenty-four hundred jobs. In case Murkowski gets nowhere with his proposal, Senator Stevens has attached a rider to the Interior Department's appropriation bill that would accomplish the same result, mandating a far higher annual cut than presently allowed.

These are shortsighted proposals, a point well made by Alaska's Democratic governor, Tony Knowles. He has told Murkowski that by exalting timber-related jobs over other economic activities in the for-est—like fishing and tourism—he will not only degrade Tongass but undermine the future economic health of southeast Alaska.

Regrettably, for political reasons, [Governor] Knowles does not dis-play the same zeal on the question of opening the wildlife refuge to oil drilling. At risk is the refuge's coastal plain—a narrow, 1.6 million-acre wilderness that flanks the Beaufort Sea. It is home to 180,000 caribou, polar bears, wolves, dozens of rare Arctic species and possibly a large undiscovered oil field.

Since 1980—despite efforts by Presidents Reagan and Bush to open up the area—Congress has kept the coastal plain off-limits to drilling. But a new breed is now in charge on Capitol Hill. Nonbinding budget resolutions passed by both houses would open up the refuge in order to help balance the budget over the next seven years. Meanwhile, Young has proposed a freestanding bill that would achieve the same objective.

The revenue argument is weak. Even if there is oil under the plain, government royalties would not surface for years. Under the most optimistic scenario, there is a 50 percent chance that the coastal plain will produce 3.5 billion barrels of oil. This would be a huge find for any oil company but only six months of United States oil consumption at best. Any number of known efficiency measures could achieve the same end without violating an innocent landscape with a vast spider-web of rigs, pipelines, drilling pods and airfields.

In recent testimony before Young's committee, Interior Secretary Bruce Babbitt attacked the economic arguments but also made a valu-able larger point. Opening up the refuge, he said, would be an ethical calamity, "the equivalent of offering Yellowstone National Park for geothermal drilling, or calling for bids to construct hydropower dams in the Grand Canyon. We can find a better way to produce energy and conserve our natural heritage."

He is right. Congress should not be seduced by its acquisitive mem-bers from Alaska.

1996 PULITZER PRIZE FOR EDITORIAL WRITING

Why Bork Is Still a Verb in Politics, Ten Years Later

LINDA GREENHOUSE

Washington, D.C.
October 5, 1997

The start of the Supreme Court's new term tomorrow falls on an anniversary the justices will surely not observe, but one that should not slip by unnoticed.

It was ten years ago tomorrow that the Senate Judiciary Committee, after three weeks of spellbinding public hearings and debate, rejected Robert H. Bork's nomination to the Court. The nomination lingered for another seventeen days before its final defeat on the Senate floor, but the committee vote of nine to five against Bork was the turning point that spelled failure for the Reagan administration's effort to install on the Court the leading conservative voice of the day.

This is no mere historical footnote. It is living history, in many ways as relevant to events on and off the Court today as it was ten years ago. The vote marked an end to a nomination but not to the explosive mix of law and politics that quickly became known as the Bork Battle.

Memories may have faded elsewhere, but to a remarkable degree, the battle still rages here. Its echoes are unmistakable in the combat zone known as the judicial confirmation process, where many Democrats see payback for Bork behind the Senate Republicans' meticulous search for any hint of "judicial activism" among Clinton administration nominees to the federal courts. "This isn't the tenth anniversary of the Bork Battle," one nominee said the other day, begging anonymity lest he offend the Republican senators who for months have failed to bring his nomination up for a vote. "It's the tenth year of the Bork Battle."

That is a judgment that Republicans themselves do not dispute. Alan K. Simpson, the Wyoming Republican, was a powerful Bork defender on the Judiciary Committee. Now retired, he was referring to the anti-Bork strategists when he said in an interview: "They wrote the text, and guess what? That's the commando booklet now for the other side." A week ago, President Clinton charged that the Senate's failure to act on his judicial nominations "represents the worst of partisan politics."

It is understandable that the losers' wounds are still raw. Year after year, the Court itself keeps serving up pointed reminders of what the stakes were and still are. Had Bork been sitting where Justice Anthony M. Kennedy, the successful nominee for the vacancy, now sits, the legal and political history of the last decade would look very different.

On the basis of Bork's own commentary and public positions, it is safe to say that *Roe v. Wade* would have been overruled and the constitutional right to privacy sharply circumscribed; burning an American flag as a political protest would be a crime rather than a First Amendment right; religion would play a greater role in public life; states would be able to impose term limits on their representatives in Congress.

In numerous five-to-four decisions addressing these and other important questions, Justice Kennedy has withheld his vote from the Court's conservative bloc; no liberal himself, Anthony Kennedy was nonetheless a nominee who commented at his confirmation hearing that the framers of the Constitution "made a covenant with the future." According to Bork's testimony, the only appropriate reference point for constitutional interpretation is the past.

For the liberal coalition that worked to defeat Bork—those who testified against him included Governor Bill Clinton of Arkansas— the ten years have brought vindication. "If I thought I was right then, I'm positive I was right now," Senator Joseph R. Biden, the Delaware Democrat who ran the hearings as chairman of the Judiciary Committee, said in an interview.

The opponents also find validation in Bork's speeches and writing of the last ten years. His best-selling *Slouching towards Gomorrah* (HarperCollins, 1996) burns with contempt for the Court and its current members, whose rulings, he proposes, should be subject to reversal by a simple majority in Congress. Bork, a former solicitor general and federal appeals court judge, asserts that the justices' infatuation with "radical individualism" and "extreme egalitarianism" has brought the Court to a "crisis of legitimacy."

It is not only the developments of the past decade that keep the Bork Battle fresh. The combatants stand on opposite sides of an unbridgeable gulf over what actually happened ten years ago: over the legitimacy of the sophisticated mobilization against the nomination, with its polling and its television spots, and over the lessons to be drawn from the campaign's success. A dozen interviews with leading veterans of the Bork Battle produced observations that could have been, and in many cases were, offered ten years ago in nearly the same words.

There remain two diametrically opposite story lines. One is Bork-the-victim. He was "the victim of a misinformation campaign waged by liberal extremists who sought to further their own agenda," in the words of Senator Orrin G. Hatch, the Utah Republican who, as a member of the Judiciary Committee he now heads, was one of Bork's chief defenders. "They knew they couldn't defeat him on his qualifications, so they distorted his writing and his views."

"They turned him into an absolute gargoyle, into a beast," said former Senator Simpson, reminiscing about an effort he called "savage." Charles J. Cooper, a Reagan administration assistant attorney general who worked on the nomination, described the opposition as "not a fair fight on substantive legal issues but a political fight pure and simple, with law and legal constructs as its topic."

According to the other story line, the stop-Bork campaign was public education at its best, a "civics lesson," in the phrase of Senator Biden and others, that informed Americans of the content and consequences of the nominee's views. "It was a legitimate effort to defeat a nominee on the basis of his views, views that were extreme," Biden said. "It was the most extensive civics lesson on the Constitution the American public has ever been exposed to."

"They say it's politics and I say it's Civics 101," said Judith L. Lichtman, president of the Women's Legal Defense Fund, which took a leading role in the campaign. "Politics only reflect what captures people's attention. Something in the body politic responded, because Bork's views opened up questions that the people thought were settled and were happy to keep settled."

"Whether you agree or disagree with the outcome, the Bork hearings were really a reflection of the best of our democratic process, a majestic debate about ideas," said Nan Aron, president of the Alliance for Justice, a coalition of liberal groups that helped organize the opposition.

One question, as another new term begins, is whether the Bork Battle changed the Court and the country in a deeper, more subtle way than a chart simply comparing Anthony Kennedy's actual votes with Robert Bork's likely votes would indicate.

Among the Bork opponents, it is an article of faith that there is a deeper meaning to the story, that the effect of successfully depicting Bork as "out of the mainstream" was to define the mainstream itself in a way that ratified the modern course of constitutional law, unenumerated rights and all. "The public repudiated not just a nominee but a vision," in Aron's words. Laurence H. Tribe, a Harvard law professor who helped Biden prepare for the hearings, said the debate "was almost a national referendum that helped crystallize a national consensus on certain constitutional principles."

The extent to which this view is correct—and there certainly is evidence that it is—also helps explain why the battle goes on. It is simply too important for either side ever to yield. Still, the premise is one that remains to be tested, case by case, in every Supreme Court term—which is why tomorrow's anniversary is as much an opening to the future as a window on the past.

1998 PULITZER PRIZE FOR BEAT REPORTING

Pulp Nonfiction
❖

MAUREEN DOWD

Washington, D.C.
September 13, 1998

The President must not lose his job.

Not over this.

Certainly, Bill Clinton should be deeply ashamed of himself. He has given a bad name to adultery and lying. He has made wickedness seem pathetic, and that's truly a sin.

Kenneth Starr, all these years and all these millions later, has not delivered impeachable offenses. He has delivered a 445-page Harold Robbins novel.

If we are going to dump our President, it should be for something big and bold and black and original. Not for the most tired story ever told.

Middle-aged married man has affair with frisky and adoring young office girl. Man hints to girl he might be single again in three or four years. Man gets bored with girl and dumps her. Girl cries and rants and threatens, and tells eleven people what a creep he is.

The dialogue in this potboiler, compiled with sanctimonious, even voyeuristic relish by Reverend Starr, is so trite and bodice-ripping that it makes *Titanic* look profound.

In fact, Monica identified with Rose, the feisty, zaftig young heroine of *Titanic*. Last January, the former intern wrote the President what she called "an embarrassing mushy note" inspired by the movie, asking her former boyfriend if they could have sex (the lying-down kind).

Despite the fact that it takes place in the most powerful spot on the planet, the romance does not sizzle.

Bill Clinton fancies himself another Jack Kennedy and invoked his idol's name last week to defend himself. But Kennedy was cool. His women were glamorous. The Rat Pack was good copy. He may have been just as immoral, but his carousing at least had style.

Mr. Clinton's escapades are just cheesy and depressing. The sex scenes are flat, repetitive, juvenile and cloying, taking place in the windowless hallway outside the Oval Office study or in the President's bathroom.

The props are uninspiring. Monica always pretends she's carrying papers to get into the Oval office, and she gives the President a frog figurine, a letter opener decorated with a frog and *Oy Vey! The Things They Say: A Guide to Jewish Wit*.

Their meetings, often when the First Lady is traveling, are more needy than erotic.

Monica recalled, "I asked him why he doesn't ask me any questions about myself, and . . . is this just about sex . . . or do you have some interest in trying to get to know me as a person?"

By way of riposte, she said, the President laughed, said he cherished their time together and then "unzipped his pants and sort of exposed himself."

When she complained to the President that she had not had any hugs for months, he quipped, "Every day can't be sunshine."

Thankfully, Clinton grew tired of his little pizza girl. She sensed he was "putting up walls."

"This was another one of those occasions when I was babbling on about something," she said of their last rendezvous, "and he just kissed me, kind of to shut me up, I think."

He didn't call. He didn't write. She began to suspect she was being "strung along." Trapped in a stereotype, Monica became the raging, vengeful Glenn Close character in *Fatal Attraction*.

"PLEASE DO NOT DO THIS TO ME," she wrote in a draft of a note to the President. "I feel disposable, used and insignificant."

She demanded a big job at the United Nations or in the business world in New York, as compensation for his ruining her life.

"I don't want to have to work for this position," she said. "I just want it to be given to me." She sent the President a "wish list" of jobs ("I am NOT someone's administrative/executive assistant") and enclosed an erotic postcard and her thoughts on education reform.

Now if the President was taking Monica's advice on education reform, that might be an impeachable offense.

She sent him a note that read: "I am not a moron. I know that what is going on in the world takes precedence. . . . I need you right now not as president, but as a man. PLEASE be my friend."

Getting nervous over her fits, Clinton reminded her, "It's illegal to threaten the President."

This is the document on which the fate of the Republic has been hanging? These are not grounds for impeachment. These are grounds for divorce.

1999 PULITZER PRIZE FOR COMMENTARY

FIVE

Life and Times

CULTURAL ARBITERS

Criticism of the arts seems destined to have a short half-life. A few years after a great pianist performs a Mozart concerto or a repertory company stages a new production of *Hamlet*, who will care what the critics said? Mozart and Shakespeare remain; comment on particular performances fades away. Of course there are exceptions. George Bernard Shaw, disguising himself (thinly) as Corno di Bassetto, wrote music criticism at the end of the nineteenth century that makes fascinating reading now. But do we expect journalistic critics today to write deathless prose? We remember them only for a witty phrase, like Dorothy Parker's comment in the *New Yorker* in 1933 on Katharine Hepburn's performance in a play called *The Lake*: "Miss Hepburn ran the gamut of emotions from A to B."

So I thought when I began looking over the work that won Pulitzer Prizes for *New York Times* critics. It turned out that I was wrong. What distinguished their prizewinning pieces was an eye for deeper truths. Their perceptions are still compelling.

Ada Louise Huxtable was a revolutionary in her way. The *Times* had never had an architectural critic until she arrived in 1963. From the start she took as her subject not just architecture as an art form but building as a crucial element in how a society functions. Does a city work? Would this skyscraper, that highway make it a better or worse place to live? Those were the kinds of questions she addressed. And she had a great impact.

Once, on an airplane, I met the inventor and principal owner of the Holiday Inns. When he heard that I worked for the *Times*, he fulminated about "that little lady who doesn't like my signs." Public officials were shaken out of their autocratic plans by Huxtable's words.

New York had for decades been the imperium of Robert Moses, a great builder who put his highways where he would, local objections be damned. He never had to face Ada Louise Huxtable. The planners of the Lower Manhattan expressway did, and lost. It was never built. Paul Goldberger followed in Huxtable's footsteps.

The other writers in this chapter were, and are, cultural critics in a more traditional sense: of music, television, books. But in the pieces collected here they all took a larger view. Who would have anticipated that a music critic, Donal Henahan, would bring medical opinion to bear on the suffocation scene in Verdi's *Otello*?

Where It Goes, Nobody Knows

ADA LOUISE HUXTABLE

Architecture
February 2, 1969

The latest word on the Lower Manhattan expressway is that it is going to be poisonous. Well, that is no surprise to a lot of us who have considered the whole idea of a Lower Manhattan expressway poisonous for some time. The warning now is that its covered stretches— which represent the result of a long and bitter battle to depress the road rather than rend Manhattan asunder with an elevated Chinese wall—will produce air-polluting fumes of more than acceptable noxiousness. One could probably do a dandy dissertation on levels of acceptable noxiousness in overpolluted New York.

The battle of the Lower Manhattan expressway, which has raged for twenty-eight years, was "settled" by the incoming Lindsay administration's "acceptance" of the road on the condition that it be built as a depressed highway, recasting it in the role of urban benefactor instead of urban assassin. (The cases of inner-city destruction by expressway are too numerous and well known to recount. Almost every one is a demonstrated environmental catastrophe.)

•   •   •

The in-and-out, over-and-under proposal that has come out of this attempt to defang the monster makes no one very happy. Ducking subways, utilities and the water table, it struggles above and below ground in a series of curious compromises of tortuous complexity, complete with enough entrances, exits and connections to turn Lower Manhattan into a concrete no-man's-land. Displaced people will now number in the low thousands rather than the high thousands. It is a question of degree; do you kill a city or maim it?

At present, the mess—and all except die-hard road lovers admit it is one—is undergoing a year's special planning study. The administration has given the problem to a highly creative architect, Shadrach Woods, hoping that the application of genius may turn up a miracle of some sort. Anyone who thinks New Yorkers lack faith has no idea of how many miracles are prayed for every day.

Meanwhile, the traffic studies pile high. One thing is quite clear, with or without them; you can go uptown, and downtown some of the time, with luck, but you can rarely go across town. That is a truth of New York life, but it is particularly true of Lower Manhattan. Cars and trucks pour off the bridges and struggle gelatinously to the tunnels and vice versa.

The traffic studies prove that most of Lower Manhattan crosstown traffic is "interstate," which means that 90 percent federal funds are available for the expressway's construction. Then they prove that most of the traffic is local after all, and that the expressway is needed primarily just to get to the other side. They prove that traffic will be routed around, rather than through Manhattan, as a result of building the expressway, and they also prove that traffic will go directly to Manhattan destinations because of it. Slice it any way you want.

Only one thing is really proved—that there is a monumental and complex traffic problem for which Nostradamus might reliably predict a future pattern. And one thing is not proved at all—that the expressway, at the expense of city-maiming, is going to solve it.

There is a Parkinson-type law that once you provide a superroute you do not just speed the already stuck cars and trucks on their way; you acquire a lot of new traffic. How much more non-Manhattan traffic will be attracted that would, or should, use Lower Manhattan as an interstate shortcut is a question that just won't go away. Or why that traffic should be dumped in Brooklyn. What will happen to the capacity of the Lincoln and Holland tunnels is another. How much more traffic can be shunted to still other congested Manhattan streets is one more.

A Port Authority statement made in favor of construction of the expressway some years ago claimed that the tunnels could, at that time, handle all traffic "which *must* travel between New Jersey and Manhattan." (Port Authority italics. Motorist vows on the necessity of their trips would ostensibly be handled by Port Authority toll collectors.) It was explained that nothing would be helped by enlarging the tunnels "and so dumping more traffic on the already overburdened streets of Manhattan."

The Port Authority's reasoning is incontrovertible. It applies equally well to the Lower Manhattan expressway.

What concerns this department most of all is something that has been least discussed: the destruction of the fabric of the city along the expressway route. There is a prevalent thought that depressing the road eliminates blight. This is not so, or only relatively so, to the degree that getting rid of a city-dividing superstructure is an improvement. But the social and physical fabric of the city along the proposed route has been deteriorating for the past twenty-eight years. This is the blight that comes from being fingered for an expressway route, with the uncertain future of the area its only certainty.

Properties are not kept up; improvements are not made. Residential and business tenants share the insecurity that sends everything down-hill. Twenty-eight years of this can do a lot of damage. Along the Lower Manhattan expressway route there once was a healthy community and its remains are still there—blighted by the expressway before it ever got built.

The route is fixed where it will do the most possible historical and architectural damage. A line on a map does not begin to indicate the amount of destruction that will take place. To get the cars on and off that "line," supporting and servicing construction must extend far beyond it. Not only will the entire north side of Broome Street go for the expressway's cross-island path but sections of many streets beyond.

The area is known to historians as the Cast-Iron District, a mid- to late-nineteenth-century structural and architectural development of particular importance to American building. Part will be destroyed and the rest irreparably damaged. The Haughwout Store on the northeast corner of Broome Street and Broadway, noted in many histories of architecture, is doomed. Greene Street, a uniquely intact enclave of iron architecture, will be hopelessly mutilated. One of the most respected critics and historians, Nikolaus Pevsner, informed a group of Americans visiting England that "there is a veritable museum of cast-iron architecture in downtown New York, a greater concentration than anywhere else in the world."

"Are you aware of this?" he asked. "Do you recognize its unique quality? Are you letting the public know about it?"

The answers to Dr. Pevsner's questions are no, no and no. The Landmarks Commission has designated the Haughwout Store and held other hearings. The highway people did go so far, a few years ago, as to commission a survey of the buildings. The city knows that some of them contain flammable materials of industries of less than good housekeeping habits, which has led to some particularly tragic fires. Hell's Hundred Acres is the catchy popular name given to the district as a result, ignoring its history, culture and some important economics.

For still another city survey came up with the information that this near miraculous nineteenth-century survival forms a valuable economic neighborhood. Small businesses of above average stability occupy irreplaceable low-rent loft space behind those handsome, rhythmic, cast-iron colonnades of shabby Victorian elegance. These necessary businesses, of the kind that the city has been losing, also give essential, hard-to-find employment to marginally skilled minority workers.

So—stack up economics, environment, sociology, art, history and people against that line across the map. If there is no guarantee, there must at least be a reasonable certainty that some problems are really going to be solved by the huge expenditure of funds and urban assets. We wouldn't bet our money on it, and what is being gambled with is the city itself.

The Crisis of the Environment

ADA LOUISE HUXTABLE

Architecture
December 29, 1969

The bulldozer approach, say the official renewal pronouncements, is a thing of the past. Total clearance is dead. We are going to save our cities and spare our pastoral splendors and make an environment that is civilized and humane.

Or are we? Everyone who believes in fairies raise his hand and Tinker Bell will live. There is no corruption in Vietnam, no mafia in Sicily, and there are no bulldozers any more.

They've all gone to Lexington, Kentucky, where they moved in at night to start demolition of a three-block historic district, or they work weekends to insure the reduction of landmarks to rubble in Santa Fe. They stand poised to demolish everything around a few token preservation blocks in Denver; they wait to level 148 acres in Pittsburgh; they bide their time for the heart of the historic communities of Salem, Massachusetts, and Hudson, New York.

Nothing much has changed except the statements of federal policy that somehow get lost in the translation at the local level, and the increasingly pious use of the word *environment*—a poorly understood concept at best.

We know that our cities are decaying, our skies are shadowed, and our ecology is threatened. That word *environment* gets a fast response now; almost as fast as the bulldozer. The protests of "consumerism" are being directed to consume and exploit the land and its resources.

But conservation is only half of the environmental picture. The bulldozer that tears up the farm or forest for the superhighway or the speculator's sprawl with its inadequate sanitation and services is clearing the way for more than the irreversible loss of the country's natural assets.

It is turning the first earth for an inexorable series of environmental disasters. It is the same bulldozer that pulverizes the urban neighborhood. What is begun with the despoliation of the land ends in the city slum. What is initiated with industrial waste finishes with industrial blight. What starts as an affront against nature becomes an affront against man.

Conservation and community are two sides of the environmental coin. For the crisis of the environment is also the crisis of cities and of the man-made world. It is a crisis of survival and the soul—and of conscience, as well.

It is odd that this rich and pragmatic country should be having a crisis of conscience. It is even stranger that the awakening of conscience should be led by its youth. The issues of conscience have been civil rights, hunger and Vietnam. Now it is the turn of the environment.

In the cities, the giant social issues of justice and opportunity for the underclass have obscured some of the specific causes of physical and human desolation. They are also issues of conscience.

There are the asocial values of real estate, for example, on which our cities are built. It is traditional to treat shelter and society as negotiable commodities; so many bags of beans to be dumped when the price is wrong. The construction on which people depend for their homes and work is conceived not as environment, or as the shaper of · cities, but as cash flow. Pollution and the cash-flow environment have a lot of ugliness in common.

Add the high cost of land, labor, materials and money, the unrealistic cost ceilings on federal aid—and the possibilities grow dim for building a proper environment at all. The only kind of housing still feasible economically is barbaric environmentally: the kind of massed, institutional barracks that have given Chicago, to cite one monumental instance, a new city-size set of social problems in its "safe and sanitary" superslums.

The renewal process has developed a curious corruption of its own. There is the game of federal program musical chairs in which local administrators of smaller cities move from one to another in an easily traced route of weekend demolition and parking lots, carrying their blinders and bulldozers with them. You might call it a new kind of professionalism. And there is the sinister and sinuous web of municipal indifference, ignorance or malpractice that feeds on renewal needs and programs, as in the searing example of Charleston, West Virginia, documented in a recent *Architectural Forum*.

These private and public practices have gotten by because they are so firmly entrenched as the economic and bureaucratic verities, and the conventional American wisdom says don't fight money or City Hall. But the verities and wisdom are being shaken up because the question is survival. What is needed is a brand of "environmentalism" akin to the current "consumerism." A nation sick to death of the kind of "progress" that exacts a terminal toll from the environment could make it stick.

1970 PULITZER PRIZE FOR CRITICISM

New Man of Music

HAROLD C. SCHONBERG

Music
December 16, 1970

He is two hundred years old today, and more alive than he ever was. He came from the provincial town of Bonn, in Germany, went to Vienna, where the action was, and within a few years changed the face of music. He also helped change the face of society. For Ludwig van Beethoven, the short, ill-tempered, boorish, domineering, bad-mannered genius, was one of the New Men of Europe. He may have been low-born, but he was superior to those around him, thanks to a special set of gifts, and he knew it. They may have been princes, archdukes, counts. But he was an artist. There were plenty of princes, archdukes, counts. There was only one Beethoven, and he let the world know it.

And so he went his own way, disregarding the conventions, laughing his arrogant laugh, and producing masterpiece after masterpiece. Even in his own day it was recognized that no musician in the world came anywhere near him, not even the great Johann Nepomuk Hummel or the even greater Ludwig Spohr.

It was also apparent that Beethoven was a symbol, and after his death in 1827 he came close to deification. Beethoven has remained a symbol. By consensus he is not only the greatest composer who ever lived but he is also a symbol of man fighting with, and triumphing over, adversity.

What could be more pulverizing to a musician than the affliction of deafness? And deafness came early to Beethoven. At the age of thirty, he knew that he was in serious trouble. Not many years after that he was living in a silent world, writing music guided only by the sounds in his inner ear.

He had a tonal vision, and it turned out to be a universal vision. Through the years, Beethoven's music has appealed to all people, on all levels, from the most unsophisticated to the most abstruse. No matter what he wrote, from the *Moonlight* Sonata and Fifth Symphony, those eternal favorites, to the C-sharp minor Quartet and the "Grosse Fuge," which inhabit a world of their own, there is something in his music that puts it apart from all others: a force, a mastery, the ultimate coexistence of content and form.

With the *Eroica* Symphony of 1805, Beethoven put music into the nineteenth century. With the Ninth Symphony of 1824 he put it into the twentieth. That thunderbolt of a chord that opens the last movement—B-flat major against D-minor—is in a way an anticipation of the polytonal music that was started by Stravinsky in his *Petrushka* of 1911.

To the last half of the nineteenth century and, indeed, to many today, the Ninth Symphony is more than a piece of music. It is an ethos. As one of the New Men, Beethoven preached a kind of democracy that would have done away with class distinctions. When he made a setting of Schiller's "Ode to Joy," with its call for universal brotherhood, and used it as the last movement of the Ninth, he also composed the first social-conscious score in history. No wonder that many nineteenth-century musicians and aestheticians saw in the Ninth Symphony, and many other Beethoven scores, not only music but also a set of ethics.

The Ninth Symphony loomed large over the century. To Brahms, it was the fearsome specter that had to be matched by any composer who wrote symphonies. To Wagner, it was an ideal of universal drama, and Wagner said that his own operas were but successors of the Ninth. To Bruckner, the Ninth was part of the musical subconscious, and the Austrian composer, whether or not he knew it, wrote a series of symphonies "in the manner of" the Beethoven Ninth. To Mahler, the Ninth was sheer trauma, but he had to follow in its footsteps. What else is the slow movement of the Mahler Fifth Symphony but an unconscious attempt to rewrite the slow movement of the Beethoven Ninth?

No great composer has ever worked in a vacuum, certainly not the assertive Beethoven. His was a success story, despite the ills of his flesh. From the very beginning he was a popular composer (also, incidentally, the greatest pianist in Europe during the few years that his hearing allowed him to play in public), one who had no trouble finding publishers and working out favorable deals with them. Any Beethoven premiere was a great event in his own day. He remained the most popular of all composers. Through the years Beethoven has been the bulwark of the repertory. He composed in all forms and was triumphant in all.

Today, two hundred years after his birth, he still remains the most popular of all composers. Conductors ultimately are judged on "their" Beethoven; pianists carry no credentials until they have conquered the *Appassionata* and the last sonatas; a string quartet is judged on the sixteen Beethoven quartets; violinists and the ten sonatas, not to mention the Violin Concerto, are inseparable. His one opera, *Fidelio*, has inexpressible power and poignancy. His colossal *Missa Solemnis* takes not only his own God but all gods and rolls them into a universal kind of religion.

His music has not dated in the least. Indeed, the world that exists two hundred years after his birth is still finding new things to admire, especially in those mysterious last quartets—those amazing five works, the omega of his creative powers. He wrote them for a future age, and they stand with Bach's *Art of Fugue* as the products of a mighty musical intellect joined to an all-encompassing vision. There are no longer any "rules" in this kind of supermusic. It is not even beautiful music. It is merely sublime. With all other Beethoven music, it has become a transcendent part of the Western heritage, along with the plays of Shakespeare and the poetry of Dante.

1971 PULITZER PRIZE FOR CRITICISM

At Last, a Welcome Public Space for Manhattan

PAUL GOLDBERGER

Architecture
May 22, 1983

It is tempting to say that there has not been a first-class public open space created in Manhattan since Central Park. It would not be true, of course—there is Paley Park, and the promenade over the East River Drive at Carl Schurz Park, and the sculpture garden of the Museum of Modern Art. But the list of decent open spaces is short—so short that it seems reasonable to wonder if we know far less than we once did about how to make civilized and comfortable outdoor places. It is certainly no exaggeration to say that most of the parks, plazas, promenades and squares that have been built in the last few years have been urbanistic catastrophes—harsh, unwelcoming spaces that seem to have been designed more with the intent of keeping people out than inviting them in.

Why this outpouring of hostility on the part of architects and landscape planners is perhaps a question better left to psychologists than to architecture critics. The builders of these odes to concrete that pass as Manhattan plazas talk constantly of security, but they never offer any evidence that there is more safety in a place that looks like a prison yard than there is in one that looks like a park. In any event, the safety they are concerned about generally turns out to be that of their plaza itself, not of the people who use it; keeping a place vandalproof is often a higher design priority than making it pleasant to be in.

Next month, however, what may be the best public space in Manhattan in a generation—and surely the finest riverfront park in New York City since the esplanade at Brooklyn Heights was completed in 1951—will open. It is the Battery Park City Esplanade, a linear park that runs for 1.2 miles along the outer edge of the ninety-two-acre landfill site on the Hudson River that will contain the immense Battery Park City development.

Battery Park City is many years from completion—the major commercial component, the four office buildings that are collectively called the World Financial Center, is only now starting, and but one cluster of three residential towers, called Gateway Plaza, has so far been finished. The esplanade is not complete, either—only the section that is tucked behind Gateway Plaza is done—but that part alone is a quarter-mile long, the equivalent of five Manhattan city blocks in length.

That quarter mile is intended to serve as a prototype for the rest of the project's open space, and to demonstrate the intention of the designers, the firm of Cooper, Eckstut Associates, to break away from the conventions that have so restricted the design of plazas and public spaces in this city in recent years. The esplanade at Battery Park City could not be more different from the norm; every inch of this quarter mile is inviting, and bespeaks a love for parks, for rivers and, most important, for the easy, relaxed social encounters that are the ideal promise that urban life offers.

To say that the Battery Park City design breaks from conventions is a bit misleading, however, for what it really does is return to conventions, at least in another, higher sense. For the essence of this design is a wise and knowing use of the very best elements of traditional New York City park design. There are hexagonal paving stones, and granite, and three familiar kinds of benches, and old-fashioned lampposts, and there are lots of trees.

But this is no tired rerun of an old park—the designers, Alexander Cooper and Stanton Eckstut, working with Amanda Burden of the Battery Park City Authority and landscape consultants Hanna/Olin Ltd. and Synterra Ltd., have varied shapes and proportions slightly, and have mixed and matched these familiar elements in new ways. It is the gift of these designers to have been able to use traditional elements in such a way as to make a place that seems fresher by far than almost any more self-consciously "modern" plaza or park.

This is perhaps the least self-conscious new public space New York City has. It looks almost as if it had been there forever—the fine granite seawalls give it an air of dignity and solidity that almost no new construction manages to have today, and there is not a single thing here that could be called shrill. This esplanade does not shout at us; it beckons warmly, quietly, gracefully. Though these designers clearly love the pure manipulation of space and the celebration of materials as much as any architect whose work is more abstract, every design decision at Battery Park seems to have been made with the ease and comfort of the esplanade's users as the paramount consideration.

A few specifics. The benches here face the river, to celebrate the view; more important, the gently curving iron rail that sits atop the granite riverfront wall is set at a height that permits bench-sitters a free and open view. The lamps are set along the river's edge, not only a good idea for reasons of security but a wonderful formal gesture, for by day the rhythms of the lampposts play off against the churning water, and by night the sparkle of the lights themselves does the same.

These benches and lampposts form a kind of outer promenade, paved in hexagonal blocks; behind it is a planter containing silver linden trees, under which are set backless benches, and behind that is an inner, asphalt walkway and another row of linden trees, and then shrubs and a pink granite wall to mark the inner border. So there are two parallel walks—an outer walk beside the water, and an inner one between a formal alley of linden trees.

If making a welcoming and pleasant public space is not easy in this day and age, making one that will work in this particular place is all the harder. For the towers of Gateway Plaza that sit beside this esplanade are institutional structures of raw concrete and brown metal panels. The buildings are the only thing ever built from an earlier master plan for Battery Park City, now wisely abandoned, and they are altogether depressing. The new esplanade not only holds its own beside them, it elevates these mediocre buildings and makes them civilized.

But the success of the Battery Park City esplanade hardly means that the tide has turned so far as public open space is concerned. If there is any doubt about that, one need only slip by the corner of Forty-sixth Street and Second Avenue, where just behind a brand-new forty-three-story condominium building, the Dag Hammarskjold Tower, sits as hostile a public open space as exists anywhere in the city.

The tower itself, designed by the Gruzen Partnership and Philip Birnbaum, is undistinguished and not a little institutional; it resembles certain publicly assisted housing projects from the mid-1960s. It is hard indeed to understand how such a harsh-looking building could be marketed as top-of-the-market luxury housing. But the tower is sheer poetry compared to its plaza, an awkward, ill-proportioned mess of concrete and brick, locked behind black iron gates and brick walls. Seating consists of backless benches that are no more than slabs of concrete; planting consists of a few scrawny trees and a lonely cluster of shrubs. The overriding image is of paving, of hard, bleak pavement.

Are we so desperate for open space in this city that even this kind of thing looks good? This landscape of desolation is considered a public amenity by the City of New York, which counts open plazas as bonuses for zoning purposes, permitting builders who provide them to increase the size of their buildings by as much as 20 percent. So this concrete yard is not only an eyesore in itself—it was a mechanism by which the builder of Dag Hammarskjold Tower, R. H. Sanbar Projects Inc., was allowed to make the tower even bigger than it otherwise would have been.

On a recent sunny day, by the way, the plaza was not even open to the public; it was entirely locked and gated, denying the public even the right of access to this unpleasant place that it had, by virtue of zoning bonuses, paid for. It was in protest against such similar closings that the Parks Council, a civic organization, brought legal action last year; in response the city has begun to show increased concern for the quality of public open space, and in one important case—the so-called plaza at Two Lincoln Square that is nothing more than a dark alley— it began legal proceedings of its own against the landlord.

But legal action to bring public access to plazas that are so badly designed that no one would want to spend any time in them anyway is not the point, encouraging as it is. What is most urgent is that the standards of public space design themselves be raised. At Dag Hammarskjold Tower, we have the latest example of how not to design a public plaza; at Battery Park City we have the most encouraging example of how to do one right. The contrast could not be more striking.

1984 PULITZER PRIZE FOR CRITICISM

Desdemona's Death Throes, Continued

DONAL HENAHAN

Music
February 24, 1985

At the risk of beating a dead soprano, I must return to a matter I thought I had dispatched quietly in a recent piece: the stifling of Desdemona in the Metropolitan Opera's *Otello*. I should have known better. For some reason, this is the sort of discussion that sends normally quiescent readers flying to their writing desks, eager to agree or disagree, often at dissertational length. Who would have thought there were so many people out there with fervent, reasoned opinions on the subject of Otello's modus operandi? In the Met production, you recall, the death weapon was a pillow wielded by the crazed Moor, but I suggested that the libretto's simple stage direction, "he stifles her," could be stretched to include more theatrically plausible possibilities, including strangling.

Doctors, of course, can be expected to hold firm views on such a matter and I heard from several. One, Dr. M. Eugenia Geib, was reminded of an inquest she held in *Opera News,* February 2, 1952, on several operatic corpses, including "some cases in which the librettist's diagnosis is scarcely tenable." Noting that Desdemona is supposedly strangled or smothered, the doctor wonders how this could be true: "It is a well-known fact that the brain cells are most susceptible to oxygen lack; the smothered individual becomes irrational, then unconscious. Finally, the vital centers of the brain are affected, causing cessation of heartbeat.

"The difficulty in accepting Desdemona as a simple case of strangulation is that she regains consciousness and speaks a few coherent words. Obviously, her brain cells are not destroyed at all. Since Otello does not restrangle her, it can scarcely be believed that she dies of oxygen lack caused by simple mechanical obstruction. It is true that in some cases the obstruction is caused not by the hands of the strangler, but by intense swelling of the throat secondary to fracture of the bones of the larynx. However, an outstanding feature of such cases is extreme difficulty in vocalizing, and the Metropolitan does not generally present Desdemonas who have that trouble. We must assume then that she dies of some other condition, probably a cerebral hemorrhage or a heart attack, no doubt brought on by the assault."

I almost hesitate to point out another possibility, that a soprano might suffer serious loss of brain cells, perhaps at birth, and still enjoy a career at the Metropolitan.

A Plainfield, New Jersey, physician, Dr. Richard M. Ball, alluding to Desdemona's prolonged "two-phase death," points out that "alas, such antemortem stamina is common in opera. But it is usually after poison, stabbing or shooting. These are believably less instantaneous deaths, so the listener can keep the poetic faith. But suffocation? No way. Your suggestion that manual throttling rather than the pillow might be more acceptable won't work either. Strangling crushes the hyoid bone, blood fills the windpipe (accounting for the so-called 'death gurgle'), and rapid swelling seals off respiration. There'd be not even a wisp of air, to say nothing of a sustained legato.

"So what shall the forensic pathologist cum operatic stage director do? I suggest both stifle and stab. Otello already has a dagger in his doublet. Let him use it twice; other operatic murderers have done it. Desdemona begs for another night, an hour, an instant. Otello, enraged, stifles (Shakespeare's word) her mewling with the pillow (which hides her face, too; Otello is something of a coward, after all), then he stabs her, and throws off the pillow, revealing a prebloodstained underside to the audience. Since Desdemona is exsanguinating, and not suffocating, she can sing now and die later. This preserves the original *soffocare*, while not shattering medical reality."

I reproduce Dr. Ball's clinical solution to the problem not only for whatever medical light it may throw, but as a fine example of how close to the surface in all confirmed operagoers lies the stage-directing impulse. I know that I, for one, often feel the urge during a performance to call a halt to some silliness onstage and offer my own astute ideas of how the scene should go.

Along that line, a Shelter Island [New York] reader named Anna Marie (surname not quite decipherable) offers her own X-rated vision of the scene: "I would rather propose a less preposterous demise for Desdemona, one which would undoubtedly allow for a few strangled notes of anguish/delight . . . that here *la soffoca* means that Otello tries to take and smother her with his love—and succeeds." It just might work, I believe, on late-night TV.

Gary Smidgall, an English teacher at the University of Pennsylvania, points out that the composer and his librettist were merely following Shakespeare in letting Desdemona live on after her stifling. "After all, it was his and not Verdi's and Boito's bright idea not to have her die 'straight off,' as you put it. In the play, thirty lines after she is smothered she comes back—momentarily resurrects—for her last Christian gesture of selfless giving. Bardolatrous MDs assure us this is all medically possible, but I don't think S. gave a damn. He expected the tremendous effect of the gesture was worth the risk of the 'picky' few not swept along by it all."

Jane Sherman of New Paltz, New York, also wants it understood that Verdi and Boito followed Shakespeare closely in letting Desdemona revive briefly in the death scene. "As for your suggestion that Emilia, Iago, Cassio and Ludovico should rush to try to save Desdemona, in the play she dies before Emilia has had time really to see what happened. And not for two pages of dialogue with Othello does she then call in the others, who could hardly be expected to apply to a thoroughly dead lady 'whatever cardio-pulmonary resuscitation techniques were known in sixteenth-century Cyprus.' "

From even deeper in the literary archives comes Kelly Graham's note of amplification: "It is commonly believed that Shakespeare based his *Othello* on Giraldi Cinthio's seventh novella of the third day of the *Hecatomonithi* (1566). This novella was supposedly taken from an actual Venetian murder in which a woman was beaten to death by pillows filled with sand by her husband and his ensign. The sand-filled pillows were used so that no bruises would show on her body. The husband and ensign then arranged for the beams of the woman's bedroom to fall upon her so that the entire incident would seem to be an accident. Perhaps this Venetian source explains the Metropolitan's production as well as the production you saw in which the bed fell upon Desdemona and Otello." Perhaps, indeed.

Yet another Shakespearean, Donald Roemer of Lexington, Massachusetts, rises to defend Verdi and Boito (neither of whom I accused of anything) but goes on to agree with me on one point, citing "the grievous error perpetrated when Desdemona lumbers down from the platform, flaps around the room, and then has somehow to be maneuvered back to the bed, where she is supposed to die. She should stay there and take her medicine." Apropos of *Otello,* Roemer fondly recalls a 1960 performance at an East German house where the Desdemona, a towering soprano bearing the first name of Brünnhilde, got out of bed, wrestled a small tenor to the death and would have won easily if the libretto had allowed her to. The tenor then had to drag the enormous body back onto the bed. Emilia entered and, as the performance was being sung in German, uttered her horrified judgment on Otello: "Dumbkopf!"

An actress, Eugenia Rawls, who portrays the nineteenth-century actress Fanny Kemble in one-woman shows, provides further insight into the question by sending along a letter that Fanny wrote just before playing Shakespeare's Desdemona for the first time: "That smothering scene is most extremely horrible. I think I shall make a desperate fight of it, for I feel most horribly at the idea of being murdered in my bed. The Desdemonas that I have seen on the English stage have always appeared to me to acquiesce with wonderful equanimity to their assassination. On the Italian stage they run for their lives around the bedroom, their Othello clutching them finally by the hair of the head, and then murdering them. But I did think I should not like to be murdered, and therefore at rehearsal got up on my knees, on my bed, and threw my arms tight around Othello's neck (having previously warned Macready, and begged his pardon for the liberty), that being my notion of the poor creature's last appeal for mercy."

So perhaps in the end, the trouble I had in suspending disbelief in that last scene of the Metropolitan's *Otello* was merely that it had an English Desdemona and an Italian director. At least there were no such serious distractions as those mentioned in a note I received from a fellow critic: "At the first performance, belief was put to an even harder suspension test: the public so much admired Otello's entrance (the double-bass passage and attendant pantomime) that it was encored! The records don't tell us whether a stagehand first came on to relight the candle he extinguishes during his advance to the bed."

And on that historical note, let the whole subject be stifled.

1986 PULITZER PRIZE FOR CRITICISM

Seducified by a Minstrel Show

MARGO JEFFERSON

Television
May 22, 1994

Who was your favorite character on *Amos 'n' Andy*? Mine was Lightning, the ineffably witless house painter. "Which way did he go, Lightning?" a policeman, hot on the track of some malefactor, would shout, and Lightning would point to the right with his left forefinger and to the left with his right forefinger, expel some raspy syllables ("Ah . . ." "Well . . ." "Dat is . . ."), then cross his eyes and expire in puzzlement. One day Lightning got stuck in a garbage can. He banged about the room futilely for some moments, trying to get out. Then, realizing that this was not to be, he sank gently down, placed his chin mournfully in his hand and murmured, "Oh, me."

Oh, me, indeed. I'm not surprised that I liked the show: seeing episodes recently at the Museum of American Broadcasting, I saw how funny it had been. But why was I so attached to Lightning (the producers spelled it Lightnin'), the figure who most embodied what an aunt of mine called, in sorrow and disdain, "the type of the ignorant Negro"?

Comedy is such a mixture of empathy and superiority, identification and alienation. Belonging to the type of the educated Negro, I found Lightning provocatively unlike me (which let me laugh at him) and yet oddly like me (which let me laugh with him). For one thing, we were both cross-eyed. For another thing, which had precious little to do with race, I was a child, and his was the comedy of regression: broad, slow gestures; grimaces and double takes; sounds that broke language into vowels, syllables and tones. Besides, what child undergoing socialization doesn't know exactly what it feels like to get caught, literally or metaphorically, in a garbage can and to try desperately to get out before the adults find you?

Oh, me.

One day at school I was chatting with a classmate, and we started recounting the last episode of *Amos 'n' Andy*. Nothing seemed more natural than that he would slip into a rendition of one of Kingfish's famous exclamations. It may have been "I'se regusted!" or "Holy mackerel!" (basso voice quavering, eyes turned heavenward); perhaps he stroked his chin and intoned, "Well, now, Sapphire..." In any case, as soon as the words came out of his mouth, I stopped enjoying myself. I smiled weakly and hurried the conversation on. But because he was white and I was black, all sorts of other things had suddenly attached themselves to Amos, Andy, Lightning and Kingfish: charged talk about "equality" and "prejudice," about what holds "us" back and how "they" like to think we behave.

I tell the story because it told me something about comedy in a nation that is not a melting pot or a mosaic but one big ethnic variety show stuffed full of mixed dialects, mixed manners and mixed motives.

In her book *American Humor,* published in 1931, the critic Constance Rourke said that our comedy sprang from a new nation's effort to devise an identity for itself in the face of a powerful, often patronizing Old World. The British saw the newly freed American as a coarse buffoon. Americans winced and admitted as much but retaliated by giving that buffoon a con man's wit and a prankster's bravado.

Comedy is about our needs, our place in the world, and how we cooperate or collide with people just as obsessed with their needs and place.

What began as comedies about rustic Anglo-Saxon buffoons in the eighteenth century became comic fantasies about Negroes in the nineteenth century, and by the twentieth had spread to include nearly every immigrant group. And the comedy of ethnicity is always tied to that of social class: of new settlers who start in the barnyard, on the street corner or in the poolroom, then make their way to the office, the living room and the cocktail lounge. Which means it is always tied to the question of who is laughing at whom and why.

The ethnic and social masks kept on rotating. Northern Irish-American actors impersonated southern African-American slaves, followed by northern African-American actors impersonating southern African-American slaves. Irish-Americans played Jewish- and Asian-Americans; Jewish-Americans played African- and Irish-Americans. In an essay called "Change the Joke and Slip the Yoke," Ralph Ellison said that for a nation of former colonials and immigrants, "the declaration of an American identity meant the taking on of a mask," one that "imposed not only the discipline of national self-consciousness, it gave Americans an ironic awareness of the joke that always lies between appearance and reality."

Which doesn't mean that the jokes were of grade-A quality. Here's a sample from *Desdemonum*, a nineteenth-century minstrel burlesque of *Othello*.

> OTEL: Wake Desdemonum, see de risin' moon,
>   Everybody's snorin', nightingale's in tune . . .
> DES: 'Tel, my duck, I hear you: Daddy's gone to bed.
>   Fotch along your ladderum, I'm de gal to wed!
> BOTH: De hour am propitious—come my darlin' flame!
>   Dey say dat in de dark all cullrs am de same.

Plenty of jokes and comic types entered vaudeville largely stripped of ethnicity though still tied to sex and status: the harridan mother-in-law, the loutish politician, the girlfriend with the face of a saint—a St. Bernard! But a lot of them kept both the thrill and the stench of ethnic difference: the way your voice, gestures and manners get interpreted out of motives that include pleasure, admiration, envy, disapproval and contempt.

If a group's status in America is fairly secure, ethnicity becomes a matter of style, artfully or awkwardly deployed. But if the group's status is perpetually up for grabs or periodically up for grabs or temporarily in question, every guffaw gets attached to a social or political judgment.

That's why *All in the Family*, the long-running CBS series that was the first postmodern whiteface minstrel show, came to television in the 1970s. Against the backdrop of the Vietnam War, the civil rights and black-power movements and feminism, it was the "counterculture" versus the "silent majority." And Archie Bunker was in the center of the fray: an oaf and yokel because he was a white hard hat and bigot.

Middle-class black viewers could feel comfortably superior on social and racial grounds. Middle-class white viewers were protected from all-out racial embarrassment because of their social distance. Women could take some satisfaction in an Edith Bunker who might be ditsy and ingratiating but had a kind heart and sometimes managed to get the last word. Jean Stapleton pulled this off well. And Carroll

O'Connor played Archie so skillfully that you couldn't help enjoying his follies, his colorful (albeit primitive) way of expressing himself. Besides, plenty of fans identified with Archie and didn't look down on him at all: minstrelsy has always managed to service an amazing variety of needs.

My favorite white minstrel show today is MTV's chronicle of two young, mean-mouthed cartoon-strip white boys, *Beavis and Butt-head*. Before I watched them I thought that only "special interest" groups like the NAACP, NOW and the Anti-Defamation League protested the way mass culture portrayed their people. Now I rather enjoy watching mainstream editorial writers and politicians who could be the fathers or older brothers of Beavis and Butt-head denounce them as dangerous and degenerate.

It must have something to do with the fact that in their own way they are very like the pair of old-time black comic stereotypes, the pair of clowns who at a various times have been called Tambo and Bones, Zip Coon and Jim Dandy, and Andy and Kingfish. They boasted and postured, insulted each other and told silly jokes in loud voices accompanied by snorts and chortles.

Like them, Beavis and Butt-head are feckless, shiftless and shameless. Their language, though white suburban in rhythm and tone (curt, short phrases instead of loopy, meandering ones; deadpan delivery instead of lavish theatrics), relies on the same puns and shrewdly butchered words that were the mainstay of minstrelsy. In old *Amos 'n' Andy* radio scripts, "repercussions" became "reconcussions," and "premeditated murder" became "prefabricated murder." In their book (the title of which cannot be reprinted here), Beavis and Butt-head turn cast of characters into "cast of caricatchers" and their acknowledgments into "uh-knowledge-mints."

But I don't think that the young classmate who unwittingly shamed me with his Kingfish imitation would have been ashamed to see me burst forth as Beavis or Butt-head. Because even if you loathe them (and I don't), they always get the last word and the last insult. This is something the blacks who peopled *Amos 'n' Andy* were never permitted, except by indirection.

Audiences were encouraged to see the *Amos 'n' Andy* cast more as real-life racial types than skilled performers. They always ended up implying, directly or indirectly, that the cosmic joke was on them. They—and by extension their people—were absurd in a way they didn't get and couldn't help. Beavis and Butt-head, on the other hand, know exactly who thinks they're absurd and they couldn't care less. They make the rules, and they break them.

Richard Pryor and Dick Gregory led those who made the black comic over, from naive prankster to hip prophet: the one who remade the rules of his comic world while breaking the rules of yours. Eddie Murphy was their most popular 1980s descendant. The 1990s brought Martin Lawrence.

Lawrence rules his world as firmly as Beavis and Butt-head rule theirs. (Since blacks spent so many years playing flesh-and-blood cartoons, it seems only fair that their comic emancipation would include rights of self-determination on a par with those of storyboard cartoons.) All three characters talk about sex, bodily fluids and bodily functions the way hyperactive kids trying to peek into a bedroom or under a bathroom stall would. They all use sturdy one-syllable Anglo-Saxonisms but in an oddly innocent way—more like rhythm markers than expletives.

On *Martin*, his Fox series, Lawrence plays a disc jockey engaged to a career girl and offers a story line that joins gentrification to folksiness. But when he does stand-up monologues as in the new film *You So Crazy*, he dispenses with the sitcom niceties and goes for polymorphous-perverse broke.

If I have been talking only about men, that is because I have had to be faithful to American comic history. The female roles in the minstrel show were fixed versions of the vamp, the termagant and the bonehead, and until late in the nineteenth century they were played exclusively by men. The type was carried into vaudeville and onto television (Amos and Andy's fussy wives and bossy mothers-in-law; Archie Bunker's fond, foolish wife and earnest, dizzy daughter). So was the tradition of female impersonation: witness Martin Lawrence's bossy country mother and raucous homegirl neighbor, Sheneneh.

A good, red-blooded, authoritative American female comic is still hard to find. That's because it is still a hard persona to create: the only two who seem to have pulled it off with steady mass-media success but with some fresh twists are Roseanne Arnold and Whoopi Goldberg. They have done it by combining old, seemingly unrelated styles with new tones and attitudes. When I watch Arnold, I see the product of a comic mating between Hattie McDaniel and Thelma Ritter: the type of the aggressive, no-nonsense black maid and mammy from 1930s and 1940s movies, and the type of the laconic, no-nonsense white maid and housekeeper from 1950s and 1960s movies. Neither was permitted a life outside her day job, and the camera and script were always reminding audiences to snicker because McDaniel was fat and dark and Ritter was bony and sallow.

But Arnold throws her weight wherever she wants to on her series: her loud, flat voice sets the pace and grounds the plot. We can't condescend to Roseanne's working-class life because she makes better jokes about her family, food and home furnishings than we could, and she fires off better one-liners about sex, death and rock-and-roll too.

Whoopi Goldberg seems to have learned her craft from Richard Pryor (the quick changes of mood and character, the physical comedy) and from Pearl Bailey (the maternal folksiness that can turn scathing in a flash), among others. But she is clearly meant for screwball comedy: the combination of slapstick and dotty wit that Lucille Ball perfected in *I Love Lucy*. Goldberg started out as a solo performer, playing characters of different ages, sexes and races without changing costume or pigmentation. Things began to falter when she went into the movies in the 1980s and got stuck in a series of lame vehicles like *Jumpin' Jack Flash* and *Burglar*. Scriptwriters and directors veered nervously between asexual slapstick and pseudo-sexual pseudo-funk.

But her recent and very popular movies have managed to put her talent to better use. Playing a psychic in that sentimental fantasy-drama *Ghost*, she bridged the usually segregated worlds of the dead and the living with a vigor that gave the movie both comic relief and common sense. The silly and funny *Sister Act*, in which she played a nightclub singer hiding out in a nunnery, had her walk the line between comic sleaze and comic celibacy. And in the 1993 *Made in America*, she and Ted Danson tucked a romantic comedy into a screwball race tale.

I hope posterity will remember them for that, not for the Friars Club roast where Danson appeared in blackface to recite gags scripted by Goldberg. Ted Danson is a good comedian, but I'm reminded of what the critic Zora Neale Hurston said about performers who used burnt cork and dialect in the 1920s: "Good comedians but darn poor niggers."

I have high hopes for Queen Latifah too. On her records and videos as well as on her more gentrified sitcom, *Living Single*, she claims a boy's traditional right to be a signifying braggart as well as social critic and a girl's right to be a comic charmer. She reminds me of Mae West, actually, and of vaudeville blues performers West admired, like Ida Cox and the young Ethel Waters. She blends satire and sex with a touch of the gangster.

Black or African-American comedy is an expanding set of performance traditions and styles, not a fixed set of sociological or cultural rules. When critics or comics speak of what constitutes "real" black comedy, they are speaking of its folk or populist traditions rather than its elite or bourgeois traditions. When folk traditions enter mass culture, they can keep their power and their edge, but they never stay "pure"; they start to call and respond to other influences. They can be flattened out, even degraded; brilliantly maintained and revised or, as with *Amos 'n' Andy*, an unsettling combination.

This is all part of the history of American culture. Paying close attention to it does amount to what Ralph Ellison called "the discipline of national self-consciousness." That's why I would no longer mind seeing *Amos 'n' Andy* reruns on television now, playing alongside *Lucy, The Jack Benny Show* and *The Honeymooners*.

Comedy is always a jostling for rights of representation: having your job laughed at, your place in the world vindicated. And now, at a moment when representations of all groups are under fire and up for grabs, more comic daring is called for.

I'm often surprised at how safely segregated or tamely integrated mainstream comedy remains. Take *P.C.U.*, the new movie send-up of political correctness on college campuses. Its merry band of politically incorrect students includes one black and several women, but no good comic use is made of that fact.

Asked about the autobiographical roots of the film recently, one of its scriptwriters reminisced about his days as a straight white man at Wesleyan University. "Early on, I was told that I should walk in a nonthreatening way," he said. "Every night I walked home from the library, I asked myself, 'Is my walk nonthreatening? How do I do this goofy, nonthreatening walk and not appear to be coming on to a girl? I mean, woman.'"

But instead of sounding a bit whiny, why not put that scene in the movie and develop it? He might have had his leading man go to an African-American cohort and request lessons on how to walk in a nonthreatening way: surely a young black male who had gotten to Wesleyan must have spent a good chunk of his adolescence mastering the art of walking down the street in a way that assured pedestrians of his good intentions. Together the two youths could then submit their walks to a panel, a girl group, of judges. Everyone would get a chance to play the fool; everyone would have a chance to get the last laugh.

And the best performer would be declared the winner. That's my idea of a divine American comedy.

1995 PULITZER PRIZE FOR CRITICISM

Norman Mailer's Perception of Jesus

MICHIKO KAKUTANI

Books
April 14, 1997

Perhaps it was inevitable that in this memoir-mad age, Norman Mailer, never a writer exactly known for his lack of hubris, would pen a novel in the form of an autobiography of Jesus.

In an interview sent out by Random House with *The Gospel According to the Son*, Mailer observed that he felt up to the dare of channeling Jesus because his own literary celebrity had endowed him with "a slight understanding of what it's like to be half a man and half something else, something larger."

"Obviously, a celebrity is a long, long, long, long way from the celestial," he said, "but nonetheless it does mean that you have two personalities you live with all the time. One is your simple self, so to speak, which is to some degree still like other people, and then there's the opposite one, the media entity, which gives you power that you usually don't know how to use well. So the parallel was stronger than I realized."

The resulting book is a sort of novelized *Jesus Christ Superstar* starring Jesus as an ambivalent pop star and guru: a silly, self-important and at times inadvertently comical book that reads like a combination of *Godspell*, Nikos Kazantzakis's *Last Temptation of Christ* and one of those new, dumbed-down Bible translations, all seasoned with Mailer's own eccentric views on God and faith and the conservation of spiritual energy.

The narrator of *The Gospel According to the Son* isn't the purposeful Son of God we met in Mark's Gospel or the forgiving Jesus described by Luke. This isn't the garrulous teacher introduced by Matthew, or the Jesus who openly proclaimed his Messiahship in John. Mailer's Jesus is an altogether more ordinary fellow: petulant, irritable and ravaged by "thoughts of lust," a carpenter who just happened to discover at the age of thirty that he had another calling.

For that matter, everything in this volume is a pale, user-friendly version of what it is in the Bible. Miracles aren't so miraculous here: in the loaves and fishes scene, we're told that Jesus "divided them exceedingly small, until there were a hundred pieces of bread from each loaf" and hundreds of flakes of fish, "a triumph of the Spirit rather than an enlargement of matter." Even Judas is given plausible human motives for his betrayal: as Mailer's Jesus tells it, Judas was angry at him for appearing to scorn the poor and for failing to lead a revolt against the Romans.

Throughout *The Gospel According to the Son*, Jesus suffers terrible doubts about his role as redeemer and worries about the dissipation of his miracle-working powers as though he were an athlete trying to conserve his energies before an important game. After restoring the daughter of Jairus to life, he wonders: "Had I drawn too deeply upon the powers of the Lord? Would it have been wiser to save His efforts for other matters?"

This Jesus is patronizing about his disciples, sarcastic about his human flock and quick to anger. "So many miracles," he complains, "so little gain." For some reason, he is also extremely sensitive to smells, be it the odor of greed radiated by the Devil, the scent of exhaustion that clings to John the Baptist or Jesus' own sometimes sour breath.

Though Mailer apparently wants to try to flesh out Jesus as a character by exploring his inner conflicts and oh-so-human problems, these efforts to make him relevant—combined with the book's flattened-out, New Agey language—have a way of making him seem less like the historical personage we have come to know as Jesus (never mind the Christian Savior), than just another chatty cult leader. Sometimes Mailer's Jesus sounds an awful lot like a guest on *Oprah*. Sometimes he sounds like Do and Ti (a.k.a. Bo and Peep, Pig and Guinea). And sometimes he sounds like Luke Skywalker, the apprentice Jedi trying to master the Force.

Mailer's Jesus suffers from repressed memory syndrome. (Although Joseph supposedly told him about his miraculous birth when he was twelve, he does not recall the discussion until he is thirty.) He complains that his mother doesn't understand him. And he feels conflicted about his identity. ("I felt as if I were a man enclosing another man within.")

To complicate matters further, the first-person narrative takes the sorts of sentiments that followers might think or say about Jesus and puts them in his own mouth. Often he sounds downright boastful.

"I could see how I wanted to be all things to all men," he says. "Each could take from me a separate wisdom. Indeed, I thought: Many roads lead to the Lord."

As for Jesus' Father, He comes across as a weary, withholding Dad. Having died and been resurrected, Jesus says he remains "on the right hand of God." "My Father, however, does not often speak to me," he adds. "Nonetheless, I honor Him. Surely He sends forth as much love as He can offer, but His love is not without limit."

In fact, as Mailer sees it, this God has had great victories, but He has also had great defeats, like the Holocaust and the death of His son. Mailer's Jesus further suggests that the words from the Bible "God so loved the world that He gave His only begotten son that whosoever believed in Him should not perish but have eternal life" were written after the fact to rationalize his death, for God "saw how to gain much from defeat by calling it victory."

No doubt this conception of God as a limited Being striving to do His best against great odds provides Mailer with a means of explaining the cruelties of history, but his portrait of God is not, essentially, a philosophical one. Rather, it is a novelist's portrait of his hero's father. Indeed Mailer's Father and Son have a lot in common: both are full of themselves, both are fond of self-dramatization, and both tend to feel put upon by their public responsibilities.

In recent years, Mailer has tried to dress his all-too-human subjects, Lee Harvey Oswald and Pablo Picasso, in the garments of heroism.

This time he has tried to do the reverse, with equally distressing results. In trying to describe Jesus and God as accessible novelistic characters, Mailer has turned them into familiar contemporary types: he has knocked them off their celestial thrones and turned them into what he knows best, celebrities.

1998 PULITZER PRIZE FOR CRITICISM

SIX

New Frontiers

REPORTING DISCOVERIES

Carr Van Anda, managing editor of the *Times* from 1904 to 1932, was an extraordinary figure who was learned in a number of scientific fields—and started the paper's strong interest in science news. Van Anda once read the text of a lecture by Albert Einstein and found what he said must be a mistake in an equation. Einstein was consulted and said Van Anda was right; he had wrongly transcribed the equation from the blackboard. Van Anda committed the *Times* in 1922 to extensive coverage of the discovery of King Tutankhamen's tomb in Egypt. In examining photographs of the inscriptions, he discovered a four-thousand-year-old forgery: replacement of the young king's signature by that of one of his military commanders. Van Anda could read hieroglyphics.

The same year as the King Tut coverage, 1922, Alva Johnston wrote science news reports that the next year won him the first Pulitzer Prize to go to an individual *Times* reporter. One of his pieces (not reprinted here) was a report of a statement by the Council of the American Association for the Advancement of Science supporting the theory of evolution against attempts to suppress its teaching in schools. Eighty years later, the would-be suppressors are still at work.

In 1929 a *Times* reporter, Russell Owen, accompanied an expedition to Antarctica led by Commander Richard E. Byrd. Owen stayed with the expedition through the frozen dark of the polar winter, reporting its frustrations and triumphs in stories that commanded big headlines on page one. "Byrd Safely Flies to South Pole and Back," one said. "Conqueror of two poles by air," Owen wrote, "Commander Richard E. Byrd flew into camp at 10:10 o'clock this morning, having been gone eighteen hours and fifty-nine minutes...[He] stepped from this plane and was swept up on the arms of the men in camp who for more than an hour had been anxiously watching the southern horizon for a sight of the plane." The breathless style and the big play of the story remind us of how daring polar exploration was in those days.

In 1937 William L. Laurence was honored for his reporting of Harvard University's tercentenary celebration. One of his stories described a discussion of recent discoveries on the atom. "Forces in Atom Exceed Magnetism," the headline said—with what turned out to be understatement. It was a fateful subject for Laurence. Eight years later he was chosen by the government to be the sole reporter to observe the beginning of the nuclear age. He watched the first nuclear test near Alamogordo, New Mexico, on July 16, 1945. Then he flew on the bomber that dropped the second atomic bomb on Nagasaki, Japan. His reports told the world that our lives had changed forever.

The science tradition at the *Times* eventually flowered in a weekly science section. Two prizewinning examples of its stories are included here: John Noble Wilford on the survival of a bird that had been at the brink of extinction, the brown pelican; and Natalie Angier on the newly discovered role of the female in evolution. It turns out that the female of the species looks for robust health in male courtiers, finding signs in courtship displays.

William J. Broad's article was part of a series by a number of reporters that won the *Times* the prize for explanatory journalism in 1986. The series examined the origins, the scientific basis and the politics of President Reagan's Star Wars program. Fifteen years and many arguments later, President George W. Bush pushed for a national missile defense system: the latest version of Reagan's dream.

Byrd Party Alone at Antarctic Base as Ship Puts Back

RUSSELL OWEN

Little America, Antarctica
February 25, 1929

The *City of New York*, flagship of the Byrd Antarctic expedition, has left for New Zealand, and if the supply ship *Eleanor Bolling*, which is en route here, should be turned back by ice, our little group on the Barrier will be beyond reach except by radio until next December.

It was with strangely mixed feelings that we stood at the edge of the ice yesterday and watched the tall white ship move slowly away and disappear in the mists that shrouded the Bay of Whales.

We felt alone, as if for the first time it was possible to realize how far away we were from the normal life of home, and yet glad that this part of the work was safely finished.

We turned inland over the trail, the dogs' tails flying like plumes as they trotted fast over the hard snow, parka hoods coated with frost, and the men laughing and joking and tipping each other over into the drifts.

Commander Byrd made the decision to send the *City of New York* back after sailing to the northeast to get soundings in uncharted waters and incidentally to lay bases on the Barrier for flights next year.

He was driven back by a severe storm.

The storm that checked his progress northward was the worst yet experienced down here, the wind blowing fifty miles an hour and lashing the waves into spray, which froze before it fell back into the sea or on the deck.

High winds prevailed outside, while there was comparative calm at the base on the Barrier, and the *City of New York* struck bad weather as soon as she pushed past the Capes. The tempest swept off the Barrier in chilling gusts, which drove the temperature down to twenty-nine below zero.

The cold air created a dense, low-hanging gloom of frost smoke, which swirled almost as high as the ship's masts and made an impenetrable curtain through which the lookout could see barely a hundred yards ahead. With big cakes of ice and small bergs floating about, the condition was disconcerting.

The wind became stronger as the ship went farther to the north and finally froze the surface of the water into a sort of slush through which it was difficult to force a way. The tops of the waves broke and as they were whipped into the air froze and fell back into the sea as ice.

In a short time vast areas of glasslike mush ice had been formed, several inches thick. The waves rolled under it, so that the surface of the sea undulated like a living thing that clutched at the sides of the vessel.

Small pans of ice formed with white, flowerlike crystals on them, pans that rapidly became larger and more threatening.

The commander determined to turn back, but when an attempt was made to tack it was found that ice had frozen around the rudder so thick that it was jammed.

With ice cutters fastened on long poles, men cut and chopped around the rudder post through the hole in the deck until the rudder could be freed, but even then turns had to be made very slowly.

Men's faces froze and their hands and feet were nipped as they worked. Dr. Coman, on lookout on the forecastle head, was caked in ice armor as the spray froze on his clothes.

In the midst of this turmoil things began to go wrong below. The steam valve in the boiler room froze in the cold draft that came down from above, but fortunately the one in the engine room stayed warm. Then a gasket blew out and later a high-pressure valve slipped.

These were quickly repaired, but without the engine the ship was almost helpless for a time.

While the wind was howling and the ship was lying well over, under only a reef, spanker, staysail and jib, Lloyd Berkner, the radio operator, was calmly sitting in his swaying radio room, communicating with the base on the Barrier and copying messages from all over the world congratulating Commander Byrd on his recent discoveries.

Down below Ralph Shropshire was working the sonic depth finder, taking regular soundings in an area where no soundings had been made before.

"The scientific results well warranted the hardships," said Commander Byrd.

Byrd Safely Flies to South Pole and Back

RUSSELL OWEN

Little America, Antarctica
November 30, 1929

Conqueror of two Poles by air, Commander Richard E. Byrd flew into camp at 10:10 o'clock this morning, having been gone eighteen hours and fifty-nine minutes. An hour of this time was spent at the mountain base refueling.

The first man to fly over the North and South Poles and the only man to fly over the South Pole stepped from his plane and was swept up on the arms of the men in camp who for more than an hour had been anxiously watching the southern horizon for a sight of the plane.

Deaf from the roar of the motors, tired from the continual strain of the flight and the long period of navigation under difficulties, Commander Byrd was still smiling and happy. He had reached the South Pole after as hazardous and as difficult a flight as has ever been made in an airplane, tossed by gusts of wind, climbing desperately up the slopes of glaciers a few hundred feet above the surface.

His companions on the flight tumbled out stiff and weary also, but so happy that they forgot their cramped muscles. They were also tossed aloft, pounded on the back and carried to the entrance of the mess hall.

Bernt Balchen, the calm-eyed pilot who first met Commander Byrd in Spitzbergen and who was with him on the transatlantic flight, came out first.

Men crowded about them eager for the story of what they had been through, catching fragments of sentences. It had evidently been a terrific battle to get up through the mountains to the plateau.

"We had to dump a month and a half of food to do it," said Commander Byrd. "I am glad it wasn't gas. It was nip and tuck all the way."

"Yes," chuckled Balchen. "Do you remember when we were sliding around those knolls picking the wind currents to help us and there wasn't more than three hundred feet under us at times? We were just staggering along, with drift and clouds and all sorts of things around us."

When the plane approached the mountains on the way south, Commander Byrd picked out the Livingston Glacier, a large glacier somewhat to the west of the Axel Heiberg Glacier, as the best passageway.

The high mountains shut them in all around as they forced their way upward, Balchen, conserving his fuel to the utmost, coaxing his engines, picking the upcurrents of air as best he could to help the plane ride upward.

Clouds swirled about them at times, puffballs of mist driven down the glacier; drift scurried beneath them; it was a wicked place for an airplane to be, hemmed in by the wall of the towering peaks on either side.

This was the time when they had to lighten ship and Byrd, looking around for what could best be spared, decided to dump some food. There was a dump valve in the fuselage tank, but he had determined to go through and did not know what winds he might face at the top of the glacier. So food was thrown overboard, scattered over the ridged and broken surface of the Livingston Glacier.

"It is an awful-looking place," Commander Byrd said.

They finally reached the hump at an elevation of 11,500 feet, as indicated by the barometer, although it might have been a little more, because of the difference in pressure inland.

But there was little space under the staggering plane, buffeted by the winds that eddied through the gigantic gorge. Once at the top, Balchen could level off for a time and then gain altitude.

Then there came into view slowly the long sweep of mountains of the Queen Maud Range, stretching to the southeast, and the magnificent panorama of the entire bulwark of mountains along the edge of the Polar Plateau.

"It was the most magnificent sight I have ever seen," Commander Byrd said. "I never dreamed there were so many mountains in the world. They shone under the sun, wonderfully tinted with color, and in the southeast a bank of clouds hung over the mountains, making a scene that I shall never forget."

Over the plateau the commander set his course for the pole. They had had a beam wind all the way in to the mountains, which held them up, but the fight to get over the edge of the plateau had used a lot of gasoline and there was some doubt as to whether there was enough to get back.

But Commander Byrd determined to go on. If they had favorable winds, coming back they would be all right, but if as much time was consumed coming in as going out, they would run out of gasoline.

He took the chance and won.

1930 PULITZER PRIZE FOR REPORTING

Drama of the Atomic Bomb Found Climax in July 16 Test

WILLIAM L. LAURENCE

September 26, 1945

Following is the first of a number of articles by a staff member of the New York Times *who was detached for service with the War Department at its request to explain the atomic bomb to the lay public. He witnessed the first test of the bomb in New Mexico and, on a flight to Nagasaki, its actual use.*

The Atomic Age began at exactly 5:30 Mountain War Time on the morning of July 16, 1945, on a stretch of semidesert land about fifty airline miles from Alamogordo, New Mexico, just a few minutes before the dawn of a new day on that part of the earth.

At that great moment in history, ranking with the moment in the long ago when man first put fire to work for him and started on his march to civilization, the vast energy locked within the hearts of the atoms of matter was released for the first time in a burst of flame such as had never before been seen on this planet, illuminating earth and sky for a brief span that seemed eternal with the light of many supersuns.

The elemental flame, first fire ever made on earth that did not have its origin in the sun, came from the explosion of the first atomic bomb. It was a full-dress rehearsal preparatory to use of the bomb over Hiroshima and Nagasaki—and other Japanese military targets had Japan refused to accept the Potsdam Declaration for her surrender.

The rehearsal marked the climax in the penultimate act of one of the greatest dramas in our history and the history of civilized man—a drama in which our scientists, with the Army Corps of Engineers as director, were working against time to create an atomic bomb ahead of our German enemy.

The collapse of Germany marked the end of the first act of this drama. The successful completion of our task, in the greatest challenge by man against nature so far, brought down the curtain on the second act.

The grand finale came three weeks afterward over the skies of Japan with a swift descent of the curtain on the greatest war in history.

The atomic flash in New Mexico came as a great affirmation to the prodigious labors of our scientists during the past four years, in which they managed to "know the unknowable and unscrew the inscrutable."

It came as the affirmative answer to the until then unanswered question: "Will it work?"

With the flash came a delayed roll of mighty thunder, heard, just as the flash was seen, for hundreds of miles. The roar echoed and reverberated from the distant hills and the Sierra Oscuro range near-by, sounding as though it came from some supramundane source as well as from the bowels of the earth.

The hills said "yes" and the mountains chimed "yes." It was as if the earth had spoken and the suddenly iridescent clouds and sky had joined in one mighty affirmative answer. Atomic energy—yes.

It was like the grand finale of a mighty symphony of the elements, fascinating and terrifying, uplifting and crushing, ominous, devastating, full of great promise and great forebodings.

I watched the birth of the Era of Atomic Power from the slope of a hill in the desert land of New Mexico, on the northwestern corner of the Alamogordo Air Base, about 125 miles southwest of Albuquerque. The hill, named Compania Hill for the occasion, was twenty miles to the northwest of Zero, the code name given the spot chosen for lighting the first atomic fire on this planet. The area embracing Zero and Compania Hill, twenty-four miles long and eighteen miles wide, had the code name Trinity.

I joined a caravan of three buses, three automobiles and a truck carrying radio equipment at 11 P.M. Sunday, July 15, at Albuquerque. There were about ninety of us in that strange caravan, traveling silently and in utmost secrecy through the night on probably as unusual an adventure as any in our day.

With the exception of your correspondent, the caravan consisted of scientists from the highly secret atomic bomb research and development center in the mesas and canyons of New Mexico, twenty-five miles northwest of Santa Fe, where we solved the secret of translating the fabulous energy of the atom into the mightiest weapon ever made by man. It was from there that the caravan set out at 5:30 that Sunday afternoon for its destination, 212 miles to the south.

These were the "mesa-men" on the march, dwellers in the "caves" in the interior of atoms, pioneer explorers of vast new continents in hitherto forbidden realms of the cosmos, builders of the civilization of tomorrow.

Here on trails hallowed by pioneers of other days, who opened new frontiers and did not rest until they conquered a continent, "covered wagons" were rolling again through the night on their way to open still newer frontiers of a continent that has no limits in space.

At our observation post on Compania Hill the atmosphere had grown tense as the zero hour approached. We had spent the first part of our stay partaking of an early morning picnic breakfast that we had taken along with us. It had grown cold in the desert and many of us, lightly clad, shivered. Occasionally a drizzle came down and the intermittent flashes of lightning made us turn apprehensive glances toward Zero.

We had had some disturbing reports that the test might be called off because of the weather. The radio we had brought along for communication with Base Camp kept going out of order, and when we had finally repaired it some blatant band would drown out the news we wanted to hear.

We knew there were two specially equipped B-29 Superfortresses high overhead to make observations and recordings in the upper atmosphere, but we could neither see nor hear them. We kept gazing through the blackness.

Suddenly, at 5:29:50, as we stood huddled around our radio, we heard a voice ringing through the darkness, sounding as though it had come from above the clouds:

"Zero minus ten seconds!"

A green flare flashed out through the clouds, descended slowly, opened, grew dim and vanished into the darkness.

The voice from the clouds boomed out again:

"Zero minus three seconds!"

Another green flare came down. Silence reigned over the desert. We kept moving in small groups in the direction of Zero. From the east came the first faint signs of dawn.

And just at that instant there rose from the bowels of the earth a light not of this world, the light of many suns in one.

It was a sunrise such as the world had never seen, a great green supersun climbing in a fraction of a second to a height of more than eight thousand feet, rising ever higher until it touched the clouds, lighting up earth and sky all around with a dazzling luminosity.

Up it went, a great ball of fire about a mile in diameter, changing colors as it kept shooting upward, from deep purple to orange, expanding, growing bigger, rising as it was expanding, an elemental force freed from its bonds after being chained for billions of years.

For a fleeting instant the color was unearthly green, such as one sees only in the corona of the sun during a total eclipse.

It was as though the earth had opened and the skies had split. One felt as though he had been privileged to witness the Birth of the World—to be present at the moment of Creation when the Lord said: Let There be Light.

On that moment hung eternity. Time stood still. Space contracted into a pinpoint.

To another observer, Professor George B. Kistiakowsky of Harvard, the spectacle was "the nearest thing to doomsday that one could possibly imagine."

"I am sure," he said, "that at the end of the world—in the last millisecond of the earth's existence—the last man will see what we saw!"

1946 PULITZER PRIZE FOR DISTINGUISHED REPORTING

Brown Pelican: A Dramatic Return from Disaster

JOHN NOBLE WILFORD

April 19, 1983

On Anacapa Island, off the California coast near Santa Barbara, the brown pelicans are nesting in profusion among the volcanic rocks this spring, a welcome sight to ornithologists who had once feared for their fate. Their eggs are firm and more thick-shelled than in years past. The early hatchlings feed lustily on the regurgitated anchovies in their parents' baggy gular pouches.

All is not completely well in this large breeding colony of pelicans, scientists report, but it is better than anyone dared hope a decade ago. Indeed, the three thousand pelicans that came to Anacapa to breed this year symbolize one of the most striking success stories in ecology. After some forty million years of survival, the brown pelican species seemed headed toward the brink of extinction, a victim primarily of mankind's heavy use of pesticides. But measures to curb pesticides appear to have saved the pelicans.

"The recovery of the pelicans is a major accomplishment in ecology today," said Dr. Ralph W. Schreiber, curator of ornithology at the Los Angeles County Museum of Natural History. "There are so many failures that it's good to have a success story."

Dr. Schreiber, an authority on pelican behavior, believes a case can now be made for removing these large marine birds from the government's endangered species list, though other experts caution that the birds' existence remains threatened by polluted waters and human invasions of their habitats. An ornithologist with the Office of Endangered Species, Jay M. Sheppard, said the removal of pelicans from the list is being considered, but no action is expected soon. He could not recall when a bird species had made a comeback warranting such action.

In any event, scientists plan to continue studying and monitoring the pelican as a useful early warning system of trouble lurking in the coastal ecosystem. As long as the brown pelicans in plentiful number are there standing solemn watch at docks, stretching their absurd physiognomies, taking flight like the prehistoric pterodactyls, gliding gracefully and making their headlong kamikaze dives for fish—as long as the pelicans inhabit the warmer coasts of North America, it is a sign that the waters still abound in fish and plankton and are relatively free of insidious pollutants.

A decade ago, the prognosis for the brown pelican in North America was grim. These birds had vanished from Louisiana, the Pelican State, and were seldom seen anymore along the Texas coast. Few, if any, chicks were hatching in California; only eight chicks hatched on Anacapa in 1971. The pelicans seemed to be holding their own in Florida, but barely, and the prospects were none too bright. And so the brown pelican, that wonderful bird whose "beak will hold more than his belican," in the words of the limerick, went on the endangered species list in 1973.

At the time, biologists already suspected pesticides as a major cause of the pelican's plight. Sometimes the effect was direct, poisoning the birds or their food supply. In other cases, sublethal doses of chemicals interrupted pelican reproduction.

Investigations found that endrin, a pesticide used for boll weevils and sugarcane borers, was responsible for massive fish kills in the Mississippi River delta beginning in the late 1950s. This coincided with the catastrophic decline in the pelican population along the Louisiana and Texas coasts, from fifty thousand to almost zero. Pelicans fish for a living, and the fishing was poor.

In an effort to bring the birds back, conservation agencies took young pelicans from Florida and set them up in colonies in Louisiana. By 1975, a population of almost five hundred birds was established, but suddenly some three hundred of them were found dead. Analysis determined they had lethal residues of endrin in their bodies. The pesticide was not only killing their food supply, it was poisoning the pelicans, too.

Dr. Schreiber doubts that pelicans will ever again thrive in Louisiana and Texas, despite the introduction of birds from Florida, because of diminished food supplies, oil spills and the loss of natural habitats to real estate development.

The effect of pesticides on pelican reproduction has been more subtle, though potentially disastrous, as Dr. Robert W. Risebrough, a University of California biologist, discovered when he visited Anacapa Island in 1969. He found only twelve intact eggs in the colony's three hundred nests; a pelican usually lays three eggs in a breeding season, each one twice the size of a chicken egg. All around were the remains of crushed and collapsed eggshells.

Pelicans, Dr. Risebrough concluded, shared a problem that was also threatening the future of bald eagles, peregrine falcons and other bird species. Pesticides in their food were causing these birds to lay eggs with shells so thin that they collapsed while being laid or during incubation. Upon further study, DDT was identified as the prime suspect. Insecticide residues found in pelican eggs were almost totally those of DDT and its metabolic products.

For some reason, scientists soon found, pelicans are particularly sensitive to DDT-caused eggshell thinning. The chemical gets in plankton that is eaten by the small fish that pelicans consume, and at each step up the food chain, the chemical seems to become more concentrated. Although the actual mechanism is not fully understood, Dr. Schreiber explained, a metabolic product of DDT, known as DDE, seems to block the process that transports calcium from the bloodstream through to the shell.

The problem was more acute in the California breeding colonies than elsewhere, scientists said, because large amounts of DDT wastes were being dumped in Los Angeles by the Montrose Chemical Company.

A few years after the use of DDT was banned in this country, in 1972, and after the company curtailed its dumping, pelicans resumed laying viable eggs on Anacapa. Dr. Daniel W. Anderson, professor of wildlife biology at the University of California at Davis, said a graduate student, Franklin Gress, recently visited the island and estimated fifteen hundred pairs of pelicans were nesting there. Though most of the cream-colored eggs looked durable, the shells were still about 20 percent thinner than normal.

"The pelican is recovering," Dr. Anderson said. "The population in California is increasing, but it's probably only half of what it was before the 1950s. Reproduction rates are still not what they should be, which is about one hatchling per breeding pair. I'm for being cautious about taking the pelican off the endangered list. A lot of things can happen."

One cause for lingering concern is the continued presence of pesticide residues in many adult pelicans. Many of the birds seen along the California coast breed on islands in the Gulf of California, near the agricultural regions of Mexico where DDT is still being used.

Another concern is over the pelican's sensitivity to fluctuations in its food supply. More than any other environmental factor, the availability of food is decisive in pelican breeding. Studies show that a hungry pelican is not an amorous pelican. The birds mate and nest only when they store up sufficient energy reserves for egg production and survival through the one-month incubation period.

Pelicans in Florida feed on more than thirty species of small fish, which Dr. Schreiber said probably accounted for the greater population stability there. On the Pacific coast the pelicans eat only anchovies. Consequently, commercial fishermen and conservationists have recently been eyeing each other suspiciously. The former view pelicans as competitors. The latter fear human overharvesting of anchovies will doom the pelicans. But so far, Dr. Anderson said, conflict has been avoided through federal regulations limiting the commercial anchovy catch.

Food shortages, whether natural or man-induced, have had some severe effects on breeding pelicans in California and Mexico, according to Dr. James O. Keith, a research biologist with the United States Fish and Wildlife Service. Pesticide residues in the pelicans may aggravate the problem.

Writing in the spring issue of *Oceanus*, a publication of the Woods Hole Oceanographic Institution, Dr. Keith noted that in ringdoves without DDT residues, a 10 percent reduction in food was sufficient to keep 50 percent of the birds from ever attempting to breed. In birds with DDT residues, the same reduction of food kept all pairs from breeding. This suggested "a similar pattern in brown pelicans," Dr. Keith said, because food shortages are common in their lives and DDT is still found in their bodies.

It was the prospect of losing these birds forever that led scientists to learn more about them. The brown pelican is now among the best-studied birds in the world.

Dr. Schreiber, for example, while a graduate student at the University of South Florida, studied the mating and nesting behavior of pelicans in Tampa Bay. He observed one male staking out a territory. The crown of its head, usually white, had turned yellow, a transformation marking its readiness to mate. It communicated its inclinations to a nearby female by repeated sideways movements of its head and long bill.

Once the female was won over, and their bond sealed, the two pelicans spent two weeks collecting sticks and grass for their nest while pausing frequently for copulation. After the eggs were laid, the two took turns on the nest for the month-long incubation. They fed the hatchlings for another three months; normally only one of the three eggs leads to a surviving bird. And for the surviving young birds life was a struggle through the first year; normally three-fourths of them perish.

Many fail to master the diving techniques that pelicans depend on for catching fish. Pelicans who get the diving knack, catching and eating 20 percent of their body weight in fish each day, usually live long lives of twenty-five to forty years. However, more than seven hundred pelicans in Florida, about 5 percent of the population there, die each year from entangling mishaps with fishing hooks and lines.

The brown pelican, which exists solely in the Western Hemisphere, is the only one of the seven pelican species to dive for its food. The others swim along, more like ducks, and gulp down fish.

1984 PULITZER PRIZE FOR NATIONAL REPORTING

Reagan's Star Wars Bid: Many Ideas Converging

WILLIAM J. BROAD

March 4, 1985

This is one part of a six-part comprehensive series on the Strategic Defense Initiative by several reporters from the New York Times, *including Wayne Biddle, Philip M. Boffey, William Broad, Leslie H. Gelb and Charles Mohr, which explores the scientific, political and foreign policy issues involved in Star Wars.*

In January 1982, Dr. Edward Teller, a physicist who played a central role in developing the hydrogen bomb, met with President Reagan to discuss new ways of trying to destroy enemy missiles and warheads during an attack.

It was the first of four meetings Dr. Teller would have with the president before the Star Wars speech of March 23, 1983. In that address Reagan called on American scientists to find ways of rendering nuclear weapons "impotent and obsolete."

No one—perhaps not even Reagan—can definitively list all the factors that ultimately prompted him to make his speech. Dr. Teller's counsel over the course of a year may have played a role. But so did the suggestions of key confidants, his science adviser, the Joint Chiefs of Staff and the National Security Council. Indeed, a confluence of people and ideas, of forces and counterforces, lay behind the speech, and a review of that history goes a long way toward illuminating the origins of the Strategic Defense Initiative, as it is officially called, and clarifying the debate that swirls around it today. Central to the story is Ronald Reagan himself. Even before assuming the presidency, he had expressed strong interest in trying to defend the nation from enemy missiles and had shown a curiosity about the powers of high technology. Newly elected to public office in 1967, Reagan became the first governor of California to visit the Lawrence Livermore National Laboratory in Livermore, California, one of the country's premier facilities for research on weapons and such exotic technologies as laser fusion. It had been founded by Dr. Teller in the 1950s.

"We showed him all the complex projects," Dr. Teller recalled in an interview. "He listened carefully and interrupted maybe a dozen times. Every one of his questions was to the point. He clearly comprehended the technology. And there was no skimping on time. He came in the morning and stayed over lunch."

In 1980 during the Republican presidential primary campaign, Reagan recalled a tour he had recently taken of the North American Defense Command, a secret installation in a hollowed-out mountain in Colorado, and said he was perplexed at the lack of space-based defense.

"They actually are tracking several thousand objects in space, meaning satellites of ours and everyone else's, even down to the point that they are tracking a glove lost by an astronaut," he was quoted as saying in the book *With Enough Shovels* by Robert Scheer. "I think the thing that struck me was the irony that here, with this great technology of ours, we can do all of this, yet we cannot stop any of the weapons that are coming at us. I don't think there's been a time in history when there wasn't a defense against some kind of thrust, even back in the old-fashioned days when we had coast artillery that would stop invading ships."

Reagan's sentiments were in step with those of the Republican Party, which in its platform, adopted on July 15, 1980, called for "vigorous research and development of an effective antiballistic missile system, such as is already at hand in the Soviet Union, as well as more modern ABM technologies." It also called for new offensive missiles and an "overall military and technological superiority over the Soviet Union."

Soon after the election, President-elect Reagan questioned Senator Harrison H. Schmitt—a former astronaut and chairman of the Senate Subcommittee on Science, Technology and Space—about the feasibility of building a space-age defense.

"The meeting lasted about twenty minutes," Schmitt recalled in an interview. "We were talking about science and technology in general. Then, about halfway through the session, he made a statement that he was concerned that we could not just keep building nuclear missiles forever—that ultimately their proliferation would get us into serious trouble. He asked what I thought about the possibility of strategic defense, especially with lasers. We spent half the conversation talking about it.

"When I later heard his speech, the phrases sounded very familiar," he said. "The words had the same ring."

In the early days of his administration, Reagan put his questions about space-based defense to a number of scientists and experts. Not the least enthusiastic was Dr. Teller, who maintained that he and his colleagues had found a novel way to end the strategy of Mutual Assured Destruction (MAD) that has dominated superpower relations for more than a third of a century.

In July 1983, a few month's after the Star Wars speech, Dr. Teller summarized his ideas in a letter to the president. Advances in nuclear-driven weapons, he wrote, "by converting hydrogen bombs into hitherto unprecedented forms and then directing these in highly effective fashions against enemy targets would end the MAD era and commence a period of assured survival on terms favorable to the Western alliance."

Dr. Teller's devices were known as third-generation weapons, their predecessors being the atom and hydrogen bombs.

Before the president's speech, Dr. Teller had also discussed such weapons with Dr. Hans A. Bethe, a Nobel laureate and longtime advocate of arms control. The two scientists were old friends turned foes. Both were in their seventies. Both had fled Europe because of the Nazi threat. Both had played pivotal roles in the birth of the nuclear era.

What divided them was how to deal with the Soviet Union. For decades Dr. Teller had put more faith in technology than in diplomacy to protect the United States from the threat of nuclear war.

In February 1983, the two men met at the Livermore nuclear-weapons laboratory. Dr. Teller tried to win over Dr. Bethe by revealing the top-secret details of what Dr. Teller considered the ultimate technical fix to the arms race. This was the nuclear X-ray laser, a device that would be based in space and whose powerful beams were meant to shoot down Soviet missiles. As the bomb at its core exploded, multiple beams would flash out to strike multiple targets before the whole thing consumed itself in ball of nuclear fire.

"You have a splendid idea," said Dr. Bethe, complimenting Dr. Teller on the physics of the unusual device. But novelty was not enough for the Nobel laureate. Soon he helped organize opposition to the X-ray laser and its exotic brethren, arguing that a defensive shield could easily be outwitted by an enemy. All it would take were simple countermeasures.

"We need to try to understand the other fellow and negotiate and try to come to some agreement about the common danger," Dr. Bethe said in an interview. "That is wha 's been forgotten. The solution can only be political. It would be terribly comfortable for the president and the secretary of defense if there was a technical solution. But there isn't any."

"Bethe sees the future in a too-easy manner," Dr. Teller said in an interview. "He was there at the birth of quantum mechanics, and he was there when we constructed the first atom bomb. Now he says there won't be anything new under the sun. Hasn't he seen enough new things?"

For decades Dr. Teller had searched for technologies that could defend the country from the threat of enemy H-bombs. "It would be wonderful," he wrote in *The Legacy of Hiroshima*, his 1962 book, "if we could shoot down approaching missiles before they could destroy a target in the United States."

Technology at the time was too feeble for the job, but Dr. Teller warned that the West should be watchful lest the needed break-throughs were made elsewhere.

"If the Communists should become certain that their defenses are reliable and at the same time know that ours are insufficient," he wrote, "Soviet conquest of the world would be inevitable."

His fear was unstated but clear. An aggressor with a good shield might be tempted to use his spear, confident he could deflect the weapon of his opponent.

In pursuit of breakthroughs over the decades, Dr. Teller has often relied on the labors of gifted young researchers at his Liver-more weapons laboratory. Some of them have fellowships from a program that Dr. Teller helps administer as a board member of the Hertz Foundation, which was founded in the 1940s by the Hertz rental-car family. Over the years the Hertz board has included such prominent conservatives as J. Edgar Hoover, director of the Federal Bureau of Investigation; General Curtis E. LeMay, head of the Stra-tegic Air Command; and Herman H. Kahn, founder of the Hudson Institute.

It now supports about 120 graduate students every year and has assets of about $14 million. According to the foundation's directory, the weapons laboratory is the largest single employer of Hertz fellows and alumni, having at least twenty-nine of them. The fellows at the laboratory, who work there while pursuing their doctorates, are some of the brightest.

According to a recent brochure, the foundation has an "express interest in fostering the technological strength of America" and "requires all fellows to morally commit themselves to make their skills and abilities available for the common defense, in the event of national emergency."

The foundation's president, Dr. Wilson K. Talley, is chairman of the Pentagon's Army Science Board and is a professor at the Univer-sity of California at Davis/Livermore, a graduate school at the weapons laboratory whose $1 million facility was built with the help of Hertz funds. Asked if the foundation had been a catalyst in Star Wars, he replied: "We've been supporting people for years all over the country in computer science, materials science and nuclear physics. We've attempted to be elitist. Only one out of fifteen who apply get a fellow-ship. And those fifteen have A-minus averages. So it's not suprising that some of the brightest brains in the Strategic Defense Initiative happen to be Hertz fellows."

Dr. Teller was once "coordinator" of the foundation's fellowship project. That job is now held by Dr. Lowell L. Wood Jr., a protege of Dr. Teller's at Livermore. The foundation's address is a post office box.

The foundation's role in the genesis of Star Wars was driven home on November 14, 1980, the day the X-ray laser first rumbled to life in a nuclear explosion beneath the Nevada desert. The test was code-named Dauphin. The inventor of the device was Peter L. Hagelstein, a Hertz fellow.

Three months later, the magazine *Aviation Week & Space Technology* carried an exclusive article that identified no sources but described the top-secret test in detail.

"The X-ray lasers based on the successful Dauphin test, when mounted in a laser battle station," it said, "are so small that a single payload bay on the space shuttle could carry to orbit a number sufficient to stop a Soviet nuclear-weapons attack."

In May 1981, Dr. George A. Keyworth II was named the president's science adviser. A nuclear physicist, he was intimately familiar with the X-ray secrets and had been strongly endorsed for the job by Dr. Teller.

Also in 1981, a group of influential scientists, industrialists, military men and aerospace executives began to meet in Washington, D.C., at the Heritage Foundation, a conservative "think tank." Their goal was to formulate a plan for creating a national system of defense. Among them were Dr. Teller, Dr. Wood and such members of the president's "kitchen cabinet" as Joseph Coors, a beer executive, Justin Dart, a wealthy businessman, and Jacquelin Hume, an industrialist.

The group's top officer was Karl R. Bendetsen, once undersecretary of the army, later chairman of the board of the Champion International Corporation, and a longtime overseer of the Hoover Institution on War, Revolution and Peace. Since the 1940s he had known Dr. Teller, who in addition to his weapons work also held a post at Hoover. The group's second-in-command was Lieutenant General Daniel O. Graham, retired from the army, once head of the Defense Intelligence Agency. All group members received security clearances so they could learn about and discuss secret details of new technologies and weapons.

But by late 1981 the group began to split over differing visions of how to carry out the task of space-based defense. Bendetsen, Dr. Teller and the Reagan "kitchen cabinet" separated into a small group to investigate sophisticated proposals that would require much more research before being ready to use, while General Graham and his group, known formally as High Frontier, emphasized systems that could be built primarily from "off the shelf."

Another factor in the split, according to General Graham, was that Dr. Teller insisted on the inclusion of third-generation weapons powered by nuclear bombs. "He wanted very much to leave in the nuclear options," the general said. "The man is carrying a load and has taken a lot of abuse as the 'father' of the H-bomb. Now he wants to see nuclear technology turn out to be the answer in the opposite direction, to save the Western world."

The split had vast implications in terms of presidential access. Bendetsen and his friends visited the White House with ease. General Graham did not.

And this division went to the heart of a dispute that today haunts the Pentagon's search for a defensive shield—the rivalry between basic scientists and applied scientists. On one side are the national laboratories, universities and contractors that carry out basic research on such directed-energy weapons as lasers and particle beams. Systems based on their results might be decades away. On the other side are contractors who want to quickly turn dollars into demonstration projects and are pushing for quick deployment of prototypes.

The winners have tended to be the barons of basic research. An example can be seen at the Sandia National Laboratory, one of three facilities in the nation for the design and development of nuclear weapons. Based in Albuquerque, New Mexico, it is about to break ground on a $70 million center to investigate Star Wars technologies, both nuclear and nonnuclear. About 10 percent of the Strategic Defense Initiative's budget is devoted to the development of nuclear weapons.

Indeed, the recommendation taken to the president by Bendetsen and his group was to start a stepped-up program of advanced research rather than trying to create a defense with "off the shelf" technology. The first meeting occurred in January 1982. Dr. Teller was present.

"The president expressed great interest," recalled a source intimately familiar with the meeting. The conversation, he said, focused on directed-energy weapons that might be used to destroy aircraft as well as missiles. There was much talk of lasers. The group told Reagan that the Pentagon was experimenting with lasers that might have only limited capacity because their wavelength was too long.

The shorter a laser's wavelength, the more destructive energy it can pour onto a target. The laser that now holds the record for short wavelength is the X-ray laser.

The January 1982 meeting at the White House had been scheduled to last fifteen minutes. It went on for an hour.

General Graham, denied access to the president, took his case to the public. In February he issued the High Frontier report, a 175-page book filled with a detailed description of the group's vision as well as color sketches of defensive battles in space.

In its foreword, General Graham recalled the group's search for "a technological end-run on the Soviets" and said it had "led inexorably to space."

"The U.S. advantage in space is demonstrated in its most dramatic form by the Space Shuttle," he wrote. "More fundamentally, the ability of the United States to miniaturize components gives us great advantages in space where transport costs-per-pound are critical. Today a pound of U.S. space machinery can do much more than a pound of Soviet space machinery. It also happened that the technologies immediately available for military systems—beyond intelligence, communication and navigation-aid satellites—are primarily applicable to ballistic missiles defense systems."

In an interview, General Graham said he was personally able to deliver the recommendations of the High Frontier panel to General John W. Vessey Jr., who soon after became the chairman of the Joint Chiefs of Staff. "He was pretty positive from the very beginning," General Graham said.

Although Dr. Teller had access to the president, it was access in which others controlled the time and agenda. His group met with the president five times in all—three times before the speech and twice afterward.

White House sources said Dr. Teller got an additional, private meeting through the following incident. In June 1982 Dr. Teller taped a segment of the *Firing Line* television program, hosted by William F. Buckley Jr., and complained that he had been denied presidential access.

"May I tell you one little secret which is not classified?" Dr. Teller asked. "From the time that President Reagan has been nominated I had not a single occasion to talk to him."

When aired on national television, Dr. Teller's comment brought an invitation from the White House. He had a private meeting with the president in September 1982, according to White House sources, although Dr. Teller refuses to confirm or deny that he had any meetings with the president on Star Wars before Reagan's speech.

Also on the *Firing Line* program, Dr. Teller and Buckley discussed why someone might invent new weapons to counter the threat of Soviet missiles.

Buckley: "I'm certainly not asking you to solve the problem of original sin. But we do know that somebody figured out how to take several hundred million tons of explosives and launch them in the Soviet Union and make them fall in the United States. Now, it is a challenge that would fall within the apparent competence of the same scientists who invented that to invent something that would frustrate that. The same people who invent fighter airplanes that get in the way—that sink submarines—are the same kind of people who invent submarines, right?"

Teller: "You have explained a good part, an important part, of my own psychology."

In the first two years of the Reagan administration, the X-ray laser was a government secret. No official was to admit that it existed. That silence was broken on January 14, 1983, when the president's science adviser, Dr. Keyworth, gave a talk at the Livermore laboratory, where the device had been invented. There he praised the "bomb-pumped X-ray laser" as being "one of the most important programs that may seriously influence the nation's defense posture in the next decades."

In the early months of 1983, the pace of presidental meetings and consultations over a national defense program began to quicken. Reagan again met with the Teller-Bendetsen group. On February 11 the president met with the Joint Chiefs of Staff. Although that meeting was scheduled to focus on the MX missile, Reagan is said to have kept the discussion centered on defensive systems for half an hour.

Robert C. McFarlane, then deputy national security adviser, Dr. Keyworth and Mr. Reagan himself have all been credited with having written the crucial parts of the March 23 speech.

After its delivery, Dr. Teller hailed the president in a March 30 article written for the *New York Times*.

"Today, a wide range of good and ingenious technical plans, ranging from simple to extraordinarily complex, challenge the widespread opinion that practical defense cannot be obtained," he said. "Mr. Reagan did not lightly accept the idea that these can be made to work. He wanted to know a vast number of details. He asked questions of his science adviser, George Keyworth, and of many other scientists, myself included. He then decided that something must and can be done."

The president's speech took some of his advisers by surprise and was later criticized by Alexander M. Haig Jr., former secretary of state. In a talk at the Livermore weapons laboratory in August 1984, he charged that the speech had been poorly timed and prepared.

"The White House guys said, 'Hey, boss, come on. You're going to make a big splash. Big P.R. You're going to look like the greatest leader in America. Get out there and give that speech.' And he did," Mr. Haig said. "But the preparation had not been made. I know the aftermath the next day in the Pentagon, where they were all rushing around saying, 'What the hell is strategic defense?' "

Critics charge that parts of the Star Wars saga have little to do with strategic defense. They point to such statements as Dr. Teller's "terms favorable to the Western alliance" and General Graham's "technological end-run on the Soviets" and say one aim is to achieve military superiority.

"What they came up with is a technical edge that looks totally pacific," said Dr. Jeremy J. Stone, director of the Federation of American Scientists.

"There's always been a school of thought that says we should try to challenge the Soviets with technology," said Dr. Sidney D. Drell, a Stanford University physicist and coauthor of a study that disparages Star Wars. "And this is clearly one way to do it."

In general, critics say that "technical edges" have always tended to disappear, leaving the world less stable and filled with more weapons. They note that it took just a few years for the Russians to catch up to the United States in A-bombs, H-bombs and multiple independently targeted warheads.

Defenders of the president's plan deny that they are searching for a technical edge and say trying to defend the nation is feasible, morally sound and a rational alternative to the idea of mutual terror.

"I've listened very hard to the arguments of the critics," said Dr. Steven D. Rockwood, associate director for defense research programs at the Los Alamos National Laboratory, the birthplace of the atomic bomb. "They're not technical, although the critics try to put technical clothing on them. They're theological or philosophical."

Defenders point to some "philosophical" statements that suggest that nuclear weapons and the "balance of terror" have played a useful role in keeping the peace between the superpowers.

General Graham says such logic is faulty. "It appears that adherence to MAD has preserved the peace or kept us from major conflict," he said. "The reality is that we can continue to say that up until the day the missiles begin to fly."

Whatever the factors that led to the Star Wars speech, an irony of the saga is that the X-ray laser, which helped bring it about, has now fallen out of official favor. In recent months, both the president and Secretary of Defense Caspar W. Weinberger have repeatedly stressed that the Strategic Defense Initiative is searching for "nonnuclear" weapons to shoot down enemy missiles.

"We have begun research on a nonnuclear defense against nuclear attack," Reagan told a group of Nobel laureates and other scientists in February. "You on the cutting edge of technology have already made yesterday's impossibilities the commonplace realities of today. Why should we start thinking small now?"

According to Pentagon officials, some of the reasons that nuclear-defensive weapons have lost their luster include: the existence of a treaty barring their predeployment in space; the time constraints of trying to quickly get them into space during an attack; the damage in space that exploding nuclear weapons would inflict on nearby satellites; and the paradox of trying to make nuclear weapons "impotent and obsolete" by means of a new generation of nuclear weapons.

Under the auspices of the Strategic Defense Initiative, billions of dollars are still earmarked to flow into the development of third-generation nuclear weapons, the X-ray laser among them. But Pentagon officials say these weapons are now seen as being useful mainly as antisatellite and "counterdefensive" weapons. An X-ray laser, for instance, might be used to knock out Soviet defensive battle stations so American retaliatory missiles could get through.

But the X-ray laser, which had been envisioned as destroying Soviet missiles and thus, as Dr. Teller put it in his letter to the president, to "end the MAD era," is no longer assigned the main job.

A lingering question no one can answer is whether Star Wars would have happened in the absence of the X-ray laser. Reagan was obviously ripe for the idea of strategic defense. And so, it seemed, was a variety of new technologies, Dr. Teller's among them.

"I can see how Edward was attracted to all this," said a scientific colleague of Dr. Teller's who has long known and respected him. "The X-ray laser was elegant. It was beautiful and elegant. It was technically sweet, just like Oppenheimer said. But is Edward an engineer? No. Is he a systems designer? No. Is he a military planner? No.

"He was enthralled with the principle and rightly so," he said. "The principle is in fact that beautiful. But he is not the kind of guy who ever got hooked on building things. His first H-bomb was the size of an apartment house. Edward is a physicist with a fantastic creative mind. He understands the beauty of a piece of music. But for God's sake, don't ask him to design a trumpet."

1986 PULITZER PRIZE FOR EXPLANATORY JOURNALISM

Hard-to-Please Females May Be Neglected Evolutionary Force

NATALIE ANGIER

May 8, 1990

What do females want? Every man who has ever rolled his eyes heavenward in apparent bafflement at this great enigma might do well to follow the example of evolutionary biologists: stop speculating and start paying attention to the evidence at hand.

In laboratories and field research stations across the United States and abroad, biologists are analyzing an evolutionary force that has long been neglected: the effect of female choice on the appearance and performance of males.

The new results indicate that many of the mysterious and seemingly irrelevant courtship rituals and male displays in the animal kingdom serve a crucial purpose of allowing a female to judge the robustness or health of her potential mate before committing herself to the union.

Biologists have suspected for years that certain flamboyant features among males, like the peacock's Technicolor tail and the bullfrog's booming moonlight sonatas, evolved for no other purpose than to allow males to curry favor with females. But many researchers dismissed the role of female choice as a minor influence in evolution of animal traits compared with the ability to elude predators or defend territory, or with warlike competition among males for access to mates.

Now the female animal is finally coming into her own in the biological arena. Galvanized by new research tools and more sophisticated evolutionary theories, biologists are designing experiments to measure precisely the features that entice females to mate with one male rather than another.

Through elaborate statistical analyses and, in some cases, laboratory manipulations, biologists who study courtship in animals are replacing what Harvard biologist Stephen Jay Gould has called *Just So Stories*— the Rudyard Kipling short stories—with rigorous data.

"We're trying to do experimental work where we manipulate characteristics, to see how changing these traits changes what the female does," said Marlene Zuk, a biologist at the University of California at Riverside. "In that way we can begin teasing apart what a female is actually choosing, not just what we think makes good sense for her to be choosing."

The latest findings, published in recent issues of *Nature* and presented at several international meetings, suggest that females of many species pay particularly close attention to telltale signs of parasitism or disease. As a result, the males often sport skin colorations or feather patterns to signal robust health, which then become accentuated or exaggerated over generations of selection by females.

Some female birds and frogs demand of their suitors in courtship a performance that pushes the males to their cardiovascular limits, perhaps as a test of the hardiness of the males' genes.

In other species, especially insects, a female will refuse a male's sexual overtures unless he offers her some sort of nuptial gift, usually a defensive chemical that she can use to protect herself or her eggs.

The long-term consequences of female choice affect the character-istics of females as well as of their mates, scientists say; daughters presumably inherit from their mothers a predisposition to favor certain masculine traits over others.

Biologists emphasize that they are just beginning to understand the complex dynamics of female choice, and that the whys and wherefores of female taste remain elusive for the great majority of species. "Female choice is more subtle than something like male-male com-petition, because it affects not only the evolution of the male, but of female preference," said Dr. Mark Kirkpatrick, a zoologist at the Uni-versity of Texas in Austin. Nevertheless, he added, "it's definitely the wave of the future in biology."

Charles Darwin proposed in 1872 that female animals could exert pressure on the evolution of their species in their mating decisions, but the theory was largely slighted for almost a century. It began its comeback in the mid-1970s, when biologists turned away from studies of amorphous group behavior among animals and instead focused on the actions and reproductive strategies of individuals in a species.

Fleshing out the ideas of Darwin and other pioneering naturalists, animal behaviorists proposed that females usually have a larger stake in reproduction than males do. The stake is especially high in female mammals that bear their young and then care for the off-spring after birth. But even for insects and fish, which invest far less time in rearing young, the amount of energy needed to produce the nutrients, fat and protein of an egg is greater than that required for generating sperm.

"Eggs are expensive," said Dr. Thomas Eisner, an evolutionary biol-ogist at Cornell University. "Sperm is cheap."

Given their greater investment in reproduction, say biologists, females have greater incentive than males to seek the best possible mate. Males that want to pass their legacy to future generations must either appeal to females, or suffer a genetic dead end.

Perhaps the most straightforward work on the fine points of female finickiness has come in species where the female seeks material help from the male in the rearing or protection of the young.

In ongoing investigations of the courtship behavior of a beetle spe-cies called *pyrochroidae*, Dr. Eisner, Dr. Jerrold Meinwald and their colleagues have determined why the male beetle goes through the peculiar ritual of displaying to a potential mate a deep cleft in his forehead. The researchers have found that stashed within the cleft is a small dose of the chemical cantharidin, familiarly known as Spanish fly.

The source of the male beetle's cantharidin is still mysterious, though Dr. Eisner suspects that it comes from eating the eggs of another insect, the blister beetle. During courtship, the male exposes his cleft to the female, she grabs his head and immediately laps up the chemical offering. Apparently placated, she allows the male to mate.

The Cornell scientists have determined that the male transfers to the female a much larger quantity of cantharidin during intercourse, and that she subsequently incorporates the chemical into her eggs, which thenceforth are protected against ants and other common predators of beetle eggs.

"The male gives her a little teaser during foreplay," said Dr. Eisner. "It's as though he's showing her a fat wallet and saying, 'There's more in the bank where that came from.' "

To prove the central importance of cantharidin, the scientists raised male beetles in the lab, where they had no access to the chemical. True to the theory, the cantharidin-free males failed dismally at mating. "Ninety percent of the males with cantharidin eventually manage to mate, but less than 20 percent of the cantharidin-free males succeed," said Dr. Eisner. "Only the ones that literally rape-mount the female get anywhere at all."

Less obvious than a nuptial gift is what a female seeks when she chooses on the basis of a male's appearance. In an experiment described in a recent issue of *Nature*, scientists from the University of Bern in Switzerland examined the impact of a male's coloration on female choice among the three-spined stickleback, a small fish.

The researchers knew that in breeding season, the male stickleback turns a bright red and, upon changing color, it displays itself before a female in a mating dance of zigs and zags. The biologists also knew that males exposed to parasites turned a dimmer shade of red, even after shaking off the parasitic disease. Their question: Did females prefer males that possessed the bright-red color signaling current and prior health?

To address the problem, they tested female responsiveness to groups of brilliant red males and dimmer, previously parasitized males under natural white light, in which the females could see the intensity of the red color, and under green light, which disguised the relative tones.

The scientists found that when females could distinguish red males from their drearier counterparts, the females almost uniformly paired up with the brighter males, although both groups of suitors performed the zigzag courtship dance with equal zest.

By comparison, females choosing males beneath a green light arbitrarily picked males of either color.

Dr. Zuk believes that female birds also are preoccupied with parasites. In experiments with red jungle fowl, the ancestors of barnyard chickens, she and Dr. Randy Thornhill and Dr. David Ligon, biologists at the University of New Mexico in Albuquerque, identified the specific ornaments that most attracted a hen to a rooster. The biologists found that hens paid closer attention to the condition of the male's comb and wattle than to any other characteristic, including size, weight, the aggressiveness of his strutting, or the state of his feathers.

The longer the comb and the brighter the wattle, the more likely the hen was to choose him over a competing rooster. As it turns out, combs and wattles are also the traits by which farmers judge the health of their flock.

"The females didn't seem to care how big the rooster was, or whether his feathers were smooth," said Dr. Zuk. "It's the fleshy parts, the wattle, the comb color and size, that can change in a matter of days depending on parasitism, and that's what the hen seemed to be looking at."

Beyond resistance to disease, another factor that females seem to find alluring is stamina. Dr. H. Carl Gerhardt, a biologist at the University of Missouri in Columbia, has analyzed the calls of gray tree frogs. Male frogs sit for days attempting to attract females by repeating a series of trilling pulses that they can vary in both length of individual pulses and timing between pulses.

Studying the physiology of the calls, Dr. Gerhardt and his colleagues discovered that male frogs consume an extraordinary amount of oxygen and deplete their body's fuel rations to generate their croons. "It's energetically demanding," he explains. "The frog reaches the same metabolic rate during calling that you get by forcing him to exercise to exhaustion. It's as though the female was asking him to push against his physiological limit."

Dr. Gerhardt also has used electronic frog calls in an attempt to determine if females are drawn to artificial sounds that exceed the calling capacity of the hardiest real frog. Generating synthetic pulses through one speaker at a normal song rate and through another at twice that rate, the team has found that female frogs leap wildly in the direction of the fast-trilling speakers, sometimes attempting to embrace the singing machine.

Other species of frog also prefer the most athletic callers, said Dr. Gerhardt. In this way, he suggested, "the females assure that they avoid the obvious wimps."

Because a male tree frog contributes nothing to the business of reproduction beyond his genes—no defensive chemicals and no caring for the young—a female selecting a male for stamina presumably hopes to gain from the exchange the probability of begetting vigorous young.

But proving that hardy males sire hardy offspring has been difficult and the subject of great contention among biologists. Some of the strongest evidence supporting the link has come lately from Dr. Anders Moller, a biologist at the University of Uppsala in Sweden. He has studied barn swallows, in which the males have tails that are about 20 percent longer than those of the female.

Dr. Moller first determined that female choice had determined the long tails of the male. He cut feathers off the tails of some male birds, and glued extra feathers to the tails of others.

When permitted to choose between the short-tails and the long-tails, the females invariably selected the more amply endowed males.

Dr. Moller next investigated possible reasons for the female preference. Like other researchers, he found a link between the chosen males and resistance to parasites. The longer-tailed males had measurably fewer blood-sucking mites on their bodies than did the short-tails.

To investigate whether the long-tailed birds had some sort of genetic resistance to the mites the biologist decided to follow the swallows through several generations. More significantly, he switched the eggs that had been fertilized by long-tailed males with those spawned by shorter-tailed males, to offset the contributions of environmental factors.

After making the switches, he infected the nests of all the birds with the same number of mites. Dr. Moller found that, as they grew,

young birds of either sex sired by the long-tailed males had significantly fewer parasites on their bodies than did the offspring of short-
tailed males.

The chicks' resistance to mites had no correlation to which nest
they were in, or to the number of parasites crawling across their foster
parents' feathers, but rather was determined by the relative parasite
load on the natural father, a strong indication that resistance is
hereditary.

Why long tails and resistance correspond remains mysterious, but
a female actively chooses the longest-tailed mate around, apparently
in an effort to bequeath to her young the best possible genetic legacy.

"About fifteen percent of males never seem to get the chance to
mate," he said. "And they are almost always the males with the short-
est tails."

Biologists warn that what is true for barn swallows may not turn
out to be true for other animals. Many of them believe that many cases
of female choice will prove to be somewhat arbitrary—that a female
pairs up with an especially loud male, for example, just because he is
the one she hears.

"The ultimate question always is, does the female really get anything out of the choice she makes?" said Robert Gibson, a biologist at
the University of California at Los Angeles who studies female choice
in the sage grouse. "Is she really making a choice, or does it just seem
that way to us? In so many cases, we still don't know."

1991 PULITZER PRIZE FOR BEAT REPORTING

SEVEN

Up Close

PRIVATE LIFE AND PUBLIC LIFE

The lead story in the *New York Times* of December 23, 1935, commanded a four-column headline at the top of page one. It began as follows:

> Colonel Charles A. Lindbergh has given up residence in the United States and is on his way to establish his home in England. With him are his wife and three-year-old son, Jon.
>
> Threats of kidnapping and even death to the little lad, recurring repeatedly since his birth, caused the father and mother to make the decision. These threats have increased both in number and virulence recently.

The story won its author, Lauren D. Lyman, a Pulitzer Prize. From the vantage point of the next century, that must seem remarkable—as does the *Times*'s big play of the news that a man who held no office was moving to England. But Charles Lindbergh was an object of fascination like no one else in that time, from the triumph of his solo flight across the Atlantic to the tragedy of his first son's kidnapping and murder.

Lindbergh was an intensely private man whose fame made him suffer the endless prying of photographers and reporters. Lyman, known as "The Deacon" and more familiarly as "Deac," had become a friend of Lindbergh's after covering him—with respect—from the time of the flight to Paris in 1927. That relationship enabled him to get what *Editor and Publisher* called "one of those rarities of modern journalism—a clear-cut, unconfirmable scoop on a story of international first-ranking." It was unconfirmable, by other papers, because

Lindbergh and his family were aboard a ship on the Atlantic when the Lyman exclusive appeared, and the ship's officers turned away wireless queries.

Today it is hard to imagine that kind of play for such a story, if it existed, in the *Times*. Celebrity journalism, degraded far below the standards of Deac Lyman and the *Times*, is the staple of television, supermarket tabloids and *People* magazine. But the human personality has not lost its fascination for the editors of the *Times* or its readers.

The prizewinning stories that follow appeared over five decades. They are highly diverse in subject and style, but they all focus on individuals. The pieces appear here as they were originally published, with just some cuts for reason of space.

The first story, by Meyer Berger, is an extraordinary example of reportorial skill. Berger was a beloved figure in the *Times* newsroom, a quiet, quizzical man. He was at his desk on September 6, 1949, when shortly before 11 A.M. the city desk told him there had been shootings in Camden, New Jersey, and assigned him to cover the story. He caught the train, spent most of the day finding out what had happened and began filing in late afternoon. He finished what was a four-thousand-word story at 9:20 P.M., about an hour before the first edition closed. Not many reporters then, or ever, could have put together the chronology of Howard Unruh's rampage with such sureness under unrelenting pressure of time.

"The Two Worlds of Linda Fitzpatrick," by J. Anthony Lukas, was a very different kind of journalism: not written under deadline pressure but produced over days of intensive exploration and reflection. Linda Fitzpatrick, who came from a well-to-do family in Connecticut, was found murdered in Greenwich Village with a hippie friend on October 8, 1967. Her parents were unhappy with newspaper reports that painted her as a hippie. Lukas was assigned to talk with them.

The parents showed him Linda's neat room in their home and said she had a nice job in Greenwich Village and lived in a pleasant hotel. But when Lukas looked into it, he found a different reality: a squalid, drug-ridden life in the Village. It was difficult for reporter and editors to deal with such a story, but they thought it was important because it threw light on the gap between parents and children at the time— the late 1960s—when that was a widespread and dangerous phenomenon. Readers saw the story that way, writing to the *Times* in large numbers about what it meant to them, parents and children.

Alex S. Jones won a prize for specialized reporting in 1987 for articles on the family dissension that brought a newspaper dynasty to an end at the *Louisville* (Kentucky) *Courier-Journal*. Barry Bingham, unable to bring his quarreling heirs to an agreement, decided to sell the paper. It was more than a private decision and private story because the general truth is that only ownership by a family committed to journalism of high quality—like the Sulzberger family at the *New York Times*—can maintain a great newspaper. After Alex Jones's reporting on the Bingham famly, the *Courier-Journal* was sold to the Gannett chain.

Isabel Wilkerson's hero is a ten-year-old boy, Nicholas Whitiker, who lives and goes to school in a black ghetto in Chicago. He is forced, Wilkerson writes, "to be a man, to answer for the complicated universe he calls family." Through the particular of that young life we glimpse the general: the grim reality of life at the bottom of American society, among people who cannot even reach for the bottom rung of the ladder.

Robert D. McFadden is a model of a less-known figure in daily journalism, the rewrite man. He takes telephone reports from several reporters who may cover a big story and weaves them together. In his account of death in Harlem he was able, stunningly, to step back and re-create the scene as it unfolded.

Then there is Rick Bragg's account of how a South Carolina sheriff unraveled the story told by Susan Smith—that a black man had taken her car and two little boys—and got her to confess that she herself had drowned them. No larger social moral here, just writing of literary quality.

The *Times* series on how race is lived in America, which won a Pulitzer in 2001, demonstrated that consciousness of race remains a prime fact of life in this country. It made the point not by generalities or statistics but by fifteen individual stories: of the white and black members of a Georgia church, of army sergeants, of workers in a slaughterhouse. The piece reprinted here describes two refugees from Cuba who were friends there, hardly affected by their different colors, but in Florida have moved into separate worlds.

Veteran Kills Twelve in Mad Rampage

MEYER BERGER

Camden, New Jersey
September 7, 1949

Howard B. Unruh, twenty-eight years old, a mild, soft-spoken veteran of many armored artillery battles in Italy, France, Austria, Belgium and Germany, killed twelve persons with a war souvenir Luger pistol in his home block in East Camden this morning. He wounded four others.

Unruh, a slender, hollow-cheeked six-footer paradoxically devoted to scripture reading and to constant practice with firearms, had no previous history of mental illness but specialists indicated tonight that there was no doubt that he was a psychiatric case, and that he had secretly nursed a persecution complex for two years or more.

The veteran was shot in the left thigh by a local tavern keeper but he kept that fact secret, too, while policemen and Mitchell Cohen, Camden County prosecutor, questioned him at police headquarters for more than two hours immediately after tear-gas bombs had forced him out of his bedroom to surrender.

The bloodstain he left on the seat he occupied during the questioning betrayed his wound. When it was discovered, he was taken to Cooper Hospital in Camden, a prisoner charged with murder.

He was as calm under questioning as he was during the twenty minutes that he was shooting men, women and children. Only occasionally excessive brightness of his dark eyes indicated that he was anything other than normal.

He told the prosecutor that he had been building up resentment against neighbors and neighborhood shopkeepers for a long time. "They have been making derogatory remarks about my character," he said. His resentment seemed most strongly concentrated against Mr. and Mrs. Maurice Cohen, who lived next door to him. They are among the dead.

Mr. Cohen was a druggist with a shop at 3202 River Road in East Camden. He and his wife had had frequent sharp exchanges over the Unruhs' use of a gate that separates their backyard from the Cohens'.

Mrs. Cohen had also complained of young Unruh's keeping his bedroom radio tuned high into the late-night hours. None of the other victims had ever had trouble with him.

Unruh, a graduate of Woodrow Wilson High School here, had started a GI course in pharmacy at Temple University in Philadelphia some time after he was honorably discharged from the service in 1945, but had stayed with it only three months. In recent months he had been unemployed, and apparently was not even looking for work.

His mother, Mrs. Rita Unruh, fifty, is separated from her husband. She works as a packer in the Evanson Soap Company in Camden and hers was virtually the only family income. James Unruh, twenty-five years old, her younger son, is married and lives in Haddon Heights, New Jersey. He works for the Curtis Publishing Company.

On Monday night, Howard Unruh left the house alone. He spent the night at the Family Theatre on Market Street in Philadelphia to sit through several showings of the double feature motion picture there—*I Cheated the Law* and *The Lady Gambles*. It was past three o'clock this morning when he got home.

Prosecutor Cohen said that Unruh told him later that before he fell asleep this morning he had made up his mind to shoot the persons who had "talked about me," that he had even figured out that 9:30 A.M. would be the time to begin because most of the stores in his block would be open at that hour.

His mother, leaving her ironing when he got up, prepared his breakfast in their drab little three-room apartment in the shabby, gray two-story stucco house at the corner of River Road and Thirty-second Street. After breakfast he loaded one clip of bullets into his Luger, slipped another clip into his pocket, and carried sixteen loose cartridges in addition. He also carried a tear-gas pen with six shells and a sharp six-inch knife.

He took one last look around his bedroom before he left the house. On the peeling walls he had crossed pistols, crossed German bayonets, pictures of armored artillery in action. Scattered about the chamber were machetes, a Roy Rogers pistol, ashtrays made of German shells, clips of 30-30 cartridges for rifle use and a host of varied war souvenirs.

Mrs. Unruh had left the house some minutes before, to call on Mrs. Caroline Pinner, a friend in the next block. Mrs. Unruh had sensed, apparently, that her son's smoldering resentments were coming to a head. She had pleaded with Elias Pinner, her friend's husband, to cut a little gate in the Unruhs' backyard so that Howard need not use the Cohen gate again. Mr. Pinner finished the gate early Monday evening after Howard had gone to Philadelphia.

At the Pinners' house at nine o'clock this morning, Mrs. Unruh had murmured something about Howard's eyes; how strange they looked and how worried she was about him.

A few minutes later River Road echoed and re-echoed to pistol fire. Howard Unruh was on the rampage. His mother, who had left the Pinners' little white house only a few seconds before, turned back. She hurried through the door.

She cried, "Oh, Howard, oh, Howard, they're to blame for this." She rushed past Mrs. Pinner, a kindly gray-haired woman of seventy. She said, "I've got to use the phone; may I use the phone?"

But before she had crossed the living room to reach for it she fell on the faded carpet in a dead faint. The Pinners lifted her onto a couch in the next room. Mrs. Pinner applied aromatic spirits to revive her.

While his mother writhed on the sofa in her housedress and worn old sweater, coming back to consciousness, Howard Unruh was walking from shop to shop in the "3200 block" with deadly calm, sporting Luger in hand. Children screamed as they tumbled over one another to get out of his way. Men and women dodged into open shops, the women shrill with panic, men hoarse with fear. No one could quite understand for a time what had been loosed in the block.

Unruh first walked into John Pilarchik's shoe repair shop near the north end of his own side of the street. The cobbler, a twenty-seven-year-old man who lives in Pennsauken Township, looked up open-mouthed as Unruh came to within a yard of him. The cobbler started up from his bench but went down with a bullet in his stomach. A little boy who was in the shop ran behind the counter and crouched there in terror. Unruh walked out into the sunlit street.

"I shot them in the chest first," he told the prosecutor later, in meticulous detail, "and then I aimed for the head." His aim was devastating—and with reason. He had won marksmanship and sharpshooters' ratings in the service, and he practiced with his Luger all the time on a target set up in the cellar of his home.

Unruh told the prosecutor afterward that he had Cohen the druggist, the neighborhood barber, the neighborhood cobbler and the neighborhood tailor on his mental list of persons who had "talked about him." He went methodically about wiping them out. Oddly enough, he did not start with the druggist, against whom he seemed to have the sharpest feelings, but left him almost for the last.

From the cobbler's he went into the little tailor shop at 3214 River Road. The tailor was out. Helga Zegrino, twenty-eight years old, the tailor's wife, was there alone. The couple, incidentally, had been married only one month. She screamed when Unruh walked in with his Luger in hand. Some people across the street heard her. Then the gun blasted again and Mrs. Zegrino pitched over, dead. Unruh walked into the sunlight again.

All this was only a matter of seconds and still only a few persons had begun to understand what was afoot. Down the street at 3210 River Road is Clark Hoover's little country barber shop. In the center was a white-painted carousel-type horse for children customers. Orris Smith, a blond boy only six years old, was in it, with a bib around his neck, submitting to a shearing. His mother, Mrs. Catherine Smith, forty-two, sat on a chair against the wall and watched.

She looked up. Clark Hoover turned from his work, to see the six-footer, gaunt and tense, but silent, standing in the doorway with the Luger. Unruh's brown tropical worsted suit was barred with morning shadow. The sun lay bright in his crew-cut brown hair. He wore no hat. Mrs. Smith could not understand what was about to happen.

Unruh walked to "Brux"—that is Mrs. Smith's nickname for her little boy—and put the Luger to the child's chest. The shot echoed and reverberated in the little twelve-by-twelve shop. The little boy's head pitched toward the wound, his hair, half-cut, stained with red. Unruh said never a word. He put the Luger close to the shaking barber's hand. Before the horrified mother, Unruh leaned over and fired another shot into Hoover.

The veteran made no attempt to kill Mrs. Smith. He did not seem to hear her screams. He turned his back and stalked out, unhurried. A few doors north, Dominick Latela, who runs a little restaurant, had come to his shop window to learn what the shooting was about. He saw Unruh cross the street toward Frank Engel's tavern. Then he saw Mrs. Smith stagger out with her pitiful burden. Her son's head lolled over the crook of her right arm.

Mrs. Smith screamed "My boy is dead. I know he's dead." She stared about her, looking in vain for aid. No one but Howard Unruh was in sight, and he was concentrating on the tavern. Latela dashed out, but first he shouted to his wife, Dora, who was in the restaurant with their daughter Eleanor, six years old. He hollered, "I'm going out. Lock the door behind me." He ran for his car, and drove it down toward Mrs. Smith as she stood on the pavement with her son.

Latela took the child from her arms and placed him on the car's front seat. He pushed the mother into the rear seat, slammed the doors and headed for Cooper Hospital. Howard Unruh had not turned. Engel, the tavern keeper, had locked his own door. His customers, the bartender, and a porter made a concerted rush for the rear of the saloon. The bullets tore through the tavern door paneling. Engel rushed upstairs and got out his .38 caliber pistol, then rushed to the street window of his apartment.

Unruh was back in the center of the street. He fired a shot at an apartment window at 3208 River Road. Tommy Hamilton, two years old, fell back with a bullet in his head. Unruh went north again to Latela's place. He fired a shot at the door, and kicked in the lower glass panel. Mrs. Latela crouched behind the counter with her daughter. She heard the bullets, but neither she nor her child was touched. Unruh walked back toward Thirty-second Street, reloading the Luger.

Now the little street—a small block with only five buildings on one side, three one-story stores on the other—was shrill with women's and children's panicky outcries. A group of six or seven little boys or girls fled past Unruh. They screamed, "Crazy man!" and unintelligible sentences. Unruh did not seem to hear, or see, them.

Alvin Day, a television repairman who lives in nearby Mantua, had heard the shooting, but driving into the street he was not aware of what had happened. Unruh walked up to the car window as Day rolled by, and fired once through the window, with deadly aim. The repairman fell against the steering wheel. The car seemed to wabble. The front wheels hit the opposite curb and stalled. Day was dead.

Frank Engel had thrown open his second-floor apartment window. He saw Unruh pause for a moment in a narrow alley between the cobbler's shop and a little two-story house. He aimed and fired. Unruh stopped for just a second. The bullet had hit, but he did not seem to mind, after the initial brief shock. He headed toward the corner drug store, and Engel did not fire again.

"I wish I had," he said, later. "I could have killed him then. I could have put a half-dozen shots into him. I don't know why I didn't do it."

Cohen, the druggist, a heavy man of forty, had run into the street shouting "What's going on here? what's going on here?" but at sight of Unruh hurried back into his shop. James J. Hutton, forty-five, an insurance agent from Westmont, New Jersey, started out of the drug shop to see what the shooting was about. Like so many others he had figured at first that it was some car backfiring. He came face to face with Unruh.

Unruh said quietly, "Excuse me, sir," and started to push past him. Later Unruh told the police: "That man didn't act fast enough. He didn't get out of my way." He fired into Hutton's head and body. The insurance man pitched onto the sidewalk and lay still.

Cohen had run to his upstairs apartment and had tried to warn Minnie Cohen, sixty-three, his mother, and Rose, his wife, thirty-eight, to hide. His son Charles, fourteen, was in the apartment, too. Mrs. Cohen shoved the boy into a clothes closet, and leaped into another closet herself. She pulled the door to. The druggist, meanwhile, had leaped from the window onto a porch roof. Unruh, a gaunt figure at the window behind him, fired into the druggist's back. The druggist, still running, bounded off the roof and lay dead in Thirty-second Street.

Unruh fired into the closet where Mrs. Cohen was hidden. She fell dead behind the closed door, and he did not bother to open it. Mrs. Minnie Cohen tried to get to the telephone in an adjoining bedroom to call the police. Unruh fired shots into her head and body and she sprawled dead on the bed. Unruh walked down the stairs with his Luger reloaded and came out into the street again.

A coupe had stopped at River Road, obeying a red light. The passengers obviously had no idea of what was loose in East Camden and no one had a chance to tell them. Unruh walked up to the car, and though it was filled with total strangers, fired deliberately at them, one by one, through the windshield.

Sergeant Earl Wright, one of the first to leap to the sidewalk, saw Charles Cohen, the druggist's son. The boy was half out the second-floor apartment window, just above where his father lay dead. He was screaming, "He's going to kill me. He's killing everybody." The boy was hysterical.

Wright bounded up the stairs to the druggist's apartment. He saw the dead woman on the bed, and tried to soothe the druggist's son. He brought him downstairs and turned him over to other policemen, then joined the men who had surrounded the two-story stucco house where Unruh lived. Unruh, meanwhile, had fired about thirty shots. He was out of ammunition. Leaving the Harrie house, he had also heard the police sirens. He had run through the back gate to his own rear bedroom.

Edward Joslin, a motorcycle policeman, scrambled to the porch roof under Unruh's window. He tossed a tear-gas grenade through a pane of glass. Other policemen, hoarsely calling on Unruh to surrender, took positions with their machine guns and shotguns. They trained them on Unruh's window.

Meanwhile, a curious interlude had taken place. Philip W. Buxton, an assistant city editor on the *Camden Evening Courier*, had looked Unruh's name up in the telephone book. He called the number, Camden 4-2490W. It was just after 10 A.M. and Unruh had just returned to his room. To Mr. Buxton's astonishment Unruh answered. He said hello in a calm, clear voice.

"This Howard?" Mr. Buxton asked.

"Yes, this is Howard. What's the last name of the party you want?"

"Unruh."

The veteran asked what Mr. Buxton wanted.

"I'm a friend," the newspaperman said. "I want to know what they're doing to you down there."

Unruh thought a moment. He said, "They haven't done anything to me—yet. I'm doing plenty to them." His voice was still steady without a trace of hysteria.

Mr. Buxton asked how many persons Unruh had killed.

The veteran answered: "I don't know. I haven't counted. Looks like a pretty good score."

"Why are you killing people?"

"I don't know," came the frank answer. "I can't answer that yet. I'll have to talk to you later. I'm too busy now."

The telephone banged down.

Unruh was busy. The tear gas was taking effect and police bullets were thudding at the walls around him. During a lull in the firing the police saw the white curtains move and the gaunt killer came into plain view.

"Okay," he shouted. "I give up. I'm coming down."

"Where's that gun?" a sergeant yelled.

"It's on my desk, up here in the room," Unruh called down quietly. "I'm coming down."

Thirty guns were trained on the shabby little back door. A few seconds later the door opened and Unruh stepped into the light, his hands up. Sergeant Wright came across the morning-glory and aster beds in the yard and snapped handcuffs on Unruh's wrists.

"What's the matter with you," a policeman demanded hotly. "You a psycho?"

Unruh stared into the policeman's eyes—a level, steady stare. He said, "I'm no psycho. I have a good mind."

Word of the capture brought the whole East Camden populace pouring into the streets. Men and women screamed at Unruh, and cursed him in shrill accents and in hoarse anger. Someone cried "lynch him" but there was no movement. Sergeant Wright's men walked Unruh to a police car and started for headquarters.

Shouting and pushing men and women started after the car, but dropped back after a few paces. They stood in excited little groups discussing the shootings, and the character of Howard Unruh. Little by little the original anger, born of fear, that had moved the crowd began to die.

Men conceded that he probably was not in his right mind. Those who knew Unruh kept repeating how closemouthed he was, and how soft-spoken. How he took his mother to church, and how he marked scripture passages, especially the prophecies.

"He was a quiet one, that guy," a man told a crowd in front of the tavern. "He was all the time figuring to do this thing. You gotta watch them quiet ones."

But all day River Road and the side streets talked of nothing else. The shock was great. Men and women kept saying: "We can't understand it. Just don't get it."

1950 PULITZER PRIZE FOR LOCAL REPORTING

The Two Worlds of Linda Fitzpatrick

J. ANTHONY LUKAS

October 16, 1967

The windows of Dr. Irving Sklar's reception room at Two Fifth Avenue look out across Washington Square. A patient waiting uneasily for the dentist's drill can watch the pigeons circling Stanford White's dignified Washington Arch, the children playing hopscotch on the square's wide walkways and the students walking hand in hand beneath the American elms.

"Certainly we knew the Village; our family dentist is at Two Fifth Avenue," said Irving Fitzpatrick, the wealthy Greenwich, Connecticut, spice importer whose daughter, Linda, was found murdered with a hippie friend in an East Village boiler room a week ago yesterday.

Mr. Fitzpatrick spoke during a three-hour interview with his family around the fireplace in the library of their thirty-room home a mile from the Greenwich Country Club.

For the Fitzpatricks, "the Village" was the Henry James scene they saw out Dr. Sklar's windows and "those dear little shops" that Mrs. Fitzpatrick and her daughters occasionally visited. ("I didn't even know there was an East Village," Mr. Fitzpatrick said. "I've heard of the Lower East Side, but the East Village?")

But for eighteen-year-old Linda—at least in the last ten weeks of her life—the Village was a different scene whose ingredients included crash pads, acid trips, freaking out, psychedelic art, witches and warlocks.

If the Fitzpatricks' knowledge of the Village stopped at Washington Square, their knowledge of their daughter stopped at the unsettling but familiar image of a young, talented girl overly impatient to taste the joys of life.

Reality in both cases went far beyond the Fitzpatricks' wildest fears—so far, in fact, that they are still unable to believe what their daughter was going through in her last weeks.

It is perhaps futile to ask which was "the real Linda"—the Linda of Greenwich, Connecticut, or the Linda of Greenwich Village. For, as the *New York Times* investigated the two Lindas last week through interviews with her family and with her friends and acquaintances in the Village, it found her a strange mixture of these two worlds, a mixture so tangled that Linda probably did not know in which she belonged.

The last weeks of Linda's life are a source of profound anguish for her parents. The forces at work on young people like Linda are the source of puzzlement for many other parents and of studies by social workers and psychologists, as they seek to understand the thousands of youths who are leaving middle-class homes throughout the country for the "mind-expanding drug" scene in places like Greenwich Village.

Until a few months ago, Linda—or "Fitzpoo," as she was known to her family and friends—seemed to be a happy, well-adjusted product of wealthy American suburbia.

"Linda is a well-rounded, fine, healthy girl," her mother, a well-groomed blonde in a high-collared chocolate brown dress, said during the interview in Greenwich. Throughout the interview, Mrs. Fitzpatrick used the present tense in talking of her daughter.

Born in Greenwich, Linda attended the Greenwich Country Day School, where she excelled in athletics. She won a place as center forward on the "Stuyvesant Team," the all–Fairfield County field hockey team, and also gained swimming and riding awards. She went on to the Oldfields School, a four-year college preparatory school in Glencoe, Maryland.

A blonde tending to pudginess, she never quite matched the striking good looks of her mother, who as Dorothy Ann Rush was a leading model and cover girl in the thirties, or of her elder sister, Cindy.

At country club dances, Linda often sat in the corner and talked with one of her half brothers; but, apparently more interested in sports and painting than dancing, she never seemed to mind very much.

According to her family, Linda's last summer began normally. In mid-June she returned from Oldfields after an active year during which she was elected art editor of the yearbook. She spent several weeks in Greenwich, then left with the family for a month in Bermuda.

"The family always takes its summer vacations together; we always do things as a family," said Mr. Fitzpatrick, a tall, athletic-looking man in a well-tailored gray suit, blue tie and gold tie clip. "Sometimes we went to Florida, sometimes to the Antibes, but for the past few summers we've rented a house in Bermuda. This time it was at Paget."

The family included seven children—Linda and nine-year-old Melissa ("Missy") from this marriage; Perry, thirty-two, Robert, thirty, Carol, twenty-seven, and David, twenty-five, from Mr. Fitzpatrick's first marriage, which ended in divorce; and Cindy from Mrs. Fitzpatrick's first marriage, which also ended in divorce. But this time only Linda and Missy accompanied their parents to Bermuda, while Cindy and her husband joined them later for ten days.

As the Fitzpatricks remember it, Linda spent "a typical Bermuda vacation"—swimming in the crystal ocean; beach parties on the white sands; hours of painting; occasional shopping expeditions to town.

On July 31 the family returned to Greenwich, where Linda spent most of August. Again, the family insists she was "the girl we knew and loved."

They say she spent most of her time painting in the studio in the back of her house. But she found plenty of time for swimming with friends in the large robin's egg–blue pool, playing the piano, and sitting with Missy.

"Linda and Missy were terribly close," their mother said, biting her lip. "Just as close as Cindy and Linda were when they were younger."

If Linda went to New York during August, the family said, it was "just a quick trip in and out—just for the day."

The "Village" Version

Friends in the Village have a different version of Linda's summer.

"Linda told me she took LSD and smoked grass [marijuana] many times during her stay in Bermuda," recalls Susan Robinson, a small, shy hippie who ran away last May from her home on Cape Cod. "She talked a lot about a fellow who gave her a capsule of acid [LSD] down there and how she was going to send him one."

Susan and her husband, David, who live with two cats and posters of Bob Dylan, Timothy Leary, Allen Ginsberg and D. H. Lawrence in a two-room apartment at 537 East Thirteenth Street, first met Linda when she showed up there some time early in August.

The Robinson apartment served this summer as a "crash pad"—a place where homeless hippies could spend the night or part of the night. Scrawled in pencil on the tin door to the apartment is a sign that reads: "No visitors after midnight unless by appointment please." It is signed with a flower.

"Linda just showed up one evening with a guy named Pigeon," Susan recalls. "She'd just bought Pigeon some acid. We were fooling around and everything. She stayed maybe a couple of hours and then took off.

"But we liked each other, and she came back a few nights later with a kid from Boston. She turned him on, too [gave him some LSD]. She was always doing that. She'd come into the city on weekends with thirty dollars or forty dollars and would buy acid for people who needed some."

David Robinson, a gentle young man with a black D. H. Lawrence beard who works in a brassiere factory, recalls how Linda turned him on on August 22. "We went to this guy who sold us three capsules for ten dollars apiece," he said. "She put one away to send to the guy in Bermuda, gave me one and took one herself. She was always getting burned [purchasing fake LSD] and that night she kept saying, 'God, I just hope this is good.' We were out in the Square [Tompkins Park] and we dropped it [swallowed it] right there. Forty-five minutes later—around midnight— we were off.

"We walked over to a pad on Eleventh Street just feeling the surge, then over to Tompkins Park, then to Cooper Union Square, where we had a very good discussion with a drunk. By then we were really flying. She was very, very groovy. At 8 A.M. I came back to the pad to sleep, and Linda took the subway up to Grand Central and got on the train to Greenwich. She must still have been flying when she got home."

That weekend in Greenwich Mrs. Fitzpatrick was getting Linda ready for school. "We bought her almost an entire new wardrobe," she recalled, "and Linda even agreed to get her hair cut."

For months Mr. Fitzpatrick had complained about Linda's hair, which flowed down over her shoulders, but Linda didn't want to change it. Then at the end of August she agreed. "We went to Saks Fifth Avenue and the hairdresser gave her a kind of Sassoon blunt cut, short and full. She looked so cute and smart. Hardly a hippie thing to do," Mrs. Fitzpatrick said.

The first day of school was only eleven days off when Linda went to New York on September 1. When she returned to Greenwich the next day, she told her mother she didn't want to go back to Oldfields. She wanted to live and paint in the Village.

"We couldn't have been more surprised," Mrs. Fitzpatrick said, fingering her eyeglasses, which hung from a gold pin at her left shoulder.

"Linda said her favorite teacher, who taught English, and his wife, who taught art, weren't coming back. She just adored them—when they went to Europe she just had to send champagne and fruit to the boat—and she couldn't face going back to school if they weren't there.

"What's more, she said there wasn't anything else she could learn about art at Oldfields. They'd already offered to set up a special course for her there, but she didn't want more courses. She just wanted to paint. She thought she'd be wasting her time at school."

Mother and daughter talked for nearly two hours that Saturday morning of the Labor Day weekend. Then Mrs. Fitzpatrick told her husband, who at first was determined that Linda should finish school.

"But we talked about it with all the family and with friends all through the weekend," Mr. Fitzpatrick recalls. "Finally, on Sunday night, we gave Linda our reluctant permission, though not our approval." Linda left for New York the next morning and the family never saw her alive again.

"After all," her mother put in, "Linda's whole life was art. She had a burning desire to be something in the art world. I knew how she felt. I wanted to be a dancer or an artist when I was young, too."

The Fitzpatricks' minds were eased when Linda assured them she had already made respectable living arrangements. "She told us that she was going to live at the Village Plaza Hotel, a very nice hotel on Washington Place, near the university, you know," her mother said.

" 'I'll be perfectly safe, mother,' she kept saying. 'It's a perfectly nice place with a doorman and television.' She said she'd be rooming with a girl named Paula Bush, a twenty-two-year-old receptionist from a good family. That made us feel a lot better."

The Village Plaza, 79 Washington Place, has no doorman. A flaking sign by the tiny reception desk announces "Television for Rental" amidst a forest of other signs: "No Refunds," "All Rents Must Be Paid in Advance," "No Checks Cashed," "No Outgoing Calls for Transients."

"Sure I remember Linda," said the stooped desk clerk. "But Paula Bush? There wasn't no Paula Bush. It was Paul Bush."

Ruffling through a pile of stained and thumb-marked cards, he came up with one that had Linda Fitzpatrick's name inked at the top in neat Greenwich Country Day School penmanship. Below it in pencil was written: "Paul Bush. Bob Brumberger."

"Yeh," the clerk said. "She moved in here on September 4, Labor Day, with these two hippie guys, Bush and Brumberger. They had Room 504. She paid the full month's rent—$120—in advance. Of course, she had lots of other men up there all the time. Anybody off the street—the dirtiest, bearded hippies she could find.

"I kept telling her she hadn't ought to act like that. She didn't pay me

any attention. But you know she never answered back real snappy like some of the other girls. She was different. She had something—I don't know, class. The day she checked out—oh, it was about September 20—I was out on the steps, and as she left she said, 'I guess I caused you a lot of trouble,' and I said, 'Oh, it wasn't any trouble, really.'

"You want to see the room? Well, there are some people up there now, but I think it'll be OK."

The elevator was out of order. The stairs were dark and narrow, heavy with the sweet reek of marijuana. A knock, and the door to 504 swung open. A bearded young man took his place again on the swaybacked double bed that filled half the room. The young man and three girls were plucking chocolates out of a box.

Against one of the light green walls was a peeling gray dresser, with the upper left drawer missing. Scrawled on the mirror above the dresser in what looked like eyebrow pencil was "Tea Heads Forever" (a tea head is a marijuana smoker) and in lighter pencil, "War is Hell." Red plastic flowers hung from an overhead light fixture. The bathroom, directly across the hall, was shared with four other rooms.

"Would you like to see Linda's room?" her mother asked, leading the way up the thickly carpeted stairway. "That used to be her room," she said, pointing into an airy bedroom with a white, canopied bed, "until she began playing all those records teenagers play these days and she asked to move upstairs so she could make all the noise she wanted."

On the third floor Mrs. Fitzpatrick opened the red curtains in the large room. "Red and white are Linda's favorite colors; she thinks they're gay," Mrs. Fitzpatrick said, taking in the red and white striped wallpaper, the twin beds with red bedspreads, the red pillow with white lettering: "Decisions, Decisions, Decisions."

Orange flashed here and there—in the orange and black tiger on the bed ("that's for her father's college, Princeton; we're a Princeton family") and in the orange "Gs" framed on the wall, athletic awards from Greenwich Country Day School.

On the shelves, between a ceramic collie and a glass Bambi, were Edith Hamilton's *The Greek Way* and Agatha Christie's *Murder at Hazelmoor*. Nearby were a stack of records, among them Eddie Fisher's *Tonight* and Joey Dee's *Peppermint Twist*. In the bright bathroom hung blue and red ribbons from the Oldfields Horse Show and the Greenwich Riding Association Show.

"As you can see, she was such a nice, outgoing, happy girl," her mother said. "If anything's changed, it's changed awfully fast."

Downstairs again, over ginger ale and brownies that Cindy brought in from the kitchen, the Fitzpatricks said they had been reassured about Linda's life in the Village because she said she had a job making posters for "Poster Bazaar" at eighty dollars a week.

"Later she called and said she'd switched to a place called Imports, Limited, for eighty-five dollars a week and was making posters on weekends. She sounded so excited and happy," Mrs. Fitzpatrick recalled.

Nobody the Times *interviewed had heard of a store called Poster Bazaar. At 177 Macdougal Street is a shop called Fred Leighton's Mexican Imports, Ltd., where, the records show, Linda worked for two dollars an hour selling dresses for three days—September 11, 12 and 13. On the third day she was discharged.*

"She was always coming in late, and they just got fed up with her," *a salesgirl said. Although Linda was given a week's notice, she left on September 14 for a "doctor's appointment" and never came back.*

Before she left, she asked the manager not to tell her parents she had been discharged, if they called. The manager said the parents did not call after Linda left, although there had been one call while she was working there.

David Robinson said Linda supported herself from then on by "panhandling" on Washington Square. "She was pretty good at it," he said. "She always got enough to eat."

Linda may have had some money left over from what her mother gave her before she left ("I gave her something," Mrs. Fitzpatrick said. "I thought she was going to be a career girl"), although she never had very much those last weeks.

Yet, David recalls, Linda frequently talked about making big money. "She had a thing about money. Once she told me she wanted to get a job with Hallmark cards drawing those little cartoons. She said she'd make forty thousand dollars a year, rent a big apartment on the Upper East Side and then invite all her hippie friends up there."

"We're a great card-exchanging family," Cindy said. "Whenever the occasion arose—birthdays, holidays, illnesses—Linda would make up her own cards and illustrate them with cute little pictures of people and animals."

From a pile on the hall table, Cindy picked out a card with a picture of a girl and an inked inscription, "Please get well 'cause I miss ya, love Linda XOX." In the same pile was a Paris street scene in pastels, two forest scenes made with oils rolled with a Coke bottle, several other gentle landscapes. "Linda was experimenting with all sorts of paints and techniques," Cindy said.

"You want to see some of the paintings she did down here?" asked Susan Robinson, as she went to a pile of papers in the corner and came back with five ink drawings on big white sheets from a sketching pad.

The drawings were in the surrealistic style of modern psychedelic art: distorted women's faces, particularly heavily lidded eyes, dragons, devils, all hidden in a thick jungle of flowers, leaves and vines, interspersed with phrases in psychedelic script like, "Forever the Mind," "Flyin High," "Tomorrow Will Come."

"Linda was never terribly boy crazy," her mother said. "She was very shy. When a boy got interested in her, she'd almost always lose interest in him. She got a proposal in August from a very nice boy from Arizona. She told me, 'He's very nice and I like him, but he's just too anxious.' The boy sent flowers for the funeral. That was thoughtful."

The Robinsons and her other friends in the Village said there were always men in Linda's life there: first Pigeon, then the boy from Boston, then Paul Bush.

Bush, the nineteen-year-old son of a Holly, Michigan, television repairman, is described by those who knew him here as "a real drifter, a way-out hippie." He carried a live lizard named Lyndon on a string around his neck. Bush, who says he left New York on October 4, was interviewed by telephone in San Francisco yesterday.

"I met Linda at the Robinsons about August 18—a few days after I got to town," he recalls. "We wandered around together. She said her parents bugged her, always hollered at her.... So I said I'd get a pad with her and Brumberger, this kid from New Jersey.

"She said she'd tell her parents she was living with a girl named Paula Bush, because she didn't want them to know she was living with a man. That was OK with me. I only stayed about a week anyway, and Brumberger even less. Then she brought in some other guy. I don't know who he was, except he was tall with long hair and a beard."

This may have been Ed, a tall hippie who the Robinsons saw with Linda several times in mid-September. Later came James L. (Groovy) Hutchinson, the man with whom she was killed last week.

Toward the end of September, Susan Robinson says Linda told her she feared she was pregnant. "She was very worried about the effect of LSD on the baby, and since I was pregnant, too, we talked about it for quite a while."

"I don't believe Linda really had anything to do with the hippies," her father said. "I remember during August we were in this room watching a CBS special about the San Francisco hippies. I expressed my abhorrence for the whole thing, and her comments were much like mine. I don't believe she was attracted to them."

However, Linda's half brother Perry recalls that during August Mr. Fitzpatrick also read a story about Galahad, a New York hippie leader, and expressed his "disdain" for him. Linda mentioned casually that she had met Galahad and that she understood he was "helping people," but her father let the remark pass, apparently considering it of no significance.

Her friends say Linda was fascinated by the scene in the Haight-Ashbury section of San Francisco. In late September she apparently visited there.

Susan Robinson recalls that she did not see Linda for some time in late September and that suddenly, on October 1, Linda turned up at her pad and said she had been to Haight-Ashbury. "She said she stayed out there only two days and was very disappointed; that it was a really bad scene; that everybody was on speed [a powerful drug called methedrine]. She said she got out and drove back."

In the first week of October, the Fitzpatricks got a postcard postmarked Knightstown, Indiana, a small town thirty miles east of Indianapolis. Mrs. Fitzpatrick did not want to show the card to a visitor because "it was the last thing I've got which Linda touched." But she said it read roughly: "I'm on my way to see Bob [her brother, who is a Los Angeles lawyer]. Offered a good job painting posters in Berkeley. I love you. I will send you a poster. Love, Linda."

Also in the first week of October a girl who identified herself as Linda telephoned her brother's office in Los Angeles but was told he was in San Francisco. She never called back.

When Linda saw Susan on October 1 she told her she had met two warlocks, or male witches, in California and had driven back with them.

"This didn't surprise me," Susan said. "Linda told me several times she was a witch. She said she had discovered this one day when she was sitting on a beach and wished she had some money. Three dollar bills floated down from heaven.

"*Then she looked down the beach and thought how empty it was and wished there was someone there. She said a man suddenly appeared. She was always talking about her supernatural powers. Once she was walking on a street in the Village with this girl Judy, and she stumbled over a broom. 'Oh,' she told Judy, 'this is my lucky day. Now I can fly away.' *"

"One of the newspapers said Linda was interested in Buddhism and Hinduism and all that supernatural stuff," Cindy said. "That's not true at all. I don't think she ever even knew what it was."

Last Friday a self-styled warlock who said he was one of the two who drove Linda back to New York was interviewed in the Village. The warlock, who called himself "Pepsi," is in his late twenties, with long, sandy hair, a scruffy beard, heavily tattooed forearms, wire-rim glasses and long suede Indian boots.

"*My buddy and I ran into Linda in a club in Indianapolis called the Glory Hole,*" *Pepsi said.* "*We took Linda along. You could see right away she was a real meth monster—that's my name for a speed freak, somebody hooked on speed.*

"*We were two days driving back. We got in on October 1 and she put up with me and my buddy in this pad on Avenue B. She was supposed to keep it clean, but all she ever did all day was sit around. She had this real weird imagination, but she was like talking in smaller and smaller circles. She was supposed to be this great artist, but it wasn't much good. It was just teeny bopper stuff—drawing one curving line, then embellishing it.*

"*It sounds like I'm knocking her. I'm not. She was a good kid, if she hadn't been so freaked out on meth. She had a lot of, what do you call it—potential. Sometimes she was a lot of fun to be with. We took her on a couple of spiritual seances, and we went out on the Staten Island Ferry one day at dawn and surfing once on Long Island.*"

Pepsi saw Linda at 10 P.M. Saturday, October 8, standing in front of the Cave on Avenue A with Groovy. She said she'd taken a grain and a half of speed and was "high." Three hours later she and Groovy were dead—their nude bodies stretched out on the boiler-room floor, their heads shattered by bricks. The police have charged two men with the murders and are continuing their investigation.

"It's too late for the whole thing to do us much good," her brother Perry said on Saturday after he had been told of her life in the Village. "But maybe somebody else can learn something from it."

1968 PULITZER PRIZE FOR LOCAL INVESTIGATIVE SPECIALIZED REPORTING

The Fall of the House of Bingham

ALEX S. JONES

Louisville, Kentucky
January 19, 1986

"It's a sad day for all of us," said Paul Janensch, executive editor of the *Courier-Journal* and the *Louisville Times*, hoarsely addressing several hundred somber coworkers who had jammed the company cafeteria to consider their uncertain future. It was 3 P.M. on Friday, January 10, the day after the abrupt announcement that the Bingham family, the glamorous and tortured clan that had owned the newspapers for almost seventy years, was selling out.

The decision to sell was a shock, but not a surprise. For two years the staff had watched as the Binghams warred with each other over the family holdings. Finally, in desperation, Barry Bingham Sr., the seventy-nine-year-old patriarch, decided to sell, hoping that his decision would somehow bring a semblance of peace to the family. What it brought initially was a blistering accusation of betrayal from Barry Bingham Jr., the son who has run the family companies since the early 1970s.

Barry Jr. resigned in anger and was in the cafeteria to speak. "In my proprietorship here," he said, "I've tried to operate these companies so that none of you would be ashamed of the man you work for."

When he had finished, the employees rose as one in a standing ovation. Many wept. But the applause was not entirely for Barry Jr., it was also for his stand against selling. And the tears were for themselves, for the uncertain future of the newspapers, for the tragedy of the Binghams and for the passing of an era.

News of the sale prompted a flood of expressions of grief, mostly from Kentuckians, mourning the end of the Bingham stewardship. Under the Binghams, the *Courier-Journal* won eight Pulitzer Prizes, establishing the newspaper as one of the finest in America.

For large families struggling with the problems of multigenerational ownership of a business, the saga of the Binghams and their failure to hold together was particularly poignant. And for the dwindling number of families still operating their own newspapers, the news from Louisville was chilling.

For the proud Binghams—a clan of southern patricians who are often compared to the Kennedys because they share a history of tragic death and enormous wealth—the pain of selling was redoubled because it may have been avoidable. It is not financial duress forcing the sale, but implacable family strife, as ancient as the struggle between Cain and Abel.

A week of interviews with the key family members, with many of their employees and with their friends has revealed the details of the Bingham family feud. From the interviews comes a portrait of a family both hugely blessed and critically flawed, a family caught in a dispute that it was unable to resolve.

"It became increasingly clear that there was just no way out of the emotional tangle we'd fallen into," Barry Sr. said. "In bringing up my children, I somehow did not get across to them that people have to make compromises."

In the drama, there is no single villain, nor a hero or healer who might have bridged the gulf of distrust and anger. In the end, a powerful gridlock developed among the three Bingham children—Barry Jr., Sallie and Eleanor. Their parents, convinced that no amicable way could be found to keep the business in the family, elected to sell all the holdings. It was a decision that Barry Sr. said he made now so that he and his eighty-one-year-old wife could face the trauma together.

In part, the roots of the crisis may lie in the family's enormous wealth that allowed the Bingham children to grow up in what Sallie calls a "golden dream," creating a generation of Binghams used to their own way. The parents' insistence on unruffled family relations and their distaste for overt emotion left Barry Jr. and his sisters without the need to forge deep relationships with each other as children— relationships they might have called upon to resolve their impasse as adults.

Running through the Binghams' story are the devastating deaths of two sons. The death of Worth Bingham, the firstborn, haunted Barry Jr., who eventually took over stewardship of the newspapers, the role intended for his older brother. In recent years, Barry Jr.'s devastating sense that he was losing the family's confidence seemed to make him dig in his heels so rigidly that he invited the decision to sell—perhaps, as Sallie says, in an unconscious wish to be delivered of his burden.

Sallie, now a determined feminist, emerged as a chief protagonist in the saga. Her resistance to Barry Jr.'s decision to remove her from the boards of the family businesses set in motion what became the final crisis.

At the end, even Eleanor, the younger and more conventional sister, who had tried to maintain her family ties, opposed her brother—as implacable in her way as the others.

Now that the decision to sell has been made, a number of media companies are competing to buy the Bingham properties—the Courier-Journal and Louisville Times Company, WHAS Inc., which includes a television station and two radio stations, and Standard Gravure, a commercial printing operation. They are expected to bring about $400 million, with the families of each of Barry Sr.'s children likely to receive about $40 million.

But the family peace that Barry Bingham Sr. and his wife, Mary, hoped for seems far, far away.

"Scale the characters down, and it's definitely Faulknerian," said Robert Bingham, the nineteen-year-old grandson of Barry Sr., comparing his family to the tortured Mississippi delta families of William Faulkner's novels.

Just as Faulkner's fictional characters plumb the past seeking explanations for the pain of the present, the Binghams tend to look far back to pick up the threads of their undoing.

The Binghams, like the Kennedys, started poor, certainly in comparison with their present great wealth. Barry Sr.'s great-great-grandfather, a Scotch-Irish immigrant, founded the Bingham School, a secondary school, in North Carolina shortly after the American Revolution. Barry Sr.'s great-grandfather was also a teacher; so was his grandfather, Robert Bingham, a Confederate soldier, who returned to North Carolina after the Civil War and worked at educating freed slaves.

But Robert's son, Robert Worth Bingham, became a lawyer and moved to Louisville in 1896, at the age of twenty-five, eventually becoming the city's mayor and a circuit court judge. He lost his first wife in 1913 when a car in which she was riding was hit by a train. Barry Sr. was seven years old when his mother died; his brother and sister not much older.

Three years later, Judge Bingham, as he was then and forever after known, married Mary Kenan Flagler, the widow of an oil tycoon with a $100 million estate. Judge Bingham signed a prenuptial agreement stating that, upon her death, he would receive $5 million from her estate. As Barry Sr. tells the story in a memo to his children, Judge Bingham insisted on the prenuptial agreement, even though without it he would have been entitled to half his wife's fortune.

Eight months after their wedding, the new Mrs. Bingham died, apparently of cardiac arrest. But her brothers accused Judge Bingham and her doctors of conspiring to poison her and the body was exhumed. An autopsy revealed that the cause of death was, indeed, cardiac arrest, and her brothers dropped the charges.

In 1918, Judge Bingham bought, for $1 million, a majority interest in the *Courier-Journal* and the *Louisville Times*, which even then were Kentucky's premier newspapers. He also acquired a forty-acre estate overlooking the Ohio River, a few miles outside Louisville, and on it a huge red-brick Georgian mansion where Barry Jr. now lives. Judge Bingham christened the estate "Melcombe," after an estate in Dorset, England, where Binghams had lived since the twelfth century. The judge had another house built on the estate, which, though generous, was smaller than the mansion and came to be called the "Little House." Barry Sr. and his wife, Mary, live there today. The judge was an ardent Democrat and a supporter of the League of Nations, and his newspapers reflected his views. In the 1930s, he backed the New Deal and President Roosevelt rewarded him in 1933 with the ambassadorship to the Court of St. James. Judge Bingham died in London in 1937 and the next ambassador was Joseph Kennedy.

By then, Judge Bingham's younger son, Barry Sr., a magna cum laude graduate of Harvard, was deeply immersed in the family business, which had grown to include WHAS Inc.—then an AM radio station—and Standard Gravure. He alone had moved back to Louisville; his brother and sister spent most of their lives in England and Barry Sr. soon bought them out.

He was thirty-two years old when his father died, a handsome, garrulous and charming man with a cello voice, and he had married Mary Clifford Caperton, a Richmond girl whom he had met while he was at Harvard and she at Radcliffe. The two are very close. Barry Sr. says that he decided to sell the family companies now rather than later so that he and his wife could face the ordeal together. "It would have been almost impossible alone," he says.

In fact, Barry Sr. says that his successful marriage and the extremely close relationship with his wife somehow contributed to what he says was his clear failure to communicate effectively with his children.

Under Barry Sr., known simply as "Senior" to his employees, the family business flourished as Louisville boomed with new industry in the postwar years and Kentucky prospered as a coal-mining and tobacco center. But the *Courier-Journal* and the *Louisville Times*, in the Southern liberal political tradition, frequently supported positions that put the papers in conflict with their more conservative readers. In their columns, labor unions found strong support and strip miners were blasted for not restoring the land.

But it was the strong stand in favor of civil rights that drew the most controversy. Barry Sr. says that one of his proudest accomplishments was that Louisville had the South's first integrated school system, a victory won largely without violence—but at a price.

"I came to Louisville in 1964," said Janensch, the papers' executive editor, "and Senior was not a beloved figure then. The Binghams were considered the liberal elite. The papers were despised as Communist. And the image of the Binghams was that they were not at all concerned with common people. Patronizing." It was only in recent years that Barry Sr. emerged in Louisville as a popular elder statesman.

For his children, life was very easy. The Binghams, Sallie recalls, had five servants including a particularly beloved nurse called Nursie by Sallie and her two older brothers, Worth and Barry Jr. "There was no other family like it," says Sallie, who adds that she remembers a family sense of being liberals under attack; of being somehow "much better looking" than other people, and of being free of the burden of "time wasted on petty boring details." These were handled by the servants and company managers. It was a family, Sallie says, in which the highest priority was placed on an absence of friction and conflict, where troublesome details of day-to-day living simply were taken care of "like magic."

She now blames what she calls the family's "smoothness" for producing a generation of children who did not have to depend on each other, and, in the case of Sallie, Barry Jr., and the youngest child, Eleanor, never created the close ties that often come with the give-and-take of childhood.

"We all seem to have some inhibitions about each other; it's very hard to express to each other the way we feel sometimes," Barry Sr.

says, somewhat ruefully. The Binghams, he says, might have been "much better off if we'd been a more Latin-type family with a lot of outbursts, tears, screams and reconciliations. But that has not been the way any of us operates."

The firstborn of this special family was Robert Worth Bingham III, as handsome and garrulous as his father and clearly heir to the top spot in the family kingdom. Barry Sr. describes Worth, who was born in 1932, as a natural athlete, a natural newspaperman, a natural leader who loved mixing with politicians and other powerful figures.

He was also a reckless, profane and overbearing personality, according to Sallie and others who were close to him. He loved to take risks, as though the family's seamless lifestyle had cheated him of being tested. As a young man he delighted in fast driving and in trips to Las Vegas, where his losses sometimes forced him to make urgent calls to the nonfamily executives who managed the Bingham holdings, asking them to replenish his bank account and not tell his parents. He was one of the Louisville businessmen who originally syndicated Muhammad Ali, then a young Louisville boxer named Cassius Clay.

Worth's younger brother by sixteen months was Barry Jr., a very different, less daredevil personality. Barry Sr. remembers his second son as having been "a merry little boy," thoroughly devoted to his older brother, as Barry Jr. himself confirms. Despite Barry Jr.'s near adoration, Worth teased his brother relentlessly. For instance, Barry Jr. was overweight until he went to college, and Worth delighted in introducing him as "Belly," rather than Barry.

Even so, Barry Jr. says that he was quite content to grow up in Worth's shadow. Explaining Barry Jr.'s yearningly tender feelings for his brother, Sallie says that Nursie once told her of a time when Worth and Barry were quite small and were gazing together at the night sky at Melcombe. "You can have the moon and all the other stars," Barry told his older brother, "but just let me have the evening star."

Sarah Bingham, whom the family called Sallie, was born in 1937 and was quickly recognized as the writer in the family, sending poems to her father during World War II and carefully printing them in a red leather book that he sent to her from London and that she still has.

Sallie says she always considered herself to be an outsider, a person apart from Worth and Barry, who were nearly inseparable. It was only later, she said, that she came to realize—and to resent—that she had been groomed by her parents for a supportive, woman's role, in contrast to her brothers, for whom management positions in the family business were assumed.

But as a child she grew particularly close to her father, and he to her, in part because she did not go away to prep school, as did her brothers. Night after night, Barry Sr. would read to her from the works of Dickens and Mark Twain. As a writer, "she was always very productive," he says. "She's a strong person and her feelings have been strongly expressed through the years."

The two other children, Jonathan, born in 1942, and Eleanor, in 1946, were raised almost as a second generation of children within the family. "Jonathan was probably the most brilliant intellectually of all," Barry Sr. says. A quiet child, he seemed drawn to science and medicine, while Eleanor was active, outgoing and gregarious. "She's never been the lonely, artistic person that Sallie was almost from the beginning," the father says.

In the Bingham tradition, Worth and Barry graduated from Harvard, and Sallie from Radcliffe, magna cum laude. Eleanor graduated from the University of Sussex, drawn to England as her aunt and uncle had been.

At college, Sallie had unusual success as a writer, and by twenty-one she had a three-book contract with Houghton Mifflin. A novel, *After Such Knowledge*, was published in 1959. In 1960, one of her short stories was selected for a collection *of Forty Best Stories from Mademoiselle*, and she seemed headed for a successful writing career. She married and moved to New York, with no intention of involving herself in the family business or returning to Louisville.

Worth and Barry Jr. also were on their way. By the early 1960s, Worth was working at the newspapers. Barry Jr., who had slimmed down as a rower at Harvard and in the marines, had developed a taste for broadcasting. He had worked as a broadcast journalist for CBS and NBC, then returned to Louisville at his father's urging to work at WHAS.

Jonathan had dropped out of Harvard and soon after, in 1964, tragedy struck—the first of the Bingham family misfortunes that draw comparisons with the Kennedy clan. Living in Louisville again, Jonathan climbed a utility pole to tap electricity into a barn at Melcombe; his intent was to illuminate a reunion of the members of his boyhood

Cub Scout troop. When he tried to make the connection, he was electrocuted. He was twenty-two.

Two years later, Worth, age thirty-four, was driving a rented car with his wife, Joan, and their two children early one morning during a vacation in Nantucket. To accommodate a surfboard, the windows of the car had been rolled down and the long surfboard protruded from both sides of the car. When Worth drove too close to a parked car, the right end of the surfboard struck the car. The surfboard, in a snapping pivot, broke Worth's neck, killing him with a sort of karate chop.

For Mary Bingham and Barry Sr., whose brother and sister had passed away in the two years between Jonathan's and Worth's deaths, the tragedies were incalculable. "There were times that I wondered if I would be able to keep on," Barry Sr. says. "Nature helps, and I drew great strength through the church." As always, he depended heart and soul on his wife.

But no one was more devastated by Worth's death than Barry Jr., Sallie says. "He sobbed and cried at Worth's funeral; it was absolutely heartbreaking."

Until Worth's death, the assumption was that he would eventually take over the newspapers, while Barry Jr. would operate the broadcast and printing companies. But at his father's invitation, Barry Jr. moved to the newspapers and in 1971, when his father retired his operating control and became chairman, Barry assumed the titles of editor and publisher, and took operating command of WHAS and Standard Gravure.

That same year, 1971, Barry Jr. learned that he had Hodgkin's disease, a form of lymph cancer that had killed his grandfather, Judge Bingham. After months of chemotherapy, the cancer went into remission and has not reappeared

But Barry Jr. was much changed from the merry boy the family knew as a child. Rail-thin and quite reserved, he became extremely cautious and, at times, rigidly inflexible—traits that played a decisive role at critical stages in the later crisis over the family holdings. He seemed to take great pleasure in the untroubled solitude of cutting wood on the family estate or in a hunting trip with a close friend.

Barry Jr., who is known to his employees as "Junior," acknowledges that he changed as a result of Worth's death and his own potentially fatal illness. But he says another reason for his austere, somewhat beleaguered manner was the burden of presiding over drooping news-paper and printing companies. "You have to have a certain personality to manage in decline," he says.

The *Courier-Journal* and the *Louisville Times* had a combined daily circulation of about 408,000 in 1973, their peak year. By last September that had fallen to 304,000, with advertising lineage down almost as dramatically. A flat Louisville economy and the steadily increasing cost of maintaining the *Courier-Journal*'s statewide circulation—it is the only daily circulated in every Kentucky county—added to the diffi-culty. So did the trend of American newspapers away from costly Sunday magazines, which Standard Gravure specialized in printing.

Profits at the Bingham companies reached a low ebb in the 1970s, of below 10 percent of revenues, and though they have rebounded, to about 12.6 percent in 1984, according to figures compiled by Henry Ansbacher Inc., all of the companies are below industry profit margins.

But while fighting a defensive economic battle, Barry Jr. mounted an aggressive one in news coverage, winning, since 1971, three of the newspapers' eight Pulitzer Prizes, and maintaining at great expense the *Courier-Journal*'s statewide reach.

Very much in the family's liberal tradition, Barry Jr. also took pride in the newspapers' support of court-ordered busing, a position that infuriated Louisville's other leaders. And he imposed rigid—some observers say too rigid—conflict-of-interest standards on his staff. He is a man who refuses to socialize with politicians, lest he be perceived as playing favorites or chilling his staff's reporting. As a result, he is considered to be somewhat isolated and aloof in Louisville. The trib-utes from people in Kentucky carried in the newspapers following the sale announcement spoke fondly of Barry Sr. None mentioned Barry Jr. And Barry Jr. struggled to live up to his dead brother, Worth. Barry Sr. says that his son is terribly burdened by the myth that has grown up around Worth, a myth that compares Barry Jr.'s perfor-mance as head of the family business with what Worth might have accomplished.

In Barry Jr.'s view, the heaviest burden has been to endure a sense that "the family was losing faith" in him. "The family becoming more critical and less supportive," he says, "that's the most debilitating expe-rience."

His mother, Mary, says she may have been the source for a dispro-portionate share of Barry Jr.'s sense of being assailed by the family—

because of her letters-to-the-editor opposing the paper's editorial positions and her defiance of Barry Jr.'s objection to her appointment to a state environmental commission. "I think I've been more outspoken about things I don't like," she says. "I have very positive ideas."

It was into this volatile atmosphere, overlaid with a veneer of Bingham smoothness, that Sallie and Eleanor returned to Louisville after many years away from home. With their arrival, the stage was set for the drama that led to the decision to sell the family business—a decision that might have been avoided if one of the family could have played the role of a healer. But, as Barry Sr. laments, there was not an effective healer among them.

Sallie came home from New York in 1977 "to be a little safer for a while," she says, after suffering "complete demoralization." She had three children, but her second marriage had broken up, and she was frustrated by a stalled writing career. "She needed some family support," Barry Jr. said, "and I certainly was willing to be part of the family to support her."

But Barry Jr. and his sister had never been close. In fact, they had barely seen each other in twenty-five years, and they continued to go their separate ways: Barry immersed in the struggle to reverse declining advertising revenue and circulation, and Sallie involved with her children, writing plays and teaching.

Eleanor came back in 1978, from California. In the decade since college, she had worked on a series of video documentaries, some financed by dividends that came each year to all family members. But a favorite project, a broadcast showing the inner workings of the Ku Klux Klan that was aired on public television, did not result in a network job, as she had hoped, and she returned to work at WHAS.

Barry Sr. made Sallie, then over forty years old, and Eleanor, in her early thirties, voting members of the boards of the family's three companies. Sallie says they viewed the appointments with delight and terror, having always regarded the businesses with awe. Barry Sr. also made Barry Jr.'s wife, Edith, a board member, and Barry Jr. supported the appointments.

For the business to survive under family ownership for another generation, Barry Sr. decided that his two daughters needed to be involved; otherwise they might lack an emotional commitment to preserve family ownership. Still, neither of the daughters was considered for management jobs by Barry Sr., who said they had never shown an interest in such roles. Sallie disagrees. She says she came to the bitter realization that the family was infused with an unspoken, perhaps even unconscious, assumption that management of the family business was men's work.

No one in the family can precisely date when relations between Sallie and Barry Jr. began to sour, but a frequently mentioned benchmark of bad feeling was publication in 1979 of an article in *Louisville Today*, a local magazine, headlined "The Bingham Black Sheep." In it, Sallie went public with some matters the family considered very private, including her resentments about the sexism she saw in the family and "the emotional distance separating both she and Eleanor" from Barry Jr. Not long afterward, Barry Sr. intervened to have Sallie made book editor, a job her mother had once filled. Barry Jr. says he had no objection to Sallie's becoming book editor, although he "disagreed on method." The woman who had held the job was moved to another post.

Tensions heightened when Sallie wrote a letter to the editor assailing Barry Jr.'s endorsement of a political candidate, and, according to Barry Sr., their relationship came to be one fundamentally of suspicion and lack of confidence. "The family has a way of making it difficult for each other," Barry Jr. says. "When your sister writes a letter to the editor denouncing the editor's endorsement, that doesn't make it any easier for you."

At board meetings, Sallie says that she asked questions—sometimes pointed ones about the poor performance of the family's printing operations—but she never cast a negative vote. Barry Jr., she says, "was completely silent at board meetings." Though there was no overt conflict, the tension between brother and sister was apparent to all.

Barry Jr.'s frustration finally surfaced a few days before Thanksgiving 1983 when Barry Sr. summoned his daughters to the Little House. He told them that Barry Jr. had issued an ultimatum: either the women family members left the boards of the three family companies or Barry Jr. could no longer go on managing them.

The elder Binghams, the sisters, Worth's widow, Joan, and the nonfamily management staff pleaded with Barry Jr. not to insist on his sisters' removal, fearing a catastrophe. But Barry Jr. was adamant. The women, he said, had to go to make room for experienced professionals. In addition, he said, the women family members were making no contribution.

"There were board meetings when my wife was doing needlepoint, one sister was addressing Christmas cards, and one sister didn't bother to attend," Barry Jr. says.

To Barry Sr. it seemed clear that Barry Jr.'s goal was to purge Sallie from the boards, not so much for what she had done, but for what Barry Jr. was convinced she would do. "He felt she would be very critical of him," Barry Sr. says. "He strongly suspected she would undermine him."

In this period, Barry Jr. also offered to turn over management of the companies to what came to be called "a regency" of nonfamily professional managers, but his father argued that the companies might as well be sold if Binghams were not going to manage them.

"He just communicated desperation," Sallie says of Barry Jr. "He looked like someone pleading to be let off somehow," contributing to her feeling now that Barry Jr. unconsciously wanted to be relieved of his burden, but did not want to be the one to force a sale.

Barry Sr. and his wife decided that, like it or not, the women had to resign from the boards as a demonstration of support for Barry Jr., who bore the burden of management on their behalf. But Sallie, bolstered by a feminist assertiveness, refused to resign.

Sallie remembers her decision to resist as a turning point in her life. "My mother has a tongue that just will take your skin off," Sallie said, recalling a moment when she says her mother accused her of "trying to destroy your brother."

But Sallie did not back down. "She said," Sallie recalls, " 'Don't you care what we think about you?' and I finally was able to say, at forty-seven, 'No, I really don't,' and mean it."

At the shareholders' meeting in March 1984, Eleanor, Mary and Barry Jr.'s wife, Edith, resigned. Sallie was voted off the boards, and remembers watching the votes being counted against her as a searing humiliation. Two or three days later, Sallie says her mother called her and suggested they go to a movie. Sallie says she responded that the two of them could not simply go on as before. Sallie and her mother have not spoken to each other since.

But Barry Sr. and top officials consider the removal to have been an extremely damaging tear to the family fabric that ultimately led to the sale.

Sallie made the first move, telling the family in July 1984 that she wished to sell to them all of her interest in the businesses. With her consent, the family asked Lehman Brothers, an investment banking firm, to appraise the companies to determine their market value and the value of her approximately 15 percent interest. Lehman Brothers finally established a value for her shares of between $22 million and $26.3 million.

Sallie considered the valuation too low, and announced publicly last January that she would consider selling to outsiders. She hired Henry Ansbacher Inc., a New York investment banking firm specializing in the sale of communications companies, to seek a buyer, and Ansbacher estimated the value of her holdings at more than $80 million.

Barry Jr., meanwhile, had begun to feel that he had lost the confidence of the rest of the family. He was suspicious of "the air of celebration" that accompanied his decision to go on a nine-month sabbatical in September 1984 to be with his wife while she completed courses for a degree from Smith College in Massachusetts. It turned out to be a relaxing interlude and he returned refreshed. "But almost immediately he stepped back into all the old pressures," his father says, "tightening up almost week by week."

Relations also began to sour between Barry Jr. and Eleanor, who remained friendly with Sallie while supporting her parents and brother. Last February, Eleanor sent Barry Jr. a letter in which, he says, she "told me she was disinterested in staying in any company with me as the head and her dependent on dividends."

The growing division between brother and sisters gave rise in March to a "stock swap" plan in which Barry Jr. would exchange his interest in WHAS for Eleanor's interest in the newspapers, leaving each with a property to run. Eleanor had said she wanted to own and operate something, and, if Sallie could be bought out, the struggle for control could end.

With the stock-swap plan on the table, Barry Sr. tried to pressure his children into compromise by issuing what he titled the "thirteen commandments," a list of directions regarding the family business that had, as the last commandment, the edict that if Barry Jr. and Eleanor could not come to an agreement, the companies should be sold. "That is not a threat, it is a fact," the document said.

To Barry Jr., the thirteenth commandment put Eleanor in the driver's seat. By her simply not agreeing to a settlement with him, he said, a sale would become inevitable—and that was her real goal. But Barry Sr. and Eleanor maintain that Eleanor's real goal was to acquire

WHAS. In the end, Eleanor agreed to the stock swap, but only if the family could reach agreement with Sallie on a buyout price. Otherwise, Eleanor wanted the family businesses sold.

Sallie, meanwhile, put a $42 million price on her shares, and the family turned it down, having made an offer of $25 million, which Sallie rejected. During the negotiations, she met with her father, who was increasingly in despair over the conflict.

"He told me that he loved me," Sallie says, adding that it was the first time she ever recalled him saying this. Barry Sr. says his daughter advised him that she did not want to have any more contact with her father until the sale question was settled, which created a break that hurt Barry Sr. terribly and colored his thinking when the breach seemed likely to persist indefinitely.

Sallie had lowered her asking price to $32 million, and Barry Jr. had reluctantly agreed to an increase in the family offer, to $26.3 million, the top value established by Lehman Brothers. Sallie spurned that offer in early December, saying that unless her price of $32 million was met, she would oppose in court a change in a family trust that was necessary for the stock swap to be accomplished.

But Barry Jr. adamantly refused to increase the $26.3 million offer. The result was a gridlock: Eleanor insisted that Sallie agree to a price before Eleanor would proceed with the stock swap. Sallie insisted on $32 million or she would fight revision of the trust, and Barry felt the company could not prudently afford to pay more than $26.3 million.

Barry Sr. and the professional staff pleaded with Barry Jr. at least to offer Sallie $28 million, arguing that Sallie's top priority was getting money to endow a foundation that she had started for Kentucky women in the arts. But Barry Jr. was not to be moved, although the debt burden involved did not seem excessive to anyone but him.

Based on a twenty-year projection that took all of the company's expenses into account, including a planned investment of $73 million in presses and other improvements, paying Sallie $26.3 million was estimated to mean a maximum indebtedness of $40 million. To offer her $32 million would have meant maximum debt of $55 million.

Barry Jr., in his own projection, predicted minimal increases in operating profits for the twenty-year period, which the professional staff regarded as unrealistically conservative.

Even using Barry Jr.'s projections, the professional staff regarded the debt as manageable.

Barry Jr. says that, because he was considering the financial security of his children and because he would be partners with Joan and Worth's children, he felt it would have been imprudent to offer Sallie more than $26.3 million. "I wanted a comfort factor," he says, noting that he could accept one year of a drop in credit rating that a $40 million debt would have prompted, but no longer.

But to his father and the professional staff, Barry Jr.'s attitude seemed to be based more on emotions than rational business judgment.

"I think he felt anything more would be a victory for Sallie and a defeat for him," Barry Sr. says.

Sallie also viewed it "very personally" and for her "it became a feminist issue of the men in the family over the women in the family," Barry Sr. says. Eleanor thought Sallie might accept $28 million, and urged such an offer.

Through it all, Barry Sr. struggled to reconcile his children. But he failed and the elder Binghams finally came to a reluctant decision, "in the small hours of the night, together," Barry Sr. says.

On Wednesday morning, January 8, Eleanor and Barry Jr. were summoned to the Little House and told by their father of his decision to sell all the properties. Barry Sr. said that the stock-swap option appeared dead, and that another proposal, strongly urged by Barry Jr. involving the sale of WHAS and Standard Gravure and the buying out of Sallie and Eleanor, would leave the newspapers financially vulnerable and unlikely to be operated in the Bingham tradition. Profits from the two nonnewspaper companies have been used to pay family members the approximately three hundred thousand dollars in annual dividends they depended upon, while the newspapers' resources supported a generous—even excessive, to some—news operation. Barry Jr. had argued that buying his sisters out would leave the newspaper in no worse financial jeopardy than the stock swap.

Barry Jr. reacted to his father's decision in fury, accusing his father of putting the wishes of Sallie and Eleanor above his own, the son who had devoted his working life to the family business. But he did not suggest reopening negotiations with Sallie by increasing the family's offer.

The decision to sell, Barry Sr. says, was "in desperate necessity to break through what had become impossible for all of us, and was best in the long run for us all: Barry, Sallie, Eleanor and the nine grandchildren."

And with the decision, the Bingham tradition in Kentucky came to an end.

1987 PULITZER PRIZE FOR SPECIALIZED REPORTING

First Born, Fast Grown: The Manful Life of Nicholas, Ten

————————————————•————————————————

ISABEL WILKERSON

Chicago, Illinois
April 4, 1993

A fourth-grade classroom on a forbidding stretch of the South Side was in the middle of multiplication tables when a voice over the intercom ordered Nicholas Whitiker to the principal's office. Cory and Darnesha and Roy and Delron and the rest of the class fell silent and stared at Nicholas, sitting sober-faced in the back.

"What did I do?" Nicholas thought as he gathered himself to leave.

He raced up the hall and down the steps to find his little sister, Ishtar, stranded in the office, nearly swallowed by her purple coat and hat, and principal's aides wanting to know why no one had picked her up from kindergarten.

It was yet another time that the adult world called on Nicholas, a gentle, brooding ten-year-old, to be a man, to answer for the complicated universe he calls family.

How could he begin to explain his reality—that his mother, a welfare recipient rearing five young children, was in college trying to become a nurse and so was not home during the day, that Ishtar's father was separated from his mother and in a drug-and-alcohol haze most of the time, that the grandmother he used to live with was at work, and that, besides, he could not possibly account for the man who was supposed to take his sister home—his mother's companion, the father of her youngest child?

"My stepfather was supposed to pick her up," he said for simplicity's sake. "I don't know why he's not here."

Nicholas gave the school administrators the name and telephone numbers of his grandmother and an aunt, looked back at Ishtar with a big brother's reassuring half-smile and rushed back to class still worried about whether his sister would make it home OK.

Of all the men in his family's life, Nicholas is perhaps the most dutiful. When the television picture goes out again, when the three-year-old scratches the four-year-old, when their mother, Angela, needs ground beef from the store or the bathroom cleaned or can't find her switch to whip him or the other children, it is Nicholas's name that rings out to fix whatever is wrong.

He is nanny, referee, housekeeper, handyman. Some nights he is up past midnight, mopping the floors, putting the children to bed and washing their school clothes in the bathtub. It is a nightly chore: the children have few clothes and wear the same thing every day.

He pays a price. He stays up late and goes to school tired. He brings home mostly mediocre grades. But if the report card is bad, he gets a beating. He is all boy—squirming in line, sliding down banisters, shirttail out, shoes untied, dreaming of becoming a fireman so he can save people—but his walk is the stiff slog of a worried father behind on the rent.

He lives with his four younger half siblings, his mother and her companion, John Mason, on the second floor of a weathered three-family walkup in the perilous and virtually all black Englewood section of Chicago.

It is a forlorn landscape of burned-out tenements and long-shuttered storefronts where drunk men hang out on the corner, where gang members command more respect than police officers and where every child can tell you where the crack houses are.

The neighborhood is a thriving drug mart. Dealers provide curbside service and residents figure that any white visitor must be a patron or a distributor. Gunshots are as common as rainfall. Eighty people were murdered in the neighborhood last year, more than in Omaha and Pittsburgh combined.

Living with fear is second nature to the children. Asked why he liked McDonald's, Nicholas's brother Willie described the restaurant playground using violence as his yardstick. "There's a giant hamburger, and you can go inside of it," Willie said. "And it's made out of steel, so no bullets can't get through."

It is in the middle of all this that Angela Whitiker is rearing her children and knitting together a new life from a world of fast men and cruel drugs. She is a strong-willed, twenty-six-year-old onetime waitress who has seen more than most seventy-year-olds ever will. A tenth-grade dropout, she was pregnant at fifteen, bore Nicholas at sixteen, had her second son at seventeen, was married at twenty, separated at twenty-one and was on crack at twenty-two.

In the depths of her addiction, she was a regular at nearby crack houses, doing drugs with gang members, businessmen and, she said, police detectives, sleeping on the floors some nights. In a case of mistaken identity, she once had a gun put to her head. Now she feels she was spared for a reason.

She has worked most of her life, picking okra and butterbeans and cleaning white people's houses as a teenager in Louisiana, bringing home big tips from businessmen when she waited tables at a restaurant in downtown Chicago, selling Polish sausages from a food truck by the Dan Ryan Expressway and snow cones at street fairs.

She is a survivor who has gone from desperation to redemption, from absent mother to nurturing one, and who now sees economic salvation in nursing. Nicholas sees brand-name gym shoes and maybe toys and a second pair of school pants once she gets a job.

She went through treatment and has stayed away from drugs for two years. Paperback manuals from Alcoholics and Narcotics Anonymous sit without apology on the family bookshelf. A black velvet headdress from church is on the windowsill and the Bible is turned to Nehemiah—emblems of her new life as a regular at Faith Temple, a Coptic Christian church on a corner nearby.

For the last year, she has been studying a lot, talking about novels and polynomials and shutting herself in her cramped bedroom to study for something called midterms.

That often makes Nicholas the de facto parent for the rest of the children. There is Willie, the eight-year-old with the full-moon face and wide grin who likes it when adults mistake him for Nicholas. There is Ishtar, the dainty five-year-old. There is Emmanuel, four, who worships Nicholas and runs crying to him whenever he gets hurt. And there is Johnathan, three, who is as bad as he is cute and whom everyone calls John-John.

That is just the beginning of the family. There are four fathers in all: Nicholas's father, a disabled laborer who comes around at his own rhythm to check on Nicholas, give him clothes and whip him when he gets bad grades. There is Willie's father, a construction worker whom the children like because he lets them ride in his truck.

There is the man their mother married and left, a waiter at a soul-food place. He is the father of Ishtar and Emmanuel and is remembered mostly for his beatings and drug abuse.

The man they live with now is Mason, a truck driver on the night shift, who met their mother at a crack house and bears on his neck the thick scars of a stabbing, a reminder of his former life on the streets. He gets Nicholas up at 3 A.M. to sweep the floor or take out the garbage and makes him hold on to a bench to be whipped when he disobeys.

Unemployment and drugs and violence mean that men may come and go, their mother tells them. "You have a father, true enough, but nothing is guaranteed," she says. "I tell them no man is promised to be in our life forever."

There is an extended family of aunts, an uncle, cousins and their maternal grandmother, Deloris Whitiker, the family lifeboat, whom the children moved in with when drugs took their mother away.

To the children, life is not the neat, suburban script of sitcom mythology with father, mother, two kids and golden retriever. But somehow what has to get done gets done.

When Nicholas brings home poor grades, sometimes three people will show up to talk to the teacher—his mother, his father and his mother's companion. When Nicholas practices his times tables, it might be his mother, his grandmother or Mason asking him what nine times eight is.

But there is a downside. The family does not believe in sparing the rod and when Nicholas disobeys, half a dozen people figure they are within their rights to whip or chastise him, and do. But he tries to focus on the positive. "It's a good family," he says. "They care for you. If my mama needs a ride to church, they pick her up. If she needs them to baby-sit, they baby-sit."

It is a gray winter's morning, zero degrees outside, and school starts for everybody in less than half an hour. The children line up, all scarves and coats and legs. The boys bow their heads so their mother, late for class herself, can brush their hair one last time. There is a mad scramble for a lost mitten.

Then she sprays them. She shakes an aerosol can and sprays their coats, their heads, their tiny outstretched hands. She sprays them back and front to protect them as they go off to school, facing bullets and gang recruiters and a crazy, dangerous world. It is a special religious oil that smells like drugstore perfume, and the children shut their eyes tight as she sprays them long and furious so they will come back to her, alive and safe, at day's end.

These are the rules for Angela Whitiker's children, recounted at the Formica-top dining-room table:

"Don't stop off playing," Willie said.

"When you hear shooting, don't stand around—run," Nicholas said.

"Why do I say run?" their mother asked.

"Because a bullet don't have no eyes," the two boys shouted.

"She pray for us every day," Willie said.

Each morning Nicholas and his mother go in separate directions. His mother takes the two little ones to day care on the bus and then heads to class at Kennedy-King College nearby, while Nicholas takes Willie and Ishtar to Banneker Elementary School.

The children pass worn apartment buildings and denuded lots with junked cars to get to Banneker. Near an alley, unemployed men warm themselves by a trash-barrel fire under a plastic tent. There is a crack house across the street from school.

To Nicholas it is not enough to get Ishtar and Willie to school. He feels he must make sure they're in their seats. "Willie's teacher tell me, 'You don't have to come by here,' " Nicholas said. "I say, 'I'm just checking.' "

Mornings are so hectic that the children sometimes go to school hungry or arrive too late for the free school breakfast that Nicholas says isn't worth rushing for anyway.

One bitter cold morning when they made it to breakfast, Nicholas played the daddy as usual, opening a milk carton for Ishtar, pouring it over her cereal, handing her the spoon and saying sternly, "Now eat your breakfast."

He began picking over his own cardboard bowl of Corn Pops sitting in vaguely sour milk and remembered the time Willie found a cockroach in his cereal. It's been kind of hard to eat the school breakfast ever since.

Once Willie almost got shot on the way home from school. He was trailing Nicholas as he usually does when some sixth-grade boys pulled out a gun and started shooting.

"They were right behind Willie," Nicholas said. "I kept calling him to get across the street. Then he heard the shots and ran."

Nicholas shook his head. "I be pulling on his hood but he be so slow," he said.

"Old slowpoke," Ishtar said, chiming in.

In this neighborhood, few parents let their children outside to play or visit a friend's house. It is too dangerous. "You don't have any friends," Nicholas's mother tells him. "You don't have no homey. I'm your homey."

So Nicholas and his siblings usually head straight home. They live in a large, barren apartment with chipped tile floors and hand-me-down furniture, a space their mother tries to spruce up with her children's artwork.

The children spend their free time with the only toy they have—a Nintendo game that their mother saved up for and got them for Christmas. The television isn't working right, though, leaving a picture so dark the children have to turn out all the lights and sit inches from the set to see the cartoon Nintendo figure flicker over walls to save the princess.

Dinner is what their mother has time to make between algebra and Faith Temple. Late for church one night, she pounded on the stove to make the burners fire up, set out five plastic blue plates and apportioned the canned spaghetti and pan-fried bologna.

"Come and get your dinner before the roaches beat you to it!" she yelled with her own urban gallows humor.

Faith Temple is a tiny storefront church in what used to be a laundry. It is made up mostly of two or three clans, including Nicholas's, and practices a homegrown version of Ethiopian-derived Christianity.

At the front of the spartan room with white walls and metal folding chairs sits a phalanx of regal, black-robed women with foot-high, rhinestone-studded headdresses. They are called empresses, supreme empresses and imperial empresses. They include Nicholas's mother, aunt and grandmother, and they sing and testify and help calm flushed parishioners, who sometimes stomp and wail with the holy spirit.

The pastor is Prophet Titus. During the week he is Albert Lee, a Chicago bus driver, but on Sundays he dispenses stern advice and thirty-five-dollar blessings to his congregation of mostly single mothers and their children. "Just bringing children to the face of the earth is not enough," Prophet Titus intones. "You owe them more."

Nicholas's job during church is to keep the younger children quiet, sometimes with a brother asleep on one thigh and a cousin on the other. Their mother keeps watch from her perch up front where she sings. When the little ones get too loud, their mother shoots them a threatening look from behind the microphone that says, "You know better."

On this weeknight, Nicholas and Willie are with cousins and other children listening to their grandmother's Bible lesson.

She is a proud woman who worked for twenty-two years as a meat wrapper at a supermarket, reared five children of her own, has stepped in to help raise some of her grandchildren and packs a .38 in her purse in case some stranger tries to rob her again. On Sundays and during Bible class, she is not merely Nicholas's grandmother but Imperial Empress Magdala in her velvet-collared cape.

The children recite Bible verses ("I am black but beautiful," from Solomon or "My skins is black," from Job), and then Mrs. Whitiker breaks into a free-form lecture that seems a mix of black pride and Dianetics.

"Be dignified," she told the children. "Walk like a prince or princess. We're about obeying our parents and staying away from people who don't mean us any good."

The boys got home late that night, but their day was not done. "Your clothes are in the tub," their mother said, pointing to the bathroom, "and the kitchen awaits you."

"I know my baby's running out of hands," she said under her breath.

This is not the life Nicholas envisions for himself when he grows up. He has thought about this, and says he doesn't want any kids. Well, maybe a boy, one boy he can play ball with and show how to be a man. Definitely not a girl. "I don't want no girl who'll have four or five babies," he said. "I don't want no big family with fourteen, twenty people, all these people to take care of. When you broke they still ask you for money, and you have to say, 'I'm broke. I don't have no money.' "

Ishtar made it home safely the afternoon Nicholas was called to the principal's office. Mason was a couple of hours late picking her up, but he came through in the end.

Nicholas worries anyway, the way big brothers do. He worried the morning his mother had an early test and he had to take the little ones to day care before going to school himself.

John-John began to cry as Nicholas walked away. Nicholas bent down and hugged him and kissed him. Everything, Nicholas assured him, was going to be OK.

1994 PULITZER PRIZE FOR FEATURE WRITING

A Killer's Only Confidant: The Man Who Caught Susan Smith

RICK BRAGG

Union, South Carolina
August 4, 1995

The case of a lifetime is closed for Howard Wells. The reporters and the well-wishers have begun to drift away, leaving the Union County sheriff at peace. He will try to do a little fishing when the police radio is quiet, or just sit with his wife, Wanda, and talk of anything but the murderer Susan Smith.

It bothers him a little that he told a lie to catch her, but he can live with the way it all turned out. Smith has been sentenced to life in prison.

Still, now and then his mind drifts back to nine days last autumn, and he thinks how it might have gone if he had been clumsy, if he had mishandled it. It leaves him a little cold.

For those nine days—from Smith's drowning of her two little boys on October 25 until she finally confessed on November 3—he handled her like a piece of glass, afraid her brittle psyche would shatter and leave him with the jagged edges of a case that might go unsolved for weeks, months or forever.

"Susan was all we had," Sheriff Wells said, sitting in his living room the other day with a sweating glass of ice tea in his hand. If he had lost her to suicide, or to madness, because he had pushed too hard, there would have been nowhere else to turn. There had been no accomplices, no confidants, no paper trails.

The manhunt for the fictitious young black man she had accused of taking her children in a carjacking would have continued. The bodies of the boys would have continued to rest at the bottom of nearby John D. Long Lake, under eighteen feet of water. The people of the county would have been left to wonder, blame and hate, divided by race and opinion over what truly happened the night she gave her babies to the lake.

Even if the car had been found, it would have yielded no proof, no clues, that everything had not happened just as she said, Wells continued. He would have been left not only with the unsolved crime but also with the burden of having driven a distraught and—for all anyone would know—innocent woman to suicide at the age of twenty-three.

Wells says he has no doubt that he and other investigators walked a tightrope with Smith's mental state and that as the inquiry closed around her, she planned to kill herself. For nine days she lived in a hell of her own making, surrounded by weeping, doting relatives she had betrayed in the worst way. "She had no one to turn to," he said.

So although he was her hunter, he also became the person she could lean on, rely on, trust. But unlike Smith, he had no way of knowing that the boys were already dead, had no way of knowing that they were not locked in a car or a closet, freezing, starving.

Someday the Smith case will be in law-enforcement textbooks. The Federal Bureau of Investigation has already asked Wells to put down in writing the procedures he used in the case, as well as any useful anecdotes from it.

But the story of how he, with the help of others, was able to bring the investigation to a close in little more than a week begins not with anything he did but with who he is.

Wells, forty-three, is the antithesis of the redneck southern sheriff. He has deer heads mounted on his wall but finished at the top of his class in the FBI Academy's training course. He collects guns but quotes Supreme Court decisions off the top of his head.

"I'm not a smart fellow," he said. But tell that to the people who work for him and around him, and they just roll their eyes. When the attention of the nation turned to Union in those nine days last fall, and in much of the nine months since, "we were lucky he was here," said Hugh Munn, a spokesman for the State Department of Law Enforcement.

People in the county say they like him because he is one of them. He knows what it feels like to work eight hours a day in the nerve-straining clatter and roar of the textile mills that dominate Union's economy: after high school, he worked blue-collar jobs until he was hired by the town's police force at the age of twenty-three.

He went on to be a deputy in the county Sheriff's Department. Then, for several years, he stalked poachers and drug peddlers as an agent with the State Wildlife and Marine Resources Division.

When his brother-in-law quit as sheriff in 1992, Wells himself ran, as a ten-to-one underdog. He promised not to operate under a good ol' boy system of favors gained and owed, and white voters and black voters liked his plainspokenness and the fact that he was neither back-slapper nor backscratcher.

He won, by just ten votes.

His mother, Julia Mae, was then in the hospital dying of cancer. She had lain there unmoving for hours but opened her eyes when he walked in after the election.

"Who won?" she asked.

His father, John, has Lou Gehrig's disease, and every day Wells goes by to care for him. The sheriff went without sleep when the Susan Smith saga began on October 25 but did not skip his visits to his father.

The Wellses have no children. Wanda suffered a miscarriage a few years ago, so they have become godparents to children of friends and neighbors. The Smith case pitted a man who wants children against a woman who threw hers away.

His investigation had to take two tracks. One, using hundreds of volunteers and a national crime computer web, operated on the theory that Smith was telling the truth. The other, the one that would build a bond between a weeping mother and a doubting sheriff, focused on her.

Wells says Smith never imagined, would never have believed, that the disappearance of her children would bring in the FBI, the state police, national news organizations. He thinks that when she concocted her story, she believed that the loss of the boys would pass like any other local crime.

Like other investigators, he was suspicious of her early on. As he talked to her only minutes after she had reported her children missing, he asked her whether the carjacker had done anything to her sexually. She smiled.

It would be months before the comprehensive history of her troubled life, of suicide attempts, sexual molestation, deep depression and affairs with married men, including her own stepfather, became known. But as bits and pieces of it fell from her lips during questioning, and as cracks appeared in her already unstable mental state, Wells began to realize that Smith, and the case, could come apart in his hands.

He had to hold her together even as he and other investigators picked her story apart, had to coax and soothe and even pray beside her, until he sensed that the time was right to confront her and try to trick her into confessing.

And he had to shield her from others, who might push too hard. Once, on October 27, a state agent accused her outright. She cursed loudly and stormed away.

After that, the people who had contact with her were limited. With the assistance of Pete Logan, a warm, grandfatherly former FBI agent now with the state police, Wells asked for her help in finding the boys, but did not accuse her.

The whole time, her family, her hometown and much of America were following her story, sharing her agony.

"She couldn't turn to her family, she couldn't ask for an attorney," said Wells. "She painted herself into a corner where no one could help her."

On November 3, he told her, gently, that he knew she was lying, that by coincidence his own deputies had been undercover on a narcotics case at the same crossroad where she said her babies had been stolen, and at the same time, and that the officers had seen nothing. Actually there had been no such stakeout.

He prayed with her again, holding her hands, and she confessed. "I had a problem telling the lie," he said as his story unfolded in his living room the other day. "But if that's what it takes, I'd do it again."

After the confession was signed, as she sat slumped over in her chair, there was still one thing he had to know.

"Susan," he asked, "how would all this have played out?"

"I was going to write you a letter," she said, "and kill myself."

He feels sorry for her, and is disgusted by the men who used her and in their own ways contributed to the tragedy. But he is not surprised that a twenty-three-year-old mill secretary could fool the whole nation, at least for a little while.

"Susan Smith is smart in every area," he said, "except life."

1996 PULITZER PRIZE FOR FEATURE WRITING

Death on 125th Street

ROBERT D. MCFADDEN

New York, New York
December 9, 1995

It was just after ten o'clock and Harlem had begun like an orchestra to tune up for another great performance. Traffic rumbled. Stores were open. Sidewalk vendors were out. And people moved briskly in the cold December morning, headed for work or shops or favorite haunts, carrying bags like responsibilities.

Across from the famed Apollo Theater, on the southeast corner of 125th Street and Frederick Douglass Boulevard, the gunman appeared out of nowhere at Freddie's Fashion Mart, a white-owned business that for months had been picketed and boycotted over a plan to expand that meant the eviction of a black-owned record shop next door. Feelings had run high. There had been threats.

The gunman was black, about thirty-five years old and six feet tall, and the police said he had on at least one occasion joined in picketing the store—protests at which the police said another demonstrator had been heard ten days ago threatening to "burn and loot the Jews." Freddie's is owned by Fred Harari, who is Jewish.

Witnesses said the gunman had the tense, quick movements of a man on a deadly mission. He carried a revolver in one hand, and in the other, a bag holding a white container of a flammable liquid, the police said.

Somehow, someone noted that it was just 10:12 A.M. when the gunman strode into Freddie's, a store at 272 West 125th Street, two doors from the corner in a two-story tan building that, on its second floor, houses the property's owner, the United House of Prayer.

The gunman immediately began shouting and waving his weapon.

"It's on now!" he screamed, some witnesses recalled. "Everybody gets out."

Others said he had ordered only black customers out—except for a security guard, no blacks were employed by the store—and there were several versions of the words he used.

"He was yelling wildly for everyone to get out," said Louis R. Anemone, the chief of department of the New York City police.

Then the gunman fired at least one shot. It was unclear if anyone was hit.

About fifteen people were in the store at the time: employees, customers and construction workers hammering and sawing in the store's expansion remodeling. Some were in the basement salesroom, while others were on the ground level. But all were trapped on the wrong side of a shrieking man who swiftly opened his bag, took out the white container and began splashing the flammable liquid over piles of clothing on tables and racks, according to the police and witnesses.

In his haste, he must have splashed some of the liquid on himself. "His clothing reeked of accelerant," Police Commissioner William J. Bratton said.

Survivors said the events were like those in a dream: fearful yet fascinating, disjointed but inexorable, as if the store where Luz Ramos, Carlotta Herring, Garnette Ramantar and others worked had somehow turned lunatic.

In the initial confusion, several people ran out the door, witnesses said, while others retreated toward the back.

The gunman apparently began setting fires around the store.

Four trapped men tried to run out and were shot. A twenty-three-year-old construction worker was hit near the spine and his spleen was shattered. A man in his twenties was hit in the abdomen by a bullet that slashed his bladder and colon. A middle-age man was hit by a shot that narrowly missed his heart. Another man suffered a graze wound of the head. Three of them staggered out, despite their wounds.

Outside, meantime, a passerby who had seen the gunman go in alerted two Twenty-eighth Precinct police officers passing on foot patrol. One officer entered the store and was fired upon by the gunman and pinned down. His partner outside radioed for reinforcements, and soon 125th Street was filled with the wailing sirens and flashing lights of police cars, emergency service units and fire engines.

Two officers from the Twenty-fifth Precinct crept carefully up to the store, crawled in and pulled their trapped comrade and one of the wounded civilians to safety. Three of the wounded men were rushed to St. Luke's Hospital Center; the fourth was taken to Harlem Hospital.

The fire in the store, meantime, was growing quickly. Feeding on stacks of clothing, the flames leaped and spread. Fabrics glowed and shriveled in their racks and piles. Sparks leaped into more flames. Tables caught fire, then the stairway to the basement. Dense smoke billowed through the store.

From a third-floor window across the street, Thomas Pierre, a voter-registration worker, saw the inside of the store suddenly engulfed. There was a burst of flames, he said, and "just like that the whole place went up."

Because of the gunshots and the intensity of the flames, firefighters had to fight the fire from outside, and police officers and other emergency workers were prevented for more than an hour from entering the building.

When firefighters and the police finally entered shortly after noon, they found four bodies on the ground floor at the back. One was believed to be that of the assailant. He had been shot in the chest, and the police, who said they had not fired any shots in the episode, called it an apparently self-inflicted wound. It was unclear who he was, though the police said he had been among the protesters at recent demonstrations at the store.

Beside his body was a revolver, and nearby, the container that had held the flammable liquid. The bodies of three women were also nearby.

In the basement, officials found four more bodies—two women and two men—all huddled at the back.

The gunman's seven victims were all believed to be employees of the store. The police and fire officials said they believed all seven had died of inhaling the noxious poisons in the fire's smoke. It was unclear if any of them had been shot, officials said. The bodies were all taken to the medical examiner's office for autopsies to determine precise causes of death.

Meantime, police investigators and fire officials began the laborious task of collecting evidence and attempting to explain the reasons for the mass murder.

"We will, over the next several days, be literally going through this very severely damaged building to recover whatever evidence we can," Mayor Rudolph W. Giuliani said at a news conference.

Throughout the afternoon, sobbing, confused relatives and friends of those who had been caught up in the incident—people killed or wounded or perhaps just missing in the confusion—gathered at the Twenty-eighth Precinct on Eighth Avenue at 122nd Street. As terrible uncertainty went on hour after hour, many could not contain their emotions. They banged on the walls with their fists, stomped their feet and screamed their anguish.

"My baby, my baby," one woman wailed. "Don't tell me I can't have my baby."

Later, two vans brought them downtown to the morgue to view the dead. For their loved ones, there was a kind of inevitability about it all, like the climax of a tragedy. One could see it coming, but there was nothing anyone could do.

1996 PULITZER PRIZE FOR SPOT NEWS REPORTING

Best of Friends, Worlds Apart

—•—

MIRTA OJITO

Miami, Florida
June 5, 2000

This is one part of a fifteen-part series entitled "How Race Is Lived in America," with reporting by Ira Berkow, Dana Canedy, Timothy Egan, Amy Harmon, Steven A. Holmes, N. R. Kleinfield, Charlie LeDuff, Tamar Lewin, Mireya Navarro, Mirta Ojito, Kevin Sack, Janny Scott, Don Terry, Ginger Thompson, and Michael Winerip.

Havana, sometime before 1994: As dusk descends on the quaint seaside village of Guanabo, two young men kick a soccer ball back and forth and back and forth across the sand. The tall one, Joel Ruiz, is black. The short, wiry one, Achmed Valdés, is white.

They are the best of friends.

Miami, January 2000: Valdés is playing soccer, as he does every Saturday, with a group of light-skinned Latinos in a park near his apartment. Ruiz surprises him with a visit, and Valdés, flushed and sweating, runs to greet him. They shake hands warmly.

But when Valdés darts back to the game, Ruiz stands off to the side, arms crossed, looking on as his childhood friend plays the game that was once their shared joy. Ruiz no longer plays soccer. He prefers basketball with black Latinos and African-Americans from his neighborhood.

The two men live only four miles apart, not even fifteen minutes by car. Yet they are separated by a far greater distance, one they say they never envisioned back in Cuba.

In ways that are obvious to the black man but far less so to the white one, they have grown apart in the United States because of race. For the first time, they inhabit a place where the color of their skin defines the outlines of their lives—where they live, the friends they make, how they speak, what they wear, even what they eat.

"It's like I am here and he is over there," Ruiz said. "And we can't cross over to the other's world."

It is not that, growing up in Cuba's mix of black and white, they were unaware of their difference in color. Fidel Castro may have decreed an end to racism in Cuba, but that does not mean racism has simply gone away. Still, color was not what defined them. Nationality, they had been taught, meant far more than race. They felt, above all, Cuban.

Here in America, Ruiz still feels Cuban. But above all he feels black. His world is a black world, and to live there is to be constantly conscious of race. He works in a black-owned bar, dates black women, goes to an African-American barber. White barbers, he says, "don't understand black hair." He generally avoids white neighborhoods, and when his world and the white world intersect, he feels always watched, and he is always watchful.

Valdés, who is twenty-nine, a year younger than his childhood friend, is simply, comfortably Cuban, an upwardly mobile citizen of the Miami mainstream. He lives in an all-white neighborhood, hangs out with white Cuban friends and goes to black neighborhoods only when his job, as a deliveryman for Restonic mattresses, forces him to. When he thinks about race, which is not very often, it is in terms learned from other white Cubans: American blacks, he now believes, are to be avoided because they are delinquent and dangerous and resentful of whites. The only blacks he trusts, he says, are those he knows from Cuba.

Since leaving Havana on separate rafts in 1994, the two friends have seen each other just a handful of times in Miami—at a funeral, a baby shower, a birthday party and that soccer game, a meeting arranged for a newspaper photographer. They have visited each other's homes only once.

They say they remain as good friends as ever, yet they both know there is little that binds them anymore but their memories. Had they not become best friends in another country, in another time, they would not be friends at all today.

They met on a bus, number 262, the one that took Joel from his home in the racially mixed neighborhood of Penas Altas to middle school, thirty-five minutes away. Achmed got on in Guanabo, and they sat together talking, as boys do, about everything and nothing.

Both grew up in orderly homes, with hardworking parents who supported the Castro government. Their fathers worked for the state oil company. Their mothers—Joel's was a nurse, Achmed's an administrator in stores for tourists—knew each other and sometimes met for coffee.

The boys' friendship was cemented through school and sport. They stood up for each other against troublemakers. "Just to know we were there for each other was good," Ruiz recalls. When his girlfriend got pregnant in high school, Achmed was the first person he told. They played soccer and baseball and ran track. Joel often stayed for dinner at Achmed's, where there was a color television and an antenna powerful enough to pick up American channels.

Because of her job, Achmed's mother had access to some of Havana's best restaurants. Every year she would take him out for a birthday dinner, and every year he would invite his best friend, Joel. "I couldn't think of anybody I would rather spend my time with," Valdés recalled.

But as they grew older, each became restless with the limitations of life in Cuba.

Achmed was in sixth grade when an aunt who had fled to Venezuela gave him a pair of white sneakers. He loved them so, he immediately wore them to school. Almost as immediately, the principal visited him at home to warn him about the troubling political implications of those foreign sneakers. At the university, too, his professors wondered why he wore foreign clothes and rode a nice bicycle. He wondered right back why he could not wear and ride whatever he wanted. When he was expelled for failing two classes, he saw it as punishment for being politically incorrect.

Before long, he found work at sea, trapping lobsters and selling them for four dollars each. In a country where most people earn less than ten dollars a month, it was a living, though not a life. When the government allowed thousands of Cubans to leave in small boats and rafts in 1994, he was ready.

His friend Joel was ready, too, though it had taken him far longer to make up his mind. Indeed, given Cuba's racial history, it is hardly surprising that black Cubans have generally been far less eager than whites to flee to America. After all, in prerevolutionary Cuba, blacks and whites had lived largely segregated, separated by huge disparities in economic and social standing. But two months after he seized power in 1959, Fidel Castro ordered whites to look upon blacks as equals and began leveling the economic and educational playing fields.

When Joel was very small, his family lived crammed into one room of an old carved-up mansion. Soon, the government gave them a three-bedroom apartment in a development that Joel's father had helped build. Before the revolution, Joel's mother had made a living cleaning white people's homes. It was Fidel, she told him over and over, who had given her the chance to become a nurse. And so Joel came to believe that it was no big deal, being black in Cuba.

As for America, he had seen the images on government television: guards beating black prisoners, the police loosing dogs or training hoses on civil rights marchers.

But as Cuba's economy fell apart in the 1990s, he began to see things differently. He left military school for a cooking program, hoping for a well-paying job at a tourist hotel. Once he graduated, the only job available was washing windows. Look around, coworkers told him, look who's getting the good jobs. The answer was whites.

He noticed, too, when he watched the American channels at Achmed's house, that some blacks seemed to live well in America. He saw black lawyers, politicians, wealthy athletes. It made him think: "It's not so bad over there. Blacks are all right."

On August 21, 1994, he climbed onto a raft and made for Florida. Like his friend before him, he was intercepted by the United States Coast Guard and sent to the American base at Guantánamo. The next year, they were freed—first Valdés, then Ruiz—and headed straight to Miami.

In Miami, Joel Ruiz discovered a world that neither American television nor Communist propaganda had prepared him for. Dogs did not growl at him and police officers did not hose him. But he felt the stares of security guards when he entered a store in a white neighborhood and the subtle recoiling of white women when he walked by.

Miami is deeply segregated, and when Ruiz arrived, he settled into one of the black urban sections, Liberty City. He had family there. His uncle Jorge Aranguren had arrived in 1980 and married an African-American. Ruiz took a job at his uncle's liquor store and started learning English.

The first thing Ruiz noticed about his new world was the absence of whites. He had seen barrios in Havana with more blacks than others, but he had never lived in a place where everybody was black. Far from feeling comfortable, he yearned for the mixing he had known in Cuba.

In Cuba, he says, he had been taught to see skin color—in his case, the color of chocolate milk—as not much more important than, say, the color of his eyes. But this was not Cuba. This was Miami, and in

Miami, as the roughly 7 percent of the area's Cubans who are black quickly learn, skin color easily trumps nationality.

Ruiz began to understand that in earnest on Valentine's Day 1996, three months after his arrival in Miami. He had gone to dinner with his uncle Ramón Suárez at Versailles, a popular restaurant in Little Havana, a bastion of white Cuban-Americans. They took three light-skinned girlfriends along. Ruiz wore one of his nicest outfits—black jeans and a red-and-green checked shirt. He was new to the country and unsure how to behave, but he felt comfortable at Versailles. After all, he remembers thinking, he was among Cubans. He knew the food, he could read the menu, and he could talk to the waiters.

The five sat in the back. Ruiz concentrated on the conversation and on his meal. More than four years later, he remembers what he ate: a breaded steak with rice and beans and fried plantains.

Shortly before midnight, the five left in a new red Nissan. One of the women drove. Suárez sat next to her, taking pictures of his nephew and the other women laughing in back. Twenty blocks from the restaurant, four police cars, lights flashing and sirens wailing, stopped them. The woman who was driving saw them first and yelled for Suárez to drop the camera.

The officers, with weapons drawn, ordered them out of the car. Terrified, Ruiz did as he was told, spreading his legs and leaning face-down on the car as the officers frisked him. It seemed like a very long time before they were allowed to go.

That was when one officer, a white Cuban-American, said something in Spanish that forever changed Ruiz's perspective on race. "I've been keeping an eye on you for a while," Ruiz recalls the officer saying. "Since you were in the restaurant. I saw you leave and I saw so many blacks in the car, I figured I would check you out."

Ruiz and his uncle stood speechless until an African-American officer approached them, apologized and sent them on their way. Afterward, his uncle said he was sure the police had been called by restaurant patrons uncomfortable with Ruiz's racially mixed group. His English teacher, an African-American, told him that white police officers liked to single out blacks driving red cars. Ruiz is not sure what to believe, but the truth is not in the details.

"Up until that day, I thought all Cubans were the same," he says. "It took a while to sink in, but that incident made me start thinking in a different way."

All at once, he had to learn how a person with dark skin should behave in this country: if an officer is following your car, do not turn your head; the police don't like it. Do not stare at other drivers, especially if they are young and white and loud. He has even learned how to walk: fast in stores, to avoid security guards; slower in the streets, so as not to attract the attention of the police. On the street, he avoids any confrontation.

He pays bills in cash because of an incident at a bank two years ago. When he asked to buy a certificate of deposit with six thousand dollars in lottery winnings, the bank officer, a white Cuban woman, looked puzzled, he recalls, and told him: "This is different. Your kind likes to spend the money, not save it." Since then he has not had a checking account.

And, of course, he avoids Cuban restaurants in white neighborhoods.

"In Cuba, I walked as if I owned the streets," he says. "Here I have to figure out where, what, when, everything."

He often finds himself caught between two worlds. Whites see him simply as black. African-Americans dismiss him as Cuban. "They tell me I'm Hispanic. I tell them to look at my face, my hair, my skin," he says. "I am black, too. I may speak different, but we all come from the same place."

He has started to refer to himself as Afro-Cuban, integrating, indeed embracing, the ways of his black neighbors. He enjoys what he calls black food—fried chicken, collard greens, grits—though he still lusts for a Cuban steak and plantains. He listens to rhythm and blues at home and at work; in the car, though, he listens to a Cuban crooner whose romantic ballads he has memorized. He dresses "black," he says, showing off his white velvet Hush Puppies and silk shirts. When he speaks English, he mimics black Miamians, but his words carry an unmistakably Spanish inflection.

Some months after the Versailles incident, when Achmed Valdés first saw his old friend, he was puzzled. "Joel has changed," he said. "He is in another world now."

Pretty much anywhere else in America, Valdés would fit nicely into the niche reserved for Hispanic immigrants. If the question of race came up, he would be called a light-skinned Hispanic. Here in Miami, such distinctions do not apply. Here he is not a member of any minority group. He is Cuban and he is white.

This, after all, is a city run by Cubans, white Cubans. Not only are the mayors of Miami and Dade County Cuban, so are seven of thirteen county commissioners and three of five city commissioners. Spanish is the dominant language heard in the streets.

Valdés's transition to this world has been seamless, so much so that he does not really think of himself as an immigrant at all. His self-image is of someone well along on a sure, quick path to the middle class, someone who would be right at home in a quiet neighborhood of well-kept houses and neatly mowed lawns. And that is where he lives, with his wife, Ivette Garcia, and his mother in a one-bedroom apartment off Seventeenth Avenue in southwest Miami.

He drives the car he likes, a 1998 Nissan that he plans to trade in soon for a newer model, says whatever is on his mind and dreams of opening his own business selling mattresses in a strip mall.

He has had to learn about punctuality and paying bills on time, but being white and Cuban, he has not had to learn how to behave. His English is tentative, but that does not matter too much here. His childhood friend may wrestle with a new identity, but when Valdés is asked how he has adapted in a strange land, he looks dumbfounded and jokes: "What are you talking about? I was born in Hialeah Hospital." Hialeah is south Florida's most Cuban city, often the first stop for Cuban exiles.

Still, he struggles the immigrant struggle. He has held a dozen jobs, from delivering Chinese food for tips to cleaning monkey cages for $6.50 an hour. Each time, he has traded up a bit, to the point where today he makes $9.60 an hour, with paid vacations and frequent overtime, to drive an eighteen-wheel Restonic mattress truck all over the state.

On weekends, however, he looks refreshed and energized, positively glowing with the middle-class knowledge of having earned his weekly respite.

It is 2 P.M. one recent Saturday, and Valdés is home from his soccer game. Before he is out of the shower, the apartment fills up with his crowd—athletic white couples, all friends from Cuba. The men drive delivery trucks. The women, like his wife, work as medical or dental assistants.

The men plop themselves on the couch and watch soccer on television. The women cluster around the kitchen table, talking about the pill. They are all in their late twenties, all still childless, focused on the English classes or professional courses that will advance their careers. The pill is pharmaceutical insurance for their dreams: eventually having children, owning businesses, buying suburban homes. It is all planned.

With some pride, Valdés shows recent pictures of his house in Cuba. When he comes to one of his father with his new wife, his mother recoils at the sight of her ex-husband with his arm around a black woman. Valdés concentrates on the coconut trees he planted in the backyard years ago. "Look how tall they are," he says, as if surprised that his house, his father, his trees have gone on without him.

The talk drifts back to Cuba, as it so often does in Miami. Like much of Miami's Cuban community, Valdés is quite conservative politically. A favorite topic is how much he says he has learned about the Cuban government since arriving here—the political prisoners, the human-rights abuses.

He listens to Miami's Cuban exile radio every day, particularly enjoying a program in which the host regularly reads the names of the men and women who have died in prison or were killed trying to overthrow the Castro government. Like most Cubans in Miami— but unlike Ruiz and most Americans—he believes that Elián González, the six-year-old shipwreck survivor, should stay in this country rather than return to Cuba with his father.

Ninety miles and four and a half years later, Valdés has ended up back in Cuba—albeit a new and improved Cuba.

"The only thing I miss from Cuba is being able to see the ocean from my windows," he says. "Everything else I need and want is right here. This is exactly the country that I always imagined."

"*Qué bolá, acere?*" ("What's up, brother?") Joel Ruiz asks a friend who has stopped to share neighborhood gossip. It is noon on a Tuesday, Ruiz's only day off.

The friend leans in the window of Ruiz's 1989 Buick, and they talk about a shoot-out in front of the friend's house the day before. Drugs, for sure. Both men know the shooters from the neighborhood, and his friend is worried that they may come back. His little daughter was in the front yard when the gunfire started.

Ruiz cuts him off politely and heads to the house of another friend, a middle-aged Cuban woman who, he says, loves him like a son. What she would really love today, though, is thirty dollars for rice and meat. "I don't have any money in the house," she says, lighting a cigarette. "It's terrible."

Having just cashed his paycheck—$175 for six days of work at the bar—Ruiz has money in his pocket. He peels off two twenties, and as he drives away, the woman yells after him, "Come by tonight and I'll make you dinner." He waves her off. He is in a rush. As always on these days of rest, relaxation is in short supply.

Like Achmed Valdés, Ruiz is a man of middle-class ambitions. He is studying English and wants to be a physical therapist. With the help of his uncles, he bought a house in Allapatah—a neighborhood of dark-skinned Latinos and African-Americans—and rents out half of it for extra income. Sure, he would like to be spending his day off hanging out, having a beer, watching sports on TV. But this day, like all his days, is circumscribed by race and the responsibilities that come with being a black man in a poor place.

For the most part, blacks are outsiders in this racially charged city, the scene of some of America's worst race riots. Blacks, especially black Cubans, lack economic and political power and resent the white Cubans who have so much of both. Steadily, relentlessly, the problems of Miami's poor have become Ruiz's, too.

When his uncle was imprisoned for drug dealing, Ruiz was shamed and told almost no one. But the uncle had helped him get started in Miami, and so he stepped in to keep his bar going and help support his little girl. When another uncle was killed by a drunken driver and left his family with no insurance, Ruiz stepped in to help the widow and her three-year-old daughter. He also sends money to his eleven-year-old son in Cuba.

His entire routine, almost his entire life, is focused on a twenty-block area around his home. Occasionally he ventures to South Beach, the fashionable zone where race is not much of an issue. Once, he went to a park in Little Havana, where Cubans, mostly retirees, gather to play dominoes and reminisce.

"But I left right away," says Ruiz, whose politics, despite a dislike of the Castro government, are more moderate than Valdés's. "I couldn't be sitting around talking about Cuba and Fidel all day."

Indeed, if his life is confined, he also feels comfortable in this place where he can be black and Cuban, where he can belong. As he drives with the windows down, he waves at people he knows, black men and women, Cubans and non-Cubans alike.

He has ambitions for the evening—some basketball, a date with his girlfriend, a black Cuban, to see *Best Man*, a film about successful black professionals.

But four o'clock finds him at the bar, Annie Mae's, getting things ready for the night. He puts beer in the cooler, sweeps the floors, cleans the bathrooms, polishes the tables and waits for the women who are supposed to run the bar when he is off. He waits, goes out for a while, then waits some more. Still no relief. He turns on the TV and begins watching the news.

"Have you noticed there are no blacks on television?" he says suddenly.

He should have been playing basketball by now, but instead he begins to play video tennis, his eyes fixed on the ball's glowing path through the darkness of the bar.

When Valdés arrived in Miami, friends and relatives did not just give him the obligatory immigrant lessons on how to fill out forms and apply for jobs. They also sent him a clear message about race, one shared by many, though not all, white Cubans: blacks in America are different from Cuban blacks. Do not trust them and do not go to their neighborhoods.

Valdés has visited his old friend's home just once. In late 1995, when he heard that Ruiz had arrived in Miami, he went to see him in Liberty City. Following his friend's directions, Valdés found the place—a small wood house set back in a huge grassy lot. A chain-link fence surrounds it, and there is an air of abandonment about it, but it does not inspire fear.

Still, he felt uneasy, the only white man in a black neighborhood. The houses were ugly, he says; the few people on the streets stared at him.

"Maybe it's just because, for us, that world is the unknown, but we felt uncomfortable," says his wife, who is as talkative as her husband is reserved. "It's like this: In Cuba I ventured out into the ocean, swimming by myself, because I knew the water, the currents. Here, when I swim, I never stray far from shore because I don't know what's out there."

One of Valdés's early jobs was delivering Ritz soda. Twice, he says, his truck was broken into in black neighborhoods. He lost sixteen cases of soda and two thousand dollars in checks. "Everywhere else you leave the truck open and nothing happens," he says.

Those experiences have left him with no interest in the black world and not a kind word for African-Americans. "They basically have kids and go on welfare," he says. "What else is there to know?"

In Cuba, he says, he grew up with blacks. It was almost impossible not to, and so he never gave it much thought. His immediate neighbors were mostly white, and he never dated a black woman—"I just don't find them attractive," he explains—but he attended racially mixed schools, and several of his soccer buddies were black.

Here, his contacts with African-Americans are limited to chance encounters at work, his relationships with blacks to those he knows from Cuba. "As far as blacks," he says, "I only trust those I know, because I know they are not delinquents."

Valdés does not flinch when expressing his feelings about blacks. He is passionate and definitive, but he can also be generous and kind-hearted, a man who shared his food with children in Guantánamo and regularly sends care packages to his friends, black and white, in Cuba.

Ruiz, he explains, is not his only black friend here. He is also friendly with Fernando Larduet, a man he knew marginally in Cuba but grew to like at Guantánamo. In a video of their time there that Valdés likes to watch to relive his daring escape from Cuba, there is an image of Valdés, who, for lack of a mirror, is gently shaving Larduet.

"It's not that I'm racist," Valdés says. "But even in Cuba, I had a vague sense blacks were different. That becomes more real here. In Cuba, everybody's the same, because everybody's poor. Not so here."

Soon after arriving in Miami, Valdés and his wife went to visit a friend at a hotel downtown. On their way, they made a wrong turn and ended up deep in black Miami.

"It was a cold night and it was really dark, even though it was early," his wife says, over dinner at a restaurant in Coral Gables, a fashionable and very white area of Miami. "People were walking around with sheets over their heads, and there was a fire in a trash can in every corner."

"And the houses were boarded up with pieces of wood to keep the cold away," her husband chimes in, barely lifting his eyes from his lasagna. "And people were smoking crack in the middle of the street."

She shudders. "We got out of there fast," she says.

The soccer field where Joel and Achmed played back in Guanabo is still a busy place, a scrum of young men vying to put the ball into a goal strung together with scraps of fish netting. On this January day, the game is still an easy mix of blacks and whites.

A few miles away, in the main plaza of the University of Havana, about two hundred students of all colors form a circle around a troupe of dancers. They are not clustered by race. At one point they form a human chain and then they, too, begin to dance, a rainbow of Cuba's best and brightest bathed in sunlight.

At first blush, Cuba might seem to be some kind of racial utopia. Unlike the United States, where there is limited cultural fusion between blacks and whites, Cuban culture—from its music to its religion—is as African as it is Spanish. But despite the genuinely easy mixing, despite the government's rhetoric, there is still a profound and open cultural racism at play.

The same black students who were part of that dancing rainbow say it is common to call someone *un negro*, or "black," for doing something inappropriate. "When a man insults a woman in the street, I will shout at him, 'You are not a man, you are black!' " said Meri Casadevalle Pérez, a law student who is herself black.

And a white mechanic named Armando Cortina explained that he would never want his daughters to marry a black. "Blacks are not attractive," he said.

Blacks, he added with conviction, commit the overwhelming majority of crimes in Cuba—a statement impossible to assess in a country that seldom publishes crime statistics. Even Cuba's racial breakdown is uncertain, with a black population thought to be as large as 60 percent.

What is clear is that while the revolution tore down most economic barriers between blacks and whites, there is inequality at the top. Blacks hold few important positions in government or tourism. They are underrepresented at the university and in the nicest neighborhoods. And the few blacks who have tried to organize around the issue of civil rights have been jailed or ostracized.

Bill Brent, a former Black Panther leader who lives in Cuba, said he had arrived full of hope that the government had found the "anti-dote to racism." Not only does racism persist, he lamented, but black Cubans lack the racial identity to do anything about it.

"The revolution convinced everyone that they are all Cuban and that their struggles were all the same, not separate or different because of their race," he said. "If a Cuban raises his voice to say, 'I am being discriminated against because I am black,' then he would be labeled a dissident."

Still, a voice of black identity can occasionally be heard.

In a sun-scorched neighborhood outside Havana, that voice reso-nates in the angry rap of Tupac Shakur. It blasts from a boom box at the feet of a group of young black men propped casually against a wall, dressed in a fair imitation of American hip-hop fashion: baggy jeans, oversize T-shirts, Nike sneakers and khaki caps with the brims turned down.

Relatives in Miami sent them the clothes and the rap tapes, they say. As they listen to the music now, it is clear they have not mastered the English lyrics and have only a sketchy sense of the song's meaning. But it does not seem to matter.

"It's about the lives of black people," says eighteen-year-old Ulysses Oliva. "It is for us. That is why we love it."

When Joel Ruiz told his mother that he, too, would be joining the migration to America, she fell to her knees and begged him to stay. Only when she realized she could not change his mind did she get up, dry her tears and cook him his favorite meal—sugar-coated ham with rice and black beans. Then she accompanied him to Guanabo and cried and cried and waved his wisp of a raft out toward the horizon.

Ruiz rarely talks about his mother; at the thought of her, his eyes seem to melt under a curtain of tears. But he says he does not for a minute regret leaving Cuba. It's not that he isn't acutely aware of the way his blackness has guided his story so far in America. He under-stands the bargain he has made. In Cuba, he says, he did not think about race, but he had no freedom and few options. Here he cannot forget about race, or his many responsibilities, and he has grown apart from his best friend. But instead of the limits, he focuses on the oppor-tunities.

"To eat a good steak in Cuba, I had to steal it from the restaurant where I worked," he says. "Here, I may not want to go to Versailles because I feel uncomfortable, but I can go anywhere else I choose, and no one can stop me at the door because it is illegal and I know my rights."

Along with his identity as a black man, he has found refuge in a community that welcomes him. And he has acquired an American vocabulary to frame his Cuban past. Thinking back, he points to instances of racism that he once shrugged off.

Once, on a bus in Havana, he got into a scuffle with a man he felt had stolen his seat. Afterward, a white friend's mother told him he had behaved like a black man.

" '*Te portaste como un negro*,' that's what she told me," he says. "Now, what could she possibly have meant by that, and how come I didn't see it then?"

Another time, at one of those special birthday dinners with Valdés, the maître d'hôtel stopped him at the door and asked, "And who is this?"

"What he really meant was, 'Who's the nigger?' " Ruiz says. "If that happened to me now, I would know."

Ruiz insists he does not dislike whites. He cites his friendship with Valdés as an example of his open-mindedness, just as Valdés uses their relationship to establish that he is not racist. And talking to the two men, watching them in one of their rare times together, it is impossible not to feel their fierce loyalty and genuine affection.

Yet both also know that theirs is now mostly a friendship of nostalgia. They are adults with ambitions and jobs and bills to pay, they point out, with little time to talk on the phone. When they do they seldom discuss anything beyond their families in Cuba or how busy they are with work.

When it comes to race, Ruiz will give his friend the benefit of the doubt. Ruiz is proud that when he turned thirty in February, Valdés ventured to black Miami for the party at Annie Mae's. "I understand that it is more difficult for him to cross the line than it is for me," Ruiz says. "It's not his thing and I respect that."

Valdés seems uncharacteristically thoughtful when discussing his friend's life. His friend, he says, has chosen to live as a black man rather than as a Miami Cuban.

"If I were him, I would get out of there and forget about everybody else's problems and begin my own life," he says. "If he stays it is because he wants to."

Ruiz thinks his friend cannot possibly understand. Even after he moved in April to an apartment south of Miami to escape the pressures of his needy relatives, Ruiz could not cast his family or his blackness aside. He spends most of his time back in Allapatah, near the bar and the neighbors who have embraced him.

"I know he would do anything for me if I ask him to, but the one thing he can never do is to walk in my shoes," Ruiz says of his old friend. "Achmed does not know what it means to be black."

Valdés and Ruiz have never talked about race. When told of his friend's opinion of blacks, Ruiz shifts uncomfortably in his seat.

"He said that?" Ruiz asks, lifting his eyebrows. "I don't know why he would think that blacks are delinquents. I know he doesn't think that of me, and I'm black. I've always been black." A pause. He thinks some more. "He grew up with blacks," he says. "I don't understand it. Maybe something bad happened to him. I am sure he is talking about American blacks."

Valdés has never told him about his experiences in Miami's black neighborhoods, just as Ruiz has never told him about the police outside the Versailles.

Yet Ruiz says he understands his friend's fear of crime in black neighborhoods. There are parts of Liberty City even he avoids. What he is wariest of, though, are white neighborhoods. Thinking back on that encounter outside the Versailles, he says: "Now I know enough to be grateful we weren't killed that night. The police could have thought Ramón's camera was a gun."

In Ruiz's new world, whites, even white Cubans, have become a race apart, and while they are not necessarily to be avoided, they must be watched and hardly ever trusted. He can no longer see himself in a serious relationship with a white woman. "Not for marriage," he says. "Not for life."

When he is working in the bar, the only man running a place where money, alcohol and loud music flow into the early hours of morning, the customers who catch his attention are the white men who sometimes wander in.

As he sat at a corner table right before Christmas, a black plastic Santa smiling down at him, Ruiz was relaxed, debating whether to leave for a quick basketball game or stay to help out.

Just then, two white men walked in. It was easy to tell they were Cuban. They walked as Ruiz does, that chest-first Cuban walk. Ruiz perked up. He trailed the men with his eyes. They ordered beers, and as they walked over to the pool table they were momentarily blinded by the light reflecting from a hanging ball of mirrored glass. Averting their eyes, they looked toward the darkness. There they found Ruiz's cold stare. He stared them down until they left.

"You see," he said, relaxing again, "this is why I can't leave this place. You never know who is going to walk in."

2001 PULITZER PRIZE FOR NATIONAL REPORTING

EIGHT

Personal Stories

AN OBJECTIVE EYE

Reporters traditionally did not write about themselves. Even when they ran into danger while on the job, editors would tell them to leave that out of the story: "We don't want to read about your troubles." But the tradition has trailed off in recent years. The word "I" has crept into columns. News stories may occasionally speak of "this reporter" or some such slightly evasive phrase. And magazine articles can be intensely personal—as the two pieces in this chapter powerfully demonstrate.

Nan Robertson was herself the subject of the *Times Magazine* article "Toxic Shock." To write about another person's close encounter with death is hard enough; to look into one's own mortality required exceptional courage as well as professionalism. Somehow Robertson managed to combine a reporter's detachment with self-examination, avoiding the mawkish. The article won national attention—and saved some lives. Women who had read it recognized the symptoms when they suddenly became gravely ill and were therefore treated promptly and correctly. Rereading Nan Robertson's piece brought tears to my eyes.

Howell Raines's magazine article, "Grady's Gift," paints a portrait of a black woman who worked for the writer's family in bitterly segregated Birmingham, Alabama—and in exploring that relationship tells much about himself and about race relations generally. It could only have been written by someone who emerged intact from that corrupted culture.

Toxic Shock

●

NAN ROBERTSON

September 19, 1982

Twenty-four hours after a glamorous New York evening, a Times *reporter lay dying, a victim of toxic shock syndrome, which left her with eight partially amputated fingers. Though therapy continues, the worst is over, and she has resumed practicing her craft.*

I went dancing the night before in a black velvet Paris gown, on one of those evenings that was the glamour of New York epitomized. I was blissfully asleep at 3 A.M.

Twenty-four hours later, I lay dying, my fingers and legs darkening with gangrene. I was in shock, had no pulse and my blood pressure was lethally low. The doctors in the Rockford, Illinois, emergency room where I had been taken did not know what was wrong with me. They thought at first that I might have consumed some poison that had formed in my food. My sister and brother-in-law, whom I had been visiting, could see them through the open emergency-room door: "They were scurrying around and telephoning, calling for help, because they knew they had something they couldn't handle, that they weren't familiar with," was the instinctive reaction of my brother-in-law, Warren Paetz.

I was awake and aware, although confused and disoriented. The pain in my muscles was excruciating. I could hear the people bent over me, blinding lights behind them, asking me how old I was, when I had stopped menstruating, and, over and over, what I had eaten for Thanksgiving dinner the previous afternoon, Thursday, November 26, 1981, and what I had had the day before.

The identical, delicious restaurant meal my mother, Eve, and I had consumed on Thursday centered on roast turkey with the classic Middle Western bread stuffing seasoned with sage that I had loved since childhood. I had eaten slowly, prudently, because I had had only three hours' sleep the night before, catching an early plane to Chicago to connect with a bus to Rockford, a city of 140,000 in north-central Illinois where all my family lives. Immediately after finishing my Thanksgiving dinner, I threw it up. It was 4 P.M. at the Clock Tower Inn in Rockford.

I thought excitement and fatigue had made me ill. Neither I nor my mother, a gutsy ninety-year-old, was overly concerned.

That was how it began: almost discreetly. I felt drained; my legs were slightly numb. The manager, apologizing all the way, drove us back to my sister's house in the hotel van. I was put to bed in the downstairs den.

I awoke, trancelike, in the middle of the night to find myself crawling and crashing up the stairs to the bathroom. The vomiting and diarrhea were cataclysmic. My only thought was to get to the bathtub to clean myself. I sat transfixed in my filthy nightgown in the empty tub, too weak to turn on the water. Warren and my sister, Jane, awakened by the noise of my passage, carried me back downstairs, with exclamations of horror and disgust at the mess I had created. Warren, an engineer who is strong on detail, remembers it as five minutes before 3 A.M.

As I lay in the darkened den, I could hear their voices, wrangling. Jane said it must be the twenty-four-hour flu: "Let's wait until morning and see how she is." Warren said: "No, I can't find a pulse. It's serious. I'm calling an ambulance. Nan, do you want to go to the hospital now?" "Yes," I said. His choice, of course, was Rockford Memorial—the status Protestant hospital in Rockford where my family's doctors practiced.

The ambulance came within a few minutes, in the wake of a sheriff's car and a fire truck. People in uniform spoke to me gently, gave me oxygen. Lying in the ambulance, I could feel it surging forward, then beginning to turn right, toward Rockford Memorial, fifteen minutes across town. I heard an emergency medical technician, eighteen-year-old Anita Powell, cry out: "Left! Left! Go to St. Anthony! She has no pulse! Rockford Memorial is fifteen minutes away—she'll be D.O.A. [dead on arrival] if we go there! St. Anthony is three minutes from here—she'll have a chance."

"Do what she says," my sister told the driver. We turned left to St. Anthony Hospital, and my life may have been saved for the second time that night, following Warren's decision to call the ambulance.

In the early hours of Friday, November 27, the baffled young medical staff on holiday emergency-room duty telephoned several physicians. One of them was Dr. Thomas E. Root, an infectious-diseases consultant for the Rockford community. He arrived at 7:30 A.M.

Dr. Root was informed about the vomiting, the diarrhea, the plummeting blood pressure. By then, a faint rash was also beginning to stipple my body. I did not develop the last of the disease's five classic acute symptoms—a fever of more than 102 degrees—until later. But Dr. Root is a brilliant diagnostician. And, incredibly, he and his colleagues had treated two similar cases within the previous year. "I think she has toxic shock syndrome," Dr. Root said to his colleagues. "Let's get going."

Most doctors have never seen, or have failed to recognize, a single case of this rare malady. Yet the St. Anthony doctors had treated two before me. The first, an eighteen-year-old who was hospitalized for six months in 1981, was left with total amnesia regarding the first weeks of her illness, but no other apparent damage. The second, a seventeen-year-old boy, who had a mild case, was out of the hospital within a week with no lasting damage.

"The most striking thing about you was your terribly ill appearance," Dr. Root recalled later. "Your whole legs and arms were blue—not just the fingers and toes. But the central part of your body, the trunk and your face, were more an ashen color. You were in profound shock. Your blood was not being pumped to your extremities. There was just almost no circulation at all. Your eyes were red, another important clue. But you were fifty-five years old and you had not worn tampons since the onset of your menopause eleven years before." Nevertheless, Dr. Root made the diagnostic leap to toxic shock syndrome.

This is the story of how, almost miraculously and with brilliant care, I survived and prevailed over that grisly and still mysterious disease. Almost every major organ of my body, including my heart, lungs and liver, was deeply poisoned. I narrowly escaped brain damage and kidney collapse. The enzyme released into my bloodstream that reflected muscle destruction showed almost inconceivable damage—an abnormally high reading would have been anything over a hundred units; I showed twenty-one thousand units. At first, the Rockford doctors thought they would have to amputate my right leg and the toes of my left foot. Because of the treatment, my legs were saved. But the dry gangrene on eight fingers persisted.

The end joints of my fingers were amputated. In all, three operations were performed. The first, at St. Anthony on January 14, 1982, was delayed in a successful effort to save more of each digit. The other operations, involving corrective surgery, took place at University Hospital in New York at the end of April and again in May. The Illinois doctors theorized that gangrene had not affected my thumbs because the blood vessels in them were larger and nearer to a major artery.

This is also the story of how—with luck and expertise—this life-threatening disease can be avoided or detected, monitored, treated and destroyed before it reaches the acute stage. Yet few physicians know how to test for it or what to do about it once the strain of a common bacterium, *Staphylococcus aureus*, releases its toxins. Toxic shock syndrome strikes healthy people like a tidal wave, without warning. Only two weeks before in New York, my internist of twenty-five years had said, after my annual physical checkup, which included a gynecological examination: "If you didn't smoke, Nan, you'd be perfect." Later, other doctors told me that smoking constricts blood vessels, further impeding circulation and thereby worsening gangrene when it occurs.

But, "Nobody should die of toxic shock syndrome," says Don Berreth, a spokesman for the United States Public Health Service's Centers for Disease Control and Prevention in Atlanta, "provided one gets prompt treatment and appropriate supportive care." This view is shared by Dr. Kathryn N. Shands, the physician who until last June headed the federal toxic shock syndrome task force at the CDC and who has studied every case reported to it from January 1980 to last June.

Toxic shock is rooted in the public mind—and in the minds of many doctors as well—as a tampon-related disease. It is true that of menstruating cases, about two-thirds occur in women under the age of twenty-five, almost all of whom are using tampons when the disease strikes. They are at very high risk.

But about 15 percent of all cases are nonmenstruating women such as myself, men and children. In this group, there has been no recorded case of a recurrence of toxic shock.

Dr. Shands warns, however, that a tristate study—conducted by the Wisconsin, Minnesota and Iowa departments of health—"showed that menstruating women who have had toxic shock syndrome and who have not been treated with an antistaphylococcal antibiotic and who continue to wear tampons have possibly as high as a 70 percent chance—horrifyingly high—of getting toxic shock again. Some people have had their second episode six months later; others as soon as one month later." The shockingly high rate of recurrence among menstruating women indicates that most doctors may misdiagnose toxic shock the first time around, or that sufferers may not seek medical aid if the case is relatively mild.

The disease was first given its present name in 1978 by Dr. James K. Todd, an associate professor of pediatrics at the University of Colorado and director of infectious diseases at Denver Children's Hospital. Writing in the British medical publication *Lancet*, Dr. Todd described seven cases of the devastating malady he called toxic shock syndrome and suggested that staphylococcus bacteria might be the cause. His patients were seven children from eight to seventeen years old; three were boys and four were girls of menstrual age. One boy died with "irreversible shock" on the fourth day after being hospitalized. One girl, aged fifteen, suffered amputation of the end joints on two toes.

By June 1980, the national Centers for Disease Control had linked toxic shock with tampon use. The findings were based on a study it had conducted after surveys of victims of the disease by the Wisconsin state health department had suggested a correlation. Publicity about the disease ballooned, spreading alarm across the nation, particularly among the estimated 52 million American women who wear tampons.

Also that June, the CDC toxic shock task force invited the major tampon manufacturers to Atlanta to brief them on the results of the studies. Shortly thereafter, the federal Food and Drug Administration (FDA) issued a ruling requesting tampon manufacturers to include warnings about their products.

As part of its surveillance, the CDC began to take cultures of women patients at family-planning clinics for *Staphylococcus aureus*—a procedure as simple as obtaining a pap smear to test for cervical cancer. It was found that 10 percent of the menstruating patients carried the bacterium in their vaginas, a statistic that still holds. "But it is not necessarily the particular strain that causes toxic shock syndrome," Dr. Shands pointed out in a recent telephone interview. Only "about 1 percent of all menstruating women," she said, "carry the poison-producing strain of the bacterium in their vaginas during their menstrual periods." Infectious-disease experts say that approximately 2 percent of the general population carry the poison-producing strain of *Staphylococcus aureus* in the mucous membranes of their noses.

In September 1980, the CDC reported that of fifty toxic shock victims contacted who had become ill during the previous two months, 71 percent had used superabsorbent Rely tampons. Of the control group of 150 healthy women 6 percent used Rely. From January through August of 1980, 299 cases had been reported. The death rate was twenty-five persons, or 8.4 percent.

Late in September 1980, after the CDC toxic shock task force had met with FDA officials in Washington about the matter, Procter & Gamble announced it would withdraw its Rely tampons from the market. (Other superabsorbent tampons, however, are still being marketed.) The company is now facing about four hundred lawsuits from the surviving victims, or the next of kin of those who died. The plaintiffs have won every one of the half dozen or so cases that have come to trial, and last month Procter & Gamble settled out of court with a woman whose original trial was the first against the company.

In October 1980, Procter & Gamble blitzed the country with advertisements encouraging women to stop using the superabsorbent Rely tampon. Then, both publicity and the number of reported cases among menstruating women fell precipitously in virtually all states. One of the few exceptions is Minnesota, where the health department has vigorously ridden herd on doctors and hospitals to count and report all toxic shock cases. There, the incidence has remained at about nine cases a year for every one hundred thousand menstruating women. The severity of the disease can range from mild to fatal. The death rate in cases *reported* in 1981 was 3.3 percent overall but the actual count is almost certainly higher, according to experts on the disease.

A National Academy of Sciences advisory panel also warned last June that toxic shock syndrome had not disappeared. . . . Indeed, the academy's experts concluded, the disease is probably underreported by physicians who don't recognize the symptoms in victims or don't report the cases they do identify to state authorities. State health agencies, however, are still giving notice of about thirty to fifty cases a month to the Centers for Disease Control in Atlanta.

Between 1970 and April 30, 1982, the Centers for Disease Control received word of 1,660 toxic shock cases, including eighty-eight deaths. Although only 492 cases were reported in 1981, down from a high of 867 in 1980, the Institute of Medicine of the National Academy of

Sciences estimated that the true number is about ten times greater, or at least forty-five hundred a year. That estimate is based on figures from Minnesota.

Last month, the *Journal of the American Medical Association* carried an article by three doctors from the Yale University School of Medicine that said a review of five toxic shock studies found flaws that could lead to biased conclusions against tampons. However, an editorial in the same issue of the journal, while agreeing that there were deficiencies in the studies (the largest of which found tampon users were up to eighteen times more likely than nonusers to develop the disease), said that "only substantial new research evidence evoking alternative explanations for the existing observations would be sufficient to negate the association between TSS in menstruating women and tampon use."

In the cases of nonmenstruating victims, *Staphylococcus aureus* can enter the body through a postsurgical wound or boil; is found inside women who have recently given birth, or anywhere on the skin. According to Dr. Root, there is no evidence that it can be sexually transmitted. In my case, among many theories, a tiny sore on the vaginal wall "may have favored the staphylococcus getting there from somewhere on your skin and then growing," according to Dr. Root. The staph was also found in my colon and urinary tract.

I was one of the dangerously ill cases. For at least four days after toxic shock struck me, the Rockford doctors did not believe I would live. Dr. Edward Sharp, a leading surgeon at St. Anthony, who would later perform the first amputation of the ends of my fingers, alternately bullied and coaxed me to fight on, and was "amazed" that I survived. "If ever anybody had a good reason to die, you did," he said later. "Your age alone! If you had been a fifteen- or twenty-year-old, it wouldn't be so unusual. Of course, this just means you're as tough as nails."

It also meant the treatment was swift and superlative, once Dr. Root decided I had the syndrome. Afterward, Dr. Root recalled: "There are two aspects to the therapy. One is the right antibiotic to treat the staphylococcus germ. Almost all staph is resistant to penicillin now." So he prescribed beta-lactamase-resistant antibiotics to inhibit and wipe out *Staphylococcus aureus* and to prevent recurrences. Last June, the National Academy of Sciences' advisory panel on toxic shock emphasized, however, that, in the disease as it usually appears in men-struation, "evidence is not available to indicate that such treatment ameliorates symptoms or shortens the course of the acute illness."

The two-pronged attack on the disease in my case began, as it would in all others, with "vigorous therapy for the cardiovascular col-lapse, the shock. And what that involves," Dr. Root said, "is massive amounts of intravenous fluid. Your body has to have a certain amount of fluid within the blood vessels, the heart, to be able to pump effec-tively."

The amount of fluid that flowed from wide-open bottles and flushed through me in the first twenty-four hours "would stagger the imagination of many physicians," Dr. Root declared. "You got approx-imately twenty-four liters, or quarts, of fluid. I think it was because of that twenty-four liters, ten of which replaced fluid lost from vom-iting and diarrhea before coming to the hospital, that your kidneys managed to make it through without being terribly damaged. You gained, with those fluids, about forty pounds in the first day. Your body blew up."

At one point, a nurse emerged from the intensive-care cubicle where I lay and blurted out to my sister and brother-in-law, "Your sister has become a conduit."

"But if we hadn't kept that adequate volume of fluid in your blood, then the kidneys would have gone and we would have lost the whole ball game because everything would have collapsed," Dr. Root explained. "The single most important thing in your therapy, in my opinion, was the incredible volume of fluid we put into you, keeping some measure of circulation going. And then, as the effects of the poison weakened, that circulation eventually picked up and was enough to restore you back to normal."

I was left, however, with eight partially dead and gangrenous fin-gers; bilateral foot-drop, a form of paralysis in both feet caused by lack of blood flow resulting in damaged nerves, which can leave the patient with a permanent limp; and severely poison-damaged muscles all over my body.

"Shock basically means that your legs and arms were getting no circulating blood anymore, that the amount of blood in your body was so depleted because, first of all, you'd lost volumes and volumes of fluid from your diarrhea and vomiting," Dr. Root told me. "Secondly, with toxic shock, the whole body is damaged, so that the blood vessels, instead of holding the fluid that's circulating through them, leak it, and the blood doesn't flow well; it gets too thick. Your body is made so that at all costs it preserves the blood flow into the brain and the kidneys and the heart. When you lose blood pressure, those organs get the blood flow and the legs and arms don't."

About twelve hours into my hospitalization I slipped into a moderate coma, from which I did not emerge for two days. My brother-in-law went to the Rockford retirement home where my mother lives to tell her I might not make it. Forever gallant, she never showed me her grief and dread during the two months I was hospitalized in St. Anthony. Her tears were secret tears. The day before I was transferred to the Institute of Rehabilitation Medicine in New York, my mother confessed, "I have cried more in the last eight weeks than I have in all my ninety years."

In the first hours, a catheter was inserted into my heart so that the doctors could judge how much fluid to give me. Another tube ran from my trachea to a respirator to enable me to breathe.

Within the week, in a profound gift of friendship, Pat Novak, a close friend since college days and a doctor's daughter, came out to Illinois from New Jersey to stay by my side until the worst was over. She kept a daily diary, which she later sent to me. These were her first impressions:

"I drove into St. Anthony Hospital and donned the gloves, mask, hat and apron required for the isolation unit. There, lost in a huge white bed, was a small face swathed in tape, with tubes from each nostril. Nan's sister, Jane, was there talking loudly, getting limited response from the brown eyes that opened occasionally as the head nodded, indicating a positive or negative response. A gurgling and hissing came from the respirator pumping oxygen directly into her lungs through the thick plastic tube in her nose.

"After asking permission of the nurses, I reached over to touch Nan. I stroked her tightly stockinged legs. Her eyes were wet with tears of welcome and gratitude. I saw the hands, fingers ending in charred and blackened tips, lifeless and distorted. Her arms were webbed in maroon rashes from her armpits to her wrists, sores and lesions and Band-Aids, wounds of the battle of the past few days."

Shirley Katzander, another dear old friend who had already become my "information central" back East, arrived from New York for a visit. "Your hands were a mummy's hands," she told me long afterward. "The fingers were black and shriveled with small, perfect black nails. I almost fainted when I saw them. Thank God you were asleep when I walked in, and could not see my face."

It was clear by then that the ends of my fingers would have to be amputated. Both thumbs had been spared from gangrene, which meant that I could possibly retain 40 percent of my hand function, using my thumbs and palms only. The day the surgeon told me he would have to amputate, I was filled with horror. I was certain I would never be able to write again. I was still on the respirator, and speechless. My friend and executive editor at the *New York Times*, Abe Rosenthal, telephoned. Pat Novak broke the news: Abe began to cry. When he had composed himself, he said something that carried me through many of the hardest days. "For Chrissake, tell Nan we don't love her for her typewriter; tell her we love her for her mind."

Then I was swept with rage, rage that fate had once again struck me down, after ten dark, troubled years following the traumatic death of my husband, Stan Levey, at the age of fifty-six. Through my long struggle and the help of others, I had finally emerged the previous summer onto what Winston Churchill had called the "broad, sunlit uplands" of life.

But now, as soon as they took me off the respirator, I began to heap my anger onto my family, the doctors and nurses. I reviled everyone who entered the room. I became imperious, demanding, argumentative, impossible. One day, when my sister materialized at the foot of the bed, I looked at her with hatred. "Go home," I said, icily.

For at least ten days I was possessed by fury, at everyone. One morning I awoke and felt for the first time cleansed and filled with hope. "You have everything to live for," I told myself. That morning in late December 1981, my recovery truly began. It has been a long road back.

Among my Illinois doctors, I shall always cherish Dr. Root, the first to diagnose me correctly, and with whom I later had many instructive and comforting talks, and Dr. Sharp, the surgeon who took a risk and decided to wait before operating on my fingers, putting me as soon as possible into physical therapy. I had dry gangrene, akin to frostbite gangrene, not the wet burn gangrene that gets infected and spreads and so must be removed immediately. Day after day until mid-January 1982, as I winced with pain, Dr. Sharp would rip away bits of the hard black sheaths around my fingers to find, triumphantly, healthy pink flesh beneath. Then the physical therapists would pull and bend the joints of my fingers to bring them back to life and flexibility. "We saved an inch of your fingers," he said later—which meant I retained a whole, middle joint on each of the eight affected digits.

Waiting to be operated on was agonizing. I longed for it to be over. Finally they had saved all the tissue they could. Dr. Sharp operated on January 14, 1982, more than six weeks after the onset of toxic shock. I awoke from the anesthesia to find my hands suspended from bedside poles, swathed in bandages like boxing gloves. The healthy thumbs stuck out.

Two days later, Dr. Sharp unwound the bandages. I was afraid. Then I forced myself to look at what my hands had become. I felt a surge of relief and surprise. I rotated the hands, front and back, and told the doctors with a smile: "I can live with this." My truncated fingers did not repel me. Nor did they shock my family and friends. "This is the worst they will ever look," Dr. Sharp said.

Meantime, the doctors and therapists were fighting to save me from foot-drop paralysis. I began to stand and walk in orthopedic shoes, with steel braces up to my knees. I exercised my legs and arms and hands obsessively, in bed and out. Under the sheets, I wore cross-shaped board splints attached to what I called "bunny boots" on my feet. I loathed them because they prevented me from turning on my side to sleep. I kept removing them. "If you don't wear them," Dr. Sharp finally warned me, "you will be a cripple for life." I wore them, after first making an enormous fuss, and was soon walking short distances—without braces, unaided and with only a slight limp when I was tired.

As yet another index of how catastrophic the sweep of toxic shock syndrome can be, I was treated by fourteen doctors during the eight weeks at St. Anthony. They ranged from cardiologists and lung specialists to a podiatrist who cut thick crusts from my toes and the soles of my feet. The cost of eight weeks' hospitalization in Rockford was thirty-five thousand dollars, not counting the doctors' fees. Ahead lay additional tens of thousands of dollars in New York, in hospital stays, additional surgery and daily outpatient therapy on my hands, which will continue for months to come.

On January 26, 1982, my brother-in-law and sister put me on a plane, homeward-bound to New York. For weeks, I had wanted to return to the city that was the center of my life and my career, and by then, thanks to my Illinois doctors, I was well enough to make the trip. I had had the good fortune to be accepted by the Institute of Rehabilitation Medicine, of New York University Medical Center, on East Thirty-fourth Street, commonly known as the Rusk Institute, after its founder, Dr. Howard A. Rusk, the great father of rehabilitation for the disabled. I went there by ambulance directly from the airport.

It is a place with miracles in every room, with people in wheelchairs crowding the halls like the pilgrims at Lourdes. During seventeen days there as an inpatient, the beneficiary of some of the most sophisticated physical and occupational therapy available anywhere, I progressed by quantum leaps. It seems incredible to me, considering the vast need, that there are only a half-dozen civilian rehabilitation centers associated with university hospitals in the United States, outside the Veterans Administration network.

I was so rare, as the first and only case of toxic shock seen at the hospital despite its worldwide reputation, that the doctors and nurses looked at me as if I were a piece of the Ark. "They will not believe your medical records from St. Anthony," Dr. Sharp had predicted, and he was right. Dr. Root had also delivered himself of a statement the day before my discharge from the Rockford hospital. "You now know more about toxic shock syndrome," said this expert, "than the majority of physicians in the United States."

For instance, the terrifyingly high rate of recurrence in menstruating victims—70 percent—indicates that most doctors may misdiagnose toxic shock the first time around, or that the sufferers may not get to a doctor if the case is relatively mild. My gynecologist in New York, Dr. Howard Berk, who has seen several hospitalized toxic shock cases some time after acute onset, said he advises his patients "to call me immediately and urgently if they have sudden high fever, vomiting or diarrhea during their menstrual period—it could point to toxic shock syndrome." Although it is most unlikely that I will ever get the disease again, because I have not menstruated for more than eleven years, Dr. Berk is monitoring me carefully. He now examines me every three months; takes cultures of my nasal mucosa and vagina for *Staphylococcus aureus*, and immediately after my discharge from Rusk began a program of local estrogen therapy to strength the vaginal walls, thus preventing irritation.

Publicity and the performance of the tampon manufacturers in warning users about toxic shock have been spotty since Procter &

Gamble took superabsorbent Rely off the market late in 1980. A new FDA ruling issued last June 22 [1981] requires a stronger warning on the outside of tampon boxes and a longer explanation of the association between toxic shock and tampons on a leaflet inside the package.

This year, International Playtex Inc., which manufactures Playtex superabsorbent tampons, has been running a television commercial that begins: "Brenda Vaccaro for Playtex tampons. If I was a mother of a teenager, I'd tell her to buy Playtex tampons. . . ."—thus aiming at the age group that is at the highest risk of getting toxic shock syndrome.

When Walter W. Bregman, president of Playtex, U.S., was asked to comment on that television advertisement, he said: "The objective of the current Brenda Vaccaro commercial is to appeal and communicate to a variety of women, both in terms of age—in other words, those both older and younger than Brenda—and those with and without children. It is not intended to reach only teenagers, and, in fact, Burke day-after recall research indicates this commercial most effectively communicates to women twenty-five to thirty-four years of age."

Government research has shown that a blood-filled tampon can provide a place for the growth of *Staphylococcus aureus*. "What we think probably happens is that the staph either grow better in the presence of menstrual fluid and a tampon, or they produce toxin better in the presence of menstrual fluid and a tampon," said Dr. Shands of the CDC toxic shock task force. The bacterium was not found on unused tampons, but could be grown on them. One study showed that the "supers" absorb more fluid, making the vaginal walls dryer and more subject to irritation. Dr. Shands pointed out that the risk of using superabsorbent tampons is greater than the risk of using less absorbent tampons. At least one case of toxic shock in women using sea sponges has also been recorded.

Testing for *Staphylococcus aureus* might be a good idea in my case, but not in many others, according to Dr. Kathryn Shands. "You could pick up *Staph. aureus* from someone else at any time," she said, by touching them or from particles of a sneeze. "In addition, you could pick it up and carry it in your nose, and you'd certainly never know it, and transfer it to your vagina at any time. So suppose you went to your gynecologist today and said, 'Please do a culture for *Staph. aureus*,' and he did and he said, 'It's negative. There's no *Staph. aureus*.' There's nothing to prevent your picking up *Staph. aureus* on Saturday."

She went on: "So in order to have some reasonably high degree of certainty that you will not develop toxic shock syndrome with this menstrual period, you would have to go in the day before your menstrual period and every day during your period and have *Staph. aureus* cultures done. And you would have to do it for every menstrual period every month. Pretty expensive for you and pretty much a waste of time. And if you multiply it by the millions of menstruating women in the United States, it becomes a ridiculous exercise: the entire health budget could be used up doing just that."

Asked if there is any way a young woman can eliminate the risk of coming down with toxic shock syndrome, Dr. Shands replied: "She could not use tampons." She hastened to add: "What we've tried to do is put the whole thing into perspective. You are more likely to be killed in a car accident than you are to get toxic shock syndrome. Not die from toxic shock syndrome, but get toxic shock syndrome. And yet people make the choice every day to drive cars. And if you want to take protective measures, you are far likelier to die from lung cancer from smoking cigarettes than you are to get toxic shock syndrome when using tampons."

From a doctor's point of view, such a perspective is no doubt reasonable. From my point of view, as I continue the torturous process of regaining the use of my hands and right leg, such statistics seem irrelevant.

The day after I was admitted to Rusk, Dr. Kristjan T. Ragnarsson, my chief physician there, did the first evaluation of me based on my Rockford medical records and his own hospital's neurological, muscle and mental tests. My first question on that day was: "Will I ever take notes again?" Dr. Ragnarsson nodded and said, "Yes." "Will I ever type again?" I persisted. His rosy face darkened. Then he smiled. "Oh, well, all you newspaper people are hunt-and-peck typists with two fingers, anyway," he responded. I said, "Dr. Ragnarsson, I have been a touch typist, using all ten digits, since I was eighteen years old." He looked somber again. I did not pursue my queries.

For a long, long time, pain was my daily companion. The worst is now over, but Dr. Ragnarsson believes it could be one to two more years, or never, before normal sensation returns to my fingertips and my right foot. The recovery time depends on how far up toxic shock struck my limbs, since the nerve endings regenerate at the rate of about an inch a month.

I have been an outpatient at Rusk five mornings a week since my discharge last February 12.

On February 13, back in my own apartment and alone after ten and a half weeks of being hospitalized, I totally panicked for the first time. Because of the long Lincoln-Washington holiday weekend, I was not immediately able to arrange for a nurse's aide to help me readjust, I could not turn a single knob on any door, or any faucet, or the stereo or the television set. I could not wash myself, dress or undress myself, pull a zipper, button a button, tie shoelaces. Punching the telephone numbers with one thumb, I called Nancy Sureck, perhaps the most maternal of all my friends, awakening her and her husband, David. "Help," I said. Nancy was at my side within the hour, taking charge. The next week I hired a wonderful nurse's aide for the mornings; afternoons, I was at Rusk; evenings, a half-dozen close women friends took turns coming in to fix dinner and pop me into bed. Harriet Van Horne, another earth mother, always arrived, like Little Red Riding Hood, with a basket of exquisite home-cooked goodies.

It was months before I could open a taxi door on my way to and from the outpatient hand clinic at Rusk. The cabdrivers of New York, with one exception, invariably sprang to my rescue with a gallantry that amazed, amused and touched me. I had decided to try a frontal, self-confident approach to all strangers in this tough city. I would hail a cab, hold up my hands, and say with a smile, "I have a bum hand— could you open the door for me?" Without an instant's hesitation, the drivers would leap around to the back door and open it with a flourish. As we approached our destination, I would hand them my wallet, tote bag or purse and they would hold up each bill and coin like a rosary or miraculous medal or baby to be blessed. "This is a dollar bill," they would say. "This is a quarter," and then return the rest of the money to its place. One driver said, "Even my wife won't trust me with her wallet," and another muttered, "Anyone takes advantage of you should be shot."

Once, in bitter cold that turned my fingers purple because I could not bear yet to wear gloves or mittens, or stick my fingers in my pockets, I could not find an unoccupied taxi. An off-duty cabbie finally stopped in the rush-hour crush for my young, beautiful occupational therapist, Gail Geronemus, while she explained why he should take me. As we reached one end of my block, we saw a fire engine blocking the other end. A policeman approached the taxi. "Back up," he commanded. "Hey, hey, this lady's come straight from surgery!" cried the driver, lying with that brilliant New York penchant for instant invention. "We've got to get her through to Number 44!" "Back up," the stone-faced cop repeated. The two men exchanged a stream of obscenities. When I had recovered from my laughter, I told the cabbie that I could make it to my apartment in the middle of the block. As usual, he hopped around to open the back door. I got to my lobby, and burst into tears of fatigue and relief.

The one and only stinker cabbie was an elderly man who refused to roll down his window or open the back door for me. I finally asked a woman on the street corner to help; she complied with alacrity and without asking why. "You roll down the window, you get a gun to your head," the driver said. When I had settled inside, he snarled, "You got only one bum hand, why didn't you open the door with the other?" I shrieked back: "Because all the fingers on both my hands have been amputated!" He almost dissolved into a heap of ashes. "I'm sorry, lady," he said, while a surge of gratifying catharsis rolled through me. I reflected later that I had finally expressed my deepest, pent-up resentments for the first time since my rages in St. Anthony.

Every day of my recovery has brought its frustrations and disasters—and its triumphs. On March 25 at the Rusk Institute's hand clinic, Gail, my occupational therapist, said, seemingly casually: "Why don't you try out our electric typewriter?" I was stunned with the enormity of her suggestion. I had thought it would be months before I would be able to attempt such a thing. I went to the typewriter. With incredible slowness and apprehension, I pecked out "Now is the time..." As the letters appeared on the paper, I began to sob. Gail and Ellen Ring, my physical therapist, rushed to my side. "Are you in pain?" they chorused. "These are tears of joy," I said.

Almost six weeks after I had begun outpatient therapy at Rusk, Gail wrote this evaluation of me: "Patient tends to protect her hypersensitive stumps by using her palms and thumbs instead of her fingers. She self-splints her hands [holds wrists, hands and fingers rigidly upright] by using her palms and thumbs instead of her fingers to complete various tasks." The tasks I could not properly perform then included picking up coins and unscrewing jar lids.

But, day by day, my occupational and physical therapists were bringing my hands back to life and function. Traumatized by toxic shock, gangrene and then surgery, my fingertips—the most sensitive part of the body, I had been told—had stiffened straight out, the opposite of a stroke victim's fingers that often curl into claws. As an outpatient, I began to wear custom-made "splints," which consisted of castlike wrist braces, leather nooses for each finger and rubber bands that passively pulled my fingers down into fists so that I could grasp objects. These splints perform much like braces on a child's teeth, without active effort on the wearer's part.

There were endless, excruciatingly boring but vital exercises at home. At the clinic, I pawed through coffee cans heaped with raw rice, kidney beans, macaroni and gravel to toughen my finger ends: this invariably set my teeth on edge. I hated the touch of metal of any kind, such as the nails I had to pick up and put in holes. But there is no way to win at physical therapy without working through pain to healing. "There are the survivors, and there are those who would rather take fifty pills and just slip under," a nurse at Rusk told me. "All human beings divide into those two groups. I have even seen babies who do not want to live—who literally pined away and died."

By early May, I was able to open taxi doors with two hands, and the doorknob crisis was over. I was buttoning my blouses and dresses in a trice with a button hook, and awkwardly cutting the top off my breakfast soft-boiled egg with a knife encased in a tube of foam that provides a wider gripping surface. By mid-June, I could punch a push-button telephone with my index finger. (I am still having trouble cutting meat.) By late July, my therapists were "thrilled" with my progress in hand strength, dexterity and range of motion.

Just as important, Dr. Barry M. Zide, a skilled young plastic surgeon at University Hospital, with which Rusk is associated, liberated me from much of my pain in two operations on my fingers last April 29 and May 26. One of my doctors at Rusk had run into Dr. Zide, a kind of Alan Alda in *M*A*S*H*—witty, irreverent and all heart as well as talent—in a hospital corridor just after failing, as had two other doctors, to remove the Illinois surgical stitches from my finger-tips without causing me agony. "No problem," said Dr. Zide. "I'll throw a nerve block in her wrists." The next day, painlessly, he took the sutures out, and I fell in love with yet another doctor.

He then told me to brace myself for more surgery. With a sinking heart, I heard him say: "I can see by the way your nails are coming in that you are set up for chronic infection as soon as the nails grow back. In addition, the unpadded skin at the fingertips will never with-stand the constant trauma of daily living. The bone below this thin skin is surely going to become exposed and infected."

First on the left hand in April and then on the right in May, Dr. Zide amputated up to half an inch of some of the fingers, removing the nailbeds and infected bone. The thicker, more resilient skin on the palm side of my fingers was then draped over the newly shaped bone. Within a week, I was making tremendous progress in the use of my hands and becoming increasingly independent in every facet of my daily life.

My story is almost over except for one crucial detail: My deepest fear did not materialize.

I have typed the thousands of words of this article, slowly and with difficulty, once again able to practice my craft as a reporter. I have written it—at last—with my own hands.

1983 PULITZER PRIZE FOR FEATURE WRITING

Grady's Gift

HOWELL RAINES

December 1, 1991

Grady showed up one day at our house at 1409 Fifth Avenue West in Birmingham, and by and by she changed the way I saw the world. I was seven when she came to iron and clean and cook for eighteen dollars a week, and she stayed for seven years. During that time every-one in our family came to accept what my father called "those great long talks" that occupied Grady and me through many a sleepy Ala-bama afternoon. What happened between us can be expressed in many ways, but its essence was captured by Graham Greene when he wrote that in every childhood there is a moment when a door opens and lets the future in. So this is a story about one person who opened a door and another who walked through it.

It is difficult to describe—or even to keep alive in our memories—worlds that cease to exist. Usually we think of vanished worlds as having to do with far-off places or with ways of life, like that of the western frontier, that are remote from us in time. But I grew up in a place that disappeared, and it was here in this country and not so long ago. I speak of Birmingham, where once there flourished the most complete form of racial segregation to exist on the American continent in this century.

Gradystein Williams Hutchinson (or Grady, as she was called in my family and hers) and I are two people who grew up in the fifties in that vanished world, two people who lived mundane, inconsequential lives while Martin Luther King Jr. and Police Commissioner T. Eugene (Bull) Connor prepared for their epic struggle. For years, Grady and I lived in my memory as child and adult. But now I realize that we were both children—one white and very young, one black and adolescent; one privileged, one poor. The connection between these two children and their city was this: Grady saw to it that although I was to live in Birmingham for the first twenty-eight years of my life, Birmingham would not live in me.

Only by keeping in mind the place that Birmingham was can you understand the life we had, the people we became and the reunion that occurred one day not too long ago at my sister's big house in the verdant Birmingham suburb of Mountain Brook. Grady, now a fifty-seven-year-old hospital cook in Atlanta, had driven out with me in the car I had rented. As we pulled up, my parents, a retired couple living in Florida, arrived in their gray Cadillac. My father, a large, vigorous man of eighty-four, parked his car and, without a word, walked straight to Grady and took her in his arms.

"I never thought I'd ever see y'all again," Grady said a little while later. "I just think this is the true will of God. It's His divine wish that we saw each other."

This was the first time in thirty-four years that we had all been together. As the years slipped by, it had become more and more important to me to find Grady, because I am a strong believer in thanking our teachers and mentors while they are still alive to hear our thanks. She had been "our maid," but she taught me the most valuable lesson a writer can learn, which is to try to see—honestly and down to its very center—the world in which we live. Grady was long gone before I realized what a brave and generous person she was, or how much I owed her.

Then last spring, my sister ran into a relative of Grady's and got her telephone number. I went to see Grady in Atlanta, and several months later we gathered in Birmingham to remember our shared past and to learn anew how love abides and how it can bloom not only in the fertile places, but in the stony ones as well.

I know that outsiders tend to think segregation existed in a uniform way throughout the Solid South. But it didn't. Segregation was rigid in some places, relaxed in others; leavened with humanity in some places, enforced with unremitting brutality in others. And segregation found its most violent and regimented expression in Birmingham— segregation maintained through the nighttime maraudings of white thugs, segregation sanctioned by absentee landlords from the United States Steel Corporation, segregation enforced by a pervasively corrupt police department.

Martin Luther King once said Birmingham was to the rest of the South what Johannesburg was to the rest of Africa. He believed that if segregation could be broken there, in a city that harbored an American version of apartheid, it could be broken everywhere. That is why the great civil rights demonstrations of 1963 took place in Birmingham. And that is why, just as King envisioned, once its jugular was cut in Kelly Ingram Park in Birmingham in 1963, the dragon of legalized segregation collapsed and died everywhere—died, it seems in retrospect, almost on the instant. It was the end of "Bad Birmingham," where the indigenous racism of rural Alabama had taken a new and more virulent form when transplanted into a raw industrial setting.

In the heyday of Birmingham, one vast belt of steel mills stretched for ten miles, from the satellite town of Bessemer to the coal-mining suburb of Pratt City. Black and white men—men like Grady's father and mine—came from all over the South to do the work of these mills or to dig the coal and iron ore to feed them. By the time Grady Williams was born in 1933, the huge light of their labor washed the evening sky with an undying red glow. The division of tasks within these plants ran along simple lines: white men made the steel; black men washed the coal.

Henry Williams was a tiny man from Oklahoma—part African, part Cherokee, only five feet three inches, but handsome. He worked at the No. 2 Coal Washer at Pratt Mines, and he understood his world imperfectly. When the white foreman died, Henry thought he would move up. But the dead man's nephew was brought in, and in the natural order of things, Henry was required to teach his new boss all there was to know about washing coal.

"Oh, come on, Henry," his wife, Elizabeth, said when he complained about being passed over for a novice. But he would not be consoled.

One Saturday, Henry Williams sent Grady on an errand. "Go up the hill," he said, "and tell Mr. Humphrey Davis I said send me three bullets for my .38 pistol because I got to kill a dog."

In his bedroom later that same afternoon, he shot himself. Grady found the body. She was seven years old.

Over the years, Elizabeth Williams held the family together. She worked as a practical nurse and would have become a registered nurse except for the fact that by the early forties, the hospitals in Birmingham, which had run segregated nursing programs, closed those for blacks.

Grady attended Parker High, an all-black school where the children of teachers and postal workers made fun of girls like Grady, who at fourteen was already working part-time in white homes. One day a boy started ragging Grady for being an "Aunt Jemima." One of the poorer boys approached him after class and said: "Hey, everybody's not lucky enough to have a father working. If I ever hear you say that again to her, I'm going to break your neck."

Grady finished high school in early 1950, four weeks after her sixteenth birthday. Her grades were high, even though she had held back on some tests in an effort to blend in with her older classmates. She planned to go to the nursing school at Dillard University, a black institution in New Orleans, but first she needed a full-time job to earn money for tuition. That was when my mother hired her. There was a state-financed nursing school in Birmingham, about ten miles from her house, but it was the wrong one.

Between the Depression and World War II, my father and two of his brothers came into Birmingham from the Alabama hills. They were strong, sober country boys who knew how to swing a hammer. By the time Truman was elected in 1948, they had got a little bit rich selling lumber and building shelves for the A & P.

They drove Packards and Oldsmobiles. They bought cottages at the beach and hired housemaids for their wives and resolved that their children would go to college. Among them, they had eight children, and I was the last to be born, and my world was sunny.

Indeed, it seemed to be a matter of family pride that this tribe of hardhanded hill people had become prosperous enough to spoil its babies. I was doted upon, particularly, it occurs to me now, by women: my mother; my sister, Mary Jo, who was twelve years older and carried me around like a mascot; my leathery old grandmother, a widow who didn't like many people but liked me because I was named for her husband.

There was also my Aunt Ada, a red-haired spinster who made me rice pudding and hand-whipped biscuits and milkshakes with cracked ice, and when my parents were out of town, I slept on a pallet in her room.

Then there were the black women, first Daisy, then Ella. And finally Grady.

I wish you could have seen her in 1950. Most of the women in my family ran from slender to bony. Grady was buxom. She wore a blue uniform and walked around our house on stout brown calves. Her skin was smooth. She had a gap between her front teeth, and so did I. One of the first things I remember Grady telling me was that as soon as she had enough money she was going to get a diamond set in her gap and it would drive the men wild.

There is no trickier subject for a writer from the South than that of affection between a black person and a white one in the unequal world of segregation. For the dishonesty upon which such a society is founded makes every emotion suspect, makes it impossible to know whether what flowed between two people was honest feeling or pity or pragmatism. Indeed, for the black person, the feigning of an expected emotion could be the very coinage of survival.

So I can only tell you how it seemed to me at the time. I was seven and Grady was sixteen and I adored her and I believed she was crazy about me. She became the weather in which my childhood was lived.

I was fourteen when she went away. It would be many years before I realized that somehow, whether by accident or by plan, in a way so subtle, so gentle, so loving that it was like the budding and falling of the leaves on the pecan trees in the yard of that happy house in that cruel city in that violent time, Grady had given me the most precious gift that could be received by a pampered white boy growing up in that time and place. It was the gift of a free and unhateful heart.

Grady, it soon became clear, was a talker, and I was already known in my family as an incessant asker of questions. My brother, Jerry, who is ten years older than I, says one of his clearest memories is of my following Grady around the house, pursuing her with a constant buzz of chatter.

That is funny, because what I remember is Grady talking and me listening—Grady talking as she did her chores, marking me with her vision of the way things were. All of my life, I have carried this mental image of the two of us:

I am nine or ten by this time. We are in the room where Grady did her ironing. Strong light is streaming through the window. High summer lies heavily across all of Birmingham like a blanket. We are alone, Grady and I, in the midst of what the Alabama novelist Babs Deal called "the acres of afternoon," those legendary hours of buzzing heat and torpidity that either bind you to the South or make you crazy to leave it.

I am slouched on a chair, with nothing left to do now that baseball practice is over. Grady is moving a huge dreadnought of an iron, a GE with stainless steel base and fat black handle, back and forth across my father's white shirts. From time to time, she shakes water on the fabric from a bottle with a sprinkler cap.

Then she speaks of a hidden world about which no one has ever told me, a world as dangerous and foreign, to a white child in a segregated society, as Africa itself—the world of "nigger town." "You don't know what it's like to be poor and black," Grady says.

She speaks of the curbside justice administered with rubber hoses by Bull Connor's policemen, of the deputy sheriff famous in the black community for shooting a floor sweeper who had moved too slowly, of "Dog Day," the one time a year when blacks are allowed to attend the state fair. She speaks offhandedly of the NAACP.

"Are you a member?" I ask.

"At my school," she says, "we take our dimes and nickels and join the NAACP every year just like you join the Red Cross in your school."

It seems silly now to describe the impact of this revelation, but that is because I cannot fully re-create the intellectual isolation of those days in Alabama. Remember that this was a time when television news, with its searing pictures of racial conflict, was not yet a force in our society. The editorial pages of the Birmingham papers were dominated by the goofy massive-resistance cant of columnists like James J. Kilpatrick. Local politicians liked to describe the NAACP as an organization of satanic purpose and potency that had been rejected by "our colored people," and would shortly be outlawed in Alabama as an agency of Communism.

But Grady said black students were joining in droves, people my age and hers. It was one of the most powerfully subversive pieces of information I had ever encountered, leaving me with an unwavering conviction about Bull Connor, George Wallace and the other segregationist blowhards who would dominate the politics of my home state for a generation.

From that day, I knew they were wrong when they said that "our Negroes" were happy with their lot and had no desire to change "our southern way of life." And when a local minister named Fred L. Shuttlesworth joined with Dr. King in 1957 to start the civil rights movement in Birmingham, I knew in some deeply intuitive way that they would succeed, because I believed that the rage that was in Grady was a living reality in the entire black community, and I knew that this rage was so powerful that it would have its way.

I learned, too, from watching Grady fail at something that meant a great deal to her. In January 1951, with the savings from her work in our home, she enrolled at Dillard. She made good grades. She loved the school and the city of New Orleans. But the money lasted only one semester, and when summer rolled around Grady was cleaning our house again.

That would be the last of her dream of becoming a registered nurse. A few years later, Grady married Marvin Hutchinson, a dashing fellow, more worldly than she, who took her to all-black nightclubs to hear singers like Bobby (Blue) Bland. In 1957, she moved to New York City to work as a maid and passed from my life. But I never forgot how she had yearned for education.

Did this mean that, between the ages of seven and fourteen, I acquired a sophisticated understanding of the insanity of a system of government that sent this impoverished girl to Louisiana rather than letting her attend the tax-supported nursing school that was a fifteen-cent bus ride from her home?

I can't say that I did. But I do know that in 1963 I recognized instantly that George Wallace was lying when he said that his Stand in the School House Door at the University of Alabama was intended to preserve the constitutional principle of states' rights. What he really wanted to preserve was the right of the state of Alabama to promiscuously damage lives like Grady's.

It is April 23, 1991. I approach the locked security gate of a rough-looking apartment courtyard in Atlanta. There behind it, waiting in the shadows, is a tiny woman with a halo of gray hair and that distinctive gap in the front teeth. Still no diamond. Grady opens the gate and says, "I've got to hug you."

Grady's apartment is modest. The most striking feature is the stacks of books on each side of her easy chair. The conversation that was interrupted so long ago is resumed without a beat.

Within minutes we are both laughing wildly over an incident we remembered in exactly the same way. Grady had known that I was insecure about my appearance as I approached adolescence, and she always looked for chances to reassure me, preferably in the most exuberant way possible. One day when I appeared in a starched shirt and with my hair slicked back for a birthday party, Grady shouted, "You look positively raping."

"Grady," my mother called from the next room, "do you know what you're saying?"

"I told her yeah. I was trying to say 'ravishing.' I used to read all those *True Confession* magazines."

Reading, it turned out, had become a passion of Grady's life, even though she never got any more formal education. For the first time in years, I recall that it was Grady who introduced me to Ernest Hemingway. In the fall of 1952, when I had the mumps and *The Old Man and the Sea* was being published in *Life*, Grady sat by my bed and read me the entire book. We both giggled at the sentence: "Once he stood up and urinated over the side of the skiff. . . ."

Partly for money and partly to escape a troubled marriage, Grady explains, she had left Birmingham to work in New York as a maid for $125 a month. Her husband had followed.

"So we got an apartment, and the man I worked for got him a job," Grady recalls. "And we got together and we stayed for thirty-one years, which is too long to stay dead."

Dead, I asked? What did that mean?

For Grady it meant a loveless marriage and a series of grinding jobs as a maid or cook. And yet she relished the life of New York, developing a reputation in her neighborhood as an ace gambler and numbers player. Through an employer who worked in show business, she also became a regular and knowledgeable attender of Broadway theater.

There were three children: Eric Lance, thirty-seven, works for the New York subway system; Marva, thirty-three, is a graduate of Wilberforce University and works in the finance department at Coler Memorial Hospital in New York; Reed, twenty-nine, works for a bank in Atlanta, where Grady is a dietetic cook at Shepherd Spinal Center. It has not been a bad life and is certainly richer in experiences and perhaps in opportunities for her children than Grady would have had in Birmingham.

At one point Grady speaks of being chided by one of her New York–raised sons for "taking it" back in the old days in Birmingham.

"He said, 'I just can't believe y'all let that go on,' " she says. "I said: 'What do you mean *y'all*? What could you have done about it?' What were you going to do? If you stuck out, you got in trouble. I always got in trouble. I was headstrong. I couldn't stand the conditions and I hated it. I wanted more than I could have.

"I always wanted to be more than I was," she adds. "I thought if I was given the chance I could be more than I was ever allowed to be."

I felt a pang of sympathy for Grady that she should be accused of tolerating what she had opposed with every fiber of her being. But how can a young man who grew up in New York know that the benign city he saw on visits to his grandmother each summer was not the Birmingham that had shaped his mother's life?

Among black people in the South, Grady is part of a generation who saw their best chances burned away by the last fiery breaths of segregation. It is difficult for young people of either race today to understand the openness and simplicity of the injustice that was done to this dwindling generation. When you stripped away the constitutional folderol from Wallace's message, it was this: He was telling Grady's mother, a working parent who paid property, sales and income taxes in Alabama for more than forty years, that her child could not attend the institutions supported by those taxes.

Even to those of us who lived there, it seems surreal that such a systematic denial of opportunity could have existed for so long. I have encountered the same disbelief in the grown-up children of white sharecroppers when they looked at pictures of the plantations on which they and their families had lived in economic bondage.

For people with such experiences, some things are beyond explanation or jest, something I learn when I jokingly ask Grady if she'd like her ashes brought back to Pratt City when she dies.

"No," she answers quite firmly, "I'd like them thrown in the East River in New York. I never liked Alabama. Isn't that terrible for you to say that? You know how I hate it."

Word that I had found Grady shot through my family. When the reunion luncheon was planned for my sister's house, my first impulse was to stage-manage the event. I had learned in conversations with Grady that she remembered my mother as someone who had nagged her about the housework. None of the rest of us recollected theirs as a tense relationship, but then again, none of us had been in Grady's shoes. In the end I decided to let it flow, and as it turned out, no one enjoyed the reunion more than Grady and my mother.

"You're so tiny," Grady exclaimed at one point. "I thought you were a great big woman. How'd you make so much noise?"

My mother was disarmed. In the midst of a round of stories about the bold things Grady had said and done, I heard her turn to a visitor and explain quietly, in an admiring voice, "You see, now, that Grady is a strong person."

Grady is also a very funny person, a born raconteur with a reputation in her own family for being outrageous. It is possible, therefore, to make her sound like some fifties version of Whoopi Goldberg and her life with my family like a sitcom spiced with her "sassy" asides about race and sex. But what I sensed at our gathering, among my brother, sister and parents, was something much deeper than fondness or nostalgia. It was a shared pride that in the Birmingham of the fifties this astonishing person had inhabited our home and had been allowed to be fully herself.

"She spoke out more than any person I knew of, no matter what their age," my sister observed. "She was the first person I'd ever heard do that, you see, and here I was eighteen years old, and you were just a little fellow. This was the first person I'd ever heard say, 'Boy, it's terrible being black in Birmingham.'"

As Grady and my family got reacquainted, it became clear that my memory of her as "mine" was the narrow and selfish memory of a child. I had been blind to the bonds Grady also had with my brother and sister. Grady remembered my brother, in particular, as her confidant and protector. And although they never spoke of it at the time, she looked to him as her guardian against the neighborhood workmen of both races who were always eager to offer young black girls "a ride home from work."

"Even if Jerry was going in the opposite direction," Grady recalled, "he would always say: 'I'm going that way. I'll drop Grady off.'"

In my brother's view, Grady's outspokenness, whether about her chores or the shortcomings of Birmingham, was made possible through a kind of adolescent cabal. "The reason it worked was Grady was just another teenager in the house," he said. "There were already two teenagers in the house, and she was just a teenager, too."

But it is also hard to imagine Grady falling into another family led by parents like mine. They were both from the Alabama hills, descended from Lincoln Republicans who did not buy into the Confederate mythology. There were no plantation paintings or portraits of Robert E. Lee on our walls. The mentality of the hill country is that of the underdog.

They were instinctive humanitarians. As Grady tells it, my father was well known among her relatives as "an open man" when it came to the treatment of his employees. I once saw him take the side of a black employee who had fought back against the bullying of a white worker on a loading dock—not a common occurrence in Birmingham in the fifties.

The most powerful rule of etiquette in my parents' home, I realize now, was that the word "nigger" was not to be used. There was no grand explanation attached to this, as I recall. We were simply people who did not say "nigger."

The prohibition of this one word may seem a small point, but I think it had a large meaning. Hill people, by nature, are talkers, and some, like my father, are great storytellers. They themselves have often been called hillbillies, which is to say that they understand the power of language and that the power to name is the power to maim.

Everyone in my family seems to have known that my great long afternoon talks with Grady were about race. Their only concern was not whether I should be hearing such talk, but whether I was old enough for the brutality of the facts.

"I would tell Howell about all the things that happened in the black neighborhoods, what police did to black people," Grady recalled to us. "I would come and tell him, and he would cry, and Mrs. Raines would say: 'Don't tell him that anymore. Don't tell him that. He's too young. Don't make him sad.' He would get sad about it."

Grady told me in private that she recalled something else about those afternoons, something precise and specific. I had wept, she said, on learning about the murder of Emmett Till, a young black boy lynched in Mississippi in 1955.

To me, this was the heart of the onion. For while some of the benefits of psychotherapy may be dubious, it does give us one shining truth. We are shaped by those moments when the sadness of life first wounds us. Yet often we are too young to remember that wounding experience, that decisive point after which all is changed for better or worse.

Every white Southerner must choose between two psychic roads—the road of racism or the road of brotherhood. Friends, families, even lovers have parted at that forking, sometimes forever, for it presents a choice that is clouded by confused emotions, inner conflicts and powerful social forces.

It is no simple matter to know all the factors that shape this individual decision. As a college student in Alabama, I shared the choking shame that many young people there felt about Wallace's antics and about the deaths of the four black children in the bombing of the Sixteenth Street Baptist Church in September 1963. A year later, as a cub reporter, I listened to the sermons and soaring hymns of the voting rights crusade. All this had its effect.

But the fact is that by the time the civil rights revolution rolled across the South, my heart had already chosen its road. I have always known that my talks with Grady helped me make that decision in an intellectual sense. But I had long felt there must have been some deeper force at work, some emotional nexus linked for me, it seemed now on hearing Grady's words, to the conjuring power of one name—Emmett Till—and to disconnected images that had lingered for decades in the eye of my memory.

Now I can almost recall the moment or imagine I can: Grady and I together, in the ironing room. We are islanded again, the two of us, in the acres of afternoon. We are looking at *Life* magazine or *Look*, at pictures of a boy barely older than myself, the remote and homely site of his death, several white men in a courtroom, the immemorial Mississippi scenes.

Thus did Grady, who had already given me so much, come back into my life with one last gift. She brought me a lost reel from the movie of my childhood, and on its dusty frames, I saw something few people are lucky enough to witness. It was a glimpse of the revelatory experience described by Graham Greene, the soul-shaking time after which all that is confusing detail falls away and all that is thematic shines forth with burning clarity.

Our reunion turned out to be a day of discovery, rich emotion and great humor. Near the end of a long lunch, my sister and my brother's wife began pouring coffee. In classic southern overkill, there were multiple desserts. Grady spoke fondly of my late Aunt Ada's artistry with coconut cakes. Then she spoke of leaving Birmingham with "my dreams of chasing the rainbow."

"I used to say when I was young, 'One day I'm going to have a big house, and I'm going to have the white people bring me my coffee,'" Grady said, leaning back in her chair. "I ain't got the big house yet, but I got the coffee. I chased the rainbow and I caught it."

Of course, Grady did not catch the rainbow, and she never will. Among the victims of segregation, Grady was like a soldier shot on the last day of the war. Only a few years after she relinquished her dream of education, local colleges were opened to blacks, and educators from around the country came to Birmingham looking for the sort of poor black student who could race through high school two years ahead of schedule.

Grady's baby sister, Liz Spraggins, was spotted in a Pratt City high school choir in 1964 and offered a music scholarship that started her on a successful career in Atlanta as a gospel and jazz singer. Grady's cousin Earl Hilliard, who is ten years younger than she, wound up at Howard University Law School. Today he is a member of the Alabama legislature. When Grady and I had lunch with the Hilliards, the family was debating whether Earl Jr. should join his sister, Lisa, at Emory or choose law school acceptances at Stanford, Texas or Alabama.

If Grady had been a few years younger, she would have gone down the road taken by her sister and cousin. If she had been white, the public-education system of Alabama would have bailed her out despite her poverty. Even in 1950, fatherless white kids who zipped through high school were not allowed to fall through the cracks in Alabama. But Grady had bad timing and black skin, a deadly combination.

At some point during our reunion lunch, it occurred to everyone in the room that of all the people who knew Grady Williams as a girl, there was one group that could have sent her to college. That was my family. The next morning, my sister told me of a regretful conversation that took place later that same day.

"Mother said at dinner last night, 'If we had just known, if we had just known, we could have done something.' " Mary Jo said. "Well, how could we have not known?"

Yes, precisely, how could we not have known—and how can we not know of the carnage of lives and minds and souls that is going on among young black people in this country today?

In Washington, where I live, there is a facile answer to such questions. Fashionable philosophers in the think tanks that influence this administration's policies will tell you that guilt, historical fairness and compassion are outdated concepts, that if the playing field is level today, we are free to forget that it was tilted for generations. Some of these philosophers will even tell you that Grady could have made it if she had really wanted to.

But I know where Grady came from and I know the deck was stacked against her and I know who stacked it. George Wallace is old, sick and pitiful now, and he'd like to be forgiven for what he, Bull Connor and the other segs did back then, and perhaps he should be. Those who know him say that above all else he regrets using the racial issue for political gain.

I often think of Governor Wallace when I hear about the dangers of "reverse discrimination" and "racial quotas" from President [George H. W.] Bush or his counsel, C. Boyden Gray, the chief architect of the administration's civil rights policies. Unlike some of the old southern demagogues, these are not ignorant men. Indeed, they are the polite, well-educated sons of privilege. But when they argue that this country needs no remedies for past injustices, I believe I hear the grown-up voices of pampered white boys who never saw a wound.

And I think of Grady and the unrepayable gift she gave with such wit, such generosity, to such a boy, so many years ago.

1992 PULITZER PRIZE FOR FEATURE WRITING

APPENDIX

CHRONOLOGICAL LIST OF *NEW YORK TIMES* PULITZER PRIZES

1918   The *New York Times*, for the most disinterested and meritorious public service rendered by an American newspaper—complete and accurate coverage of the war.

1923   Alva Johnston, for distinguished reporting of science news.

1926   Edward M. Kingsbury, for the most distinguished editorial of the year, on the Hundred Neediest Cases.

1930   Russell Owen, for graphic news dispatches from the Byrd Antarctic Expedition.

1932   Walter Duranty, for reporting of the news from Russia. (Other writers in the *Times* and elsewhere have discredited this coverage.)

1934   Frederick T. Birchall, for unbiased reporting from Germany.

1935   Arthur Krock, for distinguished, impartial and analytical Washington coverage.

1936   Lauren D. Lyman, for distinguished reporting: a world beat on the departure of the Lindberghs for England.

1937   Anne O'Hare McCormick, for distinguished foreign correspondence: dispatches and special articles from Europe.

1937   William L. Laurence, for distinguished reporting of the Tercentenary Celebration at Harvard, shared with four other reporters.

1938   Arthur Krock, for distinguished Washington correspondence.

1940   Otto D. Tolischus, for articles from Berlin explaining the economic and ideological background of war-engaged Germany.

1941   The *New York Times*, special citation for the public education value of its foreign news reports.

1942   Louis Stark, for distinguished reporting of labor stories.

1943   Hanson W. Baldwin, for a series of articles reporting a tour of the Pacific battle areas.

1944   The *New York Times*, for the most disinterested and meritorious public service rendered by an American newspaper—a survey of the teaching of American history.

1945   James B. (Scotty) Reston, for news and interpretive articles on the Dumbarton Oaks Security Conference.

1946   Arnaldo Cortesi, for distinguished correspondence from Buenos Aires.

1946   William L. Laurence, for his eyewitness account of the atomic bombing of Nagasaki and articles on the atomic bomb.

1947   Brooks Atkinson, for a distinguished series of articles on Russia.

1949   C. P. Trussell, for consistent excellence in covering the national scene from Washington.

1950   Meyer Berger, for a distinguished example of local reporting—an article on the killing of twelve people by a berserk gunman.

1951   Arthur Krock, a special commendation for his exclusive interview with President Truman: the outstanding instance of national reporting in 1950.

1951   Cyrus L. Sulzberger, special citation for his interview with Archbishop Stepinac of Yugoslavia.

1952   Anthony H. Leviero, for distinguished national reporting.

1953   The *New York Times*, special citation for its "Review of the Week" section, which "has brought enlightenment and intelligent commentary to its readers."

1955   Harrison E. Salisbury, for a series based on his five years in Russia.

1955   Arthur Krock, a special citation for distinguished correspondence from Washington.

1956   Arthur Daley, for his sports column, "Sports of the *Times*."

1957   James B. (Scotty) Reston, for distinguished reporting from Washington.

1958   The *New York Times*, for distinguished coverage of foreign news.

1960   A. M. Rosenthal, for perceptive and authoritative reporting from Poland.

1963   Anthony Lewis, for distinguished reporting of the United States Supreme Court.

1964   David Halberstam, for distinguished reporting from South Vietnam.

1968   J. Anthony Lukas, for a distinguished example of local reporting—an article on a murdered eighteen-year-old girl and her two different lives.

1970   Ada Louise Huxtable, for distinguished architecture criticism.

1971   Harold C. Schonberg, music critic, for distinguished criticism.

1972   The *New York Times*, for a distinguished example of meritorious public service by a newspaper—publication of the Pentagon Papers.

1973   Max Frankel, for his coverage of President Nixon's visit to China, a distinguished example of reporting on international affairs.

1974   Hedrick Smith, for a distinguished example of reporting on foreign affairs, coverage of the Soviet Union.

1976   Sydney H. Schanberg, for his coverage of the fall of Cambodia, a distinguished example of reporting on foreign affairs.

1976   Walter W. (Red) Smith, for his "Sports of the *Times*" column, an example of distinguished commentary.

1978   Henry Kamm, chief Asian diplomatic correspondent, for articles calling attention to the plight of Indochinese refugees.

1978   Walter Kerr, Sunday drama critic, for an outstanding example of distinguished criticism.

1978   William Safire, op-ed page columnist, for his columns on the Bert Lance affair, an example of distinguished commentary.

1979   Russell Baker, for his "Observer" column, an example of distinguished commentary.

1981   Dave Anderson, for his "Sports of the *Times*" column, an example of distinguished commentary.

1981   John M. Crewdson, for his coverage of illegal aliens and immigration, a distinguished example of reporting on national affairs.

1982   John Darnton, for his coverage of the crisis in Poland, a distinguished example of international reporting.

1982   Jack Rosenthal, deputy editorial page editor, for a distinguished example of editorial page writing.

1983   Thomas L. Friedman, for his coverage of the war in Lebanon, a distinguished example of international reporting.

1983   Nan Robertson, for her article in the *New York Times Magazine* on her experience with toxic shock syndrome, a distinguished example of feature writing.

1984   Paul Goldberger, for distinguished architecture criticism.

1984   John Noble Wilford, for national reporting on a wide variety of scientific topics.

1986   Donal Henahan, music critic, for distinguished criticism.

1986   The *New York Times*, for explanatory journalism: a series of articles on the Strategic Defense Initiative, the Star Wars program.

1987   Alex S. Jones, for distinguished specialized reporting on the dissension that dissolved a Louisville newspaper dynasty.

1987   The *New York Times*, for national reporting on causes of the *Challenger* shuttle disaster.

1988   Thomas L. Friedman, for coverage of Israel, a distinguished example of reporting on international affairs.

1989   Bill Keller, for coverage of the Soviet Union, a distinguished example of reporting on international affairs.

1990   Nicholas D. Kristof and Sheryl WuDunn, for coverage of political turmoil in China, a distinguished example of reporting on international affairs.

1991   Natalie Angier, for coverage of molecular biology and animal behavior, a distinguished example of beat reporting.

1991   Serge Schmemann, for coverage of the reunification of Germany, a distinguished example of reporting on international affairs.

1992   Anna Quindlen, for "Public & Private," a compelling column covering a wide range of personal and political topics.

1992   Howell Raines, for "Grady's Gift," an account in the *New York Times Magazine* of his childhood friendship with his family's housekeeper and the lasting lessons of their interracial relationship.

1993   John F. Burns, for courageous coverage of the strife and destruction in Bosnia, a distinguished example of international reporting.

1994   The *New York Times*, for local reporting of the World Trade Center
        bombing, pooling the efforts of the metropolitan staff as well as *Times*
        journalists covering locations as far-ranging as the Middle East and
        Washington.

1994   Isabel Wilkerson, for distinguished feature writing.

1994   The *New York Times*, for Kevin Carter's photograph of a vulture
        perching near a little girl in the Sudan who had collapsed from hunger,
        a picture that became an icon of starvation.

1995   Margo Jefferson, for her book reviews and other pieces, examples of
        distinguished criticism.

1996   Rick Bragg, for distinguished feature writing.

1996   Robert D. McFadden, for distinguished rewrite journalism, applied to
        a broad range of stories.

1996   Robert B. Semple Jr., for distinguished editorial writing on environ-
        mental issues.

1997   John F. Burns, for distinguished international reporting on the Taliban
        movement in Afghanistan.

1998   Linda Greenhouse, for reporting on the Supreme Court's work and
        its significance with sophistication and a sense of history.

1998   Michiko Kakutani, for reviewing 1997's many major literary works in
        essays that were fearless and authoritative.

1998   The *New York Times*, for a series of articles on the effects of drug cor-
        ruption in Mexico, a distinguished example of international reporting.

1999   Maureen Dowd, for the moral insight and wit she brought to bear in
        her columns on the combat between President Clinton and Kenneth
        Starr.

1999   The *New York Times*, notably Jeff Gerth, for a series of articles dis-
        closing the corporate sale of American technology to China with the
        approval of the U.S. government despite national security risks.

2001   David Cay Johnston, for penetrating and enterprising beat reporting
        that exposed loopholes and inequities in the U.S. tax code, which was
        instrumental in bringing about reforms.

2001   The *New York Times,* for its compelling and memorable series explor-
        ing racial experiences and attitudes across contemporary America, a
        distinguished example of reporting on national affairs.

INDEX

ABOUT THE EDITOR

ANTHONY LEWIS is the author of *Make No Law* and the best-seller *Gideon's Trumpet*. For his journalism he has been awarded two Pulitzer Prizes, in 1955 for a series of articles in the *Washington Daily News* that helped clear Abraham Chasanow of unjust charges by the U.S. Navy, and in 1963 reporting for the *New York Times* on the Supreme Court and the landmark *Baker v. Carr* reapportionment decision. During his nearly five-decade career writing and reporting for the *New York Times*, he served as the *Times*'s London bureau chief for eight years and a columnist for the paper from 1969 until 2001. A Visiting Lombard Lecturer at Harvard University's Kennedy School of Government, he lives in Boston, Massachusetts.